Her main pt: Culture + law interact.
The future portends a desire to "remix"
trad'l law w/ aggadic stories, so as to
reconnect w/ modes of ethics + righteousness
over + above follow) ltr ?: law.

THE MYTH OF THE *CULTURAL JEW*

THE MYTH OF THE *CULTURAL JEW*

Culture and Law in Jewish Tradition

Roberta Rosenthal Kwall

OXFORD
UNIVERSITY PRESS

UNIVERSITY PRESS

Oxford University Press is a department of the University of Oxford. It furthers the University's objective of excellence in research, scholarship, and education by publishing worldwide.

Oxford   New York
Auckland   Cape Town   Dar es Salaam   Hong Kong   Karachi   Kuala Lumpur   Madrid
Melbourne   Mexico City   Nairobi   New Delhi   Shanghai   Taipei   Toronto

With offices in
Argentina   Austria   Brazil   Chile   Czech Republic   France   Greece   Guatemala   Hungary
Italy   Japan   Poland   Portugal   Singapore   South Korea   Switzerland   Thailand
Turkey   Ukraine   Vietnam

Oxford is a registered trademark of Oxford University Press in the UK and certain other countries.

Published in the United States of America by
Oxford University Press
198 Madison Avenue, New York, NY 10016

Library of Congress Cataloging-in-Publication Data
Kwall, Roberta Rosenthal, 1955- author.
The myth of the *cultural Jew* : culture and law in Jewish tradition / Roberta Rosenthal Kwall.
    pages cm
Includes bibliographical references and index.
ISBN 978-0-19-537370-7 ((hardback) : alk. paper)
1. Jewish law—Philosophy. 2. Judaism—Doctrines. 3. Jews—Identity. 4. Culture and law. I. Title.
BM520.6.K83 2015
296.1'8—dc23
                                                                                2014030857

9 8 7 6 5 4 3 2

Printed in the United States of America on acid-free paper

Note to Readers
This publication is designed to provide accurate and authoritative information in regard to the
subject matter covered. It is based upon sources believed to be accurate and reliable and is intended
to be current as of the time it was written. It is sold with the understanding that the publisher
is not engaged in rendering legal, accounting, or other professional services. If legal advice or
other expert assistance is required, the services of a competent professional person should be
sought. Also, to confirm that the information has not been affected or changed by recent
developments, traditional legal research techniques should be used, including checking primary
sources where appropriate.

*(Based on the Declaration of Principles jointly adopted by a Committee of the
American Bar Association and a Committee of Publishers and Associations.)*

You may order this or any other Oxford University Press publication
by visiting the Oxford University Press website at www.oup.com

For my children, Shanna Kwall Hill, Rachel Kwall, Nisa Kwall, and Andrew Hill

CONTENTS

ACKNOWLEDGMENTS

This book is dedicated to my daughters, Shanna, Rachel, and Nisa, and to Shanna's husband, Andrew Hill. I am so proud of all of them and grateful for the joy they bring to my life. My husband, Jeffrey Kwall, has also played a crucial role in the development of this book. I also want to express my gratitude to my parents, Millie and Abe Rosenthal. Although my father passed away during the years I was engaged in this project, I am so grateful for his continuous encouragement and his passion for ensuring that his only child received what he termed a "good Jewish education." My mother has always been a source of comfort and support, and I am so blessed to be able to enjoy her warmth and wisdom at this point in my life.

This book has benefitted from additional sources of inspiration in addition to my early years of exposure to the Jewish tradition: the past seven years at the Spertus Institute in Chicago during which time I have been pursuing a master's degree in Jewish Studies; the many conversations I have enjoyed with Jewish professionals across the country and all over the world through my work with DePaul's Center for Jewish Law and Judaic Studies; and the countless conversations with family, friends, and acquaintances who have perspectives about Judaism that are sometimes very different from my own. I am especially grateful to the following three people who spent many hours reading and commenting on every chapter of this book: Martin S. Cohen, Edward Rabin, and my husband, Jeffrey. Each of these readers provided distinct types of feedback and all of their comments contributed substantially to this work from both a substantive and stylistic standpoint.

I also want to thank several other readers who commented on specific parts of the book and provided me with important feedback: Dean Bell, Paul Schiff Berman, Elliot Dorff, Jennifer Gong, Yosef Kanefsky, David Kraemer, Ellen LeVee, Menachem Mautner, Victor Mirelman, Daniel Nevins, Kim Treiger-Bar-Am, Ofer Tur-Sinai, and Tal Zarsky.

There have been others who have shaped my thinking about Judaism over the years, including during the time I spent researching and writing this book. For the many conversations as well as help with particular questions or concerns, I thank Jacob Bacon, Ali Begoun, David Begoun, Adena Berkowitz, Michael Broyde, Elaine Cohen, Steven M. Cohen, Alex Felch, Samuel Fraint, Richard Kahn, Peter Knobel, Asher Lopatin, Zohar Raviv, Steven Resnicoff, Joel Roth, Carol Schnitzler, Michael Schwab, Byron Sherwin, Alexi Sivertsev, Daniel Sperber, Jeremy Stern, David Wolkenfeld, and in more recent years, my children. All of these individuals have helped formulate and clarify my thinking about the important issues I discuss throughout this work. I also want to acknowledge Neil Netanel and the late Keith Aoki for reading and recommending my initial book proposal to Oxford University Press, and the various editors at Oxford who have worked with me along the way, including my copy editor Brooke Smith. And to my good friend, Deborah Tuerkheimer, a special thank you for her support and encouragement throughout this process.

Over the years, several DePaul University College of Law students have provided outstanding research assistance. They have challenged me to improve this work and facilitated my ability to do so. For these efforts, my sincere appreciation to Michael Brower, Jonathan Crowley, Aaron Fox, Kari Kammel, Mary Kane, Drew Redmond, Charles Silverman, Rebecca Stang, Tamar Shertok, and Aaron White. I am also grateful to Joe Rodgers for excellent clerical support.

I was fortunate to have the opportunity to present parts of this book in various venues over the years, including workshops at the University of Pennsylvania Law School, Tulane Law School, and the University of West Virginia. I am grateful to the faculty who attended these sessions and provided helpful comments.

Finally, I would like to express my deepest gratitude to my rabbi, Dr. Vernon Kurtz, also a professor at Spertus Institute, who read and commented on every chapter as part of my course of studies for my master's degree in Jewish Studies. He is an extraordinary teacher, rabbi, and mentor, and I am blessed to have had the opportunity to work with someone of his caliber so closely for the past several years. One of the many things I learned from Rabbi Kurtz is that it is traditional to write the following at the conclusion of a Jewish book: *Tam v'nishlam shevah le-El borei olam*–"This book is complete, praise be to God, Creator of the universe."

Roberta Rosenthal Kwall
July 2014/*Tammuz* 5774

INTRODUCTION

THE MYTH OF THE *CULTURAL JEW*

In certain circles, one often hears somebody say that he or she is "a cultural Jew." This statement usually is intended to mean that the speaker is not religious but still identifies as Jewish from a cultural standpoint. A main premise of this book is that if one identifies as a "cultural Jew," that person is inevitably molded and shaped by the Jewish tradition, which includes Jewish law. Cultural Judaism absent any connection to Jewish law is an impossibility. Why? The answer lies in the assertion that Jewish law and Jewish culture are forged together in the composition of the Jewish tradition.

Jewish religious law, known as *halakhah*, is similar to all law in that it is best understood in cultural terms and therefore through a paradigm known as cultural analysis. Cultural analysis of law sees law and culture as intertwined rather than as distinct entities developed in isolation from one another. A cultural analysis of law rejects the view that law is objectively neutral and coherent and thus lacking a relationship to its surrounding cultural environment. Instead, cultural analysis of law understands both law and culture as products of social context and historically specific circumstances. It also sees law as the product of discourse and debate, shaped in response to the push and pull of social forces.

Halakhah, like all law, both reflects and constitutes social and cultural practices. Jewish law, which is binding upon Jews according to the tradition, produces Jewish culture, and Jewish culture produces Jewish law. This interrelationship is clearly evidenced in the formation and application of the *mesorah*—which this book defines broadly as the entire chain of the Jewish tradition handed down over the generations incorporating both the strictly legal precepts formulated by the rabbis as well as the practices relating to Judaism that have developed among the people.[1] In other words, the *mesorah* embodies both the concrete legal components as well as the more amorphous yet visceral cultural elements of the Jewish tradition that have evolved over the years. As an organic legal system and set of cultural practices covering virtually every aspect of human behavior, the *mesorah* is an ideal subject for a cultural analysis study.

The view of culture this book adopts is a fluid one popular in legal academic circles. According to this view, culture embodies heterogeneous, intersecting practices and processes emerging from within and beyond its borders.[2] As a result, cultural analysis emphasizes a multiplicity of values, some of which may be perceived as foreign to the particular tradition at issue. This reality also can result in conflict among sectors of the cultural community. The problem for any cultural community, particularly a minority one, is how to balance authenticity of the cultural tradition with evolution necessitated by social forces. Significantly, cultural analysis is concerned with the preservation of cultural tradition and recognizes that change to the tradition potentially compromises its authenticity. Yet, cultural analysis also embraces the development of cultural tradition as a response to social context and therefore sees change as inevitable, and often desirable.

This book invokes cultural analysis as a tool in understanding how to approach these complex issues regarding the *mesorah*, although the analysis developed and applied herein has relevance for many types of distinct cultural traditions, especially those with a legal component.[3] There are several advantages of situating the *mesorah* within a cultural analysis framework. First and foremost, because cultural analysis emphasizes the interrelationship between

---

1. *See* STEVEN H. RESNICOFF, UNDERSTANDING JEWISH LAW 219–20 (2012). *See also* ELLIOT N. DORFF, FOR THE LOVE OF GOD AND PEOPLE 21 (2007) (discussing a theory of Jewish law that relates the law to other parts of the Jewish experience including "modern legal, social, economic, cultural, and political developments in North America and Israel").

The text preceding and accompanying this note contains examples of the many Hebrew transliterations used throughout this book. They have been made to appear in a consistent format throughout the book, even when they are contained within the body of exact quotes using different spellings. This stylistic choice was made so that non-Hebrew speaking readers will recognize the same word wherever it appears in the work.

2. *See* Naomi Mezey, *Law as Culture*, 13 YALE J.L. & HUMAN. 35, 43 (2001). This perspective contrasts with the more classic view, which sees culture as a self-contained entity composed of coherent patterns. *See id.*

3. *See, e.g.*, MUSTAFA AKYOL, ISLAM WITHOUT EXTREMES: A MUSLIM CASE FOR LIBERTY (2013). On December 15, 2013, Akyol discussed his book on CNN with Fareed Zakaria, and much of the interview concerned how, in his view, culture needs to inform the appropriate interpretation of the text of the Quran.

law and culture, this paradigm reflects an accurate understanding of the *mesorah* that incorporates both the legal and the cultural. Second, a cultural analysis of Jewish law explicitly acknowledges the human element of the law's development. *Halakhah*, as an expression of human creativity, makes a critical contribution to the identity of the Jewish people. Third, cultural analysis explains the historical reality that the *mesorah* places a high value on the preservation of its practices, customs, and laws while simultaneously encouraging the ongoing development of the tradition and its application to changing cultural conditions. A fourth advantage of employing the cultural analysis model as a means of understanding the development of the *mesorah* is that cultural analysis allows for an examination of whether and how changes in the tradition can impact the evolution, and possible disintegration, of Judaism in modernity. This last advantage lies at the heart of why cultural analysis matters to those interested in the survival of the *mesorah*.

This project contributes to the increasingly complex issue of meaningful Jewish survival in the face of escalating assimilation and arguable attrition of the Jewish people. To address the issue of Jewish survival, however, it is vital to unbundle the subject matter at stake. To what extent does the survival of Judaism depend upon survival of the *halakhah* itself (and if so, in what form)? What is the relationship between *halakhah* and the *mesorah* generally? What constitutes "Jewish identity," and to what degree can Jewish continuity be predicated on strong Jewish identity rather than religious observance?

Historically, observance of *halakhah* may have been a key element of Jewish life, but with the advent of the Enlightenment, the importance of adhering to *halakhah* began to wane for the majority of Jews, even those who otherwise maintained a strong Jewish identity. This phenomenon has taken on an entirely new complexion beginning in the latter half of the twentieth century as the following realities converged: the attraction of a stricter version of Orthodoxy for an increasing number of Jews, the ongoing reframing of *halakhah* by more liberal denominations, and the continual increase of intermarriage and growing number of unaffiliated Jews.

This book argues that the invocation of a cultural analysis paradigm is a promising way of explaining why *halakhah* must matter to those interested in meaningful Jewish survival, even if "survival" is not defined in strictly *halakhic* terms. Moreover, it demonstrates how invoking cultural analysis can facilitate the development of an evolving yet authentic *halakhah* and *mesorah*. The lesson of cultural analysis is that taken together, Jewish law and Jewish culture have enabled Jews over the centuries to preserve the particularity, and ultimately the survival, of the Jewish people.

Chapter 1 lays the groundwork for the chapters that follow by furnishing an overview of both cultural analysis and the study of Jewish law and tradition through a cultural analysis framework. It opens with a discussion of the emerging focus on law and cultural analysis in the academic world generally and identifies the salient themes of a cultural analysis approach to law. This discussion reveals that among those scholars who invoke cultural analysis, there is a general sense that law and culture should not be viewed as two distinct entities but rather as embodiments of one another. This chapter also introduces the book's central theme: how a cultural analysis paradigm provides an ideal way of understanding the historical development and ongoing evolution of *halakhah* and the *mesorah*.

Chapter 2 focuses on Jewish law from the top down. As an initial matter, it explores the relevance of Revelation and the development of *halakhah* in the biblical and post-biblical periods. This chapter continues with an examination of rabbinic authority in the period following the destruction of the Second Temple in 70 CE and illustrates how the sages reformulated Judaism during this period. It also addresses the influence of the surrounding majority Hellenistic culture on the development of early Jewish law.

Chapter 3 concentrates primarily on the medieval period and focuses on the development of the *mesorah* from the bottom up by examining the influence of the practices of the people. Just as the surrounding majority cultures influenced the rabbis in their top-down formation of *halakhah*, the same is true of the people's bottom-up practices. This chapter argues that the *mesorah* is the product of a negotiation between the rabbinic top-down law and culture and the bottom-up customs of the people. In developing this argument, it explores primarily certain life cycle events as well as practices relating to Jewish eating.

Chapter 4 grapples with the intractable questions of what is "authentic" Judaism in modernity and who gets to make this determination. It details the development of the three major denominations—Reform, Conservative, and Orthodox Judaism—that trace their roots to German-Jewish ideologies of the nineteenth century. This discussion of the denominations focuses on their distinct ideologies, histories, and approaches to lawmaking. It sets the stage for the next three chapters that explore specific, highly controversial issues of *halakhah* through a cultural analysis framework.

Chapters 5, 6, and 7 address topics that challenge the boundaries of *halakhah* in the face of arguments for increased pluralism, democracy, and fluidity. Chapter 5 explores these themes in the context of the fundamental question of "who is a Jew?" It also discusses a set of debated rulings concerning Sabbath observance, an area of vital importance given the centrality of the Sabbath in Jewish law. Chapters 6 and 7 examine restrictions on homosexuals and women, respectively. Chapter 6 addresses how the modern movements treat the tradition's ban on homosexuality that is derived from the Torah (the Five Books of Moses). Chapter 7 probes Orthodox resistance to particular types of female participation in religious services. All of the topics addressed in these chapters necessitate a careful delineation of whether, and how, to balance the particularity of the Jewish legal tradition with the social forces of modernity.

Any text applying a cultural analysis perspective to the *mesorah* must analyze the role of Israel, which occupies a unique place in the hearts and minds of many, though certainly not all, Jews. Chapter 8 examines the multifaceted relationship between Israeli and Jewish law and between Jewish law and Israeli Jewish identity. It addresses these relationships in the context of the following two extraordinarily complex questions. First, what difficulties does Israel face as a Jewish state in striking a balance between Jewish law and its secular laws? Second, what does it mean to be a Jewish state when the majority of Jews in Israel do not observe *halakhah*? These questions go to the heart of what Jewish identity means in the state of Israel.

Chapter 9 picks up where Chapter 8 leaves off by examining ways of forging Jewish identity in the Diaspora, particularly in the United States where the majority of Jews outside of Israel live. This chapter explores recent empirical evidence concerning the construction of Jewish identity in the United States, as well as certain ideological markers of Jewish identity discussed in the academic literature. It then examines current social forces that militate against a more expansive role for *halakhah* in shaping the Jewish identity of the majority of American Jews.

The final chapter illustrates how the lessons of cultural analysis can be applied to inform and mold Jewish identity and enhance the discussion concerning the survival of Judaism and the Jewish people. These lessons focus on the importance of the intersection between law and culture. The discussion illuminates the tensions between particularity and cultural fluidity and between pluralism and authenticity with respect to the *mesorah*. Drawing from the theory and insights of cultural analysis, this chapter demonstrates how the explicit synergy between Jewish law and culture can facilitate important conversations for Jews in the United States and elsewhere.

1 | CULTURE, LAW, AND THE DEVELOPMENT OF JEWISH TRADITION

The use of culture as an analytical tool is known as cultural analysis. In general terms, cultural analysis emphasizes human participation in the creation of culture[1] and focuses on "beliefs and values."[2] The use of cultural analysis necessitates a definition of culture. Professor Austin Sarat has observed that to discuss "culture is... to venture into a field where there are almost as many definitions of the term as there are discussions of it...."[3] At one time, culture was believed to be coherent and self-contained.[4] In contrast, many scholars now maintain that any given culture incorporates practices deriving from both within and outside of its borders.[5] Thus, culture manifests continual evolution as a result of a variety of internal and external influences. According to this perspective, cultural exchange is constant and inevitable.[6] As a result,

---

1. Toby Miller, *What It Is and What It Isn't: Cultural Studies Meets Graduate-Student Labor*, 13 YALE J.L. & HUMAN. 69, 70 (2001); Madhavi Sunder, *IP³*, 59 STAN. L. REV. 257, 323 (2006).

2. Austin Sarat & Jonathan Simon, *Beyond Legal Realism?: Cultural Analysis, Cultural Studies, and the Situation of Legal Scholarship*, 13 YALE J.L. & HUMAN. 3, 9 n. 30 (2001).

3. Austin D. Sarat, *Redirecting Legal Scholarship in Law Schools*, 12 YALE J.L. & HUMAN. 129, 144 (2000) (reviewing PAUL KAHN, THE CULTURAL STUDY OF LAW: RECONSTRUCTING LEGAL SCHOLARSHIP (1999)).

4. *See* Naomi Mezey, *Law as Culture*, 13 YALE J.L. & HUMAN. 35, 43 (2001).

5. *See id.* at 43; *see also* Richard Johnson, *What Is Cultural Studies Anyway*, 16 SOC. TEXT 38, 39 (1986) ("[C]ulture is neither an autonomous nor externally determined field, but a site of social differences and struggles").

6. Sunder, *supra* note 1, at 331.

interactions within and between distinct cultural traditions are "at the core of any culturally informed analysis."[7]

Cultural tradition is a major source of both individual and group identity. Cultural theorist Richard Johnson emphasizes the "who I am" and the "who we are" of culture, thereby highlighting the relevance of both individual and collective identities.[8] Further, according to some authorities, the purpose of cultural tradition is to afford groups maintaining particular identities autonomy over their communities.[9] So the operative question becomes "what does the community think is important?" The answer to this question may not always be so clear. Within a common cultural framework, culture is characterized by a sense of sharing, but it is also a product of conflict.[10] A particular community may face internal disagreements arising from the dynamic and heterogeneous nature of culture itself, given its ability to be influenced by both internal and external factors.

This reality necessitates grappling with the ultimate questions of whether, and how, preservation of cultural tradition aligns with modern sensibilities. The answers to these questions are relevant in more than just an academic sense. Individual members of particular cultural communities seek to situate their personal identities within the context of the larger community. Moreover, group identity depends not only upon a definition of the cultural tradition, but also upon its preservation. Cultural dissent and evolution of the cultural tradition in pockets of the community, particularly absent a link to the tradition, can compromise traditional values and result in the loss of something perceived as valuable by other segments of the community. Indeed, a cultural product or tradition is authentic only if it "maintains a legitimate link to the community."[11] Cultural traditions continually negotiate between preservation and modernity and between authenticity and evolution. Cultural analysis is a useful tool in understanding these dynamics.

---

7. *Id.*

8. Johnson, *supra* note 5, at 44.

9. Group rights and self-determination are related because recognition of group rights, especially when related to territory or regional autonomy, is the manifestation of self-determination. *See* Ian Brownlie, *Rights of Peoples in International Law, in* THE RIGHTS OF PEOPLES 1, 6 (James Crawford ed., 1988).

10. *See* JAMES CLIFFORD, THE PREDICAMENT OF CULTURE 10, 14 (1988) (discussing how culture's fluidity illustrates its "deeply compromised" nature).

11. SUSAN SCAFIDI, WHO OWNS CULTURE 54 (2005) (discussing cultural products).

The Emerging Focus on Law and Cultural Analysis

This book adopts a fluid definition of culture and a view of law that is steeped in the discipline of cultural analysis. Just as the classic view of culture emphasized its self-contained quality, traditionally law was understood as an objective, neutral system that does not explicitly admit factors or influences from outside of its own systematic development. In contrast, the approach embraced here understands law as a human product based on cultural influences arising in historically specific contexts. Law is a form of cultural production and its borders are porous. People create law just as they do culture.

For the most part, the connection between culture and law has been the focus of scholarly discussion in the United States only fairly recently.[12] Initially, cultural analysis was associated with the "softer" areas of legal scholarship such as feminist jurisprudence and other critical legal studies, but the "harder" traditions such as law and economics also are beginning to grapple with cultural implications.[13] Writing in the context of intellectual property law, for example, Madhavi Sunder has observed that " 'culture' is a word on everybody's lips."[14] By the last third of the twentieth century, many legal scholars began paying attention to the "imaginative life of the law and the way law lives in our imagination."[15]

Law and culture scholars focus on how law "simultaneously embodies the interests of particular groups and shapes those interests—and even shapes the identities of those who understand themselves as members of such groups."[16] When applied in the context of law, cultural analysis asks "how to talk about and interpret law in cultural terms."[17] Cultural analysis also is concerned

---

12. *See* Sarat & Simon, *supra* note 2, at 9 n.30 (explaining the rise in popularity of cultural studies and cultural analysis in the legal realm). *See* Menachem Mautner, *Three Approaches to Law and Culture*, 96 Cornell L. Rev. 839 (2011) for a discussion of a series of legal approaches that connect law and culture.

13. Sarat & Simon, *supra* note 2, at 7 n.23. Sarat and Simon welcome this trend given that "the logics of governance in the late modern era" have similarly turned from "society to culture as a way of organizing social relations." *Id.* at 7 (emphasis omitted).

14. Sunder, *supra* note 1, at 321; *see also* Dan Hunter, *Culture War*, 83 Tex. L. Rev. 1105, 1117 (2005) (noting that in intellectual property circles the discourse is all about the ownership and control of culture).

15. Sarat & Simon, *supra* note 2, at 18.

16. Paul W. Kahn, *Freedom, Autonomy, and the Cultural Study of Law*, 13 Yale J.L. & Human. 141, 150 (2001).

17. Mezey, *supra* note 4, at 36.

with cultural tradition and how the law reaffirms individual identities and values as well as the composition of groups.[18] This approach seeks to address how law reflects and shapes human beings and their world.[19]

Rather than provide a comprehensive history of cultural studies or cultural analysis, this discussion draws from those who have mined these areas previously, in order that their insights may be applied now to a new topic of focus, the Jewish tradition. The law and cultural analysis literature is varied, and no unified cultural analysis approach to the law exists; scholars working in this area incorporate several distinct approaches to the convergence of law and culture. Nonetheless, in the writings of those scholars who rely upon a more culturally nuanced approach to the law, it is possible to discern several key themes permeating the relationship between law and culture. These include a focus on (1) power relationships, (2) environment, (3) conflict, (4) multiple values, and (5) the interrelationship between law and culture.

Power, Environment, and Conflict

In general terms, cultural analysis pays attention to power and hierarchy and examines how the law sustains and reinforces relationships of power. This concern with power and hierarchy undoubtedly derives from the link that the discipline of cultural studies itself has made between culture and "questions of social stratification, power, and social conflict."[20] Thus, those who engage in the cultural study of law see legal claims as reflecting the "relationships of power that such claims sustain."[21] As retired Supreme Court justice John Paul Stevens observed: "traditions—especially traditions in the law—are as likely to codify the preferences of those in power as they are to reflect necessity or proven wisdom."[22]

An important consequence of this intellectual paradigm is that the study of law is contextualized, meaning that it is steeped in historical and cultural circumstances. Therefore, a cultural study of law rejects law's objectivity, neutrality, and coherence, and instead understands law as the product

---

18. *See, e.g.*, Asbjørn Eide, *Cultural Rights as Individual Human Rights, in* ECONOMIC, SOCIAL AND CULTURAL RIGHTS 289, 290 (Asbjørn Eide et al. eds., 2d edition, 2001).

19. *See generally* PAUL W. KAHN, THE CULTURAL STUDY OF LAW 6 (1999).

20. Sarat, *supra* note 3, at 147.

21. Kahn, *supra* note 16, at 149.

22. Adam Liptak, *From Age of Independence to Age of Ideology*, N.Y. TIMES, Apr. 10, 2010, at A1, A12 (quote originally contained in private memorandum to Justice Blackmun, 1992).

of environmental influences.[23] This view of law results from the claim that culture itself is "grounded in particular conditions of possibility."[24] Further, the increasing popularity of the postmodern perspective, which emphasizes a fluidity of meaning in a given text, requires that a cultural analysis of the law be attentive to "complex cultural borrowings, importations of new meanings, and new points of resistance."[25] This perspective also sees legal texts as "multivalent," and thus possessing the capacity to speak to new generations in different contexts.[26] Professor Paul Kahn fittingly captured this idea with the following observation: "Does one ask what the Framers said in 1789, or what they would have said 200 years later, or something in-between, such as what is the current meaning of what they said then?"[27]

This contextualized, democratic approach to the study of law breeds conflict. Culture "creates meanings that allow for the possibility of dispute and contest."[28] As a result, this approach rejects the idea of hegemony, or dominance by one social group.[29] Viewing law as hegemonic tends to reify existing power dynamics and discourage resistance.[30] A hegemonic conception of law is particularly characteristic of the top-down approach, which understands law's development from the perspectives of society's more dominant, or powerful, viewpoints. The narrative movement of legal scholarship, which gained much attention during the last part of the twentieth century, can be seen as a response by outside scholars, working in areas such as critical race,

---

23. In this respect, the cultural study of law owes a debt to the school of legal realism, although a discussion of the differences between legal realism and cultural analysis are beyond the scope of this project. *See* Sarat & Simon, *supra* note 2, at 9–13 for a nuanced discussion of this point.

24. Miller, *supra* note 1, at 74.

25. Sarat, *supra* note 3, at 148–49.

26. *Cf.* Kahn, *supra* note 16, at 146 (discussing the multivalent quality of legal texts according to this perspective and noting that "history is a wide-open field for interpretive disagreement").

27. *Id.* at 146–47.

28. Robert C. Post, *Law and Cultural Conflict*, 78 Chi.-Kent L. Rev. 485, 492 (2003).

29. *See* Susan S. Silbey, *Ideology, Power, and Justice, in* Justice and Power in Sociolegal Studies 272, 287 (Bryant G. Garth & Austin Sarat eds., 1997) (describing the idea of hegemony as "those circumstances where representations and social constructions are so embedded as to be almost invisible" or "taken for granted").

30. A hegemonic system reinforces a "structure of social control and a means by which entrenched power relations are constructed and legitimized." Paul Schiff Berman, *Telling a Less Suspicious Story: Notes toward a Non-skeptical Approach to Legal/Cultural Analysis*, 13 Yale J.L. & Human. 95, 110 (2001).

feminist, and gay legal theory, to law's hegemonic character.[31] As will be discussed shortly, narrative scholars focus on the need to introduce stories from a variety of perspectives so that legal discourse can be shaped in response to a broader array of interests rather than just the interests of those individuals who represent the mainstream perspective.

Cultural analysis understands meanings as products of conflict rather than hegemony. According to anthropology professor Sally Engle Merry, "culture is being redefined as a flexible repertoire of practices and discourses created through historical processes of contestation over signs and meanings."[32] The contestation aspect of the cultural analysis paradigm also relates to its concern for relationships of power and hierarchy because conflicts over meaning "become occasions for observing the play of power."[33] Professor Naomi Mezey agrees that "[t]o talk about the making and contestation of meaning is necessarily to talk about power."[34] Kahn notes that these contests are "often fought within, and over, the terms of legal claims for recognition of identity as well as of particular interests."[35] Those who view law through a cultural analysis lens "tend to see law as...a set of sites of social conflict, and a set of resources...for those involved in these conflicts."[36] In this regard, Sarat has observed that "because the construction of meaning through law is, in fact, typically contested, scholars show the many ways in which resistance occurs."[37]

When the law is invoked to reaffirm or enforce certain cultural values, such as meaning and practice, typically it is being used as a vehicle for advancing a particular side of an ongoing cultural contest.[38] Significantly, the battle lines can exist not only between distinct cultural groups, but also between diverse factions within a particular cultural group.[39] Sunder has examined

---

31. *See* Roberta Rosenthal Kwall, *"Author-Stories": Narrative's Implications for Moral Rights and Copyright's Joint Authorship Doctrine*, 75 S. CAL. L. REV. 1, 2–3, 8–14 (2001); *see also* sources cited in note 44, *infra*.

32. Sally Engle Merry, *Law, Culture, and Cultural Appropriation*, 10 YALE J.L. & HUMAN. 575, 577 (1998).

33. Sarat, *supra* note 3, at 140.

34. Mezey, *supra* note 4, at 47.

35. Kahn, *supra* note 16, at 150.

36. *Id.* at 149–50.

37. Sarat, *supra* note 3, at 140.

38. Post, *supra* note 28, at 492.

39. *See* Mezey, *supra* note 4, at 43–44.

the concept of "cultural dissent" within cultures and documented how an increasing number of individuals within particular cultures are seeking "to dissent from traditional cultural norms and to make new cultural meanings—that is, to reinterpret cultural norms in ways more favorable to them."[40] Cultural dissent, according to Sunder, is defined by "challenges by individuals within a culture to modernize, or broaden, the traditional terms of cultural membership."[41] Within the context of the Jewish people, for example, cultural dissent occurs between the different factions not only with respect to how Jewish law should be interpreted, but also regarding whether the law should be a component of the culture at all.

Multiple Values and the Interrelationship between Law and Culture

A cultural analysis paradigm requires law to embrace a multiplicity of values rather than reflect a unitary or purportedly objective set of ideals. Kahn observes that "[m]uch of the cultural studies of law movement has been an effort to shift the location at which we study law from the opinions of the appellate courts to the expressions of ordinary people carrying out the tasks of everyday life."[42] One notable example of this phenomenon is that despite the existence of formal speed limits, evidence suggests that police and traffic courts sometimes enforce these laws based on the geographically specific conventions of drivers.[43] Another illustration, in the context of the Jewish tradition, is furnished by the importance of custom in shaping the fabric of the tradition from the bottom up. Cultural analysis emphasizes the importance of blending the top-down and bottom-up approaches to lawmaking and thus opens the door to multiple values. It also gives a voice to the creations and practices of those who were or are inferior in social status or lost in historical struggles.

---

40. Madhavi Sunder, *Cultural Dissent*, 54 STAN. L. REV. 495, 498 (2001).

41. *Id.* at 516; *see also* Yaacov Ben-Shemesh, *Law and Internal Cultural Conflicts*, 1 L. & ETHICS HUM. RTS. 288 (2007) ("Cultural dissenters remind us that cultures are not immutable 'givens,' and that individuals have the capacity to shape, resist, and change cultural norms, values and practices").

42. Kahn, *supra* note 16, at 142.

43. Mezey, *supra* note 4, at 52 (also discussing Montana's experience with its "Basic Rule," which required only a reasonable daytime speed limit).

Therefore, from a scholarly perspective, the methodology characteristic of cultural analysis comports with the underlying premise of narrative scholarship, which emphasizes that the lawmaking process is best served when stories representing a broad range of societal perspectives are explicitly considered in the decisional calculus.[44] By attempting to focus attention on the stories of those whose perspectives have been excluded from the discourse, narrative scholars urge the need for law to incorporate as large an information base as possible. Their arguments are supported by evidence showing that compliance with law is enhanced when the public perceives that the legal decision-making process is fair and legitimate,[45] and characterized by broad-based participation.[46] This reality reinforces the emphasis that cultural analysis places upon the importance of people's participation in the creation of law as a form of cultural production.[47]

The interaction between law and culture is perhaps the most all-encompassing characteristic of the cultural analysis paradigm. According to a cultural analysis perspective, law is seen as reflecting culture as well as creating culture. Law both reflects and creates meaning, practices, and even identities. In addition, law has the capacity to reflect and constitute social forces and relationships of power. Mezey contrasts this approach with the more traditional vision of law, which understands culture "as the unavoidable social context of an otherwise legal question."[48] Instead, a cultural analysis perspective sees the law as "constitutive,"[49] meaning that law is both constituted by culture and constitutes culture.[50] In other words, law not only

---

44. *See generally* Jane B. Baron, *Resistance to Stories*, 67 S. CAL. L. REV. 255 (1994); Richard Delgado, *Storytelling for Oppositionists and Others: A Plea for Narrative*, 87 MICH. L. REV. 2411 (1988); Marc A. Fajer, *Authority, Credibility, and Pre-understanding: A Defense of Outsider Narratives in Legal Scholarship*, 82 GEO. L.J. 1845 (1994); Nancy Levit, *Critical of Race Theory: Race, Reason, Merit and Civility*, 87 GEO. L.J. 795 (1999).

45. Tom Tyler's groundbreaking research has demonstrated that the most important factor in shaping compliance with the law is public perception of right and wrong. Tom R. Tyler, *Compliance with IP Laws: A Psychological Perspective*, 29 INT'L L. & POL. 219, 225–26 (1996) (focusing on criminal justice research). Tyler proposes legitimacy as a second factor fostering voluntary compliance. In the context of legislative mandates, legitimacy derives from public perception regarding the fairness of the decision-making process. *Id.* at 231.

46. *Id.* at 232. Simply put, "People are more likely to regard as fair, and to accept, decisions in which they participated." *Id.*

47. *See supra* note 1 and accompanying text.

48. Mezey, *supra* note 4, at 35.

49. *See* Berman, *supra* note 30, at 109 (noting that "for at least the past fifteen years, sociolegal scholars have largely pursued a constitutive vision of law").

50. *See* Mezey, *supra* note 4, at 47–48.

reflects "antecedent culture" but also shapes and revises existing culture.[51] When law is seen through a cultural analysis paradigm, law is understood as both a product of, and catalyst for, cultural production. As a result of this heavily contextualized understanding of law, it is no longer regarded as a neutral, objective system. According to cultural analysis, law lacks an autonomous quality.[52]

Mezey illustrates this interdependent quality by discussing the litigation concerning the now-familiar warnings routinely given to a custodial interrogation suspect that "he has the right to remain silent, that anything he says can be used against him in a court of law, that he has the right to the presence of an attorney, and that if he cannot afford an attorney one will be appointed for him."[53] The Supreme Court in *Miranda v. Arizona*[54] developed the rule of law requiring these warnings, and they quickly became part not only of police practice, but also of our popular culture. Thirty-four years later, the Court reconsidered the *Miranda* warnings in *Dickerson v. United States*,[55] in which the Court held that the constitutional rule announced in *Miranda* could not be superseded legislatively.[56] Mezey explains the *Dickerson* decision as an example of the interdependence of law and culture. She notes that even though several members of the majority in *Dickerson* had previously sought to call the constitutional rationale of the *Miranda* decision into question,[57] "the Court found that the warnings were constitutionally required not because the Constitution demanded them but because they had been popularized to the point that they were culturally understood as being constitutionally

---

51. *See* Post, *supra* note 28, at 488–89; Mautner, *supra* note 12, at 848–56. Mautner suggests that although "the constitutive approach acknowledges…that the law not only constitutes social relations, but that social relations also constitute the law," it "identifies one element of the complex relations between law and society—law's action upon society—and focuses only on it." Mautner, *supra* note 12, at 856.

52. Mezey, *supra* note 4, at 47. Robert Cover recognized this relationship between law and culture when he observed that "the creation of legal meaning…takes place always through an essentially cultural medium." Robert M. Cover, *The Supreme Court, 1982 Term— Foreword: Nomos and Narrative*, 97 Harv. L. Rev. 11 (1983). *See also infra* notes 120–24 and accompanying text.

53. Miranda v. Arizona, 384 U.S. 436, 479 (1966).

54. *Miranda*, 384 U.S. at 479.

55. Dickerson v. United States, 530 U.S. 428 (2000).

56. *Dickerson*, 530 U.S. at 444.

57. *See* Mezey, *supra* note 4, at 56 (noting the views of Justices Kennedy, O'Connor, and Rehnquist). Also see Justice Scalia's dissent to the decision. *Dickerson*, 530 U.S. at 444 (Scalia, J., dissenting).

required."[58] In short, post-*Miranda*, law transformed culture; "in *Dickerson*, culture transformed law."[59] Together, *Miranda* and *Dickerson* illustrate the operation of a constitutive view of the law.

Mezey's discussion of the *Miranda* and *Dickerson* decisions also illustrates that it is possible to understand more fully the interrelationship between law and culture by exploring the relationship between law and cultural or social norms.[60] Indeed, social norms, which are the collective embodiment of informal rules and implicit understandings,[61] are culturally driven. Mezey's discussion of *Miranda* reveals how the development of cultural norms can be influenced by the creation and enforcement of law. Scholars describe this as law's "expressive function," indicating to people what is right or socially acceptable.[62] Sarat has remarked how "social practices are not logically separable from the laws that shape them and...are unintelligible apart from the legal norms that give rise to them."[63] In contrast, *Dickerson* shows how the development of the law can be impacted by prevalent cultural norms, and in this way, law reflects culture. According to the *Dickerson* model, law is used to enforce cultural norms that are driven by social forces.[64]

---

58. Mezey, *supra* note 4, at 57.

59. *Id.* The Court's more recent decision in *Berghuis v. Thompkins*, 130 U.S. 370 (2010), does not impact this analysis. In *Berghuis*, the Court merely examined application of the "right to remain silent" from a practical and procedural standpoint.

60. The text uses the terms "social norms" and "cultural norms" interchangeably in order to conform with the use of these terms by other legal scholars in the context of a cultural analysis discussion. *See generally* Kerry Rittich, *Engendering Development Marketing Equality*, 67 ALA. L. REV. 575 (2003).

61. The sociological and legal literature examining the development of customary practices and norms suggests that customs are most common in situations involving ongoing relationships with repetitive transactions. *See* Jennifer E. Rothman, *The Questionable Use of Custom in Intellectual Property*, 93 VA. L. REV. 1899, 1980–82 (2007). Similarly, research has shown that welfare-maximizing norms are most likely to develop in close-knit communities. *See* ROBERT C. ELLICKSON, ORDER WITHOUT LAW: HOW NEIGHBORS SETTLE DISPUTES 187, 228, 267, 283 (1991).

62. Mark F. Schultz, *Copynorms: Copyright Law and Social Norms*, in 1 INTELLECTUAL PROPERTY AND INFORMATION WEALTH 201, 206 (Peter K. Yu ed., 2007) (citing literature on this point).

63. Sarat, *supra* note 3, at 137. Sarat suggests that "law shapes society from the inside out by providing the principal categories" for a normal and cohesive social life. *Id.* at 134 (also noting Paul Kahn's "deep investment in a constitutive theory of law").

64. Post, *supra* note 28, at 485–86 (citing PATRICK DEVLIN, THE ENFORCEMENT OF MORALS 10 (1965)) (discussing Patrick Devlin's view of the relationship between culture and law). *See also* Mautner, *supra* note 12, at 844–48 (discussing the historical school in German law).

Social norms also are important because sometimes they may discourage compliance with the law. Specifically, social norms can become solidly entrenched through the exercise of bottom-up choice on the part of the people. Through this process, cultural norms have the potential not only to supplement, but even to replace, formal rules of law in certain circumstances by creating a more popular version of the legal rules. For example, changes in formal speed limits have been shown to bear little connection to the actual speed at which motorists drive.[65] Another illustration of this phenomenon is illegal file-sharing, which for many has become "a way of life."[66] This concept of bottom-up choice also has considerable significance with respect to the Jewish tradition.

Thus, law and cultural norms work in tandem in influencing human behavior. Law and culture embody one another, and therefore, we must learn to interpret law in cultural terms. As a result, "[t]hose whom the law seeks to govern may redefine the law, the law may redefine them, or both."[67] The process, overall, is a "messy" one, as candidly acknowledged by scholars working in this area.[68]

Examining Jewish Tradition through Cultural Analysis: An Introduction

The *mesorah* (Jewish tradition) embodies both an organic legal system called *halakhah* and a comprehensive set of cultural practices pertaining to the practice of Judaism. Interestingly, although cultural affiliation extends to religion in addition to ethno-racial classifications, mainstream religion has not been a focus of cultural analysis.[69] With respect to Judaism specifically, there is virtually no cultural analysis scholarship on either the *mesorah* or

---

65. *See* Robert E. King & Cass R. Sunstein, *Doing without Speed Limits*, 79 B.U. L. REV. 155, 162–68 (1999); Mezey, *supra* note 4, at 52 (discussing the experience of Montana).

66. *Speaker at Howard Law School IP Conference Proposes That Copyrights Might Be "Dead,"* Pat. Trademark & Copyright J. (BNA) No. 77, at 562 (Mar. 27, 2009) (quoting attorney John Hornick).

67. Mezey, *supra* note 4, at 60.

68. ELLIOT N. DORFF, THE UNFOLDING TRADITION: JEWISH LAW AFTER SINAI 335 (2005) (admitting that his view of Jewish law is messy; Dorff manifests a cultural analysis perspective without explicitly invoking this mode of analysis); Mezey, *supra* note 4, at 66–67.

69. *See* DAVID A. HOLLINGER, POSTETHNIC AMERICA 14 (1995) (urging more attention to "religiously defined cultures").

halakhah. This absence of an explicit connection in the literature is surprising because *halakhah*, like all law, both reflects and constitutes social forces and cultural practices.[70]

The *mesorah* is a cultural product of creative human activity intended to be transmitted to future generations, but it is also grounded in the concept of a Divine origin. This unique combination of human and Divine elements complicates the negotiation process and the struggles between different groups of Jews with respect to the authenticity of particular modes of observance.[71] Moreover, throughout history, foreign cultural influences permeated Jewish law and culture given the many years Jews lived in the Diaspora.

Judaism as it exists today is largely a function of legal rabbinic creativity in the early centuries of the Common Era known as the post-biblical Talmudic period. Several reasons support the argument that the *mesorah* presents a particularly compelling case for the application of cultural analysis. Initially, the legal component is unique in that it governs every aspect of human behavior, regulating man's relationship to God and to fellow human beings.[72] The history and functioning of *halakhah* is "as a living, religious, legal organism that is the product of [the Jews'] ongoing covenantal relationship with God."[73] In addition, throughout history Jewish law has functioned as the national legal system of the Jews, even during centuries of exile and dispersion.[74] *Halakhah* prescribes the required conduct in matters concerning ritual, ethics, business, war, sex, and virtually every other dimension of human activity. For example, most people, even non-Jews, are aware that Jewish law dictates the foods that are permissible for Jews to consume, but far fewer realize that *halakhah* also discusses the order in which one's shoes should be put on and tied.[75] Thus,

---

70. *See* Robert C. Post, *Recuperating First Amendment Doctrine*, 47 STAN. L. REV. 1249, 1272 (1995) ("All legal values are rooted in the experiences associated with local and specific kinds of social practices").

71. This phenomenon also has been true throughout Judaism's history as splinter groups continually ebbed and flowed. For a concise discussion of this phenomenon, see ELLIOT N. DORFF & ARTHUR I. ROSETT, A LIVING TREE: THE ROOTS AND GROWTH OF JEWISH LAW 227–45 (1988); *see also* LOUIS JACOBS, A TREE OF LIFE: DIVERSITY, FLEXIBILITY, AND CREATIVITY IN JEWISH LAW 93–109 (2d edition, 2000) (discussing the *halakhah*'s response to the challenges of sectarianism).

72. *See* MOSES MAIMONIDES, THE GUIDE FOR THE PERPLEXED 129 (2d edition, 1904) (translated from the original Arabic text by Dr. M. Friedlander).

73. DORFF, *supra* note 68, at 330.

74. 1 MENACHEM ELON, JEWISH LAW: HISTORY, SOURCES, PRINCIPLES 5 (1994).

75. Shabbat 61a (Babylonian Talmud). Although this matter is subject to different views that are recorded in the Talmud, one position provides that the right shoe is put on first,

the constitutive function of *halakhah* is manifest. It simultaneously reflects and creates culture as it is embedded in the daily practices of Jews. In short, *halakhah* is an all-encompassing, organic system protecting a set of practices that are integral to the survival of the Jewish people.

Another reason for applying cultural analysis to *halakhah* specifically and to the *mesorah* generally is that together, they have been developed and adapted by humans throughout the ages, as is the case with any type of cultural property. *Halakhah* and the *mesorah* have evolved considerably from their biblical origins. Although Jewish law differs from secular legal systems in that God is viewed as the ultimate Author of the laws, in practice the operation of Jewish lawmaking historically has incorporated a pronounced human element, which necessarily entails both subjectivity and fluidity of interpretation. As will be developed more fully in this chapter and those that follow, *halakhah* embodies a humanly developed tradition of interpretation that has been evolving over centuries. Significantly, it is a cultural product of creative human activity that embodies the product of human judgment about God's will. The undeniable human component of both *halakhah* and the *mesorah* is of vital importance in applying the cultural analysis paradigm to the Jewish tradition.

Moreover, Jews have faced a long history of danger regarding their ultimate survival as a people. This danger to survival presents a concern cultural analysis seeks to address given the importance of cultural tradition in shaping individual and group identity. Historically, persecution was the greatest threat to Jewish survival, and in modern times, the murder of six million Jews during the Holocaust is the paradigmatic illustration of this point. Interestingly, the current legal framework regarding international human rights "was brewed in the cauldron of World War II."[76] During the drafting

---

followed by the left; but the left shoe is tied first, followed by the right. *See also* JOEL ROTH, THE HALAKHIC PROCESS 334–36 (1986).

76. JAMES W. NICKEL, MAKING SENSE OF HUMAN RIGHTS 1 (1987). The Second World War and the Holocaust motivated the passage of the Universal Declaration of Human Rights ("UDHR"), the first document composing the International Bill of Human Rights. The framers of the UDHR often discussed these events even though the instrument itself does not refer specifically to these motivations. *See* Peter K. Yu, *Reconceptualizing Intellectual Property Interests in a Human Rights Framework*, 40 U.C. DAVIS L. REV. 1039, 1050–51 (2007). The UDHR was enacted in 1948 and does not represent binding international law given its status as a declaration rather than a covenant. However, according to many authorities, the UDHR has the force of "customary" international law and is considered an authentic interpretation of the United Nations Charter. *See, e.g.,* DAVID SHIMAN, ECONOMIC AND SOCIAL JUSTICE: A HUMAN RIGHTS PERSPECTIVE (1999).

process of the Universal Declaration of Human Rights, the delegates repeatedly condemned the numerous atrocities committed by the Nazis against the Jews during the war.[77]

With this background, it is possible to examine more fully how the five cultural analysis themes identified earlier operate in the context of both the *mesorah* and *halakhah*. This discussion begins by examining the relationship between law and power in the development of *halakhah* and the *mesorah*.

Power Relationships

Those who engage in a cultural analysis methodology understand law as sustaining and reflecting the relevant relationships of power. At the outset, *halakhah* concerns two distinct relationships of power, the first being between God and the Jewish people and the second between the people and their rabbis. *Halakhah* is rooted in the concept of Divine Revelation, which embodies a vertical model with the operative power relationship existing in a vertical line between God and the Jews. In contrast, the development and interpretation of Jewish law is within the purview of human beings. Because humans are, in theory, equal to one another, this model can be understood as a horizontal one.[78] On the other hand, between the rabbis and the people, the operative power relationship also can be seen as vertical. Simply put, the rabbis declared the law and the people obeyed. In reality, however, much of the Jewish tradition was shaped by the people's own practices or customs that often arose in a manner parallel to the exercise of lawmaking authority by the rabbis. This bottom-up phenomenon affords another horizontal dimension to the *mesorah* given that customs are not the product of either Divine authority or rabbinic leadership.

The core doctrine of Jewish law under the vertical model is Revelation by God of His will to the Jewish people at Mount Sinai. Jewish tradition maintains that through this Revelation, the Divine presence permeated the earth

---

77. *See supra* note 76. The atrocities discussed by the UDHR delegates also included forced intellectual labor. *See* ROBERTA ROSENTHAL KWALL, THE SOUL OF CREATIVITY: FORGING A MORAL RIGHTS LAW FOR THE UNITED STATES 100–01 (2010), for a discussion of Dina Gottliebova Babbitt, the Auschwitz prisoner forced to paint portraits under the direction of Josef Mengele, the infamous Nazi doctor known as the Angel of Death.

78. My friend and colleague, Dr. Zohar Raviv, was the initial inspiration behind the "vertical" and "horizontal" paradigms as used in this context. *Cf.* VERNON KURTZ, ENCOUNTERING TORAH 41–42 (2013) (discussing the vertical/horizontal model of the covenantal relationship articulated by Harold Schulweis).

with instructions, laws, and commands. As will be discussed more thoroughly in Chapter 2, the exact content of this Revelation is uncertain, and the subject of endless debate and discussion.[79] Beyond doubt, however, is the proposition that throughout history the tradition understood the Written Law, also known as the Torah or the Five Books of Moses, "as the source of authority and the starting point for the entire Jewish legal system."[80] Steven Resnicoff, writing from the perspective of an Orthodox legal scholar, has observed with respect to the Written Law that a majority of the most influential *halakhic* authorities have assumed "that the words are God's or, at least, the ones that God wants us to have."[81] Thus, Jewish law is steeped in a vertical conception of Divine authority over mankind.

According to the tradition, Revelation encompassed not only the Written Law, but also the Oral Law, which provided explanations and elaborations upon the Written Law. The part of the Oral Law that the tradition assumes God revealed directly to Moses is a product of the same vertical paradigm as the Written Law. Significantly, however, the conception of authority inherent in the Oral Law also is horizontal given that the Oral Law similarly supports a rich tradition of human interpretation in addition to its vertical source of Divine authority. That is to say, a part of the Oral Law was "committed to *halakhic* authorities" in every generation "to fashion and develop."[82] The seeds of this horizontal model for the Oral Law can be traced back to language in Deuteronomy, which provides that people must abide by the judicial verdicts that are announced by the priests or the judges in charge.[83] The tradition understands this language as applying to more than judicial verdicts so that it also invests *halakhic* authorities in subsequent generations with the authority to solve new problems.[84]

Although a more detailed discussion of the history of the Oral Law and its relationship to the Written Law will be postponed until Chapter 2, for now it is important to see how both the vertical and horizontal paradigms are present in the structure of Jewish law. Menachem Elon, the former Deputy

---

79. *See infra* Chapter 2, notes 1–20 and accompanying text.

80. ELON, *supra* note 74, at 232.

81. Steven H. Resnicoff, *Autonomy in Jewish Law—In Theory and in Practice*, 24 J.L. & RELIGION 507, 510 (2009).

82. ELON, *supra* note 74, at 193.

83. Deuteronomy 17:8–11.

84. *See* DORFF, *supra* note 68, at 31–32.

President of the Supreme Court of Israel, fittingly captured this relationship in his authoritative treatise on Jewish law:

> Thus, when we examine the views of many *halakhic* authorities, we will find that as clearly and unequivocally as they emphasized the suprahuman and divine quality of the Source of the entire *halakhah*, in the very same way and with the same emphasis they also stressed the human factor—the exclusive prerogative of the *halakhic* authorities in regard to the ongoing development and creation of the *halakhah*. The dual character of the *halakhah* is expressed in two fundamental maxims pervading the *halakhic* ambiance. On the one hand, it is a basic article of faith that "the Torah is *from*" Heaven; and on the other, it is also a basic principle that "the Torah is not *in* Heaven." The source of the *halakhah* is Heaven, but the place of the *halakhah*, and its life and development, are not in heaven but in human society.[85]

Therefore, the tradition clearly recognizes that Jewish law embodies both a Divine and a human component. These elements are represented in tandem in the law and the practices deriving from the legal content.

Further, the tradition maintains that although the Oral Law initially was received by Moses directly from God, it was handed down from one teacher to the next throughout the generations. A sage with such Mosaic ordination was considered a link in this chain of the Oral Law.[86] Due to concerns on the part of the sages that the Oral Law would be forgotten if it was not memorialized, they undertook the process of compilation and codification.[87] According to the tradition, the Mishnah emerged between 200 and 220 CE as the initial, agreed-upon written version of the Oral Law.[88] The Mishnah

---

85. ELON, *supra* note 74, at 241–42 (citing passages from the Babylonian and Jerusalem Talmuds that discuss Deuteronomy 30:12).

86. Resnicoff, *supra* note 81, at 522 (noting that "those who were ordained in this manner could trace their ordination back to Moses"). Resnicoff also asserts that the chain of Mosaic ordination was broken around the middle of the fourth century CE as a result of persecution. *Id.* at 523.

87. *See* STEVEN H. RESNICOFF, UNDERSTANDING JEWISH LAW 64–65 (2012).

88. The tradition also ascribes the editing of the Mishnah to Rabbi Yehudah, Ha-Nasi (the Prince). *See Introduction* to THE CAMBRIDGE COMPANION TO THE TALMUD AND RABBINIC LITERATURE 1, 6 (Charlotte E. Fonrobert & Martin S. Jaffee eds., 2007) [hereinafter CAMBRIDGE COMPANION] (noting also that little historical or literary evidence exists to connect this text to Rabbi Yehudah). The Mishnah can be considered the

contains Torah teachings, non-Torah laws such as rabbinical enactments, and even local customs.[89] The law's codification process generally is believed to have culminated around 500 CE with the redaction of the Babylonian Talmud,[90] regarded as the central book of Jewish law and tradition.[91]

Once the Talmud was redacted, Jewish law authorities regarded themselves as lacking the ability to reinterpret the meaning of the Written Law in ways that would contradict that which the Babylonian Talmud had established as normative Jewish law.[92] Still, legal development continued to be possible through innovative interpretation of the Talmud and creative conceptualization and application of the Talmudic principles. Thus, the *halakhic* process has a pronounced horizontal, human element despite the significance of the narrative of Revelation, with its concomitant vertical paradigm. This horizontal component necessarily entails subjectivity and fluidity of human interpretation.

The concept that *halakhah* is subject to human interpretation, even at the expense of the Divine, is illustrated by one of the most famous stories in the Talmud known as the Oven of Aknai. This narrative involves a dispute between Rabbi Eliezer and the majority of sages that purports to be

---

earliest sourcebook for the path that traditional Judaism has taken over the course of the centuries that followed its redaction.

89. At times, the meanings of the Mishnah were not clear, and frequently the application of the Mishnah's teachings to concrete cases was uncertain to rabbis of subsequent generations. *See* Resnicoff, *supra* note 81, at 527–28.

90. Professor Daniel Boyarin believes it is more accurate to speak in terms of the Talmud's "production" rather than its "redaction" because he believes the majority of elements of rabbinic Judaism were developed in the "late fifth–sixth centuries or later" and constituted work that was so substantial "as to make the term 'redaction' a misnomer." Daniel Boyarin, *Hellenism in Jewish Babylonia, in* CAMBRIDGE COMPANION, *supra* note 88, at 336, 340–42 (relying on Richard Kalmin's work for purposes of dating the production of the Babylonian Talmud). Another Talmud was redacted in Palestine. *See infra* Chapter 2, note 133 and accompanying text.

91. Resnicoff, *supra* note 81, at 528–29; *see also* Elliot Dorff, *Judaism as a Religious Legal System*, 29 HASTINGS L.J. 1331, 1334 n.9 (1978).

92. Until its demise, the supreme judicial authority for the Jewish people was the *Sanhedrin ha-Gadol*, which was composed of seventy-one rabbis with Mosaic ordination. The *Sanhedrin ha-Gadol* could issue Jewish legal rulings on Torah and non-Torah law and could also enact rabbinic legislation, all of which was viewed as binding on the Jewish people. The Roman government abolished the *Sanhedrin ha-Gadol* in the fourth century, and because the chain of Mosaic ordination also had been broken, its re-establishment became impossible. Resnicoff, *supra* note 81, at 523–24. For a discussion of how the chain of tradition and authority was shattered with the demise of the *Sanhedrin*, see DORFF & ROSETT, *supra* note 71, at 258–75 (1988).

about the ritual purity of a particular oven. In reality, however, the dispute is of much more global significance. The Talmud discloses that Rabbi Eliezer invoked various miraculous events, which culminated in the appearance of a Heavenly Voice declaring that his position is the correct one. The sages replied that the law is "not in Heaven."[93] Instead, after the Revelation, the law was to be interpreted by humans, and thus, the sages prevailed over Rabbi Eliezer. In discussing this narrative, legal scholar Samuel Levine has observed that "the sages followed their own opinion, based on the principle that the duty and authority to interpret the law was given to humans, and thus the law is determined according to human, rather than Divine, logic."[94]

A cultural analysis discourse emphasizes that the existing power structure between humans in any given place and time is a function of cultural production. This type of analysis is relevant to the horizontal model of lawmaking operative under Jewish law. The existence of the horizontal model's focus on human, as opposed to Divine, lawmaking authority was as palpable during the period of Mosaic ordination as it was after the close of the Talmudic period and afterward. Throughout history, the rabbis sought to establish their authority and power so that they could execute their role as lawmakers. With a legal system such as *halakhah*, where the root source of authority is a vertically structured model based on Divine authority, this establishment of power by the rabbinic lawmakers was critical.

Historically, the Talmudic sages forged their authority through various devices that seemed to result in an enhancement of their own powers.[95] For example, the general rule was that the sages afforded laws enacted by them the same legal consequences as biblical laws. Sometimes they accorded their own laws even greater force than biblical laws, resulting in more stringent prescriptions regarding a given law's observance.[96]

Moreover, the post-Talmudic rabbis sought to establish their power and authority, as did the rabbis of the medieval and modern periods.[97]

---

93. Bava Metzia 59b (Babylonian Talmud).

94. Samuel J. Levine, Halakhah *and* Aggada: *Translating Robert Cover's* Nomos *and* Narrative, 1998 UTAH L. REV. 465, 494; *see also* ELON, *supra* note 74, at 262–63.

95. *See* ROTH, *supra* note 75, at 46. Roth's detailed analysis contains an especially instructive chapter on the source and scope of rabbinic authority. *Id.* at 115–33.

96. ELON, *supra* note 74, at 214–15.

97. For a discussion of medieval and modern rabbinic attempts to establish judicial authority despite the break in the chain of authority from Sinai, see DORFF & ROSETT, *supra* note 71, at 303–19, 327–37.

An interesting rule of legal interpretation emerged in early post-Talmudic times illustrating the rabbinic tendency to solidify its power base. Although the *halakhic* system initially gave greater weight to the earlier authorities, the post-Talmudic authorities soon developed the rule that differences of opinion arising from the time of the middle of the fourth century onward should be resolved according to the later authorities.[98] By resorting to such rules of law-making, the rabbis of each generation sought to further *halakhic* creativity and development while simultaneously enhancing their rabbinic authority.

Environment and Conflict

The focus of cultural analysis on environment and conflict is very much inter-twined with its concern with power relationships. Significantly, the exercise of human judgment in the application of Jewish law not only produces the need for sensitivity to environmental influences but also causes conflict. Cultural analysis sees law as a product of the human condition, grounded in specific his-torical contexts, rather than as an objectively neutral system. In commenting about the Talmud's story of the Oven of Aknai, Elon has observed that even though "objective truth" was on the side of Rabbi Eliezer, "legal truth…follows the majority."[99] Elon's commentary pointedly shows that ultimately, Jewish law is not objectively neutral, but rather the product of a subjective human com-ponent. Indeed, he claims that it "would be difficult to picture a more telling illustration of the exclusive prerogative of the *halakhic* authorities to declare the law…over the divine Legislator Himself."[100]

In a fundamental sense, defining law as the product of environment and subjectivity may seem to be in conflict with the primary conception of Jewish law, given *halakhah*'s concern with timeless, enduring values. According to the most traditional perspective of Jewish law, the boundaries set by the Talmud define the parameters of the legal structure and the substantive lim-its of legal interpretation. Traditional Jewish law authorities maintain that in theory, whenever the Babylonian Talmud "reached a consensus as to a particu-lar Torah or non-Torah law, that conclusion became normative law, not to be changed by later authorities."[101] Still, even the Talmud does not constitute "a

---

98. ELON, *supra* note 74, at 268. This rule was developed in the *geonic* period. *See infra* Chapter 3, note 42 and accompanying text.

99. ELON, *supra* note 74, at 262–63.

100. *Id.*

101. Resnicoff, *supra* note 81, at 532.

clear written code of Jewish law."[102] Specifically, authorities acknowledge that it is extremely difficult to determine not only the circumstances in which the Talmud actually reaches a consensus, but also the substantive content of any given consensus in certain situations.[103] The laws have been further impacted by distinct customs, pertaining to both ritual and non-ritual matters, developed by the dispersed Jewish communities.[104] This reality has resulted in many gray areas and provided fertile grounds for disagreement over the centuries with respect to the development of *halakhah*. As will be discussed shortly, the degree of conflict has escalated substantially in modernity.

Significantly, however, even Orthodox authorities readily admit that in rendering legal decisions, the fact-sensitive nature of legal decision-making sometimes requires that new situations be considered differently from those presented in the Talmud. Resnicoff writes, "The continuous stream of significant economic, geographical, political, sociological and technological changes and scientific discoveries has...rendered the applicability of Talmudic rulings increasingly ambiguous and uncertain."[105] As a result, throughout history rabbis attempting to apply many Jewish laws have done so only by resort to the examination and consideration of diverse circumstances "involving cultural, economic, medical, political, and psychological factors."[106] Thus, although the tradition, particularly in Orthodox circles, draws a line between the prohibited changing of the law to accommodate new circumstances and the permissible application of the law to new situations, the practical applications and parameters of this distinction are not always clear.

Also, in issuing rulings, rabbis inevitably have been influenced by some of their personal approaches and perspectives on Jewish law's priorities.[107] This reality was present as early as the dawn of the first century of the Common

---

102. *Id.* at 529.

103. *Id.* at 532.

104. *See id.* at 535. Chapter 3 explores the impact of custom on *halakhah*.

105. Resnicoff, *supra* note 81, at 532.

106. *Id.* at 533–34. The role of socioeconomic factors in the development of *halakhah* has been documented by both Orthodox and historically oriented scholars. *See, e.g.*, ROTH, *supra* note 75, at 231–304 (writing about extralegal sources from an historical perspective); JACOBS, *supra* note 71 (advocating an historical viewpoint); Aharon Lichtenstein, *The Human and Social Factor in* Halakha, 36:1 TRADITION 1, 14 (2002) (acknowledging, as an Orthodox scholar, that "we can recognize the position of the human and social factor within *halakhic* decision as firmly secure"); Daniel Sperber, *Paralysis in Contemporary* Halakha? 36 TRADITION 1, 10 (2002) (writing from an Orthodox perspective).

107. Resnicoff, *supra* note 81, at 534.

Era, when two major schools of thought concerning Jewish law first emerged with the respective schools of the sages Hillel and Shammai. Talmud professor Joel Roth has observed that it cannot be denied that "the rich man's perception of the world influenced the School of Shammai" even if the members of that school were "not consciously aware" of their bias.[108]

Of course, in every generation, there were always boundaries the rabbis would not cross, no matter how much their discourse revealed significant differences of opinion. These boundaries fixed the parameters of the law in each generation. Although in certain instances the boundaries of the law were regarded as fixed and certain, more often than not, they emerged through conflict and discourse in historically specific contexts. This has been true throughout the history of *halakhah* and the *mesorah* and is no less true today. In short, the *mesorah* is designed so that discontinuous, or new, elements can be embraced as long as there is an historic basis for these elements within the body of the *halakhic* system.

In modern times, the degree of conflict has escalated given the range of issues that are capable of being debated. Prior to the Enlightenment, the Jewish community manifested a degree of insularity that minimized to some extent the nature and level of disagreement. The experience of American Jews in particular has demonstrated that enhanced opportunities for participation in the broader culture also create a greater likelihood of assimilation. This assimilation fosters exposure to the more liberal, socially democratic discourse that characterizes the worldview of moderns. This worldview is markedly different from that of the classical Jewish tradition. It is no wonder, then, that the overall context of currently debated issues looks very different in modernity than in any previous era of Jewish history.

In addition, in modern times the presence of cultural dissent has escalated as a result of shifting power dynamics. This reality is reflected in the *halakhah* on several fronts but is particularly visible in the conflicts involving gender. Whereas the female voice is noticeably absent not only in the biblical texts, but also in the texts produced in the Talmudic period and afterward, in the twenty-first century an Orthodox rabbi ordained his female protégée and invested her with the title "rabbah" (the feminine version of rabbi). Although after taking this action the rabbi negotiated with the Rabbinical Council of America and agreed he would no longer give women this title,[109]

---

108. ROTH, *supra* note 75, at 313–14.

109. *See* letter from Rabbi Avi Weiss to Rabbi Moshe Kletenik, RCA President (Mar. 5, 2010), http://matzav.com/rca-releases-statement-on-avi-weiss-weiss-says-no-more-rabba.

this story would have been unheard of in prior centuries. This unprecedented event underscores the view that contests over meaning involve power dynamics.[110] It is important to emphasize that cultural analysis reminds us about the relevance of power, environment, and conflict in law's development. If particular groups or individuals are absent from the decision-making calculus, the resulting law will look different from how it would have looked had they participated. *Halakhah* is similar to any other legal system in that the law that results in any given historical context is shaped by the voices that are allowed into the dialogue at any given time.

Multiple Values and the Interrelationship between Law and Culture

The development of Jewish law has, from its earliest beginnings, embraced a multiplicity of values that is also characteristic of the cultural analysis perspective and consistent with its parallel focus on conflict. There are at least three significant ways in which Jewish law and culture manifest multiple values. First, the sacred texts of the tradition reveal a multiplicity of meanings on their face. With respect to the Written Torah, for example, *halakhah* eschews the idea of textual fundamentalism and rejects the view that the text has a fixed and determinate meaning. Moreover, the text of the Bible incorporates "a number of views of God, a number of conceptions of sin, retribution, love, justice, and so forth."[111] In addition, the language of the original text, Hebrew, facilitates multivalent expression given that it maintains a system of verb roots—primarily consisting of three Hebrew letters—that often support multiple meanings through seven types of verb constructions known as *binyanim*. Hebrew, therefore, is a language particularly conducive to the "fullest and broadest expression of different ideas within a single expression or word."[112] Further, the consequence of a system dependent on human agency is the expectation that human agents will differ in their interpretations. Indeed, "rabbinic discussion...is replete with differences of opinion and records of divergent practice," and these differences were seen as normal and part of the sages' legacy.[113]

---

110. *See supra* note 34 and accompanying text.

111. Gerson D. Cohen, *The Talmudic Age, in* GREAT AGES AND IDEAS OF THE JEWISH PEOPLE 143, 174 (Leo W. Schwarz ed., 1956).

112. JAY M. HARRIS, HOW DO WE KNOW THIS? 215 (1995).

113. Cohen, *supra* note 111, at 165, 175.

Second, Jewish law and tradition reflect multiple values by embracing the contributions of both the rabbis and the people. Specifically, the Jewish tradition consists not only of rabbinical rulings that are the product of legal interpretation but also the practices of the people.[114] Given the absence of a legislative body and a police force, the role of custom (known in Hebrew as *minhag*) has a special significance in the development of Jewish law.[115] Professor Joshua Berman, who specializes in the Hebrew Bible, has documented how this concern for "the collective exercise of power" traces back to the book of Deuteronomy.[116] Thus, from an historic standpoint, the Jewish people have maintained a very democratic ideology in that the practices they adopted and that have become part of their lives have a special meaning and cannot be ignored by the rabbis.[117]

Third, both the rabbinic top-down and the lay-driven bottom-up components of the *mesorah* have been influenced by cultural developments both within and outside of the Jewish community. Cultural analysis reminds us that cultures are not hermetically sealed but continuously interact with the world around them, resulting in cultural borrowing. This reality is especially true with respect to the *mesorah* given that the Jewish people have been living in foreign cultures in the Diaspora since before the destruction of the Second Temple in 70 CE.[118] These cultures have exerted an enormous influence on the development and application of both *halakhah* and the *mesorah* throughout the centuries.[119]

---

114. DORFF, *supra* note 68, at 59 (discussing the views of Solomon Schechter).

115. *See id.* at 19–20. *See also supra* note 61 and accompanying text.

116. Joshua Berman, *"Culture Matters": Deuteronomy, Culture, and Collective Governance*, DEPAUL UNIVERSITY COLLEGE OF LAW CENTER FOR JEWISH LAW & JUDAIC STUDIES 1, 3 (May 13, 2010), http://www.law.depaul.edu/centers_institutes/jljs/documents/berman_culture_matters.pdf.

117. DORFF, *supra* note 68, at 51; *Cf.* Rothman, *supra* note 61, at 1946 (noting that as courts incorporate more customary law into actual decisions "a feedback loop is created in which custom influences the law, the law reinforces the custom, and the custom then becomes further entrenched").

118. *See* Isaiah Gafni, *Babylonian Rabbinic Culture*, *in* CULTURES OF THE JEWS 223, 223 (David Biale ed., 2002) (discussing how Israelites were living in Babylonia even prior to the destruction of the First Temple in 586 BCE).

119. Throughout history, Jewish law and culture have also influenced the majority surrounding cultures. Although a detailed treatment of this topic is beyond the scope of this work, the issue is given attention in other scholarly treatments. *See, e.g.*, Erich S. Gruen, *Hellenistic Judaism*, *in* CULTURES OF THE JEWS, *supra* note 118, at 77, 101 (discussing how Flavius Josephus documented the influence of Jewish practice on Greek culture); Gafni, *supra* note 118, at 248–50 (documenting that archaeological discoveries in Mesopotamia and Iran

As discussed earlier, there is a strong connection between cultural analysis and its emphasis on multiple values and use of narrative. Robert Cover's groundbreaking law review article, "Nomos and Narrative,"[120] was instrumental in shaping how the legal academy understands the relationship between narrative and law. In discussing the non-hierarchical, "radically uncontrolled" nature of narrative, Cover observed that narratives "create and reveal the patterns of commitment, resistance, and understanding."[121] Cover argued that "once understood in the context of the narratives that give it meaning, law becomes not merely a system of rules to be observed, but a world in which we live."[122] Cover's insight here demonstrates the key theme of cultural analysis that emphasizes the interrelationship between law and culture. This intersection was perhaps particularly clear to Cover given his background in Jewish law.[123] He undoubtedly understood that the *mesorah* itself is multifaceted, and incorporates not just the legal precepts, but also the narratives and folklore supporting the legal content as well as the people's practices.[124]

A significant manifestation of the *mesorah*'s multidimensional character is its use of *aggadah* in shaping the *halakhah*. The term *aggadah* sometimes refers specifically to biblical or rabbinic narrative but it "also embraces moral exhortation, theological speculation, and a great, miscellaneous variety of folklore."[125] *Aggadah* thus incorporates "the philosophical, emotional,

---

dating back to the fourth and seventh centuries CE suggest that non-Jews relied upon their Jewish neighbors to remove certain forces or spirits).

120. *See generally* Cover, *supra* note 52, at 4. Cover's article also implicitly embodies a cultural analysis approach and is especially significant given his stature in the legal academy. Cover was a professor at Yale University Law School whose expertise included legal history, constitutional law, and jurisprudence.

121. *Id.* at 17.

122. *Id.* at 4–5.

123. Cover's "reliance on Jewish sources as a basis for analyzing contemporary American legal theory" gave credibility to discussing Jewish law in the world of the secular, legal academy. Levine, *supra* note 94, at 466; *see also* Suzanne Last Stone, *In Pursuit of the Counter-Text: The Turn to the Jewish Legal Model in Contemporary American Legal Theory*, 106 HARV. L. REV. 813, 820 (1993) (observing that "Robert Cover made it respectable to draw on the Jewish tradition in public discourse").

124. Samuel Levine discusses dual usages of *halakhah*, referring to both its narrow meaning as Jewish religious law and a broader definition incorporating the idea of a "world-view." Levine, *supra* note 94, at 484–98. Levine draws on the work of Rabbi Joseph Soloveitchik, who fittingly captured this idea when he wrote that *halakhah* "penetrates into every nook and cranny of life." JOSEPH B. SOLOVEITCHIK, *HALAKHIC* MAN 94 (Lawrence Kaplan trans., 1983).

125. Robert Goldenberg, *Talmud*, *in* BACK TO THE SOURCES 129, 138–39 (Barry W. Holtz ed., 1984). According to David Stern, *aggadah* includes "a widely heterogeneous body of

religious, and social expressions that provide a context for and a deeper meaning to the legal precepts."[126] One example of *aggadah* is the Oven of Aknai
narrative discussed earlier.[127] *Aggadah* is extremely significant because it
has the power to create and "to convey national, cultural, and societal attitudes."[128] The interrelationship between *halakhah* and *aggadah*, therefore, is
important because it tellingly illustrates the *mesorah*'s reflection of a cultural
analysis paradigm in which law and culture are deeply intertwined.[129]

Cultural Analysis and the Chain of Tradition

As the foregoing discussion illuminates, in the early centuries of the
Common Era, the sages furnished a blueprint for the *mesorah*. This blueprint not only encompassed ritual law and law touching upon all aspects of
human behavior, but also a unique cultural tradition that sustained a people
in exile throughout the centuries. According to a cultural analysis paradigm, the *mesorah* affords the Jewish people their unique identity and is the
means through which they exercise their particularity. Legal scholar Paul
Berman has documented a difficult issue concerning cultural analysis generally, which can be especially problematic in the context of the *mesorah* specifically. Berman observes that if one understands a given cultural practice as
the product of human cultural production, it may be difficult to be fully
inspired by this practice or to achieve self-transformation through the
cultural system under discussion.[130] The *mesorah*, a system designed by
humans to achieve spiritual elevation, raises the question whether the

---

materials that range from extra-biblical legends and tales about the rabbis to snippets of
popular folklore and fully elaborated homilies." David Stern, *Aggadah, in* 20TH CENTURY
JEWISH RELIGIOUS THOUGHT 7 (Arthur A. Cohen & Paul Mendes-Flohr eds., 2009).

126. Levine, *supra* note 94, at 485.

127. *See supra* notes 93–94 and accompanying text.

128. Levine, *supra* note 94, at 486. According to Joseph Soloveitchik, *aggadah* can even
serve as an additional source of law because it has the power to mandate obligations. Thus, he
claims that the creation narratives, which can be considered biblical *aggadah*, teach that man
is obligated to "create." *See* Levine, *supra* note 94, at 489–92 (discussing Soloveitchik's position); *see also* SOLOVEITCHIK, *supra* note 124, at 100–01; KWALL, *supra* note 77, at 13–22
(discussing the Jewish tradition's perspective on human creativity).

129. Samuel Levine has pointed out that Cover's use of "narrative" is very similar to the concept of *aggadah*. *See* Levine, *supra* note 94, at 470, 483–84.

130. Berman, *supra* note 30, at 124 (attributing this observation to philosopher Richard
Rorty).

inevitable application of human creativity can potentially destroy the system's authenticity.

In addressing this problem, Berman has proposed an approach grounded in "a hermeneutics of meaning, faith and sympathetic interpretation."[131] He invokes Ronald Dworkin's metaphor of a chain novel, in which "every writer but the first has the dual responsibilities of interpreting and creating because each must read all that has gone before in order to establish, in the interpretivist sense, what the novel so far created is."[132] In an insightful explanation, Berman notes that "Dworkin's model requires the interpreter to treat herself as a 'partner' in the endeavor being analyzed."[133] Under this framework, the interpreter must understand the essence of the prior endeavor so she can generate new interpretations that are within the boundaries of the enterprise. Such an interpretation differs from a "suspicious" reading of the tradition because it does not seek to undermine the tradition or ignore its meaning and relevance.[134]

Interestingly, Rabbi Lord Jonathan Sacks, the former Chief Rabbi of the mainstream Orthodox synagogues in Great Britain, also has invoked Dworkin's chain novel model and has observed that it provides "an admirable way of describing the *halakhic* process."[135] This notion of a partnership between the tradition and the interpreter allows the interpreter to become a part of the interpretative enterprise but only after the interpreter has acquired a thorough understanding of the enterprise and its history.[136] In theory, this

---

131. *Id.*

132. *Id.* at 125 (quoting Ronald Dworkin, *How Law Is Like Literature, in* A MATTER OF PRINCIPLE 146, 158 (1985)).

133. *Id.* at 126.

134. *Id.* at 127.

135. Jonathan Sacks, *Creativity and Innovation in* Halakhah, *in* RABBINIC AUTHORITY AND PERSONAL AUTONOMY 123, 147–49 (Moshe Z. Sokol ed., 1992).

136. *See* Berman, *supra* note 30, at 126–27. Rabbi Sacks' reliance on Dworkin's model of legal interpretation is not surprising given that both models are "backward looking." *See* Suzanne Last Stone, *Formulating Responses in an Egalitarian Age: An Overview, in* FORMULATING RESPONSES IN AN EGALITARIAN AGE 53, 64 (Mark D. Stern ed., 2005) (discussing Dworkin's model). In other words, both models of legal interpretation confine their analysis to authoritative texts "internal to the 'law" and do not legitimize the "conscious decision to depart from prior norms in order to meet present or future needs of society." *Id.* at 64. These positions do not endorse legal creativity or reform for the sake of reform, but they do acknowledge that the historical position of the interpreter may impact legal creativity in particular instances. Note that the cultural analysis paradigm would go even further than Dworkin's model to the extent that it explicitly incorporates new understandings in the discourse.

type of partnership explains how the evolution of the *mesorah* and *halakhah* can be approached from a cultural analysis standpoint without compromising the authenticity of the tradition.

Cultural analysis explicitly acknowledges that the legal interpreter's environment always exercises an instrumental influence. Although change must be rooted in the tradition's previous chapters and therefore mindful of the integrity and coherence of the entire enterprise,[137] legal creativity will arise through the implicit differences that exist over time and space. Further, the very acknowledgement that the custodians of the *mesorah* were indeed influenced by their historic and cultural situations will of necessity produce readings of their texts that provide interpretative insight for different circumstances. In fact, the classical Talmudic sources of the Jewish tradition facilitate this approach through their preservation of minority opinions. As Rabbi Aharon Lichtenstein has acknowledged, these minority opinions "are very much alive, held in reserve where they can be culled from the shelf in a crisis."[138] On the other hand, the fact that the Jewish legal tradition historically has embraced multiple perspectives sometimes makes it difficult to determine where, in practice, the boundaries of the tradition lie.

As the next chapter explores, the genius of the Talmudic sages and their progeny lies in the rabbis' construction of an ordered legal system that was consistent with, even if not identical to, the tradition of the past. As a system of Jewish religious law, *halakhah* embodies a seamless continuity, however much it has changed in some specific forms.[139] Similarly, the cultural practices that are part of the *mesorah* also have continued to develop and evolve. Just as the worldview of the people of Israel at Sinai presumably was distinct from that of the Jews in the period of the Talmud, the same is true for Jews throughout the centuries and today. In light of this reality, a central question emerges that has profound significance for Jews in modern times. How much of the *halakhah* must be preserved in order to maintain the Jewish tradition on a more global level? This question goes to the heart of the more fundamental issue of what constitutes "Jewish identity" and whether *halakhah* is a central piece of this identity.

---

137. *See* Sacks, *supra* note 135, at 149 (describing the renewal of the "*halakhic* enterprise by adding a chapter to its continuing history but in such a way so as to preserve the integrity and coherence of the whole").

138. Lichtenstein, *supra* note 106, at 11.

139. *See* DORFF, *supra* note 68, at 33 (quoting Menahot 29b (Babylonian Talmud)).

Later chapters examine more fully the operation of the Jewish legal system and the *mesorah* generally in the context of specific challenges presented by modernity. Initially, however, it is necessary to explore in greater detail the humanly constructed nature of *halakhah*. The next chapter begins this inquiry with a more in-depth look at the development of rabbinic Judaism.

2 ORIGINS AND DEVELOPMENT OF JEWISH LAW: A TOP-DOWN VIEW

Revelation at Sinai—The Paramount Top-Down Paradigm

Chapter 1 suggests that one cannot make sense of the concept of *halakhah* (Jewish law) without understanding the relevance of the central narrative of the Written Torah—Revelation.[1] In other words, the election of Israel as the community to receive God's Revelation and laws comprises the narrative that gives Jewish law meaning, both in the biblical world and even to this day.[2] Central to this narrative is the idea of the Jewish people being in a covenantal relationship with God. Within the boundaries of the Jewish tradition, different conceptions of the Sinai covenant exist.[3] Nonetheless, as Rabbi Daniel Gordis has observed, "the centrality of law in the relationship between God and the people Israel" represents "the major message of Revelation at Sinai."[4]

---

1. *See generally* BYRON L. SHERWIN, IN PARTNERSHIP WITH GOD: CONTEMPORARY JEWISH LAW AND ETHICS 18 (1990).

2. *See* Samuel J. Levine, Halakhah *and* Aggada: *Translating Robert Cover's Nomos and Narrative*, 1998 UTAH L. REV. 465, 477.

3. Different understandings of the covenant exist within the boundaries of the Jewish tradition, but a detailed exploration of this theme is beyond the scope of this work. For an insightful and provocative account of the covenantal anthropology, see generally DAVID HARTMAN, A LIVING COVENANT: THE INNOVATIVE SPIRIT IN TRADITIONAL JUDAISM (1998).

4. Daniel Gordis, *Revelation: Biblical and Rabbinic Perspectives, in* ETZ HAYIM: TORAH AND COMMENTARY 1394, 1395 (David L. Leiber et al. eds., 2001) [hereinafter ETZ HAYIM].

The core Jewish belief is that Revelation consists of "a contentful, commanding set of instructions and admonitions from God."[5] Significantly, however, the Jewish tradition disagrees as to exactly what was revealed by God to Moses on Sinai, and the Five Books of Moses are not specific on this point. The Talmud contains the following passage:

> It has been taught: Rabbi Ishmael said, "Generalities were spoken at Sinai, details at the Tent of Meeting." Rabbi Akiva said, "Generalities and details were spoken at Sinai, repeated at the Tent of Meeting, and trebled in the steppes of Moab."[6]

According to Rabbi Abraham Joshua Heschel, "[t]he plain sense of these words is that Rabbi Ishmael held that only the general principles of the Torah were revealed at the Sinai theophany; only after the Tabernacle was built were the details communicated to Moses."[7] Heschel continues that "[i]n contrast, Rabbi Akiva held that all of the Torah, with its details and minutiae, was communicated three times, and nothing new was added at the Tent of Meeting or in the steppes of Moab."[8]

This disagreement, perpetuated by two schools of thought represented by Rabbis Ishmael and Akiva, has continued down through the ages and extends even to matters of theology. Significantly, these divergent views relate not only to the content of what was revealed on Sinai, but also to the extent to which the subsequent law is the product of Divine, or human, enterprise (or both). According to Ishmael's perspective, the Torah speaks "in human language."[9] In other words, Ishmael seemingly was inclined toward the view that God painted with broad brushstrokes and left to mankind the task of deriving the specific content of God's will. Further, the Talmudic school of thought attributed to Ishmael maintained "that there are things in the Torah that Moses said on his own authority, and that in many of the instances in which Moses heard things from on high, he transmitted the general meaning and not necessarily the actual words."[10] In contrast, Akiva maintained that "human language

---

5. *Id.* at 1398.

6. Sotah 37b (Babylonian Talmud); Hagigah 6b (Babylonian Talmud); Zevahim 115b (Babylonian Talmud).

7. ABRAHAM JOSHUA HESCHEL, HEAVENLY TORAH 378 (Gordon Tucker trans., 2005).

8. *Id.* at 378–79.

9. *Id.* at 40.

10. *Id.*

is insignificant compared to the language of Torah," which he believed to be God's language.[11] According to Akiva's approach, man can discover only the religious laws and truths already given.[12] Akiva believed that everything that was necessary to interpret God's will was inherent in the language of the text of the Torah and therefore already revealed. In sum, Ishmael can be understood as a minimalist in terms of Revelation, whereas Akiva is a maximalist.[13]

In addition to disagreement regarding the content of God's Revelation, the tradition also has acknowledged the possibility of variation as a result of individual reception at Sinai. Some believe that the presence and acceptance of the Torah by the individuals witnessing the Revelation at Sinai "shaped the very content of the Torah at the critical historical moment it took effect."[14] Some of the rabbinic literature produced during the early centuries of the Common Era reflects this idea. For example, one source states that God's voice came "to each Israelite with a force proportioned to his individual strength."[15] According to Rabbi Michael Rosensweig, this mystical-historical perspective "dramatizes the spiritual significance that *halakhah* ascribes to human singularity by revealing that the subjective inclinations of individuals invested their perspective of Torah with intrinsic worth."[16] Rosensweig's discussion of this point draws from the work of Rabbi Solomon Luria, more widely referred to as *Maharshal*, one of the great teachers of Jewish law in the sixteenth century CE. Significantly, modern theologians have taken the *Maharshal's* focus on "the role of the recipients of the Torah"[17] in formulating a pluralistic conception of Torah that has been embraced by more liberal Jewish theologians.[18]

---

11. *Id.*

12. *Id.* at 559 n.18 (editor's note).

13. Heschel devotes several chapters to defining and applying this terminology. *See id.* at 552–640.

14. Michael Rosensweig, Eilu ve-Eilu Divrei Elohim Hayyim: Halakhic *Pluralism and Theories of Controversy, in* RABBINIC AUTHORITY AND PERSONAL AUTONOMY 93, 108–09 (Moshe Z. Sokol ed., 1992) [hereinafter RABBINIC AUTHORITY].

15. Exodus 5:9 (The Midrash Rabbah) ("[T]o the old, according to their strength, and to the young, according to theirs; to the children, to the babes and to the women, according to their strength and even to Moses according to his strength.").

16. Rosensweig, *supra* note 14, at 109.

17. *Id.*

18. These theologians include Louis Jacobs, Elliot Dorff, and Arthur Green. For a discussion of their respective views on this point, see ELLIOT N. DORFF, THE UNFOLDING TRADITION: JEWISH LAW AFTER SINAI 273, 331, 460 (2005).

These conceptions of Revelation move the model from a strictly vertical one to a paradigm with varying levels of horizontal elements.

Despite the divergent views contained in the Talmud on this issue, the tradition attests to the reality that Akiva's views prevailed over those of Ishmael.[19] Throughout much of Jewish history, a large number of Jews believed that the words in the Written Torah, which appear in the Five Books of Moses, were communicated directly from God to Moses. As Chapter 4 explores, however, in the nineteenth century a distinct approach to authorship of the Written Torah emerged. This perspective, which is characterized by an historical methodology, maintains that the Written Torah should not be understood as emanating from God directly but rather as the written product of human beings produced in specific times and places.[20]

For purposes of applying cultural analysis to Jewish law, it is important to recognize that from the beginning, the rabbinic tradition always has recognized a human component to Jewish lawmaking, even while espousing a vertical model of Divine authority for the source of the subsequent laws. Thus, the cultural analysis paradigm becomes an even more compelling model to the extent the Jewish tradition itself explicitly incorporates a significant human dimension to the lawmaking process.

The Oral Law as a Supplement to Revelation and the Introduction of Rabbinic Lawmaking Authority

The parameters of lawmaking authority following Sinai become significantly more blurred according to the Talmudic tradition. Although many rabbis of the Talmudic era would have described their work as mining the contours of Divine Revelation rather than creating independently a system of Jewish law and thought,[21] the reality is that the tradition itself contains evidence of a difference of opinion on this score. Rabbi Byron Sherwin, one of Heschel's protégées, has recognized explicitly that the tradition contains divergent views concerning the level of human involvement in Jewish lawmaking.[22] Pursuant to what

---

19. HESCHEL, *supra* note 7, at 42–45.

20. DORFF, *supra* note 18, at 50.

21. *See Introduction: The Talmud, Rabbinic Literature, and Jewish Culture, in* THE CAMBRIDGE COMPANION TO THE TALMUD AND RABBINIC LITERATURE 1, 5 (Charlotte E. Fonrobert & Martin S. Jaffee eds., 2007) [hereinafter CAMBRIDGE COMPANION].

22. SHERWIN, *supra* note 1, at 219 n.28.

Sherwin denominates as the "monolithic" view, "the Torah and its command-ments are the dictates of God."[23] According to this view, "just as revelation is monolithic, devoid of any human (subjective) element, so must Jewish law—which expresses the concreting of revelation—have this quality."[24] The second view, which Sherwin calls the "dialogic" approach, sees Revelation generally as a dialogue between God and human beings with respect to both the specific revelatory event and the law that is the product of Revelation.[25] Further, regard-ing the binding nature of the law, Professor Seymour Siegel maintained that the dialogic, or minimalist, view "considerably limit[s] the scope of the dogma, and…allows for more leeway in interpretation."[26]

The classical Jewish tradition assumed that, in addition to the Written Law, God directly transmitted to Moses the Oral Law, which can be thought of, in part, as a type of guidebook to interpreting the text of the Written Law.[27] One of the first explicit references to the Oral Law appears in the story contained in the Babylonian Talmud about the proselyte who asked the great sage, Shammai, "How many Torahs do you Jews have?" Shammai replied, "We have two: The Written Torah and the Oral Torah."[28]

As is the case with the question of authorship of the Written Torah, a sim-ilar debate exists between those who maintain a more fundamentalist per-spective and those who adhere to an historical approach with respect to the authorship of the Oral Law. Specifically, the historical approach does not see the Oral Law as a series of direct commands that were also dictated by God but rather as the embodiment of the best judgment of inspired and learned humans addressing situations in their particular times. With respect to the authorship of both the Written Law and Oral Law, these distinct approaches have profound theological and legal process ramifications. That said, how-ever, even the most fundamentalist view of authorship of the Oral Law would acknowledge that the documents codifying the Oral Law produced in the early centuries of the Common Era were redacted and written by humans.

---

23. *Id.* at 19.

24. *Id.* at 20.

25. *Id.* at 24.

26. Seymour Siegel, *The Unity of the Jewish People*, CONSERVATIVE JUDAISM, Spring 1990, at 21, 25.

27. Elliot Dorff, *Judaism as a Religious Legal System*, 29 HASTINGS L.J. 1331, 1350 n.70 (1978).

28. Shabbat 31a (Babylonian Talmud).

Nevertheless, in contrast to the historical approach, a more fundamentalist perspective tends to perceive the content of these documents as being the product of a direct Revelation of God's will more so than the product of human judgment about God's will. As Chapter 4 explores more fully, this is an area of dispute today between Orthodox Judaism and the more liberal movements.

The Written Law implicitly establishes the authority of the Oral Law in Deuteronomy, in which the text authorizes the practical application of the law by judges in future generations.[29] Moreover, the Babylonian Talmud explains that every generation requires a rabbinical court to apply Jewish law to the particular circumstances at hand.[30] The precise chain of the Oral Law's transmission is delineated in the Mishnah, one of the earliest written texts of the Oral Law.[31] This chain asserts that Moses received the Oral Law from God at Sinai, and it was transmitted from Moses to Joshua, and then throughout the generations to specified categories of learned men.[32] Some scholars understand this tractate as an attempt by the rabbis of this period to legitimize their own authority and understanding of the Oral Law rather than as a "truth" about how it was transmitted.[33] Regardless of how this chain of transmission is understood, it cannot be denied that historically, Jewish law largely has functioned based on a top-down rabbinic model in which the rabbis, rather than the lay people, have been the legal decision-makers.[34]

---

29. *See* Deuteronomy 17:8–11.

30. *See* Rosh Hashanah 25a–b (Babylonian Talmud).

31. *See also supra* Chapter 1, notes 88–89 and accompanying text. The Mishnah is written in such a way as to facilitate memorization of its contents. Elizabeth Shanks Alexander, *The Orality of Rabbinic Writing, in* CAMBRIDGE COMPANION, *supra* note 21, at 38, 48.

32. Avot 1:1 (Mishnah) (The ArtScroll Mesorah Series 1984) ("Moses received the Torah from Sinai and transmitted it to Joshua; Joshua to the Elders; the Elders to the Prophets; and the Prophets transmitted it to the Men of the Great Assembly"). This tractate of the Mishnah is known as Pirke Avot (Ethics of the Fathers).

33. *See* DAVID WEISS HALIVNI, MIDRASH, MISHNAH, AND GEMARA 47 (1986) (observing that this "chain of tradition" was composed "around the first quarter of the second century for the purpose of strengthening [the sages'] authority, showing themselves to be direct successors of Moses, who received the Torah from Sinai").

34. *See* Aaron Kirschenbaum, *Subjectivity in Rabbinic Decision-Making, in* RABBINIC AUTHORITY, *supra* note 14, at 61, 70–71. *See also* Shaye J.D. Cohen, *The Judaean Legal Tradition and the* Halakhah *of the Mishnah, in* CAMBRIDGE COMPANION, *supra* note 21, at 121, 140 (demonstrating the innovative tendencies on the part of the sages of mishnaic Judaism based on the text's logic, rhetoric, and other "dominant concerns").

According to the tradition, the Oral Law functions in a variety of capacities. One such capacity is that the Oral Law provides supplementation and clarification of commands found in the Written Law. For example, the Written Law prohibits labor on the Sabbath, saying that anyone who does work on this day shall be "cut off from among his kin."[35] The Written Law explicitly designates certain prohibited activities such as, but not limited to, cooking, baking,[36] kindling of fire,[37] and wood gathering.[38] A more nuanced definition of prohibited labor is supplied by the Oral Law, specifically in the Mishnah, where the text states that the prohibited labors are "forty less one," and then enumerates the proscribed labors.[39] In formulating these additional rules, the sages were guided by the proximity in the Torah of the prohibition of work on the Sabbath and the instructions for building the Tabernacle.[40] They concluded that the tasks that were deemed essential in constructing the Tabernacle are principal categories of forbidden work.[41]

The sages sought to safeguard the Torah's commands by erecting fences around the law so as to prevent inadvertent violation.[42] This ideology of erecting fences furnishes many other areas of supplementation to the Written Law. One interesting fence concerns the length of holy days such as the Sabbath and Yom Kippur. In contrast to the secular calendar, Jewish days always begin at sundown and end at sundown.[43] Even so, the Talmud explains that because it is necessary to add "from the non-holy to the holy,"[44] the sacred holy days are inaugurated with the act of candle lighting that occurs earlier than the time of sundown, and they conclude after sundown. For those who

---

35. *See* Exodus 31:14.

36. *See* Exodus 16:23.

37. *See* Exodus 35:3.

38. *See* Numbers 15:32–36 (prescribing death as a punishment).

39. Shabbat 7:2 (Mishnah).

40. *See* Exodus 31:1–11; 31:12–17.

41. *See, e.g.,* Shabbat 103a (Babylonian Talmud) ("Even one who strikes with a hammer on the anvil while working is liable, for indeed, those who pounded the sheets of gold for the *Mishkan* [Tabernacle] did this."); *see also* Shabbat 49b (Babylonian Talmud) for general principles concerning the *Mishkan. See also infra* Chapter 5, note 73 and accompanying text.

42. In chapter 18, verse 30 of Leviticus, the Torah states "you shall keep My charge," but the Hebrew word for "keep," *shomer*, can also be translated as "guard or protect."

43. *See, e.g.,* Genesis 1:5 ("And there was evening and there was morning, a first day").

44. Rosh Hashanah 9a (Babylonian Talmud).

have always wondered, this fence explains why Yom Kippur traditionally consists of a twenty-five hour fast!

The notion of devotion to and love for the Torah is manifested by another interesting principle developed in the Oral Law: the concept of *hiddur mitzvah*. This concept is concerned with the physical beautification or embellishment of the commandments and embraces the idea of compliance with the law in a manner that extends beyond that which is required by the letter of the law. The basis in the Written Torah for *hiddur mitzvah* is the verse in Exodus stating, "He is my God and I will beautify him."[45] Specifically, the sages of the Talmud understand this verse in the Written Torah as implying that one should beautify oneself with the precepts of the Torah. The Talmud illustrates this point by encouraging beautiful objects to be used in various ritual observances.[46] The Talmud even speaks of beautiful Torah scrolls "wrapped in the purest silk" and made with the best ink and pen by "an expert scribe."[47] Interestingly, to guard against people going overboard in their endeavor of beautifying the commandments, the Talmud also provides that *hiddur mitzvah* may extend only to "a third of the sum spent on the *mitzvah* [commandment] itself."[48]

In addition to supplementing the Written Law, the Oral Law provides resolution of seeming inconsistencies on the face of the written text.[49] For example, in referring to the Passover holiday, Deuteronomy 16:3–4 states that unleavened bread should be eaten for seven days,[50] but in Deuteronomy 16:8, the text speaks of eating unleavened bread for only six days. According to the Oral Law, the reference to "the six days" is to the period in which eating unleavened bread is purely voluntary; it is only mandatory on the first day of Passover.[51]

Yet another significant function of the Oral Law is to provide instruction as to when a particular verse of the Written Law is to be understood according to a deeper, hidden meaning, rather than in a literal manner according

---

45. Exodus 15:2.

46. Shabbat 133b (Babylonian Talmud).

47. *Id.*

48. Bava Kamma 9b (Babylonian Talmud).

49. *See* Steven H. Resnicoff, *Autonomy in Jewish Law—In Theory and in Practice*, 24 J.L. & RELIGION 507, 516 (2009) (discussing the apparent inconsistencies in the Written Torah involving circumcision and the Sabbath).

50. *See, e.g.*, Exodus 12:15; Leviticus 23:6.

51. Pesahim 120a (Babylonian Talmud).

to the terms of the text. One of the most famous examples of a written verse being interpreted differently from its plain language concerns the "eye for an eye" discussion in chapter 21 of Exodus.[52] Despite the plain language of the biblical text, the Talmud clarifies that monetary restitution is the intended meaning of these verses.[53] In discussing this interpretation, Professor Barry Holtz observed that the rabbis' interpretation of these verses is the most famous example of their inclination to "reread texts in the light of their own contemporary values and beliefs."[54] In contrast, a more fundamentalist explanation is that the Oral Law accompanied the Written Law from the outset and indicated how the biblical text should be understood.

Another example of the sages' decision to ignore the plain language of the text of the Torah concerns appropriate priestly conduct in connection with burying relatives. Leviticus 21:2–3 provide a specific listing of the closest relatives for whom a priest, known as a *kohen*, may defile himself for their burial. This list includes the *kohen's* mother, father, son, daughter, brother, and a virgin sister.[55] The text continues that "he shall not defile himself as a kinsman by marriage,"[56] therefore arguably prohibiting a priest from burying his wife. Interestingly, the sages interpreted the Hebrew word translated as "relative" in Leviticus 21:2 to mean "his flesh," indicating they considered the *kohen's* wife to be his "flesh." Therefore, the sages interpreted this verse to mean that a *kohen* contaminates himself for his "unblemished wife" and therefore, a *kohen* is required to bury his wife, notwithstanding the seemingly inconsistent language to the contrary in the text.[57]

In addition to providing basic explanations of and elaborations upon the laws in the Written Law, the Oral Law is believed to contain specific hermeneutic rules as to how the early sages could derive Torah laws. The earliest collection of hermeneutic rules was associated with Hillel the Elder,[58] but most

---

52. *See* Exodus 21:22–25.

53. *See* Bava Kamma 83b (Babylonian Talmud).

54. Barry Holtz, *Midrash, in* BACK TO THE SOURCES 177, 181–82 (Barry W. Holtz ed., 1984).

55. Leviticus 21:2–3.

56. Leviticus 21:4.

57. *See* Yevamot 22b (Babylonian Talmud). The sages understand an "unblemished" wife as a woman who is not divorced and therefore qualified to be the wife of a *kohen*.

58. Hillel the Elder is believed to have died in the first century CE before the destruction of the Second Temple in 70 CE. *See* Stephen G. Wald, *Hillel the Elder, in* 9 ENCYCLOPEDIA JUDAICA 108 (Michael Berenbaum & Fred Skolnik eds., 2d edition, 2007).

authorities today refer to the thirteen principles attributed by the tradition to Rabbi Ishmael.[59] These rules are recited every day by observant Jews during the morning service.

In developing the Oral Law, the sages sometimes strained to make it consistent with, or even based upon, the Written Law.[60] This observation is an interesting one that bears upon the general question of the origin of the Oral Law. A fundamentalist perspective on this issue would conclude that both the substantive content of the Oral Law, as well as the hermeneutic rules, were revealed by God to Moses and passed down throughout the ages.[61] Modern scholarship, however, understands the relationship between the orality of post-biblical rabbinic texts and their reduction to writing as the result of a complex, orally based social process through which the oral and the written intersected with one another in an ongoing manner. Professor Elizabeth Shanks Alexander has written that the sages highly valued orality given their attempts "to craft religious ethic and mold men of wisdom and virtue in the wake of great societal upheaval."[62]

As the discussion in the following section illustrates, even if the sages were operating within a framework that assumed Revelation by God of the Oral Law in conjunction with the Written Law, the human imprint upon the Oral Law's development and redaction is palpable. In theory, the sages might have been attempting to discover Revealed truths; in practice, however, they were laying the groundwork for a new understanding of the Jewish religion that, through a "slow and gradual process,"[63] ultimately shaped the content of the *mesorah* (Jewish tradition) in the centuries to come.

---

59. *But see* HERMANN L. STRACK, INTRODUCTION TO THE TALMUD AND THE MIDRASH 25 (2004) (noting that the attribution of these thirteen rules to Rabbi Ishmael is historically inaccurate because this framework was developed centuries later).

60. *See* SAUL LIEBERMAN, GREEK IN JEWISH PALESTINE: HELLENISM IN JEWISH PALESTINE 63 (1950) (noting that rabbinic literature "abounds in...artificial and forced interpretations").

61. *See* HESCHEL, *supra* note 7, at 559 (comparing this maximalist perspective of Rabbi Akiva with that of Rabbi Ishmael's minimalist approach).

62. Alexander, *supra* note 31, at 55. She also discusses the work of Martin Jaffee demonstrating that the physical proximity between sage and disciple necessitated by oral transmission was a key element of this rabbinic culture. *Id.* at 54.

63. Jeffrey L. Rubinstein, *Social and Institutional Settings of Rabbinic Literature, in* CAMBRIDGE COMPANION, *supra* note 21, at 58, 66 (speaking of the *amoraic* period in Babylonia; *see also infra* note 76). Rubinstein also notes that, contrary to the common

The Reforms of the Sages in the Rabbinic Period: Forging a New Religion

The nature of Judaism as it is practiced today in traditional circles is markedly characterized by the reforms of the sages in the rabbinic period following the destruction of the Second Temple in 70 CE. Jewish studies historian Shaye Cohen reminds us that even before the destruction of the Second Temple, "the regimen of daily prayer, Torah study, participation in synagogue services, and observance of the commandments sanctified life outside the Temple and, in effect, competed with the Temple cult, just as the new lay scholar class, the scribes and others, in effect competed with the priests."[64] Still, after the Temple's destruction, the rabbis of this period needed to resolve how the Torah could be applied in a completely new environment. This process continued on well into the early sixth century when the Babylonian Talmud is believed to have been produced.[65] Professor Daniel Boyarin has observed that the Talmud "and its major discursive peculiarities" are "the very traits that make rabbinic Judaism what it is."[66]

Rabbinic Judaism of this period, predicated on the model of the Pharisee sect, emphasized the construction of a system of norms of holiness rather than public institutions, such as the Temple and the priesthood, that were integral to the biblical period. In contrast to the Pharisees, the rival sect known as the Sadducees responded to the destruction of the Second Temple by continuing the norms of the biblical period. The Sadducees emphasized public institutions, whereas the Pharisees stressed "the personalization of Judaism, the construction of a system of norms of holiness—and a promise of salvation—addressed not only to the collective, but to the individual as well."[67] In other words, the Judaism characteristic of the Pharisaic model "centered not around the Temple, but around the table, where all could eat like priests, and

---

understanding, it is unlikely that the rabbis banded together following the destruction of the Second Temple in 70 CE "in the pursuit of some grand, and under the circumstances grandly implausible, scheme to preserve Judaism in the absence of a Temple." *Id.* at 77.

64. SHAYE J.D. COHEN, FROM THE MACCABEES TO THE MISHNAH 210–11 (2d edition, 2006). The quotation from Cohen's book has been modified to reflect a capitalized spelling of "Temple" as used consistently throughout this text.

65. *See also supra* Chapter 1, notes 90–91 and accompanying text.

66. Daniel Boyarin, *Hellenism in Jewish Babylonia, in* CAMBRIDGE COMPANION, *supra* note 21, at 336, 340.

67. JONATHAN WOOCHER, SACRED SURVIVAL 158 (1986).

the school, where their dual Torah—the written and the oral—was taught."[68] As a consequence, the Pharisees taught that "even outside of the Temple— in one's own home—one had to follow the laws of cultic purity in the only circumstance in which they might effectively apply, namely, at the table."[69] Everyday meals, therefore, had to be eaten by ordinary people as if they were Temple priests.[70] From a cultural analysis standpoint, it is worth noting that the Pharisaic model was a very democratic one in that it called for participation by everyone, not just the priests.[71] Further, knowledge of Torah was the determining factor in qualifying for membership in the rabbinic profession, as opposed to wealth or social status.

The philosophy of the Pharisees revealed their view that the laws of the Scripture "should be expanded to cover all of life, [and] not limited to their own originally intended contexts."[72] Political science professors Bernard Susser and Charles Liebman have observed that "rabbinic Judaism...determined the basic form that Judaism would take over the course of the following two millennia of Exile."[73] Although "an impressive body of *halakhah* was already in existence long before the rabbis turned to jurisprudence," the importance of the rabbis' work during this time was in following "principles which protected legislation from inflexibility and society from fundamentalism."[74] Professor Isaiah Gafni has observed that the sages engaged in a "rabbinization of the past" through which they represented "earlier figures or institutions of Jewish history...in the image of the rabbinic world."[75] By resorting to this process, they were able to create a sense of continuity with an "untarnished past"[76] and were masters of creating new, discontinuous

---

68. *Id.*

69. Jacob Neusner, The Oral Torah 19 (1991).

70. *Id.*

71. Judah Goldin, *The Period of the Talmud, in* The Jews: Their History 119, 157 (Louis Finkelstein ed., 1970) (noting that the law was not just for the priests but for the entire "house of Jacob").

72. Robert Goldenberg, *Talmud, in* Back to the Sources 129, 130–31 (Barry W. Holtz ed., 1984).

73. Bernard Susser & Charles Liebman, Choosing Survival 28 (1999).

74. Goldin, *supra* note 71, at 163.

75. Isaiah Gafni, *Rabbinic Historiography and Representations of the Past, in* Cambridge Companion, *supra* note 21, at 295, 304–05.

76. *Id.* at 307. Gafni also notes that the rabbinization process was most prevalent during the period of the *amora'im*, who lived in the Middle Rabbinic period after the year 220 CE. *Id.* at 306, 308. *See also* Cambridge Companion, *supra* note 21, at xiv.

approaches that nonetheless arguably maintained an authentic connection to the past. Rabbi Eugene Borowitz captured the essence of rabbinic Judaism with the following observation:

> The rabbis's theological creativity operates mainly in their reshaping of the multitudinous ideas and images of biblical belief. In this process they continue the millennial Jewish experience of reinterpreting the covenant as times change and as their own intellectuality and religious sensitivity demand.[77]

Despite the innovative tendencies of the rabbis during this period, Rabbi Max Kadushin has noted the strong degree of coherence characterizing the rabbinic literature produced following the destruction of the Second Temple. Kadushin claimed that this coherence "must have been such as made for unity of thought over great stretches of time and still gave room for differences due to changed circumstances and to the divergent proclivities of individuals."[78] A famous narrative in the Talmud illustrates the same idea. According to this story, Moses visits the academy of Rabbi Akiva, who lived around 1400 years after him, and fails to understand anything that Akiva is saying. Still, Moses is comforted when Akiva cites as the source for the law being discussed the "*halakhah* transmitted orally to Moses at Sinai" because this statement indicates that Akiva and his contemporaries believed themselves to be part of the ongoing tradition dating back to Moses.[79] The implication of this narrative is "that a gap exists between the revelation Moses received and the later teachings of the rabbis."[80]

Theologically, the rabbis of this period developed the Oral Law to make Revelation a continuing reality in the lives of Jews living in the post-destruction era. Rabbi Gerson Cohen observed that "the only way that the revelation could be kept relevant to new problems was to interpret the written word so as to make it apply to the activities of the peasant and the businessman, the housewife and the servant, the schoolboy and the scholar."[81]

---

77. Eugene Borowitz, *Judaism: An Overview, in* JUDAISM: A PEOPLE AND ITS HISTORY 3, 13 (Robert Seltzer ed., 1987).

78. MAX KADUSHIN, ORGANIC THINKING 3 (1st edition, 1938).

79. *See* Menahot 29b (Babylonian Talmud).

80. Alexander, *supra* note 31, at 43.

81. Gerson D. Cohen, *The Talmudic Age, in* GREAT AGES AND IDEAS OF THE JEWISH PEOPLE 143, 177 (Leo W. Schwarz ed., 1956).

Searching the written text for meanings relevant to the present—a process known as *midrash*—provides a way for Jews to engage even today. Grounding change in Scripture facilitated the rabbis' goal of consistency, even if that process was sometimes somewhat attenuated.[82] In other words, "to achieve a serious hearing and to attain a measure of validity an idea had to be attached to a verse... [or] 'derived' from Scripture."[83] As discussed in Chapter 1, the rabbinic lawmaking process calls to mind the notion of a chain novel that depends upon change being rooted in the past so that innovations can maintain the integrity of the enterprise.[84]

A foundational example of this process concerns the rabbinic focus on prayer as a substitute for animal sacrifice, which prevailed during the biblical and Temple periods. In the Mishnaic tract Pirkei Avot (popularly known as Ethics of the Fathers or Sayings of the Fathers), the text quotes Simeon the Just, who lived prior to the destruction of the Second Temple, as saying, "By three things the world exists: by the Torah, by the service, and by the deeds of loving kindness."[85] The original context of the word for *service* as it appears in the text—*avodah*—was animal sacrifice in the Temple. After the Temple's destruction, however, the rabbis extended its meaning to include any form of worship.[86] In fact, the Talmud refers to prayer as "the service of God performed in the heart."[87] The rabbis looked to the power of personal and community prayer as the primary vehicle enabling the Jews to become close to God, in the same way that offering animal sacrifices functioned as the primary way for Jews to connect to God in the pre-destruction era.[88] This transformation reveals how the rabbis of this period forged changes to the religion while retaining a continuous and purportedly authentic connection with the Israelite religion of biblical times.

---

82. *See id.* at 175 ("Occasionally this might involve tearing a phrase out of context, emending the holy text, or...interpreting a Hebrew word as though it were synonymous with a similar-sounding Greek one!").

83. *Id.*

84. *See also supra* Chapter 1, notes 135–36 and accompanying text.

85. Pirkei Avot 1.2 (Mishnah) (Philip Blackman trans., 2000). There is some discrepancy as to whether Simeon the Just refers to Simeon I (who lived around 280 BCE) or his grandson, Simeon II (who lived around 200 BCE), although the latter is the most favored position. *See* ETHICS OF THE FATHERS 4 n.10 (Hyman E. Goldin trans. & ann., 1962).

86. *Id.* at 4 n.13.

87. Taanit 2a (Babylonian Talmud).

88. For an excellent discussion of this concept, see THE KOREN SACKS SIDDUR xxxvi–ix (Jonathan Sacks ed., 2009).

Syn·

Although synagogues, the venues of public worship, were not important centers of study for the sages, they gradually "rabbinized" them over a long period of time.[89] Moreover, the liturgy developed by the rabbis after the Temple's destruction revealed "a profound nostalgia for the Temple service and its rigid protocol and precise regulation."[90] Gradually, then, the rabbis forged a religion in which the synagogue became central, and "the stabilization and adoption of a uniform order of synagogal service permanently fixed the foundations of communal religious expression."[91] From a sociological perspective, this model provided the basis for the rich model of community worship that continues to exist to this day.

Pesach

Another paradigmatic example of rabbinic innovation following the destruction of the Temple is the re-creation of the Passover Festival. Talmud professor Baruch Bokser emphasized how Passover became the paradigm for the creation of new religious measures that nonetheless traced their roots to the biblical period.[92] In the Bible, the paschal sacrifice is depicted as the basis for a family meal. In chapter 12 of Exodus, the text states that each family is to slaughter its own lamb unless the household is too small. In that case, one household can share the lamb with a neighbor dwelling nearby.[93] Also, the Israelites were commanded to eat the Passover offering "roasted over the fire, with unleavened bread and with bitter herbs"[94] and to "not leave any of it over until morning."[95] According to Bokser, this "portrayal of a home gathering with cultic overtones provides a general model of how to perform rituals and pious activities outside of a temple."[96]

Thus, absent the existence of the Temple, the rabbis eliminated the mass pilgrimage of Jews to Jerusalem and instead emphasized the family-oriented nature of the Passover meal as depicted in the Torah. Significantly, in the

---

89. Rubenstein, *supra* note 63, at 67.

90. Cohen, *The Talmudic Age, supra* note 81, at 207.

91. *Id.* at 168–69.

92. Baruch Bokser, The Origins of the Seder 8 (1984).

93. Etz Hayim, *supra* note 4, at 380–81 (corresponds to Exodus 12:3–4).

94. *Id.* at 382 (translation of Exodus 12:8). For the most part, this book uses the English translation of the Torah that is derived from Etz Hayim. The Introduction to Etz Hayim states that this translation is from the most recent Jewish Publication Society translation, which is "considered by scholars to be the standard in the Jewish world." *Id.* at xx.

95. *Id.* (translation of Exodus 12:10).

96. Bokser, *supra* note 92, at 9.

Mishnah's account of Passover, the rabbis downplayed the paschal sacrifice in the Temple and instead elevated the matzah and bitter herbs also mentioned in the Bible.[97] In both the Mishnah and the Haggadah (the text containing the service for the Passover seder), the rabbis taught that consuming the symbolic foods and retelling the Exodus narrative were sufficient to make up for the inability to perform the Passover sacrifice after the Temple's destruction. As a result of this rabbinic reinterpretation, during the seders Jews simply point to the little shank bone on the seder plates that represents the sacrifice while nibbling on both matzah and bitter herbs.[98]

Moreover, the Passover meal itself involves innovation linked to continuity. As indicated above, chapter 12 of Exodus outlines the concept of a family meal during which time the sacrifice is consumed by members of the household. In the times of the early rabbis, however, the Greco-Roman tradition of symposia and banquets, with their emphasis on intellectual discourse, may have influenced the development of the seder's focus on storytelling and discussion. The Bible requires parents to instruct their children with respect to the Passover rite. For example, Exodus states, "And when your children ask you, 'What do you mean by this rite?' you shall say, 'It is the Passover sacrifice to the Lord, because He passed over the houses of the Israelites in Egypt when He smote the Egyptians, but saved our houses.'"[99] In this regard, the requisite textual instruction pertains to the paschal sacrifice itself rather than to the narrative of the Exodus that is the focus of the Haggadah. Although Bokser concludes that "the seder's intellectual dimension does not have a simple linear relation to the Bible," or to Greco-Roman symposia,[100] there is a level at which the rabbis began with the family meal delineated in the Bible and adapted it to their current situation by infusing it with a new meaning that was appropriate to their political and cultural milieu.

The story of the development of the Passover seder illustrates how Jewish law historically has operated in a manner that allows for its development within the context of an organic tradition. Judaism as a religion is set up so that the law essentially is the product of human judgment about God's will. In short, the entire tradition is designed so that new elements with an historic

---

97. The bitter herbs are mentioned in Exodus in conjunction with eating the Passover offering, *see* Exodus 12:8, although unleavened bread is also mentioned separately in the Bible. *See* Exodus 12:15; Leviticus 23:6.

98. BOKSER, *supra* note 92, at 8.

99. ETZ HAYIM, *supra* note 4, at 386 (translation of Exodus 12:26–27).

100. BOKSER, *supra* note 92, at 12.

basis within the body of the system can be embraced (or at times rejected). Passover, perhaps the most widely celebrated Jewish tradition today, provides a prototypical example of the rabbinic model at work.[101]

The development of the Passover seder illustrates the rabbis' outstanding abilities to delicately balance adaptation to their greater surroundings with maintenance of the Jewish tradition. As the following section develops more fully, the rabbis who lived in the Roman Empire during the Greco-Roman period had to forge their laws and tradition in the face of an overpowering Hellenistic cultural presence. From a cultural analysis standpoint, their work provides a fascinating model of the development of a minority tradition that not only borrowed from, but also reinterpreted, elements from the surrounding majority culture.

Hellenistic Influences on Early Jewish Law

Even before the conquest of Alexander the Great in the late fourth century BCE, Jews had settled in areas such as Syria, Egypt, and the lands of the Tigris and Euphrates. Still, the development of a Greek Diaspora facilitated the development of a Jewish Diaspora in areas that extended into Greece itself.[102] Greek towns appeared even in Palestine, and "the Jews of Judaea could not and did not isolate themselves altogether from the pervasive aura of Hellenism."[103] These Jews had to preserve and perpetuate their culture through the "media and methods" of the more pervasive Hellenistic culture.[104] In general, the Jews "redefined their heritage in terms of Hellenistic culture itself" by engaging "actively with the traditions of Hellas, adapting genres and transforming legends to articulate their own legacy in modes congenial

---

101. Interestingly, the Passover seder also is a perfect example of both *halakhah* and *aggadah*—the two primary components of rabbinic activity—operating together given that the Haggadah is composed of many narratives "to be discussed, pondered and explored." Holtz, *supra* note 54, at 202 (noting that "the Haggadah is more appropriately understood as a study compendium and the seder as a learning experience rather than as a 'service' "); *see also* Isaiah M. Gafni, *The Historical Background, in* THE LITERATURE OF THE SAGES 1, 15 (Shmuel Safrai & Peter J. Tomson eds., 1987) (noting how the activities of the rabbis following the destruction of the Second Temple stressed "continuity with Jerusalem and the past, while simultaneously setting up an authority structure and religious framework that clearly evolved out of a radically new situation").

102. Erich S. Gruen, *Hellenistic Judaism, in* CULTURES OF THE JEWS 77, 101 (David Biale ed., 2002).

103. *Id.* at 78.

104. Isaiah Gafni, *Babylonian Rabbinic Culture, in* CULTURES OF THE JEWS, *supra* note 102, at 223, 230.

Septuagint ✓

to a Hellenistic setting."[105] Consequently, around the third or second century BCE, the Hebrew Bible was translated into Greek to accommodate the needs of Diaspora Jews for whom Greek was the primary language.[106]

A fascinating story appearing in the Mishnah centuries later illustrates this dilemma for Jews living in these times. Rabbi Gamaliel, the patriarch of the Palestinian Jewish community of the second century CE, was asked how he could bathe in the Bath of Aphrodite, which contained a statue of the Greek goddess. His reply was, "I did not come within her limits; she came within mine."[107] The rabbi's reply is significant because he acknowledged the reality that the Jewish people must bathe, even if they must do so in an environment that is spiritually polluted. According to Arnold Eisen, the current Chancellor of the Jewish Theological Seminary, Rabbi Gamaliel's "assertion of Israelite sovereignty over the polluted Land of Israel ('she came within my limits') was essential to Jewish survival."[108]

Professor Elias Bickerman, a noted authority on the Jews of the Hellenistic period, has documented extensively the influence of Hellenistic culture on the Jewish legal system that ultimately emerged. He observed that the Pharisaic goal of bringing the Torah to everyone, and the concept that "piety was teachable and to be attained only through teaching," was a Platonic concept.[109] According to Bickerman, Hellenism introduced "the first epoch of general popular education in the Occident" and afforded citizenship rights "only after a sort of 'proficiency test' was passed."[110] As was true of the rabbinic tradition throughout its history, these outside concepts were imported into Judaism but reworked so as to comply with the precepts of the tradition. One such example is the importance the sages attributed to *everyone*

democratic?

---

105. Gruen, *supra* note 102, at 80.

106. *Id.* at 78–79 (this translation is known as the Septuagint). Although historians explain the creation of the Septuagint, as discussed in the text, some classical Jewish sources provide a different picture. *See* AMMIEL HIRSCH & YOSEF REINMAN, ONE PEOPLE, TWO WORLDS 188 (2002) (including the statement by Yosef Reinman that the Septuagint was the result of Egyptian king Ptolemy's order to translate the Torah into Greek around 250 BCE; Reinman claims this event is "recorded as an awful tragedy in Megillat Taanit, composed during Mishnaic times, not more than a century or two after the fact").

107. Avodah Zarah 3:4 (Mishnah).

108. ARNOLD M. EISEN, GALUT: MODERN JEWISH REFLECTIONS ON HOMELESSNESS AND HOMECOMING 40 (1986); *see also* Eric M. Meyers, *Jewish Culture in Greco-Roman Palestine, in* CULTURES OF THE JEWS, *supra* note 102, at 135 (noting that this narrative "attests to the sense the Jews have of participation in the discourses of the wider culture").

109. ELIAS BICKERMAN, FROM EZRA TO THE LAST OF THE MACCABEES 162 (1987).

110. *Id.*

learning Torah in order to fulfill the prefatory command to the Revelation on Sinai: "Ye shall be unto Me a kingdom of priests, and a holy nation."[111]

Further, in stressing the importance of global education, the Pharisees supplemented the Written Law, as discussed earlier. Significantly, this remarkable concept of setting the "*halakhah* alongside the written law is again Greek."[112] Bickerman has observed:

> It is the concept of the "unwritten law" (*agraphos nomos*), which is preserved not on stone or paper but lives and moves in the actions of the people. But whereas in the Greek world this notion often served to *negate* the written law, Pharisaism used the oral law to "*make a fence for the Torah*."[113]

According to some scholars, even the "chain of tradition" recorded in the Mishnah through which the rabbis traced the lineage of their authority[114] was created unilaterally by the Pharisees based on a Greek model. Professor Eric Meyers has observed that this Pharisaic tradition is "closely related to the Hellenistic philosophical schools that traced their lineage back to Plato himself."[115] Further, Meyers has discussed how the Pharisees also imitated Greek legal hermeneutics in their own development of hermeneutical principles interpreting the Oral Law.[116] He notes that the thirteen principles attributed to Rabbi Ishmael,[117] along with "other related forms of Talmudic literature, have their precise parallels in Greek legal hermeneutics."[118] Indeed, Talmud professor Saul Lieberman has explained that the rabbis of this period invoked the interpretative strategies accepted in the civilized world so that their methods would be "understood and appreciated by their contemporaries."[119]

---

111. *Id.* at 163; *see* Exodus 19:6.

112. BICKERMAN, *supra* note 109, at 163.

113. *Id.* at 163–64 (emphasis added).

114. *See supra* notes 31–34 and accompanying text.

115. Meyers, *supra* note 108, at 167. According to Meyers, this chain of tradition was an innovation that occurred "roughly parallel in time to the second-century invention of the 'apostolic succession' among Catholic Christians." *Id.*

116. *Id.* at 170.

117. *See supra* note 59 and accompanying text.

118. Meyers, *supra* note 108, at 170. *See also* LIEBERMAN, *supra* note 60, at 55–64.

119. LIEBERMAN, *supra* note 60, at 78 (this similarity also extended to interpretations of dreams).

From a theological perspective, Hellenism also played a part in the Pharisees' development of a new spiritual agenda. Bickerman notes that according to the account of Flavius Josephus, the renowned Jewish historian who lived in the first century CE, "the Pharisaic doctrine of the future life derives from the Greek teaching of the Pythagoreans."[120] The Hellenistic world popularized the notion that evil on earth can be explained by rewards and punishments that would become operative after death. This idea was foreign to the Bible. The Pharisees adopted the Hellenistic doctrine of resurrection but gave it a spin that was consistent with the Torah. Therefore, whereas "among the Pythagoreans each soul must automatically return to new life after death, each according to its merit…the Pharisees substituted the single event of the Last Judgment, whose day and scope God would determine."[121] The Pharisaic sages "dovetailed the new Hellenistic idea into the structure of biblical ideas" and forged a doctrine that developed into a staple of Jewish belief.[122]

The reinterpretation of the Jewish religion that emerged in Jewish Palestine provided "a fertile setting for a constructive symbiosis between Jewish and Hellenistic cultures."[123] The leaders of the Jews in Hellenistic Palestine saw "no inherent contradiction between a Hellenized lifestyle and a Jewish practice."[124] An interesting example of this is furnished by "the presence of mythological Greek images on the sarcophagi of the sages," suggesting "that burial in such containers did not contradict rabbinical Judaism."[125] Meyers has observed that "the manner in which the Jews accommodated" to living in the Hellenistic world culture "became the paradigm for future accommodation to other major world civilizations, such as Rome, Byzantium, Islam, and Christianity."[126]

Scholars have emphasized that the notion of adaptation by assimilating selected ingredients from the surrounding culture has been the key to the survival of the Jewish religion throughout the ages. Jewish history professor David Biale has written that "for every period of history, interaction with the non-Jewish majority has been critical in the formation of Jewish culture."[127]

---

120. *See* BICKERMAN, *supra* note 109, at 165.

121. *Id.*

122. *Id.*

123. Meyers, *supra* note 108, at 174.

124. *Id.* at 161.

125. *Id.* at 171.

126. *Id.* at 136.

127. David Biale, *Preface* to CULTURES OF THE JEWS, *supra* note 102, at xv, xx.

Susser and Liebman have observed that "Judaism...learned from and was enriched by the many cultural legacies it inherited from the dozens of countries through which Jews passed."[128] They posit that the source of "Jewish cultural creativity" may be in its multidimensional confrontation "with so many of the world's greatest cultures."[129] According to Gerson Cohen, Judaism "was able to survive as a living culture...precisely because of its ability to translate its culture; that is, to accept as a positive value a considerable degree of assimilation."[130]

Biale concurs that throughout history the Jews were able to construct their particular identities through their "profound engagement with the cultures of their environment," but he notes two "seeming paradoxes" resulting from this phenomenon:

> On the one hand, the tendency to acculturate into the non-Jewish culture typically produced a distinctive Jewish subculture. On the other hand, the effort to maintain a separate identity was often achieved by borrowing and even subverting motifs from the surrounding culture.[131]

The cultural analysis paradigm reminds us that what was true for Jewish culture generally also was true for Jewish law specifically because these societal elements are completely intertwined. Talmud professor Joel Roth has observed that "borrowings from other legal systems, whether consciously or unconsciously...often incorporate the sociological reality into the Jewish legal system, sometimes intact and sometimes modified."[132] In other words, both Jewish law and Jewish culture reflected and was shaped by the reality of assimilation and acculturation.

Rabbinic Law in the Post-Talmudic Period

Ultimately, the rabbinic culture that emerged in Babylonia, rather than Palestine, had the greatest impact on the development of Jewish law throughout the centuries to come. On a comparative level, Babylonian Jews enjoyed

---

128. SUSSER & LIEBMAN, *supra* note 73, at 88.

129. *Id.*

130. GERSON D. COHEN, JEWISH HISTORY AND JEWISH DESTINY 151 (1997).

131. Biale, *Preface, supra* note 127, at xxi.

132. JOEL ROTH, THE HALAKHIC PROCESS 303 (1986).

far more cultural autonomy than their Palestinian counterparts, who had to face an overpowering Hellenistic cultural presence. Although two Talmuds were redacted, one in Palestine and the other in Babylonia, the latter surpassed the former in importance.[133]

The rabbis who lived in Babylonia during the early centuries of the Common Era crafted and propagated "a self-image that would project this culture as being the embodiment of the one unique and ancient model of true, unadulterated Israelite tradition, with uncontaminated roots going back to First-Temple Jerusalem and the days of the prophets."[134] Despite the appeal to many of this image, the reality suggests otherwise given that the Babylonian rabbinic culture, like any culture, was subject to outside influences. Boyarin has documented a "shared cultural milieu" between the Hellenistic and Christian traditions and the rabbinic culture in Babylonia.[135] In this context, he posits that rather than thinking in terms of one culture's influence on another, it is more accurate to think of "shared and overlapping cultures…in different variants."[136] In this regard, Boyarin's theory embraces a particularly fluid view of culture that is characteristic of cultural analysis.[137]

With respect to the rabbinic culture of Babylonia specifically, the surrounding Middle Persian attitudes and the doctrines of Zoroastrianism, the Persian Empire's official religion, were especially strong cultural influences. Professor Yaakov Elman's study demonstrates that the Babylonian Talmud itself testifies to substantial "Jewish acculturation to the Persian way of life, mores, and culture."[138] These Persian outside influences also impacted the developing *halakhah* and rabbinic theology.[139]

Regardless of these cultural realities, the sages succeeded "in securing a near-universal acceptance of their Babylonian Talmud as the definitive expression of rabbinic Judaism."[140] By the beginning of the Jewish Middle

---

133. *See Introduction* to CAMBRIDGE COMPANION, *supra* note 21, at 1, 8–9. *See also supra* Chapter 1, note 90.

134. Gafni, *supra* note 104, at 223, 253.

135. Boyarin, *supra* note 66, at 336–37.

136. *Id.* at 349.

137. *See* Naomi Mezey, *Law as Culture*, 13 YALE J.L. & HUMAN. 35, 43 (2001).

138. Yaakov Elman, *Middle Persian Culture and Babylonian Sages: Accommodation and Resistance in the Shaping of Rabbinic Legal Tradition, in* CAMBRIDGE COMPANION, *supra* note 21, at 165, 166.

139. Elman's study provides an extensive examination of these topics. *Id.*

140. Gafni, *supra* note 104, at 253.

Ages, the Talmudic literature informed the dominant mode of Jewish practice.[141] This period can be defined as the one spanning the seventh to the eighteenth centuries. The emancipation of the Jews and the beginning of modernity tend to mark the end of this time frame.

During the Jewish Middle Ages, Jewish law and culture developed in Islamic and Christian environments.[142] In the Muslim Mediterranean basin, all Jews—the rabbis, their dissenters, and the people at large—adopted Arabic language and culture just as the earlier Jews of Palestine embraced Greek culture by both owning and transforming it.[143] Saadia Gaon, who lived in Babylonia under Muslim rule during the ninth and tenth centuries, translated the Bible into Arabic, which "helped to accelerate the process of the adaptation of rabbinic Judaism to the canons and tastes of intellectual Arabic society."[144] Moses Maimonides, one of the most renowned Jewish philosophers, also was a product of Islamic culture. In discussing the environment in which Maimonides lived in the twelfth century, Menachem Kellner, a scholar of medieval Jewish philosophy, has observed, "Just as today many Jews, even those learned to one degree or another in Judaism, use essentially alien categories in their own understanding of Judaism...so Maimonides' audience lived in a culture suffused with elements of Greek and Muslim thought and very likely understood at least portions of their own faith in terms of categories borrowed from the host society."[145]

Bernard Lewis, a scholar of Oriental Studies, has observed that during the Middle Ages, Jewish law was heavily influenced by the mores and norms of the dominant Islamic and Christian cultures. Further, differences in these respective cultures impacted Jewish law in different ways. He illustrated this general point by looking to the law of marriage:

> One of the clearest and most striking differences between Christian and Islamic usage is that while Islam permits polygamy and concubinage, Christianity bans both. In the Christian world the Jews adopted

---

141. *See* David Biale, *Introduction to Part Two: Diversities of Diaspora, in* CULTURES OF THE JEWS, *supra* note 102, at 305.

142. *Id.*

143. *See generally* Raymond P. Scheindlin, *Merchants and Intellectuals, Rabbis and Poets: Judeo-Arabic Culture in the Golden Age of Islam, in* CULTURES OF THE JEWS, *supra* note 102, at 313.

144. COHEN, *supra* note 130, at 153.

145. MENACHEM KELLNER, DOGMA IN JEWISH THOUGHT 45 (1986).

and practiced monogamy to the point of making it a rule of law; in the Muslim world most Jewish communities practiced, or at least permitted, polygamy and concubinage until almost the present day.[146]

The influence of Christianity was particularly prominent among European Jews during the Middle Ages. As early as the ninth century, small groups of Jews migrated from Italy to France and Germany. These groups ultimately grew into the prominent Ashkenazic Jewish culture of Northern, and eventually Eastern, Europe.[147] The Ashkenazic Jews developed their culture and ritualistic laws in the High Middle Ages within the milieu of Christianity, resulting in an interesting process that involved both borrowing and polemics, a process termed "inward acculturation" by Jewish history and religious studies professor Ivan Marcus.[148] For example, as discussed in Chapter 3, these Jews responded to persecutions and the ensuing pogroms "by developing a cult of martyrdom and rituals to memorialize the dead, elements of which they adapted from Christian imagery."[149]

With respect to adherence to the ritualistic precepts of the tradition, once again the *halakhists* of this period sought "to justify the legality of the adjustments in terms of the ancient tradition" so that although there were deviations from older practices, "Jewish life was made to appear as a continuation of that of earlier times."[150] In this sense, therefore, the function of Jewish law was to balance "the necessity for adjustment to new conditions and the preservation of Jewish identity."[151] One interesting illustration of this process involves the rabbinic inclination to permit trading in wine prepared by Gentiles, while maintaining the prohibition against personal consumption of such beverages. The rationale behind this distinction was the socioeconomic reality that "the use of wine for business was an economic necessity, and to grant permission for this purpose did not imply any social contact with non-Jews" which,

---

146. Bernard Lewis, The Jews of Islam 82, 196 n.21 (1987).

147. Biale, *supra* note 141, at 306.

148. Ivan G. Marcus, *A Jewish-Christian Symbiosis: The Culture of Early Ashkenaz, in* Cultures of the Jews, *supra* note 102, at 449, 461. *See also infra* Chapter 3, notes 25–27 and accompanying text.

149. Biale, *supra* note 141, at 306–07. *See also infra* Chapter 3, notes 125–49 and accompanying text.

150. Jacob Katz, Exclusiveness and Tolerance 45–46 (1961).

151. *Id.* at 46.

it was feared, would lead to intermarriage.[152] Nevertheless, the Talmudic prohibition is clear in that it applies to both trading and consumption.[153]

Another revealing example of this process involves the prohibition of interest. The Torah contains three separate prohibitions outlawing lending with interest among Jews.[154] Rabbi Hillel Gamoran published an extensive scholarly treatment of these prohibitions and their historical interpretations as they apply to loans between Jews. He notes that these biblical prohibitions must be understood in the context of protections for the poor rather than regulation of commerce.[155] Gamoran examines in detail buying on credit as one of the violations of the biblical prohibitions. Although the Mishnah prohibits credit sales among Jews,[156] the sages were already finding ways to circumvent the prohibition and allow for the development of trade and commerce.[157] The rabbis manifested additional latitude later in Talmudic times.[158] As was the case with trading in wine by Gentiles, by the Middle Ages the rabbis had significantly loosened the strictures concerning buying on credit in order to legalize the practices of the people and to allow Jewish law to coexist with the economic realities of the times.[159] Very simply, the Jewish people "lived in a credit society" and "to abandon interest would imperil their livelihoods."[160] In this situation as with others, the problem was solved through creative legal interpretation.

Both the medieval and the modern centuries reflected the same type of cultural exchange between the Jews and their host cultures as occurred during the Talmudic period. This reality "demonstrates how the culture of a minority group like the Jews can never be separated from that of the majority surrounding it."[161] The process, repeatedly, was a complex one that mediated

---

152. *Id.* at 46–47.

153. *Id.* at 46 ("The Talmudic sources do not make any distinction between the Gentile's wine as an object of trade and as a commodity for personal consumption").

154. *See* Deuteronomy 23:20–21; Exodus 22:24; Leviticus 25:35–37.

155. HILLEL GAMORAN, JEWISH LAW IN TRANSITION 5–8 (2008).

156. *See, e.g.,* Bava Metzia 5:2 (Mishnah).

157. GAMORAN, *supra* note 155, at 20 ("[I]f the 'regular' price of the goods already included the cost of credit, then the transaction was allowed").

158. *Id.* at 31, 66 (discussing the complicated and not completely defined Talmudic concept of the *tarsha* as a means of circumventing the prohibition concerning credit sales).

159. *Id.* at 62–93.

160. *Id.* at 179.

161. Biale, *supra* note 127, at xx.

between "adaptation and resistance."[162] This adaptation also produced a wide range of divergent religious practices and customs, a point that will be addressed more fully in Chapter 3.[163] Yet, despite the existence of diversity among the Jews as a whole during this time, there remained a compelling uniformity of legal practice that served as a "testimony not only to the power of the classical texts but also to the authorities who were its custodians."[164] In his study of the early modern period, Dean Bell remarked that "Jews appear to have had a remarkable ability to engage the world around them," to adapt to the majority's customs while infusing them with Jewish meaning, and to retain their own religion.[165]

Although the Jews incorporated and revamped aspects of their surrounding culture throughout history, up until the emancipation the majority continued to adhere to traditional practices and maintained their religious heritage. Jacob Katz, in his study of the Jews between the years 1770 and 1870 in Europe, noted that in the early part of this period, the Jews were still socially and culturally isolated, tightly organized, and reliant on their religion as a mighty "force for unification."[166] By the second half of the nineteenth century, however, Jews were no longer culturally isolated, the economic isolation was ameliorated if not completely gone, and they "were divided among themselves in point of religion."[167] Significantly, however, Jews still adhered to the practice of maintaining "exclusively Jewish family ties."[168]

This chapter emphasizes the role of religious leaders in interpreting and developing Jewish law. The composition of Jewish law, however, always has considered the practices of the people, and in this regard, it embraces a critical insight of cultural analysis. The following chapter examines this bottom-up participatory process in more detail.

---

162. *Id.* at xix.

163. One division familiar to many Jews even today is that of the Eastern European Ashkenazic Jews and their Sephardic brethren, whose roots can be traced to the Iberian Peninsula in the period preceding the expulsion of the Jews from Spain. *See generally* Benjamin R. Gampel, *A Letter to a Wayward Teacher: The Transformations of Sephardic Culture in Christian Iberia, in* CULTURES OF THE JEWS, *supra* note 102, at 389.

164. Biale, *supra* note 141, at 309.

165. DEAN BELL, JEWS IN THE EARLY MODERN WORLD 232 (2007).

166. JACOB KATZ, OUT OF THE GHETTO 213 (1973).

167. *Id.* at 213–14.

168. *Id.* at 214. In contrast, today intermarriage among American Jews exceeds 50 percent. *See infra* Chapter 9, notes 27–30 and accompanying text.

3 THE NORMS OF JEWISH LAW OBSERVANCE: A BOTTOM-UP VIEW

Introductory Themes

Chapter 2 illustrates that through the sages' direct development of *halakhah* (Jewish law), Judaism always has manifested a significant human involvement in the law's evolution. Moreover, by recognizing the role of custom (known in Hebrew as *minhag* or *minhagim* in the plural) and even communal enactments in the formation of the tradition, Judaism extends this human dimension to incorporate the bottom-up practices of the lay people, a quality that is characteristic of cultural analysis. This pluralistic dimension of Jewish law's development contrasts markedly with the perceived exclusivity of many of the more traditional practices.

This chapter addresses how these bottom-up practices have influenced the development of the *mesorah* (the Jewish tradition) on both a legal and cultural level. It develops two primary arguments. First, the substance of the bottom-up customs reflects a blend of rabbinic culture, including the texts and laws, and the cultures of the nations in which the Jews lived. Second, on a global level, the *mesorah* reflects a negotiation between the bottom-up folk practices and the rabbinic top-down sources. This chapter explores the nature of this negotiation in the context of customs, particularly as they pertain to certain life cycle rituals and food.

Although the focus of this chapter is on custom rather than communal enactments, it is worth noting that beginning in the tenth century[1] and continuing until the emancipation of the Jews toward the end of the eighteenth century, Jewish law was determined and applied by virtue of local authorities. As a result, enactments promulgated by the various Jewish communities became an important source of legal authority. Significantly, they generally were accorded the same authority as the *halakhah*.[2] This was the case even when these communal enactments actually contained provisions that were inconsistent with *halakhah*.[3] This phenomenon may seem surprising unless one keeps in mind that the lay and religious leaders of these communities were not working in opposition to one another.[4] On the contrary, the majority of people believed in the authority and primacy of *halakhah*, and the communal enactments were seen as a vehicle for perpetuating the law and the *mesorah* across time and space.[5] One salient caveat, however, is that in general, communal enactments were not able to supersede *halakhah* with respect to matters of religious law.[6] At times, however, the line between the religious and civil spheres was difficult to draw,[7] and legislative authority did, in practice, sometimes extend to matters affecting religious law.[8]

One particularly interesting example of this blurring occurred in connection with a ruling that Israeli jurist Menachem Elon terms "one of the most significant enactments in post-*geonic* legislation."[9] Elon is referring to the ruling of the twelfth-century *halakhic* authority Jacob b. Meir (known

---

1. 2 MENACHEM ELON, JEWISH LAW: HISTORY, SOURCES, PRINCIPLES 883–84 (1994) (noting that this increase in the power afforded to the local Jewish communities was the result of the waning of the former center of authority in Babylonia that had previously exercised spiritual hegemony over the entire Diaspora).

2. *See id.* at 699–701. Elon notes the revolutionary character of this development. *Id.* at 713. *Cf.* STEVEN H. RESNICOFF, UNDERSTANDING JEWISH LAW 79 (2012) (noting the Talmudic requirement that any new communal legislation required rabbinic approval).

3. ELON, *supra* note 1, at 736.

4. *Id.* at 782.

5. *Id.* at 779. Elon discusses the various mechanisms by which Jewish law attempted to bridge the communal enactments and *halakhic* authority. *Id.* at 751–78. One of these measures required that in order for an enactment to be valid, the majority of the people must be able to comply with its provisions. *Id.* at 762–63.

6. *Id.* at 707, 712.

7. *See id.* at 710.

8. *Id.* at 711.

9. *Id.* at 789. See also *infra* note 42 and accompanying text for a discussion of the *geonic* period.

more widely as *Rabbenu Tam*)[10] restricting the ability of a husband to inherit from his deceased wife's estate by requiring the return of her dowry to her original heirs or donors if she died within twelve months after the marriage occurred, without leaving a surviving child.[11] The significance of this ruling was that it contradicted biblical law regarding a husband's inheritance rights.[12] Although *Rabbenu Tam* eventually changed his mind about this particular ruling, by that time his ruling had already been widely accepted and was subsequently adopted and extended by three significant medieval Jewish communities.[13]

The emancipation of the Jews in Europe eventually resulted in a diminished need for communal legislation given that the Jews were becoming absorbed into the mainstream culture, legal and otherwise.[14] The emancipation did not, however, continue to affect the course of custom, which has continued to thrive and influence the development of Jewish law and tradition.[15] Elon defines *minhag* as "particular normative behavior that has been continuous and unquestioned."[16] These behaviors "were invented at a specific time, in a particular Jewish community, and then were either preserved locally or adopted by other Jews and disseminated so that they became widely practiced customs."[17] Given this bottom-up and varied nature of *minhag*, the rabbinical authorities developed numerous measures involving interpretative methods and Scriptural support to integrate custom into the *halakhic* system.[18] This is particularly true with respect to matters of civil law, where custom has

---

10. *Rabbenu Tam* was the grandson of *Rashi*, the renowned eleventh-century French *halakhic* authority. For a discussion of the origin of the appellation *Rebbenu Tam*, see IVAN G. MARCUS, THE JEWISH LIFE CYCLE 265 n.26 (2004).

11. ELON, *supra* note 1, at 787, 836.

12. Previously, the *halakhah* took the position that a husband remains his wife's heir regardless of when she dies. *Id.* at 837.

13. These three communities were known by the acronym of *Shum*, standing for the Hebrew names of the communities of Speyer, Worms, and Mainz. *Id.* at 787, 838. This legislation also became the basis for similar enactments in other locales that further limited a husband's inheritance rights. *Id.* at 796, 838–39 (discussing thirteenth-century enactments in Spain).

14. *See id.* at 824.

15. *Id.* at 897. The Talmud contains numerous discussions of custom. For example, the Talmud addresses matters such as general and local custom, customs unique to particular individuals, and the appropriate practice for one who travels and encounters conflicting geographic customs. *Id.* at 933–35.

16. *Id.* at 885.

17. MARCUS, *supra* note 10, at 25.

18. ELON, *supra* note 1, at 937.

the ability to override *halakhah*.[19] With respect to religious law, on the other hand, because the legal strictures are considered obligatory, *halakhah* cannot be changed through the will of the people, at least in theory.[20] The following discussion illustrates, however, that this rule is not as clear-cut in practice. Moreover, the people always retained the power to develop more stringent practices than *halakhah* required.[21]

Several of the customs examined in this chapter pertain to topics that are relevant to all human beings, such as birth, death, and food. Still, the customs that are the focus of this discussion have a particular content and history specific to the Jewish people. One rite of passage explored below, ritual circumcision, is a ceremony unique to the Jewish religion.[22] The contribution of the bottom up to the development of all of the customs discussed is highly significant from a cultural analysis standpoint.

As was the case with the laws that were promulgated by the rabbinic elite, at every point in history, the people's practices and customs were heavily influenced by the local customs of the surrounding cultures. One colorful example of this phenomenon concerns the origin of the custom of wearing costumes on the Jewish holiday of Purim, a day marking the triumph of the Jews' survival in ancient Persia in the face of threatened destruction by a villain known by the name of Haman.[23] Historically, a carnival-like atmosphere accompanied the celebration of Purim. Some believe that beginning in late medieval Germany, the Jews borrowed for this celebration a Christian custom of wearing costumes that dates back to the Roman carnival.[24]

In his study of Jewish life cycle rites, Professor Ivan Marcus notes that the dynamic process resulting in the perpetuation of the Jewish tradition

---

19. *Id.* at 942, 944. *See also id.* at 888, 893, 911–29. *Cf.* RESNICOFF, *supra* note 2, at 77–78 (noting that "commercial transactions are governed by custom" and such customs are "default terms" in Jewish law contracts "similar to the way in which Article 2 of the Uniform Commercial Code treats industry customs as default terms in contracts for the sale of goods").

20. ELON, *supra* note 1, at 904.

21. *See infra* notes 55–58, 151–83 and accompanying text.

22. Although non-Jewish males can be circumcised, the particulars of ritual circumcision are unique to the Jewish religion. The roots of this ceremony are found in the Torah. *See infra* note 87 and accompanying text.

23. This narrative is recorded in the Book of Esther, contained in the Hebrew Bible.

24. *See* Ivan G. Marcus, *A Jewish-Christian Symbiosis, in* CULTURES OF THE JEWS 449, 484 (David Biale ed., 2002). Others dispute this origin of the costume custom and argue that it originated entirely from within the tradition. *See Purim Costumes—A History—Reasons and Origins* (Feb. 25, 2010), http://www.vosizneias.com/50116/2010/02/25/.

consisted of the following two steps: an initial negotiation by the Jews with their majority cultures, during which they adapted some customs and rejected others; and a transmission of the products of these negotiations to the next generation. This two-step dynamic process, which Marcus calls "inward acculturation," has repeated itself throughout history across the globe.[25] Although the Jews typically adapted the customs of their respective majority cultures to suit their unique Jewish communities, institutions, and patterns,[26] this reality of adaptation provided an important foundation for the creation of a unique Jewish subculture in the areas in which they lived.[27]

Equally important, the bottom-up practices also had a strong basis in the biblical and rabbinic traditions, legal and otherwise, even if the people sometimes modified or adapted the authoritative positions in certain respects. Thus, the Jewish folkways, traditions, and customs usually were "deeply rooted in Jewish sources" such as the Torah, the Talmud, and other official texts of the tradition.[28] As the Russian Jewish folklorist S. Ansky[29] has observed, Jewish "folklore" is like the Bible in that it is "the product of the Jewish spirit; it reflects…the same loftiness and depth of Jewish thought."[30] Thus, the people's bottom-up practices manifested a synergy between the rabbinic tradition and the ways of the surrounding cultures. The resulting cultural products of this synergy varied depending on place and time. Significantly, despite considerable uniformity of the tradition overall, there never has been a unified series of practices among the Jewish people who have lived throughout the majority of their history in the Diaspora. This point is underscored from early on by the development of distinct traditions and

---

25. MARCUS, *supra* note 10, at 4. *See also supra* Chapter 2, note 148 and accompanying text.

26. MARCUS, *supra* note 10, at 8. *See also* LOUIS GINZBERG, ON JEWISH LAW AND LORE 70–71 (1955) (discussing folkloristic literature of European Jews).

27. *See supra* Chapter 2, note 131 and accompanying text.

28. Shalom Sabar, *Childbirth and Magic, in* CULTURES OF THE JEWS, *supra* note 24, at 671, 712.

29. David Biale, *A Journey between Worlds, in* CULTURES OF THE JEWS, *supra* note 24, at 799. Ansky was born Solomon Rappoport but adopted a Russian-sounding name that "drew from the Yiddush custom of forming last names from the first name of one's mother." *Id.* at 799.

30. *Id.* at 843 (quoting S. Ansky, 1 *Dos yidishe etnografishe program* at 10 (L.I. Shternberg ed., Petrograd 1914)) (also quoted in David G. Roskies, *Introduction* to ANSKY, THE DYBBUK AND OTHER WRITINGS xxiv (David G. Roskies ed., trans., Yale University Press 2002) (1992)). According to Biale, Ansky "clearly intended his characterization of Jewish folklore as an 'oral tradition' to usurp the rabbinic idea that the Talmud was the oral law." *Id.*

customs among Eastern European, or Ashkenazic Jews; the Sephardic Jews who came from Spain, Portugal, and other areas; as well as the Jews who settled in North Africa.[31] In large part, these differences are attributable to the influences of the distinct surrounding cultures in which these groups of Jews were living.[32] These groups continue to maintain numerous distinct traditions even today.

In short, the bottom-up practices represent a blend of the customs of the surrounding majority cultures and the laws promulgated by the elite rabbinic culture, as negotiated by the general population in distinct locales and times. Marcus has observed that "Jews did not do everything that the rabbinic documents said they should, and, conversely, they did some things that are not mentioned in rabbinic texts and others that the rabbis explicitly opposed but had no power to stop."[33] The reality of which Marcus speaks suggests that the *mesorah*, particularly with respect to custom, generally also reflects the results of a negotiation between the rabbis and their followers. On a theoretical level, the rabbinic leadership clearly had the ultimate say concerning the legal validity of the people's practices,[34] but the rabbis' role in this matter often was complex.

The relationship between the rabbis and the people regarding the evolution of *minhag* produced several distinct scenarios.[35] Sometimes the rabbis simply overruled the people's practices because they deemed them to be foolish or performed in error.[36] This chapter does not address these types of

---

31. *See* Lucette Valensi, *Multicultural Visions, in* Cultures of the Jews, *supra* note 24, at 888 (discussing the "cultural tapestry" of North African Jews).

32. *Cf.* Rachel Biale, Women and Jewish Law 51 (1984) (noting that the ban on polygyny—the practice of having multiple wives—issued by medieval Ashkenazic authority *Rabbenu* Gershom was not accepted by the Sephardic Jews who lived in Islamic countries where polygyny was practiced). Rachel Biale also notes that when the state of Israel was established, the close proximity between Ashkenazic and Sephardic Jews created problems resulting from their differing practices in this matter. Although Israel banned polygyny, those Jews who arrived in Israel with more than one wife were permitted to retain these marriages. *Id.*

33. Marcus, *supra* note 10, at 28.

34. Aaron Kirschenbaum, *Subjectivity in Rabbinic Decision-Making, in* Rabbinic Authority and Personal Autonomy 61, 70 (Moshe Z. Sokol ed., 1992).

35. *Cf.* Barry Freundel, Contemporary Orthodox Judaism's Response to Modernity 34–35 (2004) (describing the authority centers of *halakhah* as three concentric circles with community practice or *minhag* being the outermost circle).

36. Kirschenbaum, *supra* note 34, at 70. *See also* Elon, *supra* note 1, at 939–40 (discussing the nullification of the customs of allowing a minor holding a Bible to complete a prayer quorum and of requiring women to refrain from work during the entire evening following the completion of the Sabbath).

situations because the focus of the discussion is on the tradition's incorporation of the people's practices rather than its marginalization of their customs. Instead, this discussion emphasizes the development of the *mesorah* by virtue of the following three themes concerning the role of the people: (1) popular *validation* of biblical and rabbinic texts, law, and authority through the bottom-up practices; (2) rabbinic *reliance* on the bottom up in determining, ascertaining, or at least informing the law; and (3) rabbinic *toleration*, and even facilitation, of bottom-up practices absent a formal legal endorsement of the people's customs.

Before illustrating the operation of these themes, it may be helpful to provide some additional background drawn from a variety of subjects. An example from the medieval period illustrates the operation of the community validation process, or more specifically in this case, the failure of such process. Rabbi Isaac ben Jacob Alfasi,[37] a well-known *halakhic* authority whose life spanned the majority of the eleventh century, blew the shofar on the Sabbath in Fez, Morocco, when it coincided with Rosh Hashanah.[38] He did so despite the fact that this practice was approved only for the Temple in Jerusalem, with a few notable exceptions.[39] By blowing the shofar under these unusual circumstances, Alfasi may have been trying to equate his locale with that of the Temple in Jerusalem. His students refused to accept this practice, perhaps due to its relative singularity.[40] Had his community embraced this custom, however, this practice would have become the norm for this particular area and perhaps others as well.

---

37. Alfasi is known by the Hebrew acronym *Rif.* The use of Hebrew acronyms, especially for renowned rabbinic scholars, became popular in medieval times and has continued to grow in modernity. *See* Sol Steinmetz, Dictionary of Jewish Usage: A Guide to the Use of Jewish Terms 128 (2005).

38. Ari Z. Zivotofsky & Ari Greenspan, *Shofar on Shabbos* (July 30, 2009), http://halachicadventures.com/wp-content/uploads/2009/09/Shofar-on-shabbat.pdf.

39. One such exception was made by the renowned Talmudic sage, Yochanan Ben Zakai, who established Yavneh as the new center of Judaism following the destruction of the Second Temple in Jerusalem. One of Ben Zakai's rulings was that the shofar could now be blown on Rosh Hashanah when it fell on the Sabbath (prior to the Temple's destruction, this could be done only in Jerusalem, not in the provinces). *See* Rosh Hashanah 4:1 (Mishnah); Rosh Hashanah 29b (Babylonian Talmud) (quoting Ben Zachai as saying "Let us first blow and afterwards we will consider whether this practice should continue in the future"). *See also* David Silverberg, *Surf a Little Torah*, The Israel Koschitzky Virtual Beit Midrash, http://www.vbm-torah.org/archive/salt-chagim/rosh%20hashana-9.htm (Rosh Hananah 2006).

40. *See* Rosh Hashanah 29b (Babylonian Talmud) (Steinsaltz commentary); Zivotofsky & Greenspan, *supra* note 38.

This example shows that community conduct sometimes has the potential for abrogating rabbinic rulings if the people are unable—or perhaps even unwilling—to abide by the law.[41] Conversely, the people have the power to validate the law through their acceptance of rabbinic rulings. Especially in the *geonic* period following the redaction of the Babylonian Talmud,[42] the people themselves actively participated in the validation of the Talmud's authority by virtue of their embracing and reaffirming the Talmud's tradition and worldview. As Professor David Biale has observed, "The culture of the Talmud became increasingly the culture of the folk."[43] This process, however, was a slow one.[44] Professor David Kraemer has written that "in recent decades, scholarship has come more and more to recognize that the rabbis in late Antiquity were a small and, to a large extent, elitist group whose ideas and practices were hardly shared by Jews at large."[45] With time, a remarkable consistency in legal practice developed across the Diaspora despite the differences in local customs and surrounding cultures.[46] This outcome is a testament not only to the power of the tradition and its rabbinic authorities, but also to the people's inclination to accept and validate the tradition. The words of the Rabbi Abraham Isaac Kook furnish a twentieth-century example of the same point. Rabbi Kook stated that when

---

41. RESNICOFF, *supra* note 2, at 81 (noting also that some authorities believe the rabbinic legislation becomes void automatically while others require a formal repeal). *See* FREUNDEL, *supra* note 35, at 35 ("Non-acceptance by a majority of the nation is ultimately a veto that cannot be overridden."). *Cf.* LOUIS JACOBS, TREE OF LIFE 228 (1984) (discussing how laws can fall into de facto suspension due to the people's lack of observance).

42. The *geonic* era followed the Talmudic period and lasted roughly from the seventh to the eleventh centuries. This era is named after the heads of the Jewish academies living in the Islamic world during this time who were known as *geonim*. *See* Raymond P. Scheindlin, *Merchants and Intellectuals, Rabbis and Poets, in* CULTURES OF THE JEWS, *supra* note 24, at 316, 321 (noting that because "the *geonim* put a permanent stamp on many aspects of Jewish religious life…it is only appropriate" that this era of Jewish history is known as the *geonic* period).

43. David Biale, *Introduction to Part Two: Diversities of Diaspora* to CULTURES OF THE JEWS, *supra* note 24, at 305, 310 [hereinafter Biale, *Introduction to Part Two*]. Biale also observes that by the Middle Ages, although the Talmud remained a book studied by a small elite rabbinic culture, it "came to shape popular Jewish culture, not only through its laws but also through its maxims and legends." David Biale, *Preface* to CULTURES OF THE JEWS, *supra*, at xxvi.

44. *See, e.g.*, Biale, *Introduction to Part Two, supra* note 43, at 306.

45. DAVID C. KRAEMER, JEWISH EATING AND IDENTITY THROUGH THE AGES 7 (2007).

46. David Biale, *Introduction to Part Two, supra* note 43, at 309. Raymond Scheindlin notes that the triumph of the rabbinic tradition over the competing Karaite sect that relied on the text of the Bible in lieu of the authority of the rabbis is attributable, in part, to the Islamic government's recognition of the Rabbanites "as the authoritative voice for Jewry as a whole."

changes in the law need to be enacted in Israel, they "will have the same force as a law of the Torah" provided "they are approved by a majority of the generally recognized *halakhic* authorities of Israel *and then accepted by the community.*"[47]

An early rabbinic source contains a narrative involving the well-known Babylonian sage Hillel illustrating rabbinic reliance on the people's practices in ascertaining the law. The story concerns the appropriate protocol for the Passover sacrifice when it falls on the Sabbath. As discussed in more detail in Chapter 5, observance of the Sabbath entails numerous restrictions on daily activity, including a prohibition on carrying from one domain to another.[48] Therefore, a question was raised as to what happens if someone forgot to bring the knife needed to perform the sacrifice prior to the onset of the Sabbath given that carrying the knife would be forbidden. Hillel could not recall the law but proclaimed that in order to determine the protocol, the practices of the people should be determinative because "if they are not prophets, they are the descendents of prophets" and therefore will know the proper conduct in this matter.[49] When this investigation was performed, it was revealed that the people would place the knife in the wool of the lambs to be sacrificed, or between the horns of the goats, in order to avoid carrying the implement. Hillel then recalled that this was indeed the law that he had learned from his teachers.

Elon has observed that this narrative furnishes an example of custom supplementing the law in that it involves a bottom-up practice that served to preserve a long-forgotten law.[50] Indeed, the concept that the practice of the people governs when there is uncertainty as to a law is prominent within the Jewish tradition.[51] This concept is embodied in the Talmudic precept of "go out and see what the people are doing," which is invoked in the absence of a

---

Scheindlin, *supra* note 42, at 322. During the period of the seventh through thirteenth centuries, the Jews of the Muslim world constituted the vast majority of world Jewry. *Id.* at 317. The Rabbanites were eventually able to suppress, although not completely eliminate, the Karaites. *Id.* at 322.

47. ELON, *supra* note 1, at 824 (emphasis supplied). Rabbi Kook, who died in 1935, was the first Ashkenazic Chief Rabbi of the Land of Israel (prior to the establishment of the state).

48. Shabbat 7:2 (Mishnah). *See infra* Chapter 5, note 73 and accompanying text.

49. Pesahim 4:13–14 (Tosefta). A somewhat different version of this narrative also is found in both the Jerusalem and Babylonian Talmuds. *See* Pesahim 66a (Babylonian Talmud); Pesahim 6:1 (Jerusalem Talmud).

50. ELON, *supra* note 1, at 902.

51. JACOBS, *supra* note 41, at 206. *See also* ELON, *supra* note 1, at 881–82.

clear-cut *halakhic* ruling.[52] The underlying idea is that the popular practice of the people can serve as a basis for a decision in these circumstances. This view is a testament to "the creative power of the people"[53] and thus is very much aligned with the philosophy of cultural analysis.

In contrast, it is also the case that when custom is in opposition to the *unanimous* opinion of the legal authorities, it will not prevail. In the words of a fifteenth-century *halakhist*, "For if we were to abolish laws prohibiting certain things as a result of the (contrary) *minhag*, then one by one all prohibitions will be permitted and the whole of the Torah set at naught."[54] Thus, in theory a distinction exists between allowing custom to resolve an uncertainty concerning the law and a modification of the law based on the practices of the people. In practice, however, because religious leaders do consider the people's practices in determining the law, such modification is inevitable.

When the people's practices are more stringent than the existing *halakhah*, little difficulty exists from a *halakhic* standpoint.[55] In fact, the Mishnah discusses the binding character of local customs that operate to extend the law. One such example concerns whether work may be done on the eve of Passover before noon, which the Mishnah states is governed by local custom.[56] A more recent example is that despite the absence in the Talmudic tradition of a requirement that Jewish males wear a head covering, known as a *yarmulke*,[57]

---

52. ADIN STEINSALTZ, THE TALMUD: A REFERENCE GUIDE 136–37 (1989).

53. ELON, *supra* note 1, at 885.

54. JACOBS, *supra* note 41, at 207 (quoting R. Solomon b. Simeon Duran, in *Teshuvot Rashbash*, nos. 419 and 562, quoted by Kahana *Mekhkarim*, 115).

55. Elon discusses this concept extensively. *See* ELON, *supra* note 1, at 909–11. Elon also notes that "*halakhic* authorities viewed customs that establish new prohibitions as a type of vow taken by the public, and, on that basis, explained their binding force." *Id.* at 934. An excellent example of an increased stringency stemming from the people concerns the expanded waiting period following bloody discharge that women in the early centuries of the Common Era followed before ritual immersion and resumption of sexual relations with their husbands. *See generally* Niddah 66a (Babylonian Talmud); *see infra* Chapter 6, notes 7–10 and accompanying text. Some scholars believe that this stringency was the result of the influence of the Jews' Persian neighbors. *See* Yaakov Elman, *Middle Persian Culture and Babylonian Sages: Accommodation and Resistance in the Shaping of Rabbinic Legal Tradition, in* CAMBRIDGE COMPANION TO THE TALMUD AND RABBINIC LITERATURE 165, 176 (Charlotte E. Fonrobert & Martin S. Jaffee eds., 2007) [hereinafter CAMBRIDGE COMPANION].

56. *See* Pesahim 4:1 (Mishnah). Jacobs observes that such purely local customs "found their way into *halakhah*, the rationale for this being the mystical idea that customs adopted by a 'holy people' are 'Torah' almost in the sense of a divine revelation." JACOBS, *supra* note 41, at 207. The earliest collection of local customs is the *Sefer hamanhig* by Abraham b. Nathan of Lunel, who was born in the early thirteenth century. *Id.*

57. *See* Nedarim 30b (Babylonian Talmud) (Note 11, Schottenstein edition, 2000).

this practice now is regarded as obligatory in certain segments of the Jewish community.[58] This development illustrates how more stringent customs, typified by a bottom-up approach, can indeed acquire the force of law. This chapter's discussion of food provides additional examples of *halakhah's* ultimate incorporation of more stringent popular customs.

On the other hand, it is often the case that the people's practices are more lenient or simply divergent. This situation, while also common, can be dangerous for the maintenance of the *mesorah* for the reasons expressed by the medieval *halakhist* quoted above. As discussed earlier, however, if people will not follow a particular law, it will fall into disuse. Therefore, in theory as well as in practice, rabbinic leaders always have taken the people's customs into account in one way or the other. The history of the development of *halakhah* reveals that in every age and locality, local custom enjoyed a prominent position. Indeed, an important part of rabbinical training was familiarity with local customs so that religious leaders could make appropriate decisions.[59]

The Jewish tradition also reveals a significant degree of rabbinic toleration of bottom-up practices, even absent their formal validation as legal rulings. Sometimes this toleration took the form of passive agreement; other times the rabbis actively participated in the perpetuation of these practices. An interesting example of this phenomenon is furnished by the practice of medieval French and German communities reciting the evening prayers in the synagogues long before nightfall. This practice flatly contradicted the *halakhah* requiring the recitation of these prayers at night.[60] The rabbis attempted to defend this practice in various ways. Thus, Israel Isserlein, the greatest *halakhic* authority in Germany in the fifteenth century, was forced to condone the practice of reciting the evening prayers so early in the afternoon that many hours still remained until nightfall, despite the lack of legal

---

58. *See* Naomi Maya Stolzenberg & David N. Myers, *Community, Constitution, and Culture: The Case of the Jewish Kehilah*, 25 U. MICH. J.L. REFORM 633, 658–59 (1992).

59. *See, e.g.*, Marcus, *supra* note 24, at 452–54 (discussing the emerging Ashkenazic community in the Middle Ages); Moshe Rosman, *Innovative Tradition, in* CULTURES OF THE JEWS, *supra* note 24, at 519, 534 (discussing the Polish-Lithuanian Commonwealth in early modernity).

60. *See* JACOBS, *supra* note 41, at 110–11 (noting also that a main reason for this practice probably is attributable to the fact that in these northern countries the sky became dark late in the evening during the summer months, during which time people did not wish to leave their homes to attend daily synagogue services).

authority for this practice.[61] Isserlein advised against making the people feel guilty for their unlawful conduct and even encouraged scholars to join in the community custom unless their personal practices were characterized by extraordinary piety.[62]

The remainder of this chapter concentrates on particular types of customs. This discussion illustrates how the Jewish people not only borrowed elements from the surrounding cultures in creating customs, but also adapted these elements based on rabbinic sources and traditions. It also demonstrates how the *mesorah* generally incorporates certain customs as a result of a negotiation between the people's creative contributions to the tradition and the rulings of their rabbis. This negotiation involved popular validation of the top down, along with rabbinic toleration of, and even reliance on, the people's practices. The customs examined tend to focus on the medieval period during which time many *minhagim* originated. Therefore, this discussion also serves as a bridge between Chapter 2's primary focus on the Talmudic period and Chapter 4's investigation of the major Jewish movements in modernity.

Popular Validation of Rabbinic Authority in Shaping Bottom-Up Practices: Childbirth

Ritual entails the merger of gestures and words, "joined as expressions of the inner being."[63] As ritual has the potential for expressing multiple layers of meaning, it can be thought of as the substantive embodiment of an enriched daily existence.[64] Cultural analysis suggests that the line between popularized ritual and *halakhah* is indeed a fuzzy one. Especially with respect to prophylactic ritual designed to provide defenses against unknown forces of death and destruction, historically the components of religion, popular ritual, and science blended together. Thus, "amulets, blessings, incantations, and prayers" all represented weapons in the survival for life.[65] These weapons were

---

61. *Id.* at 111.

62. *Id.* at 112.

63. MARCUS, *supra* note 10, at 10.

64. *Id.*

65. Haym Soloveitchik, *Rupture and Reconstruction: The Transformation of Contemporary Orthodoxy*, Tradition 28:4 at 1, 10 (1994). *See also* Rosman, *supra* note 59, at 519, 528–29 (discussing the medieval Polish-Lithuanian Commonwealth).

formulated based on Jewish sources as well as elements from the host societies, as Jewish tradition and culturally driven innovation merged together in the Diaspora over the course of the centuries.

Even the rabbis, including those who lived during the Talmudic era, practiced to some extent activity that to an outsider would have been more akin to "magic" than ritual.[66] It is therefore not surprising that the lay population would also be drawn to such practices. This section demonstrates how certain folk practices drew from the normative biblical and Talmudic rabbinic sources in fashioning distinctly Jewish prophylactic measures. In this sense, then, these measures represent a popular validation of rabbinic authority and tradition. This mixture of rabbinic and popular folk culture, "enhanced by the trends and practices of the surrounding society,"[67] is especially reflected in the prophylactic rituals with respect to childbirth and circumcision that are the focus of this and some of the following sections.

The widespread use of amulets during childbirth and at other times illustrates this point. Although the use of amulets and other prophylactic folk measures is not exclusive to Judaism, their specific content in Jewish communities typically manifested particular Jewish themes that were meaningful to those who used them.[68] For example, in eighteenth-century Germany, the childbirth amulet for a female featured the Hebrew words for the three particular commandments incumbent on women: ritual immersion prior to resuming sexual relations with one's husband after menstruation, setting aside a portion of dough before baking bread, and kindling Sabbath lights prior to the onset of the day of rest.[69] In fact, the Talmud states the violation of these three laws cause women to die in childbirth.[70] These representations exemplify the importance of the top-down sources of authority to the masses in fashioning their bottom-up practices.

In addition, the significance the Jewish tradition ascribes to fire and light furnishes a particularly important motif for childbirth. Fire has long been considered a sacred symbol of fertility and life.[71] During the Talmudic era,

---

66. MARCUS, *supra* note 10, at 35.

67. Sabar, *supra* note 28, at 672.

68. *See id.* at 682.

69. *Id.*

70. Shabbat 31b (Babylonian Talmud).

71. *See* Proverbs 20:27 ("The lifebreath of man is the lamp of the Lord"). JEWISH PUBLICATION SOCIETY, TANAKH 1633 (1999) [hereinafter JPS TANAKH]. Many childbirth amulets also featured depictions of women lighting the Sabbath candles because, according

the rabbis permitted lighting candles during labor and delivery even on the Sabbath day, on which it is otherwise biblically forbidden to light a fire.[72] Similarly, it was not permissible to extinguish a fire in a room in which there was a newborn, or to remove anything burning. Even in more modern times, some Ashkenazic Jews still considered it bad luck if someone smoking a cigarette left such a room.[73]

Often the bottom-up practices derived from biblical sources, which are clearly viewed as authoritative by the rabbinic tradition. For example, biblical figures played a prominent role in matters regarding children and fertility. In this regard, the prophet Elijah probably is the most universally popular persona, undoubtedly due to his biblical status as a miracle worker.[74] In Islamic countries, Joseph was also especially popular among both Jews and Muslims.[75] The Jews in Islamic lands likely elevated Joseph because of his difficult circumstances as a child and great success as an adult.[76] The rabbis delved deeply into the sources in order to justify both his popularity and the consequent production of many tangible objects emphasizing his connection to fertility, children, and good luck in general.[77] One Talmudic passage refers to Joseph and his progeny as fruitful over whom "the evil eye has no dominion."[78] Professor Shalom Sabar has observed that "the association of Joseph with protection continues to this day in Israel, especially among families who emigrated from Islamic lands."[79] Childbirth amulets in many geographic locations often contained the names of biblical couples, particularly the patriarchs

---

to German Jewish folklore, light was believed to expel demons who would otherwise destroy the delight of Friday night, the onset of the Sabbath. Sabar, *supra* note 28, at 682.

72. *See* Shabbat 128b (Babylonian Talmud). *See infra* Chapter 5, note 72 and accompanying text.

73. Sabar, *supra* note 28, at 708.

74. *Id.* at 704 (noting that "a survey of the items assembled in the Archives of the Jewish Folktale in Haifa reveals that there are more stories concerning Elijah than any other hero of the Jewish people."). *See also infra* notes 96–104 and accompanying text.

75. Joseph is the only biblical character to whom the Quran devotes a full *sura*, or chapter. Sabar, *supra* note 28, at 682.

76. *Id.*

77. *Id.* at 700.

78. Berakhot 20a (Babylonian Talmud). *See also* Berakhot 55b (Babylonian Talmud).

79. Sabar, *supra* note 28, at 704.

and matriarchs. In contrast, Joseph's mother Rachel is rarely mentioned given that she died giving birth to Joseph's brother Benjamin.[80]

This image of Joseph as a protector par excellence was augmented by the motif of fish, which serves as a symbol of fertility in several cultures. In Jewish communities, however, the power of fish in this regard may have stemmed from Jacob's blessing to Joseph's sons, Ephraim and Manasseh, which is translated as they should be like "teeming multitudes upon the earth."[81] In Hebrew, the word translated as "teeming" is *yidgu,* which is a derivative of the Hebrew word for fish (*dag*). Essentially, then, the verse means the boys should "multiply like fish."[82] The Talmud also contains a reference to the lack of power the evil eye has over Joseph as well as over the fish in the sea.[83] Based on these sources, even twentieth-century amulets for the home and childbirth contain images of fish.[84]

Thus, the Jews drew heavily from their distinct tradition in fashioning defensive measures to cope with critical times of transition such as childbirth. The circumcision ceremony, discussed below, is another time of transition, and many of the rituals developed in connection with this rite also can be understood in similar terms. In addition, however, the ritual circumcision ceremony also drew significantly from the elements of the surrounding cultures in which the Jews lived and therefore furnishes an excellent study of how outside culture impacted the formation of the Jewish tradition.

The Influence of Outside Cultural Elements: Circumcision

Circumcision, the cutting and removal of the foreskin of the penis, is performed on the eighth day after a boy's birth, absent a medical reason requiring the postponement of this rite.[85] This ceremony is known in Hebrew as the *brit,* although in colloquial language it is often pronounced *bris* among Jews

---

80. *Id.* at 683 (discussing childbirth amulets in Eastern Europe).

81. ETZ HAYIM: TORAH AND COMMENTARY 297 (David L. Leiber et al. eds., Rabbinical Assembly 2001) (translating Genesis 48:16) [hereinafter ETZ HAYIM].

82. *See* Sabar, *supra* note 28, at 703. Sabar also notes that in Morocco, the Jews would throw a live fish at the feet of a bride and groom to symbolize their wish for the couple's fertility. *Id.*

83. *See* Berakhot 20a (Babylonian Talmud); *supra* note 78 and accompanying text.

84. *See* Sabar, *supra* note 28, at 692, 694, 702.

85. *See* MARCUS, *supra* note 10, at 42.

of Ashkhenazic descent. Although circumcision is commonly practiced in many cultures, in the Jewish religion the *brit* ceremony marks a male's entry into the covenant established between God and the Jewish people. In the ancient Near East, "the association between cutting something and making a covenant or an agreement has deep cultural roots."[86] The Torah states that God commanded Abraham to circumcise every male at the age of eight days. This rite is intended to be a sign of the covenant between God and Abraham and any male who is not circumcised "shall be cut off from his kin" as he has broken God's covenant.[87] Thus, a father has the religious obligation to circumcise his son.

Although the origins of the *brit* are biblical, very little about the actual content of the ceremony as it is practiced today is found either in the Torah or the Talmud. In late antiquity, the rabbis prescribed the particular prayers and blessings in connection with the *brit*.[88] Despite the presence of this and numerous other practices that were formulated by the rabbinic leadership, many of the components that ultimately became part of the ceremony were the result of the people's adaptations of customs from their surrounding cultures in the early and modern periods.[89]

Marcus has discussed how many of the currently familiar aspects of the *brit* were drawn largely from the Christian baptism ceremony, a development that is not all that surprising in light of the fact that baptism itself replaced circumcision in early Christianity.[90] Over the course of time, the *brit* came to include a godfather, who was given the honor of holding the baby during the ceremony. The traditional name for this person is *sandeq,* which "reflects the late Greek term for godfather at an Orthodox Christian child's baptism or christening."[91] Marcus notes that another way in which the *brit* began to

---

86. *Id.* at 45.

87. ETZ HAYIM, *supra* note 81, at 90–91 (translating Genesis 17:9–14). *See also* Leviticus 12:3 (noting the command of circumcision on the eighth day). Jewish baby girls traditionally are named in the synagogue during the Torah service as soon after the birth as possible. In addition, today many families celebrate the birth of a daughter with creative and participatory naming ceremonies in the home in addition to the traditional naming performed at a synagogue. *See* Carl N. Astor, *The Jewish Life Cycle, in* THE OBSERVANT LIFE 239, 246–47 (Martin S. Cohen & Michael Katz eds., 2012).

88. MARCUS, *supra* note 10, at 49.

89. *See generally id.* at 46–47.

90. *Id.* at 52.

91. *Id.* at 50 (noting that this person also is referred to as the *ba'al brit*, translated as "partner to the covenant"). There were, however, significant differences between the Jewish *sandeq*

resemble a Christian baptism in medieval Europe was through the adoption of the custom of adding two other godparents (one male and one female) to the honorees. In this way, two men (the *sandeq* and an additional male godfather) and one woman were honored, which was the same formula as that adopted for baptisms for males.[92]

The evening prior to the circumcision was generally believed to be the most dangerous night for the baby and his mother, given that this time represented "the last opportunity for the demons to attack the male child before the protective ceremony of circumcision would take place."[93] At one time, in Jewish communities throughout the Diaspora, all-night vigils were held to protect the infants from evil spirits.[94] Similar to the prophylactic measures utilized in connection with childbirth, many of the measures invoked for this night and the day of the ceremony itself were drawn from the Jewish sources. Thus, during the evening prior to the *brit*, psalms and other prayers would be recited, including the most sacred of all Jewish prayers, the *Shema*.[95]

The prophet Elijah earned a prominent place in connection with the circumcision rite given his status as the "guardian angel" of children according to Jewish folklore.[96] This role actually was derived from the rabbinic interpretation of a biblical verse. In Malachi 3:1, Elijah is called *Mal'akh ha-Berit*, the Angel of the Covenant, and the rabbinic tradition interpreted this to mean "circumcision."[97] These sources, in combination with Elijah's supernatural powers as a miracle worker,[98] earned him a special physical and spiritual place at both the *brit* and the preceding vigil.

---

and Christian godparents. The latter were intended to have an ongoing relationship with the child, unlike the *sandeq* whose importance was limited to the *brit* itself. Moreover, Jews typically selected relatives for this honor, rather than people outside the family circle, a practice more typical in Christian circles. *Id.* at 43.

92. *Id.* at 52–53 (noting also that for the baptism of a girl there were two female sponsors and one male).

93. Sabar, *supra* note 28, at 671.

94. *Id.* at 696. Jewish legend depicts Lilith as the primary enemy of infants. See *id.* at 673–74 for a more complete discussion.

95. *Id.* at 697. *See also infra* note 145 and accompanying text.

96. Sabar, *supra* note 28, at 707.

97. *Id.* at 705 (noting also that the Hebrew word *brit* means both covenant and circumcision). *See also* MARCUS, *supra* note 10, at 51, for a further discussion of this tradition.

98. See, for example, the narrative in which Elijah revives a young boy who had fallen gravely ill, which is recounted in 1 Kings 17:17–24, in JPS TANAKH, *supra* note 71, at 757.

Some Sephardic Jews, such as those from Morocco, actually call the vigil "The Night of Elijah the Prophet."[99] In addition, in Sephardic communities the vigil featured a special tray with candles[100] and protective plants called Elijah's tray or candelabrum.[101] Moreover, at every *brit* a special chair is reserved for Elijah.[102] Many distinct local customs have arisen in connection with Elijah's chair, and in some locales it was even regarded as a holy object.[103] Even today, when the infant arrives at the place of the ceremony, the person charged with performing the *brit* (known in Hebrew as the *mohel*) greets him with the traditional welcoming greeting in Hebrew, and the infant is placed on Elijah's chair.[104]

There is also much evidence to suggest that the nighttime vigil owed "some of its coloring to Christian customs that marked the night before a newborn child's baptism."[105] The term *wachnacht* appeared in medieval Germany in the sixteenth century to designate a meal in the parents' home on the evening before the *brit*. This tradition was an adaptation of the German Christian custom with the identical appellation on the night prior to a child's baptism. Marcus notes that another sign of this derivation is the preparation of special cakes that were similar to those baked by Christians to appease the evil spirits and protect the Christian child on the evening prior to his or her baptism.[106] Interestingly, both Jews and Christians believed that the presence of food could mollify evil spirits, thus explaining the practice of a festive meal on the evening prior to a significant transitional event such as a *brit* or baptism.[107]

In a fascinating study of the pre-circumcision vigil, Professor Elliott Horowitz reveals the historical development of this custom in greater detail. Horowitz demonstrates how the vigil changed in accordance with the norms of the religious cultural sensibilities of both Jews and Christians

---

99. Sabar, *supra* note 28, at 707.

100. Recall the protective power of light and fire. *See supra* notes 71–73 and accompanying text.

101. Sabar, *supra* note 28, at 708–09.

102. *See id.* at 709; MARCUS, *supra* note 10, at 51, 58.

103. *See* Sabar, *supra* note 28, at 711.

104. MARCUS, *supra* note 10, at 58.

105. *Id.* at 47.

106. *Id.* Marcus also describes the efforts that the rabbis made to anchor these practices in Jewish biblical sources. *See id.*

107. *Id.* at 48.

in early modern Europe.[108] Although his study is focused primarily on the Italian version of this rite, known as the *veglia*, it illustrates how in both Italy and central Europe the nature of the vigil underwent an increasing process of sacralization that mirrored the majority religious culture. When this rite emerged initially in the Middle Ages,[109] its character was largely festive and even bawdy. Women and men often engaged in eating, drinking, mixed dancing, and even gambling as they passed away the long hours of the night. Thus, the vigil was representative of late medieval Europe's popular religious culture, which did not object to merging the sacred and the profane.[110] Horowitz notes that the vigil "maintained itself as a popular tradition, untouched by the religious authorities, and hence an authentic expression of the religion of the people."[111]

By the seventeenth century, however, the vigil began to take on the quality of a much more somber and religious event, due to the "intervention of rabbinic and communal authorities who came to regard as problematic forms of festivity that had previously been tacitly tolerated if not explicitly endorsed."[112] This trend was a reflection of the Church's growing tendency to separate the realms of the sacred and the profane to a much greater degree than had been the case in medieval times.[113] Yet, as accounts of these vigils show, the people continued to demonstrate a resistance to completely embracing a more serious and pious atmosphere. This reality attests to the power of the tradition of the people.[114]

The continued presence of more festive elements of the vigil illustrates yet another important theme concerning *minhag*. Often, the rabbis were not able, or willing, to reformulate substantially or eliminate the customs of the people because they were too firmly entrenched. In these instances, the religious leaders passively tolerated practices they nonetheless found to be problematic. In some cases, the rabbis even found themselves in the position of providing active assistance or justification.

---

108. Elliott Horowitz, *The Eve of the Circumcision: A Chapter in the History of Jewish Nightlife*, 23:1 J. Soc. Hist. 45, 46 (1989).

109. The pre-circumcision vigil was known at least as early as the thirteenth century. *Id.* at 47.

110. *Id.* at 51.

111. *Id.*

112. *Id.* at 46.

113. *Id.* at 52.

114. *Id.* at 56 (noting that the sacral observances did not replace the traditional rites, but "simply took their place alongside them in a decidedly subordinate manner").

Rabbinic Toleration: Childbirth, Circumcision, and Martyrdom

With respect to folk practices lacking a specific basis in the *halakhah*, Rabbi Louis Jacobs has noted the tendency among *halakhists* to accept "even dubious practices that had become too deeply rooted to be banned by simple rabbinic edict" and subsequently to endeavor to "discover some warrant for them in the *halakhah*."[115] This section explores representative examples of such rabbinic toleration. The discussion not only concentrates on the previously discussed critical transitional periods of childbirth and circumcision, but also incorporates a treatment of the cult of martyrdom that developed in the Middle Ages. All of these areas entailed considerable top-down toleration, and even facilitation, of bottom-up practices.

Recall that the customs surrounding birth and circumcision drew heavily from the rabbinic tradition and normative Jewish sources, even if the rabbinic authorities did not always approve of the specific content of the folk culture. The rabbinic response of toleration perhaps can be understood as an acknowledgment of the reality that the people's "folkloristic beliefs"[116] represented a stronger form of unification than even the traditional and official practices of Judaism. The official representatives of *halakhah* often collaborated with their communities in trying to satisfy the people's needs.[117] For example, in Islamic countries, Jewish law authorities would inscribe the writings on the amulets used in connection with these rites. In so doing, they would "wash themselves in preparation and observe the same laws of purity required for writing a Torah scroll" or other sacred text.[118] In Eastern Europe, where a stringent interpretation of the Second Commandment's prohibition on "graven images" resulted in the avoidance of figurative representations, boys in schools of Jewish learning typically made childbirth amulets using a paper cut technique that was popular among Jews and their neighbors. The willingness of these students to facilitate this form of folk practice also suggests some degree of acquiescence by their rabbinic teachers.

The customary practice in eighteenth-century Germany of placing a Torah scroll taken from the Ark of the local synagogue in the delivery room

---

115. JACOBS, *supra* note 41, at 210.

116. Sabar, *supra* note 28, at 672.

117. *Id.* at 712.

118. *Id.*

furnishes another fascinating example of this point. Given that the Torah is the most sacred object in the Jewish tradition, people believed that its presence in the delivery room would facilitate an easy delivery and protect both mother and child. Clearly the rabbis must have given their explicit permission for this practice or the Torah scrolls would have remained in the synagogues. This permission is particularly significant in light of the tradition's position that human exposure to certain blood causes ritual impurity.[119] Although the rabbis knew that a Torah scroll is not susceptible to ritual impurity,[120] the practice still raised questions concerning "'proper usage,' if not official law, for both the Ashkenazic and Sephardic authorities whose communities followed this custom."[121]

Another example of rabbinic toleration is found in connection with the storage location of Elijah's chair in certain synagogues. As already discussed, Elijah's chair gave rise to many distinct local customs in connection with the *brit*. In Islamic countries, when this chair was not in use at a *brit*, it was generally stored in the synagogue in the most holy of places—inside the Ark of the Torah.[122] This proximity to the Torah scroll imbued the chair with additional spiritual sanctity, a result that the rabbinic leaders clearly either encouraged or, at the least, did not oppose.

One of the most interesting examples of rabbinic tolerance is found in Horowitz's study of the pre-circumcision vigil. He notes that in Germany, it was customary to drink wine and eat meat on this night even when the rite fell on the days preceding the ninth day of the Hebrew month of *Av*, a fast day commemorating the destruction of the two Temples in Jerusalem as well as other tragedies in the history of the Jewish people. The ninth of *Av* is considered the saddest day in the entire Jewish calendar, and its observance entails numerous prohibitions on the actual day of the fast, in addition to various other forbidden activities for the preceding three weeks.[123] One set of prohibitions entails the custom of refraining from eating meat and drinking wine for the

---

119. Examples include menstrual blood and blood connected with childbirth. *See supra* note 55.

120. *See* Berakhot 22 (Babylonian Talmud).

121. Sabar, *supra* note 28, at 678.

122. *Id.* at 710. In contrast to European synagogues, in synagogues of Islamic countries the Ark was not a separate piece of furniture but rather an actual room (or several large niches) on the side of the synagogue closest to Jerusalem. *Id.*

123. Food restrictions in connection with the ninth of *Av* date back to the Mishnah. *See* Taanit 4:7 (Mishnah).

nine days prior to the fast. Yet, the popularity of the vigil tradition in Germany resulted in the *halakhic* authority Jacob Reischer allowing his constituents a degree of latitude, thus requiring them to eliminate *either* meat or wine, but not both, during these vigils.[124]

Throughout history, the ninth of *Av* has been regarded as a communal day of mourning, a time to remember those who perished as a result of persecution. During the Middle Ages, the Ashkenazic Jews living in Europe responded to persecutions "by developing a cult of martyrdom and rituals to memorialize the dead," and as discussed more fully below, they adapted many of these elements from Christian imagery.[125] Although but for "a few extreme instances" the permissibility of committing voluntary martyrdom is questionable under Jewish law,[126] we know for a fact that the Ashkhenazic community during this time exhibited a pattern of martyrdom over the course of centuries. This pattern not only resulted in the deaths of individuals, but also extended to parents killing their own children to prevent them from being raised as Christians. In documenting this period of history, Professor Haym Soloveitchik has noted that parents "even recited a blessing on the murder of themselves and of their own children, as they would on the performance of other divine commandments."[127] Despite "the magnitude of this *halakhic* breach," the rabbinic response was to survey all of the available *halakhic* literature in order to compile a tenuous case for condoning suicide as a response to religious persecution.[128] Moreover, as no such case could even be made for killing one's children under these circumstances, the response was simply "audible silence."[129]

The Role of Persecution: Death and Mourning

Many of the familiar Jewish rituals performed today in connection with the deaths of relatives and friends are derived from northern European Ashkenazic culture beginning in the twelfth century. The "Jewish cult of

---

124. *See* Horowitz, *supra* note 108, at 56.

125. Biale, *Introduction to Part Two, supra* note 43, at 306–07; *see also* MARK R. COHEN, UNDER CRESCENT AND CROSS 174–75 (1995) (discussing the origins of the Ashkenazic Jewish tendency toward martyrdom); MARCUS, *supra* note 10, at 222–23.

126. Haym Soloveitchik, *Religious Law and Change: The Medieval Ashkenazic Example*, 12:2 AJS REVIEW 205, 208–09 (1987).

127. *Id.* at 209.

128. *Id.* at 209–10.

129. *Id.* at 210.

the dead" essentially began with the anti-Jewish riots and subsequent acts of martyrdom that occurred in the Rhineland in 1096, accompanying the call to the First Crusade.[130] As the persecutions spread geographically, a greater number of elements were added to the developing rituals. These rituals represent not only a response to historical circumstances, but also a significant borrowing from the surrounding Christian cultures.[131]

For example, the custom in Germany of reciting annually the names of local martyrs on the anniversary of their deaths, and the lighting of candles in their memory, was derived from the "Christian monastic practice of compiling and reading necrologies" accompanied by the lighting of candles.[132] Eventually, this practice in Judaism was expanded to include the anniversary of the death of an individual's own parents and other close relatives as a result of the German riots and massacres during the fifty years prior to the Black Death in 1348–1350.[133] The observance of the anniversary of the death of a relative is called *yahrtzeit*, and it is marked by attending services to recite a particular prayer known as the mourner's *kaddish,* and by lighting a candle at home that burns for the entire day. Although the Talmud contains some discussion of practices to be observed on the anniversary of the death of a parent or teacher, most of the currently observed institutionalized memorial practices developed in medieval Germany as a response to historical realities.[134] Interestingly, the term *yahrtzeit* is taken from the same term used by German Christians to recall the souls of the departed on the anniversary of their deaths.[135]

---

130. Marcus, *supra* note 10, at 224–25.

131. *See supra* note 25 and accompanying text; *see also supra* Chapter 2, notes 148–49 and accompanying text.

132. Marcus, *supra* note 10, at 230. The Christian necrologies listed the dead according to their date of death. Similarly, the names of Jewish martyrs were preserved in memorial books, a practice adapted from the monasteries that preserved the dates of death of their members that were recited on their "birthdays"—"the day the saint died and was born to eternal life." *Id.* Marcus also notes that "these practices reflect the Jews' close awareness of their Christian neighbors' rites that they sometimes turned into a cultural polemic." *Id. See also* Yosef Hayim Yerushalmi, Zachor 46 (1982).

133. *See* Marcus, *supra* note 10, at 236; Marcus, *supra* note 24, at 464.

134. Marcus, *supra* note 10, at 235–36.

135. In the German language, *yahr zeit* appears as two words. *Id.* at 236. Observance of *yarhtzeit* initially was resisted by Sephardic Jews, given its Ashkenazic origin. Jacobs, *supra* note 41, at 214 n.26.

From a liturgical standpoint, the *kaddish* is the most well-known prayer associated with remembering the dead. The word *kaddish* means "sanctified," and the text of the prayer is about the sanctity of God rather than those who are no longer living. Although some lines of the prayer may be traced back to the days of the Second Temple (before 70 CE),[136] Rabbi Louis Jacobs has written that the "institution of the mourner's *kaddish* originated in folk custom."[137] Historians are in general agreement that "the custom of a son reciting *kaddish* during the first year after his father's death originated in Germany in the thirteenth century at a time of persecution by the Crusaders."[138]

Another component of the memorial liturgy is the *yizkor* memorial service, the basis for which is derived from an early medieval Palestinian text referring to giving charity and remembering the dead on Yom Kippur, the Day of Atonement.[139] Although originally *yizkor* was recited only on Yom Kippur, after the persecutions in the German Empire culminating in the Black Death, three additional recitations were added during the course of a year.[140] Marcus notes that in some respects, the *yizkor* service combines elements from both the Christian All Souls' Day and the Christian All Saints' Day, during which days special masses are held and candles lit. In the Jewish tradition, different prayers are said during the *yizkor* service for one's relatives and for the martyrs, and the *yizkor* days are also marked by lighting a memorial candle that burns for the entire day.[141]

The influence of Christianity upon Jewish customs was present not only in terms of remembrance, but also at the time of actual death. Thus, although the Talmud recommends that one whose life is in danger as a result of serious illness should perform a confession of sin,[142] the presence of a rabbi at this confession is related to the Church's ceremony of last rites.[143] This concern for the presence of a rabbi was especially prominent in early modern

---

136. MARCUS, *supra* note 10, at 239.

137. JACOBS, *supra* note 41, at 214.

138. *Id.*

139. MARCUS, *supra* note 10, at 226–27.

140. *Id.* at 225. These additional three times coincided with the three major Jewish festivals: Passover, Shavuot (Pentecost), and Sukkot (Tabernacles).

141. *Id.* at 232–33.

142. Shabbat 32a (Babylonian Talmud).

143. *See* MARCUS, *supra* note 10, at 199. *See also* New Advent, Extreme Unction, http://www.newadvent.org/cathen/05716a.htm (last visited July 8, 2014) (discussing New Testament origins of last rites).

Italy, where the attitudes of the Jews of that country mirrored those of their Catholic neighbors following the Council of Trent.[144]

Traditionally, Jews also recite the *Shema* right before death. This prayer, beginning with the verse in Deuteronomy "Hear O Israel! The Lord is our God, the Lord alone," is considered the foundational prayer in the Jewish liturgy.[145] This practice is ancient, but the precise nature and onset of its origin are debatable.[146] Marcus notes that the Jews who perished in the massacres of 1096 in the Rhineland are depicted as reciting this verse upon their own death, or upon witnessing the death of other martyrs. The practice then spread to other Ashkenazic Jews at the moment of their deaths.[147] In the world of medieval Ashkenazic Jewry, the martyrs represented the epitome of religious piety. The Jewish communities of this time constructed "an entire ideology about themselves as a pious community," and the recitation of the *Shema* upon dying was, according to Marcus, "one of many ways that the dead of 1096 affected the broader culture of medieval European Jewish memory expressed in liturgical rites and gestures."[148] This development was largely regional in nature given that such practices were not prevalent among the Jews living in Islamic countries at this time.[149]

The foregoing discussion examines representative areas in which the people validated rabbinic law and culture through their customs, and the rabbis, in turn, tolerated and at times even facilitated popular practices lacking credible *halakhic* standing. In some instances, however, the rabbis willingly adopted popular stringencies that developed from the bottom up. Many of

---

144. Elliott Horowitz, *Families and Their Fortunes, in* CULTURES OF THE JEWS, *supra* note 24, at 573, 587–88. The Council of Trent teaches that the ceremony of last rites is of biblical origin. *See* New Advent, *supra* note 143. *See also* MARCUS, *supra* note 10, at 199 ("In descriptions of early modern Italian-Jewish death rites, the institution of deathbed confession betrays Christian surroundings.").

In his essay focusing on the Jews of early modern Italy, Horowitz notes another interesting death ritual performed by the four sons of the revered Venetian rabbi Samuel Aboab in 1694. Perhaps inspired by the Catholic world in which they lived where "extravagant gestures of deferential respect" surrounded them, the sons kissed their dead father's feet. Horowitz, *supra*, at 621–22.

145. ETZ HAYIM, *supra* note 81, at 1024–25 (translating Deuteronomy 6:4). *See also supra* text accompanying note 95.

146. For a more complete discussion of this point, see MARCUS, *supra* note 10, at 200–01.

147. *Id.*

148. *Id.* at 201.

149. *Id.* at 228.

these stringencies involve customs concerning *kashrut,* the Jewish dietary laws. David Kraemer has written that Jewish eating is and has always been "a 'negotiation,'...a struggle on the part of individual Jews and the community over where the boundaries of Jewish identity should be laid."[150] Thus, the topic of eating practices serves as an appropriate conclusion for this chapter about bottom-up practices.

Rabbinic Reliance on the Bottom Up: Increasing Stringencies in *Kashrut*

In his seminal article on the increasing stringencies of Orthodox practice in the twentieth century, Haym Soloveitchik observed, "The simple fact is that the traditional Jewish kitchen, transmitted from mother to daughter over the generations, has been immeasurably and unrecognizably amplified beyond all *halakhic* requirements."[151] In another article concentrating on the medieval period, Soloveitchik demonstrates that in the context of the Jewish kitchen and eating practices generally, many of the current norms were developed during the twelfth and thirteenth centuries in the Ashkenazic culture of Northern Europe, particularly France and Germany.[152] This region's Ashkenazic *halakhic* commentators are known as the *tosafists,*[153] and their work has had a strong and lasting influence on the development of Jewish law. The connection between the canonized literature, such as the Talmud, and the practices of the people in this place and time is particularly relevant for this discussion. Specifically, Soloveitchik demonstrates that as is the case with so many areas of Jewish law and life, when the people's practices diverged from the written word, the rabbis radically interpreted *halakhah* in order to accommodate the law to the lived reality. Further, as the Franco-German community was in a state of "intense religiosity,"[154] this accommodation usually meant enacting increased stringencies. Soloveitchik's study extends well beyond the kitchen and Jewish eating practices, but his remarks about this topic are illustrative of his overall thesis.

---

150. KRAEMER, *supra* note 45, at 5.

151. Soloveitchik, *supra* note 65, at 2, 37 n.18.

152. Soloveitchik, *supra* note 126, at 206, 216, 220.

153. *Id.* at 207.

154. *Id.* at 212.

Jews are not permitted to eat meat and dairy products together,[155] and today, kosher kitchens maintain separate eating and preparation implements for meat and dairy. Yet, many Jews, including those who are observant, would be surprised to learn that there is little basis in the *halakhah* for separate dishes for meat and dairy, let alone "separate sinks, dish racks, towels, table-cloths, and even separate cupboards."[156] Haym Soloveitchik, the son of Rabbi Joseph Soloveitchik, perhaps the most revered Modern Orthodox leader of the twentieth century, recalls his own "shock" when he realized this discrepancy between the letter of the law and normative Jewish practice after studying Yoreh De'ah, a *halakhic* compilation dating back to the early fourteenth century.[157] He writes that "if food is served cold, there is no need for separate dishware altogether."[158] Still, as Soloveitchik immediately acknowledges, notwithstanding the content of the Yoreh De'ah, serving cold cuts on a "dairy" dish is simply *treif* (not kosher).[159]

The intersection of law and culture that produced much of the complex dietary regulations is a fascinating study of rabbinic reliance on popular practices in fashioning *halakhah*. Kraemer has written a comprehensive study of this topic that merits a careful reading for those interested in the history of Jewish eating and the relationship between food and Jewish identity.[160] *Kashrut* is a complicated area that incorporates numerous subtopics. The following discussion, which draws largely from Kraemer's study, focuses mainly on the subject of physical separation for meat and dairy dishes and other accoutrements.

The Torah says relatively little about the general prohibition of mixing meat and dairy. In three separate verses, the Torah states, "You shall not boil a kid in its mother's milk."[161] During early Talmudic times, the sages interpreted this injunction to require physical separation with respect to cooking meat and milk together when these foods "give taste" to the pots in which they are cooked.[162] Kraemer notes the lack of clarity with respect to

---

155. *See infra* note 161 and accompanying text.

156. Soloveitchik, *supra* note 65, at 2.

157. Soloveitchik, *supra* note 126, at 220.

158. *Id.; see also* Soloveitchik, *supra* note 65, at 2.

159. Soloveitchik, *supra* note 126, at 220.

160. *See* Kraemer, *supra* note 45.

161. Exodus 23:19; *Exodus* 34:26; Deuteronomy 14:21 (translation from Etz Hayim, *supra* note 81, at 474, 544, 1074).

162. *See, e.g.,* Hullin 111b (Babylonian Talmud); Zevahim 96b (Babylonian Talmud).

the precise meaning of "giving taste" and posits that the language seems to reflect concern "for the transmission of the taste of one category of food to the other."[163] In analyzing the Talmudic sources, Kraemer asserts, "There is evidently no concern whatsoever if dishes or other utensils had not been used on the same day" or if "at some point in the transmission chain, the food and utensil/dish were not hot."[164] Further, given that the consumption of meat was rare during this time, the cause for concern in Talmudic times was relatively limited. In fact, the topic of separation was not a major focus until the High Middle Ages,[165] the period of time that is the focus of Soloveitchik's previously discussed study.

The early *halakhic* interpretations that surfaced in both the Ashkenazic and Sephardic communities were lenient compared to today's standards. These rulings seem to require some degree of separation of cooking utensils, but there are uncertainties concerning whether utensils used to cook meat must be immersed in boiling water before they can be used for dairy *on the same day,* or whether immersion is necessary for a dairy use at any point in the future.[166] Regarding the use of pots for dairy following meat, the medieval commentators manifested divergent views concerning process and procedure, with some authorities requiring a more stringent separation in practice.[167] Still, at this time, the practice of maintaining permanently separate dishes and utensils for meat and dairy was not widespread.[168]

Significantly, Kraemer, like Soloveitchik, acknowledges that the pietist movement that began to emerge in Germany in the twelfth and thirteenth centuries eventually impacted not only the people's practices concerning separation of dishes, but ultimately also the perspectives of *halakhic* authorities. Jewish law codes written during the sixteenth century reveal that community practices, if not the actual letter of the law, reflected increasing stringencies concerning separation.[169] Thus, by this time Rabbi Moses Isserles noted that the prevailing custom was for Jewish households to have two separate

---

163. KRAEMER, *supra* note 45, at 100.

164. *Id.* at 101 (defining "not hot" as "less than a temperature that might scald the hand").

165. *Id.* at 102.

166. *Id.* at 102–03.

167. *Id.* at 104–07.

168. *Id.* at 107.

169. *Id.* at 107–08 (discussing the codes of Joseph Caro and Moses Isserles). *See also infra* Chapter 4, note 143 and accompanying text.

knives, with the one used for dairy being clearly designated as such.[170] The focus on knives is understandable given that they were the most important utensil as they were used for cooking, serving, and eating.[171] With respect to washing meat and dairy dishes together, however, the codified laws allowed more leniency than modern normative practices.[172] German sources from the early sixteenth century reveal that overall the customs of the people concerning separation were far more stringent than those required by their rabbinic authorities.[173]

By the middle of the eighteenth century, the practice of complete separation had become widespread among the Jews.[174] Significantly, such separation was driven by the bottom-up practices of the people rather than the top-down leadership. In short, "rabbinic codifications pertaining to the separation of Jewish kitchens into 'meat' and 'dairy' lag well behind popular practice."[175] The development of kosher kitchen customs is one of many illustrative examples of how bottom-up practices substantially impacted the development of halakhah from the top down.[176]

Another food custom manifesting a similar pattern of increased stringency is the customary waiting period between consuming meat and dairy. The Talmud discusses washing one's hands and either wiping or rinsing one's mouth as well as waiting some unspecified period of time after eating meat before consuming dairy.[177] It does not, however, contain much in the way of specificity concerning these practices. Later rabbinic authorities offered various interpretations and halakhic recommendations regarding the necessary waiting periods between consuming meat and dairy foods. Maimonides, the celebrated medieval Sephardic authority, determined in his code of Jewish law that dairy is prohibited after eating meat for the amount of time equivalent to eating another meal, approximately six hours, on the theory that such

---

170. KRAEMER, supra note 45, at 108.

171. Id. at 114.

172. Id. at 108–09, 116–17.

173. Id. at 109–10.

174. Id. at 110–12.

175. Id. at 111.

176. See id. at 117 ("The practice of maintaining separate dishes may be seen as a part of a more prevalent tendency in post-medieval Jewish practice to choose the more stringent route—in regulations pertaining to eating and in many other matters as well.").

177. Hullin 104b–105a (Babylonian Talmud).

a waiting period is necessary due to the meat that remains between one's teeth.[178] In the view of Maimonides, therefore, simply wiping and washing are insufficient when dairy follows meat. Maimonides's ruling was embraced by later Sephardic authorities who understood the six-hour wait to be a matter of *halakhah* rather than custom.[179]

In contrast, among Ashkenazic Jews the custom had been to wait only one hour between meat and dairy.[180] Indeed, earlier medieval Ashkenazic authorities such as *Rebbenu Tam* had ruled very leniently on the waiting period.[181] By the sixteenth century, the six-hour waiting period still was not widespread among the Ashkenazic masses despite the fact that by this time keeping separate dishes and other utensils for meat and dairy already was becoming a popular practice.[182] Eventually, however, the standard custom became six hours, despite some variants among particular Jewish communities such as the Dutch, who wait one hour, and German Jews, who wait three.[183] In other words, as with keeping separate dishes and utensils, the bottom up eventually embraced a more stringent mode of practice and this custom prevailed.

As formalized denominations of Judaism began to develop in the nineteenth century, their respective practices of observance came to be characterized by distinct rabbinic legal interpretations as well as by variable bottom-up practices. One example, relevant to the waiting period discussion, is that those Conservative Jews who keep kosher typically wait three hours after eating meat before consuming dairy while Orthodox Jews adhere to the six-hour wait.[184] The following chapter explores the histories, ideologies, and lawmaking patterns of the major movements of Judaism in the modern period.

---

178. KRAEMER, *supra* note 45, at 88–89 (citing Maimonides, Mishneh Torah, at 9:28).

179. Rabbi Doniel Neustadt, *Weekly Halacha*, TORAH.ORG, http://www.torah.org/advanced/weekly-halacha/5762/kisisa.html (last visited July 8, 2014).

180. KRAEMER, *supra* note 45, at 91 (citing Moses Isserles, who recognizes and accepts the one-hour custom but expresses a preference for the six-hour stringency).

181. *See id.* at 87–88.

182. *Id.* at 120.

183. *See id.* at 97; Neustadt, *supra* note 179, at 1.

184. KRAEMER, *supra* note 45, at 97.

4 THE BIRTH OF JEWISH DENOMINATIONS IN MODERNITY AND THEIR DIVERGENT VIEWS ON JEWISH LAW

Throughout the medieval period, nearly all of the traditional Jewish community agreed that observance of *halakhah* (Jewish law) was essential and of unquestioned importance.[1] In other words, the integrity of the *halakhic* system was accepted by virtually everyone within the mainstream of the religion. The notion of someone claiming to be a believing Jew but denying the concept that the Torah came from heaven was entirely unknown in the medieval period.[2] Moreover, as historian Marc Shapiro has noted, the medieval period lacked the current denominations we have today, and therefore, even the most "radical philosophers...all seem to have lived in accordance with Jewish law, even if their view of its significance diverged drastically from that of the Talmudists."[3] As developed more fully in the following discussion, the Enlightenment era and modernity brought increasing options for participation in the surrounding cultures for Jews. This development led to the birth

---

1. *See generally supra* Chapter 3. That is not to say that legitimate theological differences did not exist between the medievals. *See, e.g.,* BYRON L. SHERWIN, *Philosophies of Law, in* IN PARTNERSHIP WITH GOD: CONTEMPORARY JEWISH LAW AND ETHICS 25–26 (1990) (discussing the Lurianic mystics of the medieval period who rejected the monolithic view of the medieval philosophers by instead claiming the Torah reflects the imperfections, change, and fluctuations of an earthly existence).

2. *See* Julius Guttmann, *The Principles of Judaism,* CONSERVATIVE JUDAISM, Fall 1959, at 1, 3 (asserting that, in medieval times, denial of the *Torah min Ha-Shamayim* ("Torah from Heaven") dogma would place a Jew "outside the pale of Judaism").

3. MARC B. SHAPIRO, THE LIMITS OF ORTHODOX THEOLOGY 28 (2004).

and growth of divergent factions among the Jews who understood the process, and importance, of *halakhah* very differently.

This chapter focuses on the European origins of the various modern movements of Judaism and emphasizes their historical development in the United States with particular attention to the post-Holocaust twentieth century. The discussion of each movement examines their respective ideologies, histories, and lawmaking processes, an approach consistent with this book's thesis that culture and law are inextricably intertwined. This chapter also showcases the divergent views of the movements concerning the development and relevance of *halakhah*. Chapters 5 through 7 build on this discussion by examining specific areas of dispute, both within and between the movements, that have arisen as a result of this landscape.

In medieval times, Jewish life generally thrived in "a self-imposed and tolerated ghetto" within the Christian and Muslim domains of Europe, Asia, and Africa.[4] Rabbi Gerson Cohen observed that despite the well-documented hostilities among the three major religions, they each maintained a familiar framework characterized by revealed truth, a detailed regimen for daily existence, and the fundamental premise "that no differences existed between the secular and the sacred."[5] Due to these commonalities, the medieval period furnished a very suitable environment for Talmudic culture. Specifically, the "God of Israel and his moral values became the law of the nations."[6]

By the eighteenth century, this climate changed as the French Revolution set the terms for national identity by "re-organizing former corporate groups, such as the Jews, into equal, rights-bearing individuals as the price of citizenship."[7] In 1789, as the French National Assembly debated the emancipation of the Jews, Count Stanislas of Clermont-Tonnerre declared, "The Jews should be denied everything as a nation, but granted everything as individuals. They must be citizens."[8] This period generally marked the beginning of

[handwritten margin note: destroy cmty promote indiv.]

---

4. Gerson D. Cohen, *The Talmudic Age, in* GREAT AGES AND IDEAS OF THE JEWISH PEOPLE 143, 211 (Leo W. Schwarz ed., 1956).

5. *Id.*

6. *Id.* at 212.

7. Suzanne Last Stone, *Formulating Responses in an Egalitarian Age: An Overview, in* FORMULATING RESPONSES IN AN EGALITARIAN AGE 53, 55 (Marc D. Stern ed., 2005).

8. David Biale, *Introduction to Part Three: Modern Encounters, in* CULTURES OF THE JEWS 725, 725 (David Biale ed., 2002). Biale also cautions, however, that the process of emancipation did not proceed with equal rapidity throughout Europe and in the Muslim world. *Id.* at 727.

today's modern era that is characterized by a variety of related ideals and ideologies such as nationalism, equality, personal autonomy, and liberal toleration.[9] Rabbi Byron Sherwin has noted the irony that "modern liberal religion embraced Enlightenment ideas to provide a foundation for their beliefs and practices" given that "a major goal of the French and German Enlightenment in the eighteenth century was the subversion of religious authority and tradition."[10] Enlightenment thinkers "wanted to replace religious obligations with individual autonomy, religious law and ritual with rational thought and…particularistic interests with universalistic concerns."[11]

Enlightenment ideologies did not sit comfortably with the medieval Talmudic culture that resisted the norms of equality and personal autonomy. Thus, Immanuel Kant called for the "euthanasia of Judaism," given his perception that Judaism was a religion of law and "devoid of ethics."[12] As the philosophies that shaped the Enlightenment era began to take hold among the general population, Jewish culture, practice, and philosophy began to experience a significant sea change. The intellectual and political climate of nineteenth-century Germany rendered many German Jews especially interested in participating in German culture and education.[13] Some Jews desiring to become part of mainstream society sought to define "Judaism" in terms of the dominant culture rather than according to the traditional Jewish framework. In this milieu, the Reform movement introduced universal ethical monotheism as a conceptual basis for Judaism.

Reform Judaism
Ideological Predicate

Christian theologians played a part in the development of the concept of ethical monotheism as a basis for Judaism. Julius Wellhausen, in seeking to answer "what is Christianity," a fairly typical question for a liberal Protestant

---

9. *See* Stone, *supra* note 7, at 55.

10. Byron L. Sherwin, *The Assimilation of Judaism: Heschel and the "Category Mistake,"* JUDAISM, Fall/Winter 2006, at 40, 42, http://www.ajcongress.org/site/DocServer/ Assimilationofjudaism.pdf?docID=2124.

11. *Id.*

12. *Id.*

13. *See* W. GUNTHER PLAUT, THE RISE OF REFORM JUDAISM xiv–xv (2d prtg., 1969) [hereinafter THE RISE].

theologian in the nineteenth century, also sought to answer the question "what is Judaism" given that Jesus was a Jew.[14] According to Wellhausen's narrative, universal ethical monotheism—which he believed to be the Judaism of the early prophets such as Isaiah and Micah—was the authentic biblical version of Judaism. He claimed that this version of Judaism was uncorrupted by the focus on law, ritual, and particularism characteristic of the priesthood.[15] Wellhausen argued that Jesus and his teachings restored this authentic form of prophetic Judaism.[16]

[handwritten margin note: wow! I never realized this was Wellhausen's view]

Wellhausen's view of Judaism is important because of his influence on the early Reform movement that warmly embraced his ideas. In Reform Judaism, the idea of prophetic Judaism is very pronounced.[17] Early Reformers manifested a concern with the immediate—as opposed to futuristic—redemption of the human spirit in the form of the "perfectibility of the human race."[18] In his renowned study of the rise of Reform Judaism, W. Gunther Plaut noted that broad universalism accompanied Reform's distinct Messianic vision. This tendency "combined the visions of the prophets with the dreams of man's brotherhood which the American and French Revolutions had proclaimed."[19] Reform's embrace of the universal resulted in a reduction of parochialism and, as the following section discusses, eventually led to a rejection of what came to be known as Jewish nationalism.[20] Given this background, it is not surprising that Reform Judaism historically has encouraged social action far more than the other movements on both a theoretical and practical level.[21]

From the outset, the Reformers condemned assimilation and instead called for strong, distinct religious Jewish identity among the movement's adherents. They were strong proponents of Jewish education, and their early leaders, such as Leopold Zunz, advocated a new type of Jewish study that came to be known as the "Science of Judaism."[22] This discipline, which became an

---

14. *See* Sherwin, *supra* note 10, at 42.

15. *Id.* at 43.

16. *Id.*

17. *See* THE RISE, *supra* note 13, at xvi (Reform Judaism was "prophet-directed").

18. *Id.*

19. *Id.* at xvi–xvii.

20. *Id.* at xvii.

21. *See* JONATHAN SARNA, AMERICAN JUDAISM 151, 195–96, 308 (2004).

22. THE RISE, *supra* note 13, at 16.

integral component of Reform's structure, urged that Judaism be studied as a systematic science "for its own sake and not for any special purpose or definite intention."[23] This approach departed significantly from the traditional view that study is a necessary part of worship. Reform's receptivity to the idea that the study of Judaism should be treated as a science was supported by its acceptance of biblical criticism. Embraced by Protestant scholars in the nineteenth century, biblical criticism maintains that the Five Books of Moses is a composite document rather than the product of a literal transmission from God to Moses.[24] This view also represents a substantial departure from the tradition's cornerstone position concerning the origin of the Written Torah.

Scholars have observed that the ideology of Reform Judaism manifests three distinct stages.[25] The first stage was characterized primarily by a call for reform that was grounded in the classical sources of the tradition. The second stage reflected a pronounced antagonism to *halakhah* and Jewish particularity. The third, and current, stage reveals an inclination to embrace, and perhaps even endorse, *halakhic* practice, although in a different way from the other two major denominations.

Historical Development

The initial Reform Jewish leaders in the early nineteenth century were very proud of their Jewish heritage and approached all that they did within a classic Jewish framework. These Reformers regarded themselves as thoroughly Jewish and educated in the classical Jewish sources, which they used to bolster their ideological positions. They insisted that the tradition was significant and that change had to be accomplished organically from within the bounds of the tradition.[26] These Reformers believed that the Jewish tradition historically was receptive to the development, and even change, of *halakhah*.[27] Consistent with their support of universal ethical monotheism, they invoked the ethical commandments of the biblical prophets as their primary source of authority for change.[28]

---

23. *Id.* at 107 (quoting Immanuel Wolf).

24. *Id.* at 111–12.

25. *See* Moshe David Herr & Theodore Friedman, *Oral Law, in* 14 THE ENCYCLOPEDIA JUDAICA 454, 456 (Michael Berenbaum & Fred Skolnik eds., 2d edition, 2007).

26. THE RISE, *supra* note 13, at xix.

27. *Id.* at 112.

28. *Id.* at xix.

Reformers at this time did not reject the Talmud but instead approached it from a critical perspective. In other words, they "selected from, rather than rejected, its dicta."[29] This aspect of Reform's ideology was steeped in Kant's emphasis on personal autonomy, an ironic tendency given his call for the "euthanasia of Judaism."[30]

Kant

Several members of the Reform community in Hamburg, Germany, established the New Israelitish Temple Association in 1817, thus effectuating the birth of formal worship consistent with a Reform outlook.[31] The term "Temple" was selected to avoid conflict with the prior Hamburg synagogue. The innovations it introduced included prayers and the sermon in German, choral singing, and the use of an organ on the Sabbath. Again, these Reformers relied on the Talmud to support these changes, and they believed they were upholding the continuity of the *mesorah* (the Jewish tradition).[32]

In contrast to these early Reform efforts, the second phase of Reform displayed a pronounced anti-*halakhic* stance.[33] Beginning in Frankfurt, Germany, in the middle of the nineteenth century,[34] this version of Reform urged the overhaul, and even abandonment, of sacred ritualistic practices rather than gradual, organic change. For example, Samuel Holdheim, the principal proponent of radical Reform Judaism in Germany, advocated changing the Jewish Sabbath to Sunday and abolishing circumcision.[35] Holdheim also believed that resort to the authority of the tradition was counterproductive and that it deserved little, or even no, weight in matters of contemporary relevance.[36] This anti-*halakhic* perspective gradually became a prominent feature of Reform's ideology in Europe, and eventually in the United States where the movement adopted the 1885 Pittsburgh Platform, which significantly influenced its development for decades to come.[37] The explicit principles adopted by the Platform stated that only the

---

29. *Id.* at xviii–xix.

30. *See supra* note 12 and accompanying text.

31. THE RISE, *supra* note 13, at 31.

32. *Id. See also* Herr & Friedman, *supra* note 25, at 456 (noting reliance on the Talmud and Jewish law codes as support for these changes).

33. Herr & Friedman, *supra* note 25, at 457.

34. THE RISE, *supra* note 13, at 50.

35. *Id.* at 122, 190, 209.

36. *Id.* at 112.

37. According to Jonathan Sarna, the Pittsburgh Platform "remained the most important statement of Reform Jewish beliefs until it was superseded in 1937" by the Columbus

"moral laws" of Judaism are binding and rejected all ceremonies that "are not adapted to the views and habits of modern civilization."[38] The Platform further declared, "We hold that all such Mosaic and Rabbinical laws as regulate diet, priestly purity and dress originated in ages and under the influence of ideas altogether foreign to our present mental and spiritual state."[39] In short, the Platform explicitly renounced the binding nature of *halakhah*, thus marking a clear, and heretofore unprecedented, break with the tradition.

Additionally, given its origins in the Enlightenment era, the universality characteristic of Reform manifested an anti-nationalist approach that eventually became anti-Zionist in nature.[40] The Pittsburgh Platform reflected this classical anti-Zionist perspective through its explicit rejection of nationalism: "We consider ourselves no longer a nation but a religious community, and therefore expect neither a return to Palestine... nor the restoration of any of the laws concerning the Jewish state."[41] In the wake of the Second World War, however, this classical perspective of Reform was substantially, if not completely, obliterated.[42] The era of Reform's classical anti-Zionist character drew to a close when its Cincinnati and New York seminaries merged in 1950 and the movement "reacquired the full force of Jewish peoplehood."[43] Still, Plaut observed that "Reform's early failure to find a workable compromise between Jewish universalism and Jewish nationalism" was its greatest weakness and represented "its greatest missed opportunity."[44]

The 1950 merger also "brought the period of Reform's radicalism decisively to a close"[45] and began a shift to the right in the movement. Paralleling its changing stance on Zionism, the previous classical Reform position manifesting an antipathy to *halakhah* also changed over time. In the late nineteenth and early twentieth centuries, the German Reform Jews in the

---

Platform. SARNA, *supra* note 21, at 150. *See also id.* at 253–54 (discussing the Columbus Platform).

38. W. GUNTHER PLAUT, THE GROWTH OF REFORM JUDAISM 34 (1965) [hereinafter THE GROWTH] (Third Principle of Pittsburgh Platform).

39. *Id.* (Fourth Principle of Pittsburgh Platform).

40. *See* THE RISE, *supra* note 13, at 133.

41. THE GROWTH, *supra* note 38, at 34.

42. *See* SARNA, *supra* note 21, at 254.

43. THE GROWTH, *supra* note 38, at 350. *See also* SARNA, *supra* note 21, at 249–55 for a discussion of this postwar shift in Reform Judaism.

44. THE GROWTH, *supra* note 38, at 144.

45. *Id.* at 350.

United States often embraced acculturation and assimilation in response to the influx of Eastern European Jews whom they believed threatened their "hard-won status."[46] This response on the part of the laypeople was consistent with the increasing radicalization of Reform's leaders during this period. After the Second World War, however, the pendulum began to swing back in the opposite direction among American Jewish liberals as more traditional patterns of thought and practice began to emerge.[47] This trend is reflected in the increasing attention to ritual and tradition in the Reform platform statements crafted in 1937, 1976, and 1999.[48] By 1965, Plaut observed that the era associated with the goals of the Pittsburgh Platform represented "the outward swing of the pendulum rather than the climax and goal" of the Reform movement.[49]

This shift to the right represents the third, and current, phase of Reform Judaism. The movement's Central Conference of American Rabbis ("CCAR") has noted in its publications that in recent decades many of its synagogues and members have reinstituted ritual and other practices previously abandoned such as the wearing of traditional garments for prayer, including *yarmulkes* (skullcap head coverings), *tallitot* (prayer shawls), and *tefilin* (phylacteries).[50] Also more common are the celebration of traditional ceremonies for life cycle events such as the Bar and Bat Mitzvah, marriage, death, and conversion.[51] Moreover, since the middle of the twentieth century, Reform prayer books have contained an increasing amount of Hebrew and other elements of the traditional liturgy.[52] Much discussion also has surfaced in the Reform movement about creating a specific code of practice governing Reform Judaism.[53]

---

46. *Id.* at xxi. *See also id.* at xxii (noting that the German Jews, "already firmly in the camp of change, now felt forced to quicken their pace of acculturation").

47. *Id.* at xxiv.

48. *See* ELLIOT N. DORFF, THE UNFOLDING TRADITION 446–48 (2005) [hereinafter UNFOLDING TRADITION]. Dorff notes that "[w]hile the Pittsburgh Platform . . . had emphasized the ways in which Jews and Judaism should be part of a universal, human culture, the 1999 statement focuses on affirming Jewish tradition, albeit in dialogue with modern culture and within the boundaries of personal autonomy." *Id.* at 449.

49. THE GROWTH, *supra* note 38, at ix.

50. Phylacteries are small black leather boxes traditionally worn by men during the weekday morning prayer service. The boxes contain parchment inscribed with verses from the Torah.

51. *See* UNFOLDING TRADITION, *supra* note 48, at 452.

52. *Id.* at 445.

53. *See* Herr & Friedman, *supra* note 25, at 457. *See also infra* notes 65–67 and accompanying text.

As discussed in the following section, the CCAR does issue *responsa* (Jewish legal opinions) in response to questions presented by individual congregational rabbis.[54] Typically, however, the answers provided are intended to be advisory in nature, rather than binding legal rulings.[55] Thus, despite Reform's abandonment of the ideological and practical anti-*halakhic* perspective that was prominent in the second phase of its development, autonomy of individual practice remains the hallmark of Reform's position on Jewish law.

Interestingly, this shift to the right noticeable in Reform since the middle of the twentieth century has been accompanied by a growth of alternative, or renewal, Jewish movements that can be categorized as left of Reform because they embrace ideologies that many see as completely outside the pale of the Jewish tradition. In general, the renewal movements take a more individual-istic approach to the tradition, and typically see the tradition as a vehicle for addressing the personalized spiritual needs or the moral challenges confront-ing humanity today.[56] These alternative movements also include Humanistic Judaism, officially founded in 1963 by Rabbi Sherwin Wine, which embraces Judaism on a cultural level but eliminates the need for belief in God, and of course, the observance of *halakhah.*[57]

Whether these movements are "outside the pale" of the Jewish tradition is completely subjective. Arthur Green, ordained as a Conservative rabbi and now a notable proponent of Jewish renewal, suggests they are not by remind-ing his audience that the current leaders of existing liberal forms of Judaism were originally seeking something different from literal belief "in the revealed authority of Judaism and its practices."[58] Moreover, the Orthodox see the Reform and Conservative movements as outside the boundaries of the tradi-tion; and Conservative Judaism, at least on a theoretical level, views Reform Judaism's unwillingness to embrace the binding nature of *halakhah* as out-side of the tradition's framework. Reform, in turn, has ruled that Humanistic Judaism is outside the pale.[59]

---

54. *See infra* notes 68–72 and accompanying text.

55. Herr & Friedman, *supra* note 25, at 457.

56. *See* UNFOLDING TRADITION, *supra* note 48, at 456–63 for a discussion of two promi-nent Jewish renewal thinkers, Arthur Waskow and Arthur Green.

57. For a brief description of the Humanistic Jewish movement, see http://www.shj.org/ (last visited July 8, 2014).

58. UNFOLDING TRADITION, *supra* note 48, at 460 (quoting ARTHUR GREEN, JUDAISM FOR THE POST-MODERN ERA (1995)).

59. *See infra* notes 71–72 and accompanying text.

These realities raise complicated questions as to the boundaries of the *mesorah*. Indeed, the early Reformers as well as the proponents of Conservative Judaism firmly believed that the *mesorah* always has been subject to evolution and change, but that change must be accomplished organically and with a basis in the tradition. Chapter 2 demonstrates how changes to the tradition were the backbone of the Talmudic era. The legal components of the *mesorah* should be understood in the cultural context in which they emerged, and therefore, it is impossible to deny the impact of changing cultural realities upon the development of the *mesorah*. That said, although individual Jews may question, and perhaps even deny, God's existence, a movement such as Humanistic Judaism whose core concept embodies the rejection of the Divine may be difficult to situate within the tradition. Moreover, because these renewal movements typically do not manifest a concern with issues of Jewish law, they do not embrace the fundamental cultural analysis insight that Jewish culture and Jewish law must be understood as a unit. As the following section illustrates, the mainstream Reform movement is ideologically distinct from these newer movements as reflected by its concern with, and discussion of, Jewish law on a formal basis. On the other hand, many individuals affiliated with Humanistic Judaism and other renewal movements strongly identify with Jewish culture and are even engaged in the practice of certain Jewish traditions. These renewal movements raise the global issue of the current relationship between the *mesorah* and the Jewish people collectively.

Lawmaking

In the 1960s, the Reform movement established a committee to craft *responsa*.[60] Plaut has observed that from its inception, the basic dilemma of Reform is answering the question of who has the authority to change or reject *halakhah* given the human origin and historically specific conditioning of the law.[61] This unresolved issue remains "a chief problem of the movement."[62] Historically, Reform elevated the ethical-religious content of Judaism above the ritual or ceremonial aspects "but it could not fully resolve the question of differentiation: which *mitzvot* [commandments] were divine obligations and

---

60. UNFOLDING TRADITION, *supra* note 48, at 445.

61. THE RISE, *supra* note 13, at xviii; THE GROWTH, *supra* note 38, at 236.

62. THE RISE, *supra* note 13, at xviii.

which were not?"[63] This dilemma clearly is reflected in Reform's controversy over ritual guides and codes.[64] Despite a growing demand for a Reform guide or even code of law,[65] mid-twentieth-century Reform leaders such as Solomon Freehof "eschewed the creation of a guide or code, and instead counseled trust in the evolutionary genius of an organically growing Reform movement."[66] More recently, however, the CCAR Press has published numerous guides to religious observance within the contours of the Reform movement.[67]

Reform *responsa* do cite the classical Jewish sources and codes, but the interpretations of the law differ substantially from more traditional perspectives. For example, in 1999, a *responsum* (singular form of *responsa*) was issued on the subject of whether a particular congregation could observe the Jewish festival of *Shavuot* (commemorating God giving the Jewish people the Torah) for two days on a particular occasion so as to accommodate the logistical preferences of its Confirmation class in that year.[68] The congregation asking this question followed the Reform tradition of observing all the Jewish festivals (holy days) for only one day, in contrast to Orthodox and Conservative synagogues that adhere to the rabbinic tradition of the two-day festival. The *responsum* contains a lengthy discussion of the Jewish law pertaining to the particular calendar issue in question and to the Jewish law concerning whether rabbinic enactments such as the two-day festival can be overturned. Noting existing conflict on these issues, the *responsum* affirms Reform's decision to continue to adhere to its practice of one-day festivals, and urges the congregation in question to refrain from designating the second day as a holy day on this one occasion because that is not the general practice of this particular congregation (the *responsum* notes, however, that many Reform congregations do observe two-day festivals, particularly Rosh

---

63. *Id.* at 95–96.

64. *Id.* at 96.

65. *See* THE GROWTH, *supra* note 38, at 236 (attributing this increased demand "to the large influx of East European Jews into the ranks of Reform, who brought with them a remembrance of practical *mitzvot* and who [were now searching] for new forms and new rationales").

66. *Id.* at 239.

67. *See, e.g.,* CENT. CONFERENCE OF AM. RABBIS, GATES OF THE SEASONS: SHAAREI MO-EID (Peter Knobel ed., 1986) (providing detailed guidance on observance of the holy days of the Jewish calendar); CENT. CONFERENCE OF AM. RABBIS, GATES OF SHABBAT: SHAAREI SHABBAT (Mark Dov Shapiro ed., 1991) (providing guidance for observing the Sabbath).

68. *See* CENT. CONFERENCE OF AM. RABBIS *RESPONSA*, THE SECOND FESTIVAL DAY AND REFORM JUDAISM (1999), http://ccarnet.org/responsa/nyp-no-5759-7/.

Hashanah).[69] Orthodox authorities never would have interpreted the Jewish sources in the same way as this Reform *responsum*, and neither would the Conservative movement's lawmaking body.[70]

This *responsum* concerning the second day of the festival is fairly typical of Reform *responsa* in that it functions in an advisory capacity on ritual and other matters. Sometimes, however, these *responsa* are concerned with establishing policy for the movement. One such example is the 1991 CCAR *responsum* on whether a particular Humanistic congregation can become a member of the Union of American Hebrew Congregations, the Union of Reform congregations. Given that Humanistic Judaism operates independently of the traditional Jewish theistic framework, the *responsum* concluded that "the Congregation's system of beliefs" was "outside the realm of historical Reform Judaism."[71] The opinion was not unanimous because three members of the Committee dissented and the controversy took on a very public quality. Ultimately, the Board of Trustees of the Union "overwhelmingly refused to admit the Congregation."[72]

Orthodoxy in Modern Times
Ideological Predicate

Whereas the Reform movement rejected the binding nature of Jewish law, the classical tradition continued to adhere to the precepts and methods of legal interpretation as they were understood throughout the centuries. Specifically, the party line of the tradition understood the Written Torah as the word of God, and the interpretive Oral Law as binding. The fact that the ideology of those who believed in the binding nature of the Torah was

---

69. *Id.*

70. Of course, it is also true that Conservative lawmaking looks different from that of Orthodox. *See infra* notes 205–18 and accompanying text. *See also infra* Chapter 5. For example, although there is no dispute among Orthodox lawmaking authorities that the second days of the Festivals are holy days, there are divergent opinions in the Conservative movement on this issue. Still, the vast majority of Conservative synagogues in the United States, and virtually all in England, celebrate the second day of the festivals. *See* David Steinberg, *Conservative Judaism and Halakhah* (May 10, 2004), http://www.adath-shalom. ca/hekel.htm#4.%20Yom%20Tov%20Sheni%20in%20Conservative%20Judaism.

71. Cent. Conference of Am. Rabbis *Responsa*, Humanistic Congregation (1991), http://data.ccarnet.org/cgi-bin/respdisp.pl?file=4&year=5751.

72. *Id.*

distinct from that of the Reformers should not obscure the fact that ideological divisions were developing even among those who would later come to be categorized as Orthodox. Although the interpretation of Jewish law always had been the subject of dispute, the Enlightenment created new contexts for this conflict. It furnished a paradigm shift for how areas of ideological and even legal disagreements would be played out. As a result of the Enlightenment, the contested issues were not just about the legal interpretation of the classical sources; they also included matters governing the social relationships between Jews and non-Jews in a world in which Jews were gaining a degree of equality and opportunity they had not previously experienced.

For Eastern European Jews, the age of Enlightenment dawned more slowly than for their brethren in Germany. In his treatment of culture's role in shaping Jewish identity in Europe, Jewish studies professor Jay Harris noted the distinct social, economic, cultural, and political conditions facing nineteenth-century Lithuanian Jewry and how the relative absence of a burgeoning movement interested in religious reform impacted the course of Orthodoxy's development in that region.[73] According to Harris, the pervasive influence of the eighteenth-century scholar, Elijah ben Soloman Zalman, known more widely as the *Vilna Gaon*, was even more significant than these other external factors.[74] The *Vilna Gaon* espoused the notion that the cultivation of human understanding and rationality was necessary to discern the deeper significance of the Written Torah.[75] Therefore, he attributed "to Torah scholars throughout the generations an essential role in determining the latent significance of the Written Torah" and emphasized "the role of the rational human interpreter in establishing meaning and controlling the applied significance of the text."[76] For the *Vilna Gaon*, properly applied human reasoning led to the discernment of "unshakable truth…approved by the divine author of multivalent Scripture and the creator of human intellect."[77] In other words, he believed the human role in interpreting and even creating the law was palpably clear.

---

73. Jay M. Harris, How Do We Know This? 234–37 (1995).

74. *Id.* at 235.

75. *Id.* at 238.

76. *Id.* at 239. Harris notes that although the *Vilna Gaon* "had not encountered Jewish reformers who would conclude that [his theory] gave them license to change the meaning the sages generated," he doubts "it would have mattered if he had." *Id.*

77. *Id.*

The Hasidic movement developed in Eastern Europe in response to the prevailing view that Judaism had become the exclusive property of the elite Talmudic scholars such as the *Vilna Gaon* and his disciples. Plaut observed that in Eastern Europe, Enlightenment was "diverted into the Messianic sweep of Hasidism."[78] The primary message of Hasidism was that simple, common folk (who constituted the vast majority of Jews) could "approach God directly through heartfelt prayer and an outpouring" of their souls.[79] Their leader, Rabbi Israel ben Eliezer, known more widely as the *Baal Shem Tov*, taught that every Jew could have a relationship with God and that this could be accomplished by infusing even the most mundane acts with the proper attention to devotion to God. Moreover, Hasidism taught that such devotion was more important than rote performance of ritual. The Hasidic philosophy emphasized joy, faith, and fervent prayer accompanied by song and dance. This perspective was indeed revolutionary, and met with strong disapproval by the established rabbinic authorities of the time. One denunciation of the Hasidim by the more traditional Eastern European rabbinic authorities claimed, "They conduct themselves like madmen, and explain their behavior by saying that in their thoughts they soar in the most far-off worlds.... Every day is for them a holiday. When they pray...they raise such a din that the walls quake...And they turn over like wheels, with the head below and the legs above."[80] This statement, made around 1772, was a reference to the fact that some of the more extreme Hasidic sects turned somersaults in their synagogues in the early days.[81] Although the Hasidim modified certain customs and even made some ritual modifications, by and large their changes did not represent the same type of departure from the traditional norms as was the case with the Reformers. Hasidic Jews remained observant, but they sought to infuse Judaism with what they believed to be a missing spirituality.

Today, the Hasidim are regarded as one of the three groups composing the *Haredim*, the name presently used for describing the most right-wing of Orthodox Jews. The other two groups are the *Mitnagdim*, who trace their origin to the world of the *Vilna Gaon* that competed with the Hasidic

---

78. THE RISE, *supra* note 13, at xv.

79. SUE FISHKOFF, THE REBBE'S ARMY 17 (2003).

80. A LIFE APART: A BRIEF INTRODUCTION TO HASIDISM, http://www.pbs.org/alifeapart/intro.html (last visited July 8, 2014).

81. FISHKOFF, *supra* note 79, at 17.

groups in Europe, and the Jews of Middle Eastern origins that have become a large presence in Israeli society since the latter half of the twentieth century.[82] Significantly, however, the groups that compose the *Haredim* today, and even during the early years of modernity in Europe, do not represent the whole story of the Orthodox movement. Sociologist Samuel Heilman has noted that although Orthodoxy as a movement has been, and is, perceived as maintaining that "there was only *one* way to be a Jew and that this way was the Orthodox one," the reality is that from the inside, unanimity never has existed concerning what it means to be legitimately Orthodox.[83] Thus, while the Hasidim and *Mitnagdim* of Eastern Europe were engaged in a struggle of their own, a young rabbi in Germany named Samson Raphael Hirsch was developing a distinct approach to Orthodoxy.

Born in Germany in 1808 and having studied both in a prominent yeshiva (school of Jewish learning) as well as the University of Bonn,[84] Hirsch perceived that both of the major Jewish movements of his day were problematic. The traditionalists adhered to *halakhah* but had lost the religion's essential spirit. The Reformers were well intentioned, but their ignorance of the tradition rendered their efforts to help the Jews dangerous. In words that may resonate today, Hirsch asked, "And today, when, despite a thousand shades and variations of difference, these two opposing elements are alike in the one great respect, that they are both in the wrong—what shall be done?"[85]

Hirsch's answer to this dilemma was to urge Jews to rediscover their tradition through careful study of the classical Jewish sources (the Bible and the Talmud) while simultaneously embracing their emancipation and participating in their surrounding environment. In articulating an ideology that called for a deep understanding of the foundational elements of Judaism and adherence to the precepts of Torah, while maintaining a visible presence in the public sphere, Hirsch laid the groundwork for the current Modern Orthodox sector. He became the spokesman for Orthodoxy in Germany, where the Jews had experienced the benefits of the Enlightenment before their Eastern

---

82. SAMUEL C. HEILMAN, SLIDING TO THE RIGHT 4–5 (2006). For a pioneering look at the theological perspective of the *Mitnagdim* as a contrast to that of the Hasidim, see ALLAN NADLER, THE FAITH OF THE *MITHNAGDIM*: RABBINIC RESPONSES TO HASIDIC RAPTURE (1997).

83. HEILMAN, *supra* note 82, at 3.

84. SAMSON RAPHAEL HIRSCH, THE NINETEEN LETTERS 4 (1960) (*Introduction* by Jacob Breuer).

85. HIRSCH, *supra* note 84, at 127.

European brethren.[86] Hirsch's version of Orthodoxy was distinct from the more rigid Eastern European variety, and the essence of these differences remain visible in the various Orthodox communities today, particularly in the United States and in Israel.

Hirsch's ideological position was driven by his understanding of the mission of the Jews. To Hirsch, the "chosen" element of the Jews' historical existence meant that God "has the sole and exclusive claim to Israel's devotion and service" rather than the commonly misunderstood notion that Israel "has a monopoly on God's love and favor."[87] The mission of the Jewish people, according to Hirsch, was to affirm to the world that "God is the only creative cause of existence, and that the fulfillment of His will is the only goal of life."[88] Thus, Hirsch focused on the study of the Bible and the Talmud for the sole purpose of ascertaining "the duties of life which they teach."[89] This very practical purpose of study underscored Hirsch's entire ideological predicate: "There is no science which trains the mind to a broader and more practical view of things than does the Torah, pursued in this manner."[90] Once the Jewish mission is understood in this way, it becomes easy to see how Hirsch reconciled the Jews' position in modernity. If the Jews practiced what the Torah teaches, there is no doubt that they would interact with their non-Jewish neighbors so that they would love, support, and sustain them economically and spiritually:

> [P]ractice righteousness and love as your Torah bids you do. Be just in deed, truthful in your speech, bear love in your heart for your non-Jewish brother, as your Law teaches you. Feed his hungry, clothe his naked, console his mourners, restore his sick, help his helpless, assist him with counsel and deed in time of need and sorrow—unfold the whole noble breadth of your Israeldom.[91]

Moreover, Hirsch maintained that the Jews' spiritual unity deriving from their distinct mission was in no way compromised by their acceptance

---

86. THE RISE, *supra* note 13, at xiv–xv.

87. HIRSCH, *supra* note 84, at 96.

88. *Id.* at 54.

89. *Id.* at 99.

90. *Id.*

91. *Id.* at 104.

of citizenship in the various nations in which they lived.[92] He cautioned, however, that emancipation was not to be viewed as an end toward a more comfortable life that would afford greater economic opportunities. Rather, emancipation should be welcomed as a means to achieve "a greater opportunity for the fulfillment" of the Jews' mission: "the realization of a noble and ideal life."[93]

As this discussion reveals, although Orthodoxy may be perceived by both Jews and non-Jews as a monolithic entity, the reality always has been quite different. The following section illustrates that much of the interesting history of Orthodoxy in the modern era revolves around areas of conflict within Orthodoxy itself. Orthodox Judaism "has from its earliest beginnings in nineteenth-century Europe been at its root a reactive and oppositional movement, shaped by what it fights against."[94] Significant from a cultural analysis standpoint, this reactive nature of Orthodoxy "has been constituted by selective retrievals from [the] tradition, elements that emphasize and reinterpret whatever is needed to meet the challenges of the day and place in which its adherents find themselves."[95] This was the situation of Orthodoxy in its inception as a movement,[96] and it continues to the present. From a historical standpoint, however, the Holocaust substantially impacted the growth and development of Orthodox Judaism in the United States and elsewhere. The next section examines this phenomenon more fully.

Historical Development

Scholars of Jewish history believe that the "Third Great Cycle in Jewish History" began in the last half of the twentieth century, following upon the heels of the Holocaust.[97] Even as late as the period just prior to World War II, Orthodoxy of any version was believed "destined to be at best a minority

---

92. *Id.* at 107.

93. *Id.* at 111.

94. HEILMAN, *supra* note 82, at 189. *See also* HARRIS, *supra* note 73, at 211.

95. HEILMAN, *supra* note 82, at 189. *See also* SARNA, *supra* note 21, at 76–77 (discussing the innovation around 1830 of sermons in English by traditionalist Isaac Lesser in the United States).

96. Professor Sarna notes that the earliest use of the term "Orthodox" in the United States occurred in the 1840s by Jews opposing the innovations of Reform. SARNA, *supra* note 21, at 87.

97. HEILMAN, *supra* note 82, at 15.

orientation among Ashkenazic Jews," regardless of whether they were living in Europe or the United States.[98] Moreover, the Orthodox communities of Europe were the hardest hit by the horrors of the Holocaust, particularly those that were the most uncompromising in their religion. These groups lacked the professional, language, and other survival skills that would give them at least a small chance of survival in the death camps.[99] For many Jews, the Holocaust served as an "orienting event" that significantly changed their worldview.[100] Heilman claims that particularly for Orthodox Jews in America, the Holocaust "undoubtedly not only set their future direction but also...*reframed* and redefined their past."[101]

Although the state of Israel was destined to attract and retain a significant percentage of the world's Orthodox population following the war, the United States also was on the brink of becoming a major center of the world's Orthodox population. For those Orthodox survivors who found their way to the United States, two paths seemed open. One approach was to cling to the insular ways of the past out of fear that the American experience required even "greater vigilance and more powerful strategies" to prevent the dismemberment of the tradition.[102] A second approach was to embrace all that America had to offer while maintaining a strong allegiance to the tradition.

In the aftershock years immediately following the Holocaust, many Orthodox survivors were almost "invisible"—advised to keep silent by their leaders both in the United States and in Israel.[103] Within a short time, however, the silence gave way to a religious resurgence that was fueled by a desire to demonstrate that the surest way to ensure future survival was to bear witness to the faith in the most visible manner possible. Moreover, veneration for those who had perished became enmeshed in this institutional Orthodox survivor guilt. Thus, "after the war the European Orthodoxy that had

---

98. *Id.* at 20.

99. *Id.* at 21 ("In effect, those who had been expert in parochial Jewish crafts and scholarship and nothing more were lost in great numbers, as were those sectarians who had remained totally within the precincts of Judaism."). For a poignant account of one survivor's tale that lends anecdotal support to Heilman's claims, see ROBERTA ROSENTHAL KWALL, THE SOUL OF CREATIVITY 100–01 (2010) (detailing the story of Dina Gottliebova Babbitt who escaped death because of her artistic talents).

100. HEILMAN, *supra* note 82, at 15 (quoting Rabbi Irving Greenberg).

101. *Id.*

102. *Id.* at 22–23.

103. *Id.* at 23.

suffered death and destruction became 'stronger' in the imagined memory of the survivors."[104] Orthodoxy thus was remembered in an idealized state, rather than the reality that it had been losing followers and even arguably contributed to the decreased ability of its adherents to survive in the Nazi death camps.[105] This veneration was strongest among the most religious of the Orthodox and resulted in a reinterpretation of the tradition in a "more religiously demanding" form deriving from the perceived superiority of their murdered ancestors.[106]

On the other hand, an alternate response to the Holocaust flourished after the war among Orthodox Jews in the United States. Following the ideology of Samson Raphael Hirsch, Jews who denominated as "Modern Orthodox" embraced the notion that the best way to ensure continuity of the tradition was to engage with modernity and contemporary culture while maintaining an equally firm commitment to a Torah-true lifestyle. Heilman has termed this state of duality characteristic of the Modern Orthodox as "contrapuntal-ism."[107] He notes that this approach was a popular one in the United States for at least thirty years after the war.[108] Over time, however, the Modern Orthodox approach has been greatly overshadowed by a visible push to the right in the Orthodox community, both in the United States and in Israel.[109]

In his insightful study of how the American Orthodox community has changed significantly since the aftershock years, Heilman identifies numerous factors that have contributed to this shift in the American Orthodox community. Although his study reveals the complexity of this phenomenon, a few of the most significant causes are useful to consider at this point.[110] Perhaps the most global cause is that the worldview and lifestyle of the

---

104. *Id.* at 29.

105. *See supra* notes 98–99 and accompanying text.

106. *See* Heilman, *supra* note 82, at 27–30; *see also* Sarna, *supra* note 21, at 275, 296–97, 300.

107. Heilman, *supra* note 82, at 40.

108. *Id.* at 41.

109. *See also* Sarna, *supra* note 21, at 305–06. According to a comprehensive 2013 study of Jews in the United States, ultra-Orthodox Jews outnumber Modern Orthodox Jews by a 2-to-1 ratio. *See* A Portrait of Jewish Americans—Pew Research Religion & Public Life Project (2013), http://www.pewforum.org/2013/10/01/jewish-american-beliefs-attitudes-culture-survey/ [hereinafter Pew Report] (last visited July 8, 2014) (follow "Chapter 3: Jewish Identity" hyperlink).

110. These causes are summarized more fully in the first chapter of Heilman's book and explored in greater detail throughout his study. *See* Heilman, *supra* note 82, at 15–61.

contrapuntalists resulted in a decline of Modern Orthodox men entering the rabbinate because they frequently chose other more lucrative professions for which they were equipped as a result of their strong secular educations. This lack of leadership left a vacuum that the more right-wing rabbis began to fill. As a result, the rabbinic leadership gradually became less inclined to permit the desired *halakhic* modifications that were essential to maintaining a contrapuntalist approach to Orthodox Judaism.

Moreover, with increasingly fewer Modern Orthodox rabbis and educators as role models, the children of Modern Orthodox families became increasingly educated by those who did not see the benefit of Modern Orthodoxy's emphasis on engagement with the contemporary culture. This trend coincided with the growing popularity of a post–high school but pre-college educational experience in Israel, where the Orthodox norms historically were far more stringent than in the United States.[111] Heilman notes that "the Israeli sojourners thus returned to America not only with a new set of orthodox behaviors and values but with a studied alienation from the kind of Judaism that had been normative for them prior to their Israel experience."[112]

Also significant, by the latter part of the twentieth century, American culture had undergone a radical shift to the left, making it difficult for even those who theoretically embraced contrapuntalism in theory to continue to believe in its benefits on a practical level.[113] Further, Modern Orthodox Jews looked to the escalating degree of assimilation and intermarriage among non-Orthodox Jews to reinforce their growing suspicions of whether contrapuntalism really could work in the United States. On the other hand, the growing numbers of evangelical Christians impacted Orthodoxy's slide to the right in a favorable way because the growth of the Christian right legitimized the ability of the more right-wing sectors of Orthodoxy to maintain with public conviction their views in this country.[114]

In this environment, the demands of Orthodoxy increased substantially. For example, day school educations (whose schools employed educators with an increasingly right-wing perspective) became mandatory and replaced the after-school model, the practices of keeping kosher became more strict, and

---

111. *Id.* at 112–22.

112. *Id.* at 119.

113. *See, e.g., id.* at 42.

114. *Id.* at 59–61.

even the clothing of those claiming to be Orthodox became increasingly more modest. Thus, in the 1970s it was not unusual for Orthodox Jews claiming to keep strictly kosher to eat a tuna salad sandwich in a non-kosher restaurant. Today this practice is frowned upon. Eventually, those who were "Orthodox in name only" soon exited from the movement. By the latter part of the twentieth century, it was no longer comfortable for Jews who attended a synagogue (albeit an Orthodox one) only on the High Holidays to consider themselves Orthodox Jews.[115] With their departure from the movement, the "centrist" Orthodox Jews soon became the "left," thus reinforcing the already steady pace of Orthodoxy's slide to the right.[116]

This well-known slide to the right so aptly documented by Heilman's study entails not just a more demanding level of religious observance, but also a more pronounced tendency toward an enclavist and isolationist stance with respect to American culture.[117] This tendency is particularly apparent among certain Orthodox groups in New York, an important phenomenon given the popular perception that Orthodoxy in New York "still sets the tone and informal standards of the movement."[118] On the other hand, perhaps spurred by the renowned outreach efforts of the Chabad-Lubavitch movement discussed below, an increasing number of adherents of the right-wing sectors of Orthodoxy currently are beginning to understand the importance of tempering their isolationist tendencies for the purpose of reaching out to non-Orthodox Jews so they can bring them into the fold.

The history of Orthodoxy, particularly in the United States, reveals that many of the schisms previously in existence in Europe also are present today. The current conflict between Modern Orthodoxy and its more right-wing version mirrors a similar conflict that existed between the approach of Samson Raphael Hirsch and the Eastern European *Mitnagdim* in earlier years. In 2011, a rabbinic contributor to an American ultra-Orthodox newspaper sang the praises of Hirsch's Torah philosophy, followed by the observation that the Modern Orthodox, whom he calls historical revisionists, operate in a "foolish

---

115. *Id.* at 44.

116. *Id.* at 49.

117. *See id.* at 56–57. Heilman's chapter "Orthodox Jewish Calls from the Walls"—a study of the posters in four Orthodox communities in New York—makes for fascinating reading on this point. *See id.* at 211–95.

118. *Id.* at 213. For a brief historical account of New York's appeal to the Jewish immigrants, see SARNA, *supra* note 21, at 153–54.

and underhanded" manner when they "disguise and taint Rav [Rabbi] Hirsch's approach and try to paint him in Modern Orthodox clothing."[119] This article provoked a sharp response in an Orthodox blog declaring that the author of the article hates his fellow Jews and owes Modern Orthodox Jewry an apology.[120]

Adding yet another dimension of conflict within Orthodoxy is a growing rift between those who denominate as Modern Orthodox and an even more liberal version of Orthodoxy called Open Orthodox. This left-wing Orthodox contingent is fueled by a blog entitled Morethodoxy authored by several Open Orthodox rabbis as well as a *"maharat"* (a woman who was ordained as an Orthodox rabbi by a rabbinic leader in a story well known in the Modern Orthodox community).[121] Open Orthodoxy is rapidly making waves within the more conventional Modern Orthodox community and even among those Orthodox Jews further to the right. Open Orthodoxy also is being watched with interest among segments of the Conservative Jewish community, some of whose members believe that the core philosophies of the leaders and laity of Open Orthodoxy are not all that distinct from their own.

In September 2011, Rabbi Yitzchok Adlerstein, a prominent Modern Orthodox rabbi who is an adjunct professor at Loyola Los Angeles Law School, wrote an essay in the Modern Orthodox blog Cross Currents that explicitly called for the expulsion of the "Far Left" wing of Orthodoxy from the Rabbinical Council of America, the rabbinic "umbrella group of Modern Orthodoxy."[122] Rabbi Adlerstein stated, "To avoid erosion of Torah values and practice, the rest of the community must define the approach of the Far Left as so different, that it can no longer be called Orthodox as the rest of us know it."[123] A few months later, Adlerstein allowed his friend

---

119. Rabbi Avrohom Birnbaum, *Addressing Our Youth with "Old Wine in a New Vessel,"* YATED NE'EMAN (Aug. 7, 2011), http://yated.com/content.asp?categoryid=0& contentid=430.

120. Rabbi Harry Maryles, *Torah and Mada—A Forbidden Mixture?*, EMES VE-EMUNAH (Aug. 15, 2011), http://haemtza.blogspot.com/2011/08/torah-and-mada-forbidden-mixture. html.

121. *See supra* Chapter 1, notes 109–10 and accompanying text.

122. Yitzchok Adlerstein, *Modern Orthodoxy at a Crossroads*, CROSS CURRENTS BLOG (Sept. 27, 2011), http://www.cross-currents.com/archives/2011/09/27/ modern-orthodoxy-at-a-crossroads-2/. Rabbi Adlerstein's essay initially was published in 39 *Ami Magazine* (2011).

123. *Id.*

and fellow Modern Orthodox rabbi, law professor Michael Broyde, to publish a response in Cross Currents that vehemently disagreed with an expulsion of the Far Left.[124] A reader of these two posts—written by two good friends and colleagues—will easily understand the extent to which Modern Orthodoxy experiences conflict on issues deemed significant for the group's membership. Around the same time as these two posts were written, the same right-wing Orthodox rabbi who labeled the Modern Orthodox sector "historical revisionists" published an essay in which he argued for Open Orthodoxy's expulsion from the entire pale of Orthodoxy and accused the Open Orthodoxy clergy of "using—nay, abusing—language to deceitfully try bringing Reform Judaism into their synagogues…under the guise of Orthodox."[125]

Rounding out this discussion of current conflict prevalent in Orthodoxy is a recent schism beginning in the latter part of the twentieth century between the most widely known Hasidic group, Chabad-Lubavitch, and other Orthodox groups. Although the international growth of Chabad was facilitated by Orthodoxy's growth,[126] Chabad's fame and appeal derives from its unique mission of bringing Judaism to the masses and reaching out to Jews everywhere. In a sense, Chabad's approach is diametrically opposed to the isolationist one that characterizes many other ultra-Orthodox groups, including those that are Hasidic. "Chabad" is an acronym of the Hebrew words for wisdom, comprehension, and knowledge.[127] The name "Lubavitch" derives from the town in White Russia where four of its original rabbinic founders (known as *rebbes*) were based.

Chabad's theology emphasizes that a Jew's purest expression of love for God is manifested by offering to help other Jews strengthen their relationship with the Divine. Hence, outreach to Jews is the sine qua non of Chabad's existence.[128] Although Chabad-Lubavitchers maintain scrupulous observance of the tradition, the group's leaders are comfortable associating with non-observant Jews; indeed, this association is critical to Chabad's

---

124. Michael Broyde, *Modern Orthodoxy Is Always at the Crossroads*, Cross Currents Blog (Nov. 9, 2011), http://www.cross-currents.com/archives/2011/11/09/modern-orthodoxy-is-always-at-the-crossroads/.

125. Avrohom Birnbaum, *When*, Yated Ne'eman (Oct. 25, 2011), http://www.yated.com/when.0-466-0-.html. *See also* Birnbaum, *supra* note 119.

126. Fishkoff, *supra* note 79, at 25.

127. *Id.* at 18.

128. *Id.* at 20–21.

mission. Under the leadership of their seventh, and last, *rebbe*, Menachem Mendel Schneerson, Chabad grew into an international empire and has been described as being more similar to a Jewish movement than a Hasidic sect given its distinct philosophy and liturgy.[129] Schneerson's death in 1994 exacerbated already-existing differences among his followers on the critical issue as to whether he is the Messiah—the Redeemer of Israel—who, according to the biblical prophecies, would lead the Jewish people into an era of universal peace.[130] This topic is significant because it represents more than just an internal division among Lubavitchers; it also causes conflict between Lubavitchers and other Orthodox Jews,[131] as well as Jews of other denominations.

Although this discussion has focused mainly on historical conflict among Orthodox Jews in the United States, it is worth noting that much of the above description applies equally, if not more so, to the current situation in Israel. Instances of public conflict concerning religious matters among Jews in Israel frequently highlight the divide between the Orthodox and secular Jews, but the last decades of the twentieth century have witnessed "mounting dissension among the various groups" comprising the ultra-Orthodox communities there.[132] The increasing numbers of Jews from distinct Orthodox and Hasidic traditions compounds this dissension. In addition, conflict results from the divide between Jews from Ashkenazic, or Eastern European, backgrounds and the Sephardic Jews whose roots can be traced to the Iberian Peninsula in the period preceding the Expulsion of the Jews from Spain.[133] Thus, in any discussion of conflict among Orthodox Jews, the unique situation of those Jews in Israel must be incorporated into the picture for a full appreciation of the scope of the issue.[134]

---

129. *Id.* at 25 (discussing the view of New York University professor Lawrence Schiffman).

130. *Id.* at 264.

131. *See* DAVID BERGER, THE REBBE, THE MESSIAH, AND THE SCANDAL OF ORTHODOX INDIFFERENCE (2001).

132. Lawrence Kaplan, *Daas Torah, in* RABBINIC AUTHORITY AND PERSONAL AUTONOMY 52 (Moshe Z. Sokol ed., 1992) [hereinafter RABBINIC AUTHORITY].

133. *See, e.g.*, Or Kashti, *Ashkenazi Parent: Sephardi Girls Have a Bad Influence on Our Girls*, HAARETZ (Dec. 24, 2009), http://www.haaretz.com/print-edition/news/ashkenazi-parent-sephardi-girls-have-a-bad-influence-on-our-girls-1.1513 (discussing protest against the decision by the Israeli government's Education Ministry and its High Court to end the segregation between Sephardic and Ashkenazic students).

134. *See also infra* Chapter 8.

Lawmaking under Orthodox Standards

Even the most traditional authorities of Jewish law acknowledge the humanly derived component of the Oral Law.[135] This dependence on human mediation illustrates the importance of interpretative creativity from the outset of the tradition's development.[136] A particularly complicating factor regarding the *halakhic* process is the classification of a law as either biblical (*de-oraita*) or rabbinic (*de-rabbanan*). Although the sages gave their own laws the same force as biblical law (and sometimes even greater force),[137] generally speaking biblical laws are interpreted more strictly than rabbinic laws.[138] A continuing problem, however, is the nature of this classification. Laws that are explicitly stated in the Torah are classified as biblical; laws that are "clearly the product of legislation by the *halakhic* authorities are rabbinic."[139] Laws that fall into a doubtful area, however, are more problematic and have continued to generate debate throughout the centuries.[140] This complexity is largely a function of the dualistic character of the Oral Law as being partially the product of Divine Revelation and partially the product of human interpretation.

Despite the importance of human interpretation in the law's development and operation, an Orthodox perspective maintains that the text of the Talmud

---

135. *See supra* Chapter 1, notes 82–85 and accompanying text.

136. As to the degree of creativity present in this approach, Louis Jacobs has documented how the post-Talmudic *halakhic* authorities, all of whom were operating according to an approach that currently would be classified as Orthodox, have continually demonstrated creativity and imagination in the application of the law. *See* LOUIS JACOBS, A TREE OF LIFE: DIVERSITY, FLEXIBILITY, AND CREATIVITY IN JEWISH LAW (2d edition, 2000). For an Orthodox perspective on this same point, see Jonathan Sacks, *Creativity and Innovation in Halakhah, in* RABBINIC AUTHORITY, *supra* note 132, at 123. Recall also the discussion of the *Vilna Gaon. See supra* notes 74–77 and accompanying text.

137. *See supra* Chapter 1, notes 95–96 and accompanying text.

138. 1 MENACHEM ELON, JEWISH LAW: HISTORY, SOURCES, PRINCIPLES 212 (1994).

139. *Id.* at 208.

140. *Id.* at 211. *See also* Daniel S. Nevins, *The Use of Electrical and Electronic Devices on Shabbat,* 76 (2012), http://www.rabbinicalassembly.org/sites/default/files/public/halakhah/teshuvot/2011-2020/electrical-electronic-devices-shabbat.pdf (emphasizing Rabbi Gordon Tucker's observation that the distinction between biblical and rabbinic law often is "misleading" because "so many of the rules declared 'biblical' by the rabbis are not in fact clearly stated in the Bible"). Thus, what is termed "biblical" law "is actually rabbinic!" *Id.* That said, however, Nevins (a Conservative rabbi) writes that "biblical law has greater authority than rabbinic law, even if it is the rabbis who declare and define these laws." *Id. See also* JOEL ROTH, THE HALAKHIC PROCESS 13–48, 153–204 (1986) for a detailed treatment of this topic.

defines the substantive limits of legal interpretation.[141] Thus, given that the traditional Orthodox perspective is bounded by the parameters of this conventional
halakhic framework, the degree to which creativity can be exercised is limited
to areas that are not settled by the Talmud (although recall that different views
exist as to what the Talmud leaves open). In other words, the Talmud sets the
parameters but consensus is not so clear as to the nature of these boundaries.[142]

On a strictly legal level, following the sealing of the Babylonian Talmud,
the development of Jewish law was impacted substantially by the creation of
certain Jewish legal codes. Among the most important codes of Jewish law
are the twelfth-century work by the philosopher Moses Maimonides, the
Mishneh Torah, as well as the sixteenth-century work by Yosef Caro, the
Shulhan Arukh (the title of which means "the Set Table"). Moses Isserles
authored a subsequent commentary to the Shulhan Arukh called the Mappah
("the Tablecloth"). Caro's Code reflected the customs and traditions of the
Sephardic Jews, whereas Isserles's commentary drew from the Ashkenazic
tradition. Over time, the works of Caro and Isserles began to be published
together and became known as the Code. Newer printings of the Code also
have incorporated other subsequent commentaries.[143]

Initially, there was opposition to codifying Jewish law.[144] In his volumi-
nous treatise on Jewish law, Israeli jurist Menachem Elon discusses the struggles concerning the Code's eventual acceptance as binding law in both the
Sephardic and Ashkenazic traditions. Elon emphasizes the many supplemen-
tal commentaries to the Code as a factor contributing toward its universal
acceptance.[145] Further, he posits that persecutions against European Jewry
during the seventeenth century accelerated the perceived need for a codification of the law, which also contributed toward the Code's acceptance.[146]
Rabbi Louis Jacobs has written that the invention of the printing press also
played a vital role in the Code's authoritative stance due to its unprecedented
dissemination.[147] Interestingly, Samson Raphael Hirsch observed that the

---

141. *See supra* Chapter 1, note 92 and accompanying text.

142. *See supra* Chapter 1, notes 101–04 and accompanying text.

143. *See* Steven H. Resnicoff, *Autonomy in Jewish Law—In Theory and in Practice*, J. LAW &
RELIGION, 507, 530–31 (2008–09).

144. *See, e.g.,* SHERWIN, *supra* note 1, at 32 (discussing the opposition of the sixteenth century Polish *halakhist* Solomon Luria to Isserles).

145. 3 MENACHEM ELON, JEWISH LAW: HISTORY, SOURCES, PRINCIPLES 1407–19 (1994).

146. *Id.* at 1420.

147. JACOBS, *supra* note 136, at 153.

Code, "originally intended only as a compendium for the learned," partially
fell into the hands of the laity, resulting in an emphasis on prayer and observance to the exclusion of the additional significance of the religion.[148] Today,
the Code continues to govern the religious practices for the majority of mainstream Orthodox Jews.

Many Orthodox thinkers adhere to the view that *halakhah* embodies a
sense of absolute truth that comes from the inner workings of a pure legal system untainted by outside influences. This perspective is evident in Hirsch's
discussion of the great minds of the medieval and early modern periods. For
example, Hirsch is rather critical of Maimonides, one of the most revered
Jewish law authorities, whom he claims was "brought up in the environment of uncomprehended Judaism and Arabic science" and thus "entered
into Judaism from without, bringing with him views of whose truth he had
convinced himself from extraneous sources."[149] Although Hirsch apparently
believed that Maimonides's understanding of Judaism was influenced by
his surrounding culture, he names a few other authorities whom he asserts
"stood with their intellectual efforts entirely within Judaism, and built it up
out of its own inner concepts."[150]

Thus, although an Orthodox perspective on *halakhah* clearly acknowledges a "human" component to Jewish law, lawmaking still is seen as ideally
executed within a pure, untainted system embodying the internal essence
of the religion.[151] Cultural analysis takes issue with this reality. Moreover,
according to an Orthodox perspective, Torah law does not evolve to accommodate society although it can forever be applied to address new social
realities.[152] This perspective asserts that a person's own ethical views are an
insufficient reason to depart from God's clear command,[153] but its proponents

---

148. HIRSCH, *supra* note 84, at 122–23.

149. *Id.* at 119.

150. *Id.* at 121–22. In this respect, Hirsch singles out the medieval philosophers Judah
Halevi and Rabbi Moses ben Nahman ("Nachmanides").

151. *See also* HARRIS, *supra* note 73, at 234–49 for a discussion of this phenomenon in the
context of Lithuanian Orthodoxy.

152. Orthodox authorities maintain that the non-Torah law does evolve to accommodate a
number of societal needs. *See, e.g.,* Resnicoff, *supra* note 143, at 537–38 (discussing custom).
As discussed in the following section on Conservative Judaism, those who take the historical approach to Jewish law's development would assert that even Torah law has evolved, and
should evolve, to accommodate social needs.

153. *Id.* at 515.

sometimes recognize that the boundaries of God's command are not always so readily clear.[154] In practice, therefore, these complicated realities present challenges for the Orthodox view that "once the meaning of Torah law is established ... that law, being divinely authored, cannot be overruled by a person simply because it offends that person's sense of morals."[155]

In contrast, some Orthodox thinkers reveal a perspective that is not inconsistent with cultural analysis. Recently Asher Lopatin, the president of Yeshivat Chovevei Torah, wrote, "The knowledgeable person reading the limited number of authoritative sources enters their world with a potentially infinite number of values, of ideas and ideologies, of *cultural genes* inherited from parents, teachers, and the world around us."[156] Although Lopatin stops short of embracing extralegal factors other than the primary sources as the basis for Jewish law's development, his interpretative vision clearly acknowledges a significant cultural influence on the interpreter.

In practice, much of the lawmaking that takes place within all segments of Orthodoxy occurs at the level of individual rabbinic leaders who advise their communities based on opinions issued by greater rabbinic authorities. Indeed, throughout the centuries, rabbis issued *responsa* to questions presented by correspondents, and these *responsa* constitute an important component of Jewish law.[157] As Heilman's research so palpably demonstrates, today much of this lawmaking is being executed increasingly at the highest levels by authorities representing the right end of Orthodoxy. Indeed, large numbers of Orthodox Jews in the United States, including those who self-denominate as Modern Orthodox, seek both advice on *halakhic* issues and guidance on social matters from members of ultra-Orthodox rabbis in Israel who are more culturally sheltered than their American counterparts.[158] This reality results not only in the creation of an increasing number of *halakhic* stringencies, but also in the adoption of stringent positions by rabbis operating within

---

154. *See supra* note 142 and accompanying text.

155. Resnicoff, *supra* note 143, at 512 (discussing the Orthodox perspective).

156. Asher Lopatin, *To the Editor*, CONSERVATIVE JUDAISM, Spring 2012, at 97, 98 (emphasis added).

157. Robert Goldenberg has analogized *responsa* to appellate court decisions, noting that they do "not necessarily uncover great new amounts of precedent" but instead "provide an authoritative interpretation of texts that the inquirer has already cited." Robert Goldenberg, *Talmud, in* BACK TO THE SOURCES 129, 160 (Barry W. Holtz ed., 1984).

158. Resnicoff, *supra* note 143, at 538 (noting that these "religious rulings seem to be increasingly out of step with cultural developments in the United States").

a particular cultural context (such as the yeshiva world in Israel) who seek to couch their advice as binding legal rulings for people living in a very different cultural environment (such as Modern Orthodox Jews in the United States).[159]

Moreover, the concept of consensus is seen as an essential value in the development of *halakhah*, despite the myriad of legal, ritual, and even ideological differences among the various sectors of Orthodoxy.[160] Therefore, especially when an issue is being considered that is seen as a significant departure from the status quo, even more moderate Orthodox authorities resort to the consensus trope rather than advocate for reform, even if the tradition contains a basis for a different position.[161] This phenomenon is particularly evident in matters concerning increased ritual participation for women, a topic explored in further detail in Chapter 7.

The Conservative Movement
Ideological Predicate

In nineteenth-century Europe, certain rabbis began to see Judaism as too limited in its ideological outlook and too confined in practice for modernity. This group also believed, however, that the Reformers were going too far in their attempts to stray from the ritualistic norms. A German rabbi named Zacharias Frankel was the leader of this middle-ground group.[162] In 1845, Frankel departed from the Reform Frankfurt Rabbinical Conference in disgust over its proposal to abandon Hebrew for prayer.[163] He then began to articulate an historical approach to the study and development of *halakhah*

---

159. See *id.* at 538–46 (discussing instances of authorities banning books written by Orthodox rabbis as well as a music concert designed for Orthodox Jews whose proceeds were designated for a worthwhile Jewish charity).

160. See Michael J. Broyde & Shlomo B. Brody, *Orthodox Women Rabbis? Tentative Thoughts That Distinguish between the Timely and the Timeless*, HAKIRAH, FLATBUSH J. JEWISH L. & THOUGHT 25, 25–27 (2011) (discussing the spectrum of Orthodox thought).

161. See Shlomo Riskin, *Torah Aliyyot for Women, in* DANIEL SPERBER ET AL., WOMEN AND MEN IN COMMUNAL PRAYER: *HALAKHIC* PERSPECTIVES 361–62 (Chaim Trachtman ed., 2010) (expressing concern that changes in prayer and Torah reading "could lead to further divisions in the already fragmented Orthodox community"). *See also* Broyde & Brody, *supra* note 160, at 55 (noting that the requisite consensus for female ordination does not exist).

162. HARRIS, *supra* note 73, at 190.

163. THE RISE, *supra* note 13, at 87–89.

that differed substantially from the path recommended by even the more moderate Orthodox leader Samson Raphael Hirsch.[164] Until this time, Jewish law was studied and interpreted only through the Talmud and the commentaries of subsequent rabbinic scholars. The historical approach also relies upon these primary sources, but in addition incorporates "the same methods used to study other ancient civilizations such as cross-cultural studies, linguistic comparisons and analysis, and in the twentieth century, archeology."[165] In this regard, the historical method embraces a methodology steeped in cultural analysis for the study of *halakhah* because it understands the law in the overall cultural context in which it develops, rather than as an autonomous entity.

Traditionally, the theological predicate of *halakhah* is God's direct communication to the Jews in the form of the Revealed Written Law, the Torah.[166] In contrast, the historical approach maintains that the Torah should not be understood as emanating from God directly but rather as the written product of human beings produced in specific times and places.[167] By rejecting the idea that the Torah was literally transmitted by God to Moses, the historical approach's view of the Written Law introduced a new dynamic regarding the origin and consequent application of the law. Specifically, Revelation is seen as the product of *both* Divine and human elements. According to many scholars who adhere to this historical perspective, God still is viewed as the ultimate Author of the Torah because the composers of the actual text are seen as either inspired by God or responding to their experiences of God.[168] Those who maintain an historical approach to *halakhah* posit that the Five Books of Moses were "produced by a series of…inspired [human] authors who were influenced in their work by the conditions which obtained in their

---

164. *See* HARRIS, *supra* note 73, at 190–202 for a comprehensive discussion of the development of Frankel's theory of Jewish law.

165. UNFOLDING TRADITION, *supra* note 48, at 48.

166. *See supra* Chapter 1, notes 79–81 and accompanying text; *supra* Chapter 2, notes 1–20 and accompanying text.

167. UNFOLDING TRADITION, *supra* note 48, at 50.

168. For a description of the various theories of Revelation within the Conservative movement and their implications for how the formation of the text of the Torah is understood, see ELLIOT DORFF, CONSERVATIVE JUDAISM: OUR ANCESTORS TO OUR DESCENDANTS 96–150 (1996). *See also* Joel Roth, *Musings toward a Personal Theology of Revelation*, CONSERVATIVE JUDAISM, Fall 2012, at 22, 31 (arguing that the Torah's "sanctity is entirely based on God's providence working through natural processes").

day."[169] In other words, this perspective understands Revelation by defining it not as God's direct communication to mankind but rather "as a complicated and complex process of divine-human encounter and interaction."[170]

The historical approach also sees the content of the rabbinic literature produced during the Talmudic era as largely a function of human output rather than the result of direct Divine Revelation. This perspective embraces the view that Jewish law is binding because it is a system that maintains the importance of keeping God's commandments, but that the essence of those commandments "can only claim to be true within the confines of the human condition and within the parameters of specific historical conditions."[171] Thus, the Conservative movement maintains that in every generation, the oral tradition was shaped both by rabbinic authority and "the generally accepted views, values, and practices of devoted Jews."[172] The communal aspect of the law's authority derives from the notion of Catholic Israel, an ideological concept especially prominent in the early discourse of the Conservative movement.[173] As will be explored below, the historical approach to the origins of the Written and Oral Law results not only in a substantial theological shift from the Orthodox perspective, but also in a shift with respect to the process of lawmaking.

The next section's historical overview details how the Conservative movement was rooted in the idea of "conserving" the tradition. In contrast to Reform, Conservative Judaism places the burden of proof on those who desire change rather than the other way around.[174] From the movement's inception, its objective was to facilitate the vitality of traditional Judaism in a modern context.[175] In this regard, there is a similarity to the views of Samson Raphael Hirsch discussed earlier. Nevertheless, the ideology of Conservative Judaism is very different from Modern Orthodoxy (or any Orthodoxy) given its explicit adoption of the historical approach to the law's origins and development. Moreover, Conservative Judaism not only espouses an ideology

---

169. JACOBS, *supra* note 136, at 224.

170. *Id.*

171. SHERWIN, *supra* note 1, at 29.

172. UNFOLDING TRADITION, *supra* note 48, at 59.

173. *Id.* at 58 (discussing the views of Solomon Schechter, who originated the concept of Catholic Israel). *See also infra* note 185 and accompanying text.

174. UNFOLDING TRADITION, *supra* note 48, at 50.

175. *Id.* at 1.

that is distinct from that of Orthodox Judaism, but also often endorses more liberal legal interpretations as a result of its ideology. For example, the Conservative movement sometimes has modified—or even eliminated—certain ritual practices, creating areas of dispute with Orthodox Judaism (the next three chapters illustrate this point more fully). These changes often occur as the result of the Conservative movement's conscious exercise of its lawmaking process, but sometimes they arise through popular consensus or even through a combination of top-down and bottom-up means.[176] The Conservative movement's well-known philosophy is that Jewish law is both binding and evolving.[177]

Yet, given the admission that the *halakhic* process inevitably is influenced by human, and hence subjective, judgment, it is easy to understand how the theological concept of binding law can recede in practice. Rabbi Julius Guttmann put the matter even more starkly:

> For without the belief in *Torah min Hashamayim* [Torah from Heaven] it is impossible to insist upon the performance of the *mitzvot* [commandments] without substantial changes in the method of performance or in the contents of the *mitzvot*. The moment this belief totters, the absoluteness of the *mitzvot* itself is shattered.[178]

Guttmann's observation is similar to that of cultural analysis scholar Paul Berman, discussed in Chapter 1, who questions whether and how a cultural practice that derives from human production can fully inspire those who are members of the cultural tradition in question.[179]

Historical Development

Although Conservative Judaism traces its ideological roots to Europe through the Breslau Seminary headed by Zacharias Frankel, as an institutional movement Conservative Judaism essentially began in the United States. In 1887, the Jewish Theological Seminary ("JTS") was established in

---

176. *Id.* at 3.

177. *See* Avi Hein, *Women in Judaism: A History of Women's Ordination as Rabbis*, http://www.jewishvirtuallibrary.org/jsource/Judaism/femalerabbi.html (last visited July 8, 2014).

178. Guttmann, *supra* note 2, at 17.

179. *See supra* Chapter 1, notes 130–34 and accompanying text.

New York based upon the principles of positive historical Judaism embraced by the Breslau Seminary. From the beginning, JTS included a rather mixed coalition covering a wide spectrum of "middle of the road" thinkers.[180] Rabbi Solomon Schechter is considered the institutional founder of the Conservative movement.[181] Born and educated in Europe, Schechter served as the president of JTS in New York from 1902 until 1915, during which time he was responsible for securing the institution from both an organizational and economic standpoint.[182]

Yet, Schechter did not consider his work to be the establishment of a movement per se, as he often referred to the "Conservative tendency" rather than the Conservative movement.[183] In fact, the movement he originally envisioned was a cross-denominational one that included all traditional synagogues (as opposed to those accepting Reform's Pittsburgh Platform that rejected the traditional practices Schechter espoused). When the Union of Orthodox Hebrew Congregations was established, Schechter realized that those institutions identifying as Orthodox would not accept his cross-denominational effort, so in 1913 he established the United Synagogue of America, the eventual umbrella organization of the Conservative movement.[184]

Schechter's philosophy was heavily steeped in the notion of *klal yisrael*— the community of the People of Israel. He referred to this community as Catholic Israel, and to him, it included all those who embraced the religion's traditional practices. Schechter understood Jewish law to be shaped both by rabbinic interpretation as well as the practices of Catholic Israel—the committed people. In other words, according to Schechter, "[i]t is the rabbis' ongoing interpretation of the Torah and the changing practices of Catholic Israel that determine the content of Jewish law."[185] His philosophy embodies the cultural analysis insight that law should incorporate a multiplicity of values according to a top-down and a bottom-up approach.[186]

---

180. Sarna, *supra* note 21, at 184.

181. Unfolding Tradition, *supra* note 48, at 57.

182. JTS still is sometimes called "Schechter's Seminary," and many Conservative day schools are part of the Solomon Schechter Day School system, in recognition of his early efforts with respect to the movement. *Id.*

183. *Id.* at 58.

184. *Id.* at 59. *See also* Sarna, *supra* note 21, at 189–93 for an account of the Conservative movement's separation from Orthodoxy at this time.

185. Unfolding Tradition, *supra* note 48, at 60.

186. *See supra* Chapter 1, notes 42–47 and accompanying text.

Schechter's avid Zionism was one manifestation of his concern for Catholic Israel. At this time, Zionism was rejected not only by Reform Jews,[187] but also by many Orthodox Jews who believed that the establishment of a Jewish state should wait for the coming of the Messiah.[188] In contrast, from its inception, the Conservative movement was founded upon a strong sense that the Jews must have their own nation in their homeland.[189]

During World War I, the majority of Jewish soldiers chose to attend Conservative services, a phenomenon that "proved...to be a harbinger of the future."[190] By the 1940s and early 1950s, the Conservative movement gained the largest number of affiliated American families. According to Jonathan Sarna, the renowned historian of American Judaism, between the years 1945 and 1965 the Conservative movement "increased the number of its congregational affiliates by 450, more than the number of new Reform and Orthodox synagogues combined."[191] The reasons for the movement's success during this period reflect sociological trends prominent in American society as a whole. Significantly, during this time the United States generally was moving toward the middle of the road from an ideological standpoint, and Conservative Judaism's "middle-of-the road message, simultaneously religiously authentic yet lacking stringencies perceived as offensive, seemed well suited to this cultural milieu and felt in touch with the times."[192] Further, the Conservative movement was very youth focused and appealed to the growing number of suburbanites. It particularly resonated with those suburban housewives who "experienced a heightened sense of religious status" within

---

187. *See supra* notes 40–44 and accompanying text.

188. UNFOLDING TRADITION, *supra* note 48, at 58.

189. Schechter's Catholic Israel stance also had consequences from the standpoint of lawmaking, especially because he did not clearly articulate how the operation of Catholic Israel's input should work from a practical perspective. *Id.* at 61. Moreover, because he was less concerned with theology than with rabbinics, his ideology arguably lacked a compelling basis for adherence to the ritual. Although he understood Jewish law to be binding upon the Jewish people, he believed the source of particular legal rulings reflected a combination of both the Divine and the human. Schechter believed in Revelation, but his conception of what this concept means is not entirely clear. This philosophy can give rise to a "messy" situation in practice. *See also infra* notes 205–18.

190. SARNA, *supra* note 21, at 213 (discussing the history of the ABRIDGED PRAYER BOOK FOR JEWS IN THE ARMY AND NAVY OF THE UNITED STATES (1917)).

191. *Id.* at 284.

192. *Id.* at 285.

Conservative synagogues as a result of the movement's allowing men and women to sit together during prayer.[193]

As the twentieth century continued, however, the numbers affiliated with Conservative Judaism began to dwindle. Some of this decline is attributable to a countercultural movement that began in the late 1960s and years later morphed into a quest for worship in small, informal venues with strong lay participation and group singing. Thus, by the late twentieth century, the preferable model of an American synagogue became more participatory and less performance oriented, a trend that ran counter to the format of many large Conservative synagogues. As a corollary of this phenomenon, a new trend emerged in the form of independent prayer groups, or *minyanim* (the plural of the Hebrew word *minyan*—referring to a quorum of ten Jewish males above the age of thirteen necessary to recite certain Hebrew prayers and read from the Torah publicly). These independent *minyanim* typically are lay-led and follow the pattern of a very traditional service, although usually they are more egalitarian in nature than Orthodox protocol allows. In recent years, this trend has become especially popular among traditional Conservative Jews who find many Conservative synagogues lacking in sufficient ritual and observance.[194]

Conservative synagogues have been losing more traditionally oriented members not only to independent *minyanim* but also to Modern Orthodoxy. A significant problem is the movement's failure to impart a clear sense of *halakhic* obligation among its members. As a result of this problem, as well as the slide to the right on the part of the Orthodox, adherence to the ritualistic content of *halakhah* among Conservative Jews is far more lax than among the Orthodox. In fact, the personal religious practices of many Conservative Jews actually are closer to that of their Reform brethren, who openly acknowledge their autonomy in determining how to practice Judaism. This reality poses a barrier for some traditional Conservative Jews wanting to be part of a community that takes the Sabbath and dietary laws more seriously than do the majority of affiliated Conservative Jews. Indeed, Bruce Phillips, a sociologist of American Jewry, has noted that those Jews who have attended Camp Ramah, the Conservative movement's official summer camp mandating

---

193. *Id.* at 286.

194. Based on a national survey undertaken in 2007, 46 percent of those who attend independent *minyanim* grew up in Conservative synagogues. *See* ELIE KAUNFER, EMPOWERED JUDAISM 64 (2010).

serious *halakhic* observance by its campers, comprise "a significant segment of middle-aged members in Orthodox synagogues."[195]

At the other end of the spectrum, in recent years the Conservative movement has been losing its less-traditional adherents to Reform. One explanation for this phenomenon stems from the resurgence of tradition among Reform synagogues. Given that many Conservative Jews operate fairly close to Reform Jews on a personal level, the infusion of more Hebrew and tradition at the institutional level makes Reform a more appealing option than in previous years. Moreover, Jews who grew up Conservative but marry a non-Jewish spouse often elect to join Reform synagogues—should they affiliate at all—because they offer a more welcoming environment for intermarried couples in light of Reform's position that the children of non-Jewish females can be considered Jewish under certain circumstances.[196] In light of the high rate of intermarriage among American Jews,[197] these numbers can be quite significant. Although some Conservative synagogues are now beginning to reach out more directly to intermarried couples,[198] the movement's current position aligning with the tradition's precept that religion is determined by the mother's status may discourage affiliation among some families.[199]

No discussion of the history of the modern movements would be complete without some attention to the Reconstructionist movement, pioneered by Rabbi Mordecai Kaplan. Kaplan, the son of a traditional Lithuanian rabbi, immigrated to the United States in 1889 and was educated both in

---

195. Bruce Phillips, *American Judaism in the 21st Century, in* CAMBRIDGE COMPANION TO AMERICAN JUDAISM 409 (2005) (commenting on sociologist's Marshall Sklare's findings).

196. *See infra* Chapter 5 where this issue is discussed more fully.

197. Today intermarriage among American Jews exceeds 50 percent. *See infra* Chapter 9, notes 27–30 and accompanying text.

198. In the June 2012 issue of the Chicago *JUF News* (the magazine published by the area's Jewish Federation), an advertisement for Congregation Beth Shalom, one of the largest suburban Conservative synagogues in the greater Chicago area, claimed that it is a "Conservative, egalitarian, interfaith welcoming congregation." This wording clearly is designed to send a message—and one that not all Conservative synagogues would endorse.

199. The statistics maintained by the Conservative movement do reveal that enrollments in many Conservative day schools have declined since the early 1990s. Statistics furnished to the author by Elaine Cohen, former Schechter Day School Network Director, as an e-mail attachment (June 20, 2012, 1:20 p.m. CST) (on file with author). Nonetheless, enrollments at the various locations of Camp Ramah, the movement's official overnight camp, are on the rise, and new locations in Georgia and Colorado, as well as day camps for younger children, have opened in recent years. Studies also show that Conservative Jews, like those of other denominations, are experiencing a renewed interest in ritual observance, despite the reality that individual variation in this area seems to be the norm. *See* SARNA, *supra* note 21, at 326.

yeshiva and secular settings. He received his ordination from JTS, where he taught for much of his life. Over time, however, Kaplan began to develop a theory of Judaism that placed the Jewish people, rather than God, at the center of the religion. As a consequence, he saw Judaism as an entire civilization including "land (meaning Israel), history, language, literature, religious folkways, mores, laws, and art" rather than just a set of prescribed legal rules and rituals.[200] Kaplan, though personally observant, thus spurred a "Copernican Revolution in Jewish legal theory" by explicitly positing that because *halakhah* is developed by people rather than being the product of Divine command, humans possess "the power and even the duty to evaluate it and apply it to the needs and sensibilities of the times."[201]

Although the number of official adherents to the Reconstructionist movement always has been comparatively small, Kaplan's vision of Judaism probably resonates with a significant number of Jews, particularly Jewish Americans.[202] Sarna has observed that "Reconstructionism's significance lies…in the critical questions that it raised and the important debates that it stimulated within *all* movements of Judaism."[203] From the standpoint of cultural analysis, Kaplan's theory represents the most explicit adoption of a cultural analysis approach to Jewish law. Through its express endorsement of the law as the creation of the Jewish people, rather than the product of Divine command, it understands the *entire mesorah* as "very much a cultural document."[204] Indeed, as will be discussed more fully below and in subsequent chapters, Kaplan's belief that the tradition has a vote but not veto power has had a marked impact in the Conservative movement's lawmaking process.

---

200. SARNA, *supra* note 21, at 245.

201. UNFOLDING TRADITION, *supra* note 48, at 75. *See also* JONATHAN WOOCHER, SACRED SURVIVAL 178 (1986) (calling Kaplan's vision a "Copernican revolution which places the people, and not God, at the core of the Jewish religious experience").

202. *See* SARNA, *supra* note 21, at 246; UNFOLDING TRADITION, *supra* note 48, at 75 (noting that "even though Kaplan probably articulated how most modern Jews understand Jewish law, few lay Jews want to admit to such a theology"). Professor Sarna also notes that the Reconstuctionist movement is the only completely homegrown American movement. SARNA, *supra* note 21, at 243. *See also* Jay P. Lefkowitz, *The Rise of Social Orthodoxy: A Personal Account*, COMMENTARY 37, 40 (Apr. 2014) (noting the relevance of Mordecai Kaplan to Modern Orthodoxy).

203. SARNA, *supra* note 21, at 247. For a brief discussion of Kaplan's influence specifically on Reform thinkers, see *id.* at 249, 251.

204. *Id.* at 246 (quoting NEIL GILLMAN, CONSERVATIVE JUDAISM: THE NEW CENTURY, 78 (1993)).

Lawmaking under the Conservative Movement

As previously noted, the ideological underpinning of the historical approach has resulted in a lawmaking process that is more liberal than that which currently exists under Orthodoxy. Although Conservative Judaism claims to regard *halakhah* as binding upon Jews, adherents of the movement's historical approach sometimes are willing to revisit and reject legal precedents that Orthodox authorities regard as conclusive, including rules perceived as having been settled by the Talmud. In other words, according to Conservative authorities, the rabbis of the Talmud may not be the final arbiters of Jewish law because the law, as a human system, must be allowed to develop in response to changing human conditions.[205] The movement also opposes the claim that the codifications of Jewish law are "authoritative and binding," but instead sees these texts as furnishing guidance.[206] As a result, this viewpoint allows "for the possibility of a subjective and a social element in *halakhic* decision."[207]

On a practical level, the Rabbinical Assembly, the international association of Conservative rabbis, established in 1927 a Committee of Jewish Law that was charged with the responsibility for adopting legal positions considered *halakhically* acceptable by the movement.[208] In 1949, a notable change occurred with respect to the Committee's lawmaking process when it adopted a formal proposal that the "decisions of the Law Committee shall be presented in the form of a traditional *responsum* indicating its relationship to relevant *halakhic and other material*."[209] With the adoption of this proposal, the Committee explicitly approved the propriety of considering extralegal factors in addition to the classical Jewish law authorities. Further, this decision was reflected in the change of the Committee's name from the Committee on Jewish Law to the Committee on Jewish Law and Standards ("CJLS").[210]

---

205. *See* JACOBS, *supra* note 136, at 222.

206. SHERWIN, *supra* note 1, at 32, 45, 225 n.115 (noting the Conservative movement's position on this issue). *See also supra* note 143 and accompanying text.

207. SHERWIN, *supra* note 1, at 32.

208. Herr & Friedman, *supra* note 25, at 457

209. *Id.* (emphasis added).

210. *Id.*

As a result of this explicit change, the CJLS now bases its Jewish law decisions on more than past Jewish law precedents. According to Elliot Dorff, the current chair of the CJLS, Jewish law "requires rabbis first to study those precedents within their historical contexts and then to weigh them together with contemporary circumstances (economics, demographics, etc.) and a host of other Jewish forms of expression (stories, theology, history, morals, etc.) to make a considered, wise and clearly Jewish judgment about what they think God wants of us now."[211] In addition, Jewish law "mixes things up further by taking into account past and current Jewish customs."[212] Moreover, the historical approach to *halakhah* is inclined to call for changes in the law when the status quo "results in the kind of injustice that reasonable persons would see as detrimental to Judaism itself."[213] Thus, the operation of lawmaking under this historical approach is made by balancing precedent, including a healthy respect for the tradition, with a consideration of extralegal factors that focus on current circumstances. Still, despite the fact that the Conservative movement sees itself as a "big tent" with room for differing viewpoints, there are certain *halakhic* standards for the movement that cannot be abdicated by individual rabbis. Thus, the CJLS has adopted three Standards of Rabbinic Practice to which all Conservative rabbis must adhere. These standards prohibit a Conservative rabbi from officiating at an intermarriage, require a Jewish writ of divorce, known as a *get*, before remarriage pursuant to Jewish law, and define Jewish membership according to the mother's religion or a *halakhic* conversion.[214]

The CJLS currently is composed of twenty-five members and represents a range of viewpoints. It often issues diverse, and sometimes even contradictory, opinions.[215] The CJLS members even have the option of voting

---

211. UNFOLDING TRADITION, *supra* note 48, at 332.

212. *Id.* It is important to underscore that this view of Jewish law is one of many variations embraced by the Conservative movement. *See generally* UNFOLDING TRADITION, *supra* note 48, for a comprehensive treatment of theories of law within the Conservative movement.

213. JACOBS, *supra* note 136, at 221. In this regard, the views of Conservative thinkers in the United States were very influenced by Justice Benjamin Cardozo, who called for the consideration of socioeconomic factors into the lawmaking process. *See* BENJAMIN N. CARDOZO, THE NATURE OF THE JUDICIAL PROCESS (1921).

214. UNFOLDING TRADITION, *supra* note 48, at 405. *See generally infra* Chapter 5 for a discussion of the third standard mentioned in the text. It should be noted that the Conservative movement has a distinct lawmaking body governing matters for Conservative Jews in Israel, known as *Masorti* (traditional). Sometimes *Masorti* rulings are stricter than the ones issued by the CJLS. *See, e.g., infra* Chapter 5, note 86.

215. *See, e.g., infra* Chapter 6, notes 64–67 and accompanying text.

affirmatively for contradictory opinions,[216] presumably to give congregational rabbis a choice of perspectives. Six votes are needed in order for a given opinion to be considered official by the CJLS. This approach underscores how, in practice, Conservative Judaism embraces a multiplicity of values and approaches. Further, according to the internal dynamics of the Conservative movement, individual congregational rabbis act as the *mara d'atra*, the teacher of the local community, and they have the responsibility for determining how the law can best be applied in particular synagogue communities.[217] In exercising this role, Conservative rabbis consider the decisions of the CJLS, but individual rabbis have the authority to rule otherwise, subject to being required to adhere to the three Standards of Rabbinic Practice mentioned earlier.[218]

In sum, those who take the historical approach assert that Torah law has evolved, and should evolve, to accommodate social needs. In other words, the Conservative movement's approach to lawmaking embraces the idea that what is considered *halakhic* is largely a human decision and interpreted through a cultural lens. These points are a major source of disagreement between the mainstream Orthodox and Conservative legal perspectives.

The Law and Culture of Postdenominationalism

As the foregoing discussion illustrates, the development of various denominations is a defining characteristic of Judaism in modernity. The reality of denominations necessitates a concern, on the part of religious leaders as well as the laity, with appropriate boundaries. Throughout the history of Judaism, particularly in the United States where the distinct movements have flourished, Jews from all of the movements have been concerned with where the lines should be drawn, and how inclusive or exclusive their respective movements should be.[219] As Heilman's discussion of Orthodoxy's slide to the right demonstrates, in this struggle for denominational identity and definition,

---

216. *See, e.g., infra* Chapter 6, note 67 and accompanying text.

217. *See* UNFOLDING TRADITION, *supra* note 48, at 484.

218. *See supra* note 214 and accompanying text. This path has been embodied in the structure of the CJLS since 1985. *See* UNFOLDING TRADITION, *supra* note 48, at 405 (discussing Rabbi Gordon Tucker's paper concerning individual rabbinic autonomy).

219. SARNA, *supra* note 21, at 183–84, 366–68.

those at the margin tend to help redefine the mainstream.[220] This is true not just for Orthodoxy but also for the other denominations.

According to the 2013 Pew Research Religion & Public Life Project ("the Pew Report"), the most comprehensive national survey of the Jewish population since 2000,[221] denominational affiliation is the norm among those Jews in the United States who say they are Jewish when asked about their religion. The Pew Report shows that 40 percent of such Jews identify as Reform, 22 percent Conservative, 12 percent Orthodox, and 19 percent claim no denominational affiliation.[222] Yet, despite these numbers and the reality that the institutional and ideological divisions among the three major movements remain strong, there are indications that a postdenominational milieu is the wave of the future, with the divisions grouped along the lines of "traditional versus progressive" rather than specific denominational affiliations. Specifically, traditional Jews can be characterized as individuals whose lives by and large are shaped by, and revolve around, the *halakhah*. In the final chapter of Heilman's book, entitled "Toward a Postmodern American Orthodoxy," he notes that "the atmosphere of postmodernism that has marked Western civilization since the 1980s" has the capacity to blur the distinct versions of Orthodoxy, resulting in individuals selecting their particular Orthodox mode depending on the time and place.[223] Moreover, this group of traditionally oriented Jews includes not just those who self-denominate as Orthodox, but also observant Conservative Jews, as well as an in-between group known as "Conservadox." Many of these individuals gravitate toward Orthodox, including Open Orthodox, synagogues to find a community, despite the fact that they are not necessarily Orthodox from an ideological perspective.[224]

On the ground, these realities reinforce the blurring of already gray boundaries between the margins of the Orthodox and Conservative movements. From the standpoint of ideology, one perceptive Modern Orthodox commentator has published an article in *Tradition Magazine*, a premier academic Orthodox journal in the United States, arguing that yeshivas should

---

220. *See also id.* at 193.

221. *See* Pew Report, *supra* note 109 (follow "Chapter 3: Jewish Identity" hyperlink).

222. *Id.*

223. HEILMAN, *supra* note 82, at 304–05.

224. *See also* Lefkowitz, *supra* note 202 (discussing the phenomenon of "social Orthodoxy"); *infra* Chapter 10, notes 23–24 and accompanying text.

consider exploring a degree of Talmudic study from a critical, academic per-spective.[225] In essence, this article calls for a significant paradigm shift with respect to the traditional study of Talmud. The very fact of its publication in this venue points to the potential for further blurring of long-standing divi-sions regarding the educational methodology of Orthodox and Conservative institutions that historically have appeared unalterable.

On the other hand, progressive or liberal Jews may be guided by, and even observant of, *halakhah*, but their daily existence is not governed by *halakhic* norms in the same way as their more traditional counterparts. It is a well-known fact that despite the difference in formal prayer services, few differences exist "in the private lives and orientations" of most members of Conservative and Reform synagogues.[226] The 1990 and 2000 National Jewish Population Studies reveal that Conservative and Reform Jews "share much in their patterns of *personal* observance" and overall outlook on issues such as interfaith marriage, same-sex marriage, ordination of gay rabbis, and whether Jewish membership should be determined by either one's mother or father.[227] Although the Pew Report reveals a substantial difference between

---

225. David C. Flatto, *Tradition and Modernity in the House of Study: Reconsidering the Relationship between Conceptual and Critical Methods of Studying Talmud*, TRADITION, Winter 2010, at 1, 1–20.

Even more recently, an initiative entitled Project TABS (Torah and Biblical Scholarship) has created a website devoted to Jewish biblical study in "a historical and contextual approach." Although TABS appears to be unaffiliated with any particular movement, most of the contributors (including the founders) self-identify as Orthodox. The website contains a recent essay by Zev Farber, a Modern Orthodox rabbi, in which he affirms the need for critical Torah study and calls for an "honest conversation" in his community on this topic. *See* Zev Farber, *Avraham* Avinu *Is My Father: Thoughts on Torah, History, and Judaism*, http://the-torah.com/torah-history-judaism-introduction/ (last visited July 8, 2014). Farber's essay in TABS has been extremely controversial within Orthodoxy and has been the subject of much discussion and criticism, even within the Open Orthodox blog Morethodoxy. By Farber's own admission in the Morethodoxy blog, his work in TABS is intended to be a "conversa-tion starter." *See* Zev Farber, *The Torah, The Torah.com, and the Recent Tumult in Context*, MORETHODOXY (July 25, 2013), http://morethodoxy.org/tag/rabbi-david-steinberg/.

226. THE GROWTH, *supra* note 38, at 350–51.

227. UNFOLDING TRADITION, *supra* note 48, at 454–56. Indeed, Rabbi Paul Menitoff, the former Executive Director of the CCAR, maintains that on these matters, most Conservative Jews agree with the more liberal views of Reform Jews. *Id.* at 454 (discussing Menitoff's views). *See also* Pew Report, *supra* note 109, (follow "Chapter 6: Social and Political Views" hyperlink) (showing that among Conservative Jews, 80 percent believe homosexuality should be accepted by society and 14 percent say it should be discouraged; among Reform Jews, 92 percent believe it should be accepted and 4 percent say it should be discouraged). *See also* STEVEN M. COHEN & ARNOLD M. EISEN, THE JEW WITHIN 37–38 (2000) (noting the diminishment of ideological divisions among moderately affiliated Jews).

Conservative and Reform Jews in terms of certain markers of observance, this difference still is not as significant as that which exists between Conservative Jews and those who self-denominate as Modern Orthodox.[228]

For now, institutional differences still exist between the Conservative and Reform movements that are very much ideologically driven[229] despite similarities between segments of the laity. Yet, whether the differing ideologies of these respective movements will continue to support distinct institutions in the future is somewhat of an open question as new generations of Jews determine affiliations more by their peers than by ideology or their parents' affiliation. Moreover, the *halakhic* lines that characterize the current Conservative movement possibly may continue to shift to the left in the future, further blurring existing ideological and *halakhic* distinctions.[230]

---

228. *See* Pew Report, *supra* note 109, (follow "Chapter 4: Religious Beliefs and Practices" hyperlink) (discussing observance of markers such as lighting Sabbath candles, keeping a kosher home, and refraining from handling money on the Sabbath).

229. *See* UNFOLDING TRADITION, *supra* note 48, at 455 for a listing of differences.

230. *See, e.g., infra* Chapter 6, note 167 and accompanying text.

5 FOUNDATIONAL CONFLICTS: "WHO IS A JEW" AND SABBATH LAWS

A cultural analysis perspective is characterized by conflict and multiple values. This chapter and the two that follow examine some important areas of dispute in the interpretation and application of Jewish law. All of the issues discussed in these chapters are significant from a cultural analysis standpoint because they illuminate how the traditional Jewish law texts can be reinterpreted, and in some cases even rejected, based on a cultural analysis of the law. They also illustrate an underlying dilemma of invoking cultural analysis. Specifically, this methodology seeks to preserve a tradition's integrity and authenticity while simultaneously justifying the development of the tradition in response to cultural change.

This chapter explores these themes in two contexts: first, the global discussion of "who is a Jew" according to Jewish law; and second, a ritually oriented discussion concerning observance of the Sabbath, a cornerstone of the Jewish tradition. The issue of membership in the Jewish religion became an especially contested one in 1983 when the Reform movement unilaterally abandoned the traditional matrilineal principle that determines Jewish personal status from the standpoint of *halakhah* (Jewish law) exclusively according to the mother's religion. In doing so, the Reform movement adopted the patrilineal principle and ruled that children of a Gentile mother and a Jewish father can be considered Jewish, subject to certain criteria. Both the Conservative and Orthodox movements strongly contest Reform's ruling. With intermarriage significantly on the rise, this issue is tremendously important to the Jewish community.

The second topic addressed in this chapter involves modifications to *halakhah* with respect to Sabbath observance that were made by the Conservative movement in 1950. Specifically, the discussion focuses on rulings concerning permission to drive to the synagogue and to use electricity on the Sabbath, practices long deemed forbidden by Jewish law. The Conservative movement's Committee on Jewish Law and Standards ("CJLS") issued conflicting rulings with respect to these issues, resulting in the ability of individual congregational rabbis to decide for themselves which position to follow. By allowing, and indeed even embracing, this process, Conservative Judaism welcomes a strong degree of disputation among its own adherents.[1] Equally significant, however, is the degree of conflict these decisions spurred between the Conservative and Orthodox movements. The nature of this conflict is typical in that it reflects not only different bottom lines in some instances, but also different reasoning processes even when Orthodox authorities are in agreement with the more traditional positions of the CJLS. In light of the Sabbath's central importance to Jewish law and culture, the existence and nature of this conflict is especially significant.

Before exploring these two areas of conflict, however, it is useful to lay some additional groundwork. Although Chapter 1 introduces the operation of dispute generally and in the context of the Jewish tradition specifically, a fuller treatment is provided in the following discussion as a prelude to the examination of the specific areas of conflict addressed in this chapter and those that follow.

Parameters of Conflict

Cultural analysis scholars remind us that cultural dissent occurs as a result of challenges by individuals seeking to broaden, modernize, and otherwise reframe the boundaries of foundational issues within the cultural tradition.[2] Moreover, in light of the inherently dynamic nature of culture, particular groups can struggle with both internal conflicts and pressures imposed by externalities. As a result, cultural traditions continually seek to negotiate the balance between evolution and preservation. That said, however, sometimes

---

1. For an insightful discussion of this diversity, see ELLIOT N. DORFF, UNFOLDING TRADITION (2005).

2. *See supra* Chapter 1, note 41 and accompanying text.

particular sectors of a given cultural tradition advocate for changes that can compromise traditional values and result in a loss of something perceived as valuable by other sectors of the community. Although cultural analysis embraces conflict and multiple perspectives, it also is concerned with safeguarding cultural tradition. Therefore, selectivity with respect to change is a competing value of the cultural analysis paradigm with respect to negotiating the line between evolution and preservation.

Cultural analysis understands law as a cultural product that evidences human creativity. With respect to Jewish law specifically, the *mesorah* (Jewish tradition) embodies a cultural analysis perspective because it includes not just the top-down concrete legal components, but also the bottom-up practices of the people that are seen as the cultural elements of the tradition. Given the undeniable human component of the Jewish tradition—with respect to both its strictly legal and seemingly cultural elements—the *mesorah* in its entirety can be understood as a cultural product of creative human activity that represents the product of human judgment about God's will.

Further, a cultural analysis perspective of Jewish law understands preservation of the *mesorah*—both its legal and cultural components—as vital because, as an expression of the Jewish people, it is the vehicle through which Jewish particularity is expressed and maintained. As Chapter 4 illustrates, the three major Jewish movements in modernity reflect three distinct approaches to the importance and application of Jewish law. Stated in categorical terms, these three approaches can be summarized as follows: Jewish law informs Jewish life but is not binding upon Jews; Jewish law is binding, but its interpretation should mesh with modernity in a way that preserves its authenticity yet allows for its evolution; and Jewish law is binding, and modernity is not a significant factor in its interpretation (although current realities can influence its application). Given these diverse perspectives, conflict exists surrounding the importance and application of Jewish law. These differences are reflected in struggles both among the movements and even internally within each particular movement.

Chapter 4 also highlights conflict within Orthodoxy from an historical perspective. The picture of Orthodoxy painted in that chapter may be surprising given the rather widespread public perception that Orthodoxy is monolithic. Chapter 4 discusses significant schisms among Orthodox sectors despite their larger commonalities. Some of the points of conflict discussed are ideological, such as the differences in lifestyle between Modern Orthodox and the *Haredim* (ultra-Orthodox), and the theological differences between

Chabad-Lubavitchers and other Orthodox Jews. Other points of conflict involve perceived boundary pushing by those Jews following the Open Orthodox approach. On the whole, however, with respect to fundamental areas of ritual observance, there is not a significant degree of variability among those who self-denominate as Orthodox. For example, despite some arguable differences in observance at the margins, keeping kosher and the Sabbath are hallmarks of Orthodox Jewish observance.

The nature of contested discourse within Orthodoxy, therefore, generally has a different flavor from that which is produced by certain controversial changes adopted by the Reform and Conservative movements. These changes often involve modifications to, or even outright rejections of, long-settled legal positions or traditions. When these changes involve foundational practices and are fueled by changing societal norms, the resulting conflicts can be particularly pronounced.

Further, the traditional *halakhic* process maintains a distinction between biblical and rabbinic law, and holds that biblical law generally has greater authority than rabbinic law.[3] Still, the boundary between these classifications is unclear and often itself the product of conflict. Moreover, although in theory *halakhah* that is the result of a Talmudic consensus cannot be changed (at least according to the traditional perspective), in practice it is often difficult to determine whether and how the Talmud has reached a consensus.[4]

In light of these parameters of the *halakhic* process, the abandonment of an explicit precept in the Written Torah represents the most radical type of change to the Jewish legal system. The least radical changes involve a choice between two options, each of which has strong support in the tradition. An intermediate scenario involves the adoption of a practice that is supported by some basis in the legal tradition, despite a developed consensus against this particular practice. Another intermediate but more difficult scenario is presented by changes to, or modifications of, the tradition that involve either a reinterpretation or abandonment of a rabbinic law or a law that is understood as resting at the intersection between biblical and rabbinic law. This chapter and the two that follow explore important examples of conflict resulting from these types of changes to *halakhah*.

---

3. See *supra* Chapter 4, notes 137–40 and accompanying text.

4. See *supra* Chapter 1, notes 101–04 and accompanying text.

Conflict between Reform and Other Movements:
Who Is a Jew from Birth?

The answer to the question of what it means to be a member of the Jewish people is one that has changed over time, and currently is widely contested. Until the second half of the second century BCE, the terms used to designate the people who are today referred to as "Jews" were understood as referencing the Judaeans, an ethnic-geographic category of people living on their ancestral land (notwithstanding their allegiance to the religious traditions contained in the Torah, including worshipping the God of the Judaeans).[5] Gradually, however, this ethno-geographic self-definition came to be supplemented with political, and more importantly for this discussion, religious definitions, making it possible for those not born in the land itself to be considered part of the people.[6]

Chapter 2 discusses in detail the impact of the Hellenistic culture upon the development of Jewish law and culture during this period. Professor Shaye Cohen has remarked that the Judaeans, "influenced by the Greek culture, and at the same time in opposition to it, … redefined Judaism (Jewishness) so that it too could become a portable culture."[7] In this environment, conversion to Judaism "emerged as an analogue to conversion to Hellenism"[8]—a vehicle through which the forces of assimilation could be resisted as Jewish citizenship and way of life became open to other peoples.[9]

Early on, no formal conversion was deemed necessary for Gentile women who married Jewish men; the existence of the marriage established their social conversion, and this status lasted as long as the marriage was intact.[10] Significantly, toward the late first and second centuries CE, the notion of female personhood began to emerge, and with it, the idea that Gentile women who married Jewish men still had to formally convert in order to be considered Jewish.[11] Cohen notes that the rabbinic texts of the second century CE

---

5. SHAYE J.D. COHEN, THE BEGINNINGS OF JEWISHNESS 70, 96 (1999).

6. The formation of a political community made it possible to extend citizenship to non-natives. *Id.* at 105. Although the end of the Hasmonean empire (the ruling dynasty of Judea) obviated the importance of this political definition of Jewishness, it nonetheless had an influence upon later reflections on the meaning and process of Jewish conversion. *See id.* at 105.

7. *Id.* at 134.

8. *Id.* at 135.

9. *Id.* at 138.

10. *Id.* at 170, 265.

11. *Id.* at 170.

"unambiguously attest for the first time...the conversion of women."[12] This development was critical for the sages' adoption of the matrilineal principle, which also was documented for the first time during this same period.[13] This principle establishes that according to rabbinic law, the child of a Gentile mother and a Jewish father is Gentile; conversely, the child of a Jewish mother and a Gentile father is Jewish. Thus, religious status follows the mother. The connection between this principle and the ability of women to convert to Judaism in their own right is clear: "since the Gentile woman was now a person whose Jewishness could be determined without reference to her Jewish husband," her children are Jewish if she converts; otherwise, her children are Gentile regardless of her husband's Jewishness.[14]

A traditional Orthodox perspective probably would emphasize that the rabbis of this period determined that, according to biblical law (including both the Written and the Oral Law), Jewish religious status is based on matrilineal descent. Yet, the adoption by the rabbis of the matrilineal principle is surprising in that it represents a departure from the biblical and Second Temple practice according to which patrilineal descent determined the status of children of mixed marriages.[15] In his exhaustive study of its origins, Shaye Cohen writes that the matrilineal principle is not specifically attested in either the biblical or Second Temple period, despite the fact that certain biblical passages provide "scriptural hooks" upon which it can be based after the fact.[16] Instead, the principle appears in the Mishnah, a rabbinic text believed to have been produced around 200 CE.[17]

At the end of his extensive analysis, Cohen has no single governing explanation for the appearance of the matrilineal principle or why the rabbis would have decided to break with the previously established practice. He rejects a rabbinic inclination to restrain intermarriage as an explanation, given the relatively low occurrence of this phenomenon among Jews at this time, and he supposes that if intermarriage were a concern, the rabbis would

---

12. *Id.* at 223.

13. *Id.*

14. *Id.* at 306–07.

15. *Id.* at 305.

16. The particular biblical hooks Cohen discusses are Exodus 21:4 and Deuteronomy 21:15. For an extensive analysis of these passages as they relate to this topic, as well as other possible explanations for the matrilineal principle, see COHEN, *supra* note 5, at chapter 9.

17. *See* Kiddushin 3:12 (Mishnah).

have required a bilateral system demanding that both parents be Jewish.[18] Of course, one logical explanation for the adoption of the matrilineal principle is that as Jews became increasingly scattered, it was more difficult to define Jewish status according to geographic criteria or through a system of patriarchal clans. Designating Jewish status through the mother's line arguably was helpful because she could always be identified, unlike the father. In the final analysis, however, Cohen asserts, "On an issue as complex and diffuse as the rabbinic matrilineal principle, we must allow for a multiplicity of motives."[19]

The matrilineal principle remained an unchallenged precept of the *mesorah* until 1983, when the Reform movement adopted the Patrilineal Resolution, governing only North American Reform Jews. The Patrilineal Resolution stipulates that with respect to determining the religious status of children of mixed marriages, "the same requirements must be applied...regardless of whether the mother or the father is Jewish."[20] These requirements provide that any child of a mixed marriage with one Jewish parent "is under the presumption of Jewish descent," and this presumption of Jewish status "is to be established through appropriate and timely public and formal acts of identification with the Jewish faith and people."[21] In other words, children of mixed marriages are presumed to be Jewish as long as they publicly manifest a positive and exclusive Jewish identity.[22] This manifestation can be accomplished by observing *mitzvot* (commandments) that commit the child and his or her parents to Jewish life. This Patrilineal Resolution not only altered the established practice concerning matrilineal descent, but also added additional requirements for membership for children with Jewish mothers and Gentile fathers who were, according to *halakhah*, considered Jewish regardless of whether they publicly displayed a positive and exclusive Jewish identity.

---

18. COHEN, *supra* note 5, at 305, 307.

19. *Id.* at 306.

20. Committee on Patrilineal Descent, *The Status of Children of Mixed Marriages*, http://www.jewishvirtuallibrary.org/jsource/Judaism/patrilineal1.html (last visited July 8, 2014).

21. *Id.*

22. Shaye Cohen observes that the opinion of R. Yom-Tov Algaze of Jerusalem in the eighteenth century actually foreshadows Reform's position. Algaze interpreted the Talmud's matrilineal principle to be applicable only when the child was raised by the mother and given a Jewish identity. Cohen also notes that this view garnered some support by authorities in the eighteenth, nineteenth, and twentieth centuries. *See* COHEN, *supra* note 5, at 321–22.

Following the issuance of the Patrilineal Resolution, the Reform movement issued a *responsum* (legal opinion) addressing the *halakhic* and other justifications for the movement's new position.[23] The *responsum* emphasizes the uncertain basis of the rabbinic adoption of the matrilineal principle, the current social climate with escalating rates of intermarriage, and the adoption and application of past and current eligibility criteria for the Israeli Law of Return (discussed in greater detail shortly), which, according to the *responsum*, embodies a perceived similar line of reasoning.[24] The *responsum* also stresses that by adopting the requirement of public acts of Jewish identification for *all* children of mixed marriages, the movement is taking a more strict line than the current *halakhah*. The *responsum* observes that these more stringent requirements "will lead to a firmer commitment to Judaism on the part of these individuals and that it will enable them to become fully integrated into the Jewish community."[25] Yet, it acknowledges the need for flexibility in determining the necessary "appropriate and timely public and formal acts" deemed sufficient to establish this identity in any given case.[26]

The boundaries of the Reform movement's position on patrilineal descent were tested in 1995 with a question concerning whether a Jewish man and his son could be members of a Reform congregation, and the son enrolled in the synagogue's religious school, when the father is married to a Catholic woman who is raising their daughter as a Catholic.[27] The *responsum* initially determines that the husband cannot be denied membership in the congregation because he is Jewish. That said, because he is allowing his daughter to be raised as a Catholic, he is ineligible to serve in any congregational position of leadership. With respect to the son, however, the *responsum* concludes that his being raised in a dual religion household results in a denial of the presumption of his Jewishness because the application of this presumption now depends "as much if not more upon the quality of the child's religious upbringing as it does upon the circumstances of his or her birth."[28] The bottom line is that

---

23. Cent. Conference of Am. Rabbis *Responsa*, Patrilineal and Matrilineal Descent (1983), http://ccarnet.org/responsa/carr-61-68/ [hereinafter Patrilineal Descent].

24. *See infra* notes 45–49 and accompanying text.

25. Patrilineal Descent, *supra* note 23.

26. *Id.*

27. Cent. Conference of Am. Rabbis *Responsa*, The Dual Religion Family and Patrilineal Descent (1994), http://ccarnet.org/responsa/tfn-no-5755-17-251-258/.

28. *Id.*

the *responsum* questions "whether such a family is capable of transmitting an *exclusive* Jewish identity to one of its children."[29] The *responsum* also notes that according to the Patrilineal Resolution, its decision would be identical if the boy had a Jewish mother rather than a Jewish father.[30] As a result of this decision, the child was required to undergo a formal conversion process prior to being considered Jewish, although he was allowed to enroll in the congregation's religious school to begin a course of study that will enable him to strengthen his Jewish identity.[31]

Reform's departure from the matrilineal principle is a source of significant conflict among the movements. The essence of this conflict reflects both theological and socio-cultural considerations. A traditional Orthodox perspective represents the theological critique. This view, as noted above, maintains that biblical law mandates the matrilineal principle, and therefore, the sages' understanding of this concept cannot be altered regardless of whether sociological considerations arguably militate in favor of a different conclusion today. Rabbi Avi Weiss, the founder of the Open Orthodox movement, articulated an interesting twist to this view. Emphasizing that patrilineal descent undermines the significance of the covenantal relationship upon which the entire Jewish religion is based, Weiss writes:

> In that covenant, God says to the Jewish people, "you are mine, no matter what." In the new Reform covenantal relationship, Jews tell God: "You, God, belong to us, but only if we choose You."[32]

For Jews who adhere to the traditional theological framework, Reform's position concerning the patrilineal principle is completely untenable and a perversion of the *mesorah*. According to this perspective, sociological realities do not alter long-standing tradition that derives from Divine command.

A theologically based objection to the patrilineal principle leaves no room for incorporating historical or sociological considerations into the decision-making calculus. In contrast, Shaye Cohen, who was ordained as

---

29. *Id.*

30. *Id.*

31. *Id.* The *responsum* reflects that there was a disagreement among Committee members issuing the *responsum* as to whether the son should be required to convert before enrolling in the congregation's religious school. The Committee unanimously agreed, however, that conversion was required prior to the boy's Bar Mitzvah. *Id.*

32. Avi Weiss, *The Insurmountable Divisiveness of Patrilineality*, SH'MA J. 7 (Mar. 1994).

a Conservative rabbi at the Jewish Theological Seminary (JTS), argues that the matrilineal principle "was not revealed to the people of Israel by Moses at Mount Sinai but…created by historical Jews living in historical times."[33] That said, Cohen is not advocating the adoption of Reform's change; rather, his view is that "historical argumentation" can be used as justification for changing laws and practices that are otherwise deemed to be in need of change.[34] On the other hand, he admits that history is irrelevant to those who either dispute "the very principles" on which his historical account is premised or who "accept his arguments but contend that [his] historical theories have no consequences for those who wish to be faithful to tradition and to observe normative rabbinic law."[35]

As would be expected, rabbinic leaders of the Conservative movement, steeped in a positive, historical approach to *halakhah*, tend to accept an historical account of the matrilineal principle. Nevertheless, at this point in time, the majority of these rabbis still discount the relevance of this history in determining the *halakhah* on this matter. The Conservative movement has proscribed Reform's position in one of its three standards of rabbinic practice.[36] Rabbi Vernon Kurtz, a former member of the CJLS and past president of the Rabbinical Assembly, has written that the Patrilineal Resolution answers the question of "what is a Jew" rather than "who is a Jew." To Kurtz, born in Canada, "who is a Jew" is a question of status in much the same way as is the issue of American citizenship. An individual might act, walk, and talk like a Jew through the public display of a positive and exclusive Jewish identity, but unless one satisfies the traditional definition of membership, the privileges of Jewish status should be unavailable.[37] Perry Netter, another Conservative rabbi who has written publicly about this issue, criticizes the Patrilineal Resolution on socio-cultural grounds. Netter observes that "the folly of the patrilineal descent decision lies in the hope that this policy will

---

33. COHEN, *supra* note 5, at 348.

34. *Id.*

35. *Id.*

36. *See supra* Chapter 4, note 214 and accompanying text. This standard was approved by the CJLS in 1985 and formally adopted by the Rabbinical Assembly at its 1986 Convention. Carl N. Astor, *The Jewish Life Cycle*, in THE OBSERVANT LIFE 255 (Martin S. Cohen & Michael Katz eds., 2012).

37. Vernon Kurtz, *Who—Not What—Is a Jew?*, SH'MA J. 3 (Mar. 1994).

affect the behavior of intermarrieds and their offspring and keep them in the Jewish fold."[38]

Part of what underlies the marked conflict on this issue is the centrality of the topic. Clearly, denominations differ with respect to their applications of Jewish law, and even their views on the relative importance of Jewish law. That said, prior to 1983, all denominations were in agreement on the boundaries of membership. The Patrilineal Resolution unilaterally altered the playing field concerning this issue. Even some Reform rabbis sharply disagree with their movement's position on patrilineality, based on its impact on the global Jewish community. For example, Rabbi Donald Tam, a self-denominated "Liberal Jew . . . committed to the world view which grew out of the Enlightenment," sees the Patrilineal Resolution as "more harmful than helpful to the cause of Jewish unity and continuity."[39]

Although the composition of group membership arguably transcends other important issues of conflict that operate at the level of individual synagogue and personal observance, there may be additional sociological causes of the marked conflict surrounding the patrilineal principle. Writing ten years after the Patrilineal Resolution, Netter posits that the severity of the conflict in the years following its adoption was the result of "shared impotence in the face of the rising tide of indifference, intermarriage, conversion out, and the projected disappearance of American Jews."[40] Put starkly, he sees "the internecine strife which followed the decision" as "a displacement for much deeper fears, insecurities and a crippling sense of inadequacy."[41]

Regardless of the original and ongoing causes of the conflict surrounding the Patrilineal Resolution, its existence continues to present complexities for Jews, both in the Diaspora and in Israel. As a matter of Jewish religious law, the answer to "who is a Jew" is very clear and has been the same for nearly two thousand years. In contrast, the response to "what is a Jew" requires evaluating the Jewish membership issue from the standpoint of the broader category of "peoplehood." This approach is not linear and will almost always entail a messier application, a process familiar to cultural analysis scholars. The

---

38. Perry Netter, *Non-lineality Means the Destruction of Judaism*, Sн'ма J. 5 (Mar. 1994).

39. Donald A. Tam, *Patrilineal Dissent*, Sн'ма J. 2 (Mar. 1994). In the same issue of this journal, Reform Rabbi Clifford Librach calls the Resolution "a colossal blunder." *See* Clifford E. Librach, *Patrilineality—A Colossal Blunder*, Sн'ма J. 3 (Mar. 1994).

40. Netter, *supra* note 38, at 5.

41. *Id.*

Reform *responsum* discussed above addressing the situation of the dual religion household illustrates the potential for such messiness within the context of North American Reform Jews.

Significantly, however, Reform's change of the criteria of membership from a linear religious perspective to one based on peoplehood has created the need to address numerous issues beyond those that arise in its own movement. Conservative Jews and sometimes even Orthodox Jews want to marry individuals considered by Reform Judaism to be Jewish but who are not Jewish according to *halakhah*. This situation presents difficulties for non-Reform clergy, and their congregants, when it comes to issues such as performing wedding ceremonies, family membership (and leadership positions) in synagogues other than Reform, and attendance at non-Reform Jewish summer camps and day schools by the offspring of such unions. Conservative Rabbi Harold Schulweis wrote about his experience with "Lucy Cohen," an educated, active Reform Jew whose mother was not Jewish. When one of his congregants wanted to marry Lucy, and he had to explain that a formal conversion ceremony would be necessary before such a wedding could take place in the Conservative movement, Lucy left his office slamming the door in the rabbi's face.[42] Further, when the individual in question is a male, he might be surprised to learn that even though he might have been circumcised at birth, his formal conversion will require a ritual reenactment that requires taking a drop of blood from the site of the circumcision.[43]

The situation created by the Patrilineal Resolution becomes even more complex when Reform's current policy is considered in light of Israel's Law of

---

42. *See* Harold M. Schulweis, *When Lucy Cohen's Mother Is Not Jewish*, SH'MA J. 4 (Mar. 1994).

43. This ceremony is known as *hatafat dam brit*. *See* Anita Diamant, *The Covenant of Circumcision*, MY JEWISH LEARNING, http://www.myjewishlearning.com/life/Life_Events/Conversion/Conversion_Process/Circumcision.shtml (last visited July 8, 2014.

A brief article authored by a proponent of the matrilineal principle furnishes a personal example of other difficulties created by Reform's Patrilineal Resolution. The author's brother is an active and affiliated Reform Jew who married a non-Jew. This situation placed the author in an uncomfortable position as he struggled with how to relate to his brother's children within a Jewish context (such as attending a Bar or Bat Mitzvah ceremony or a *brit*, a religious circumcision) given that they are being raised as Jewish but are not Jewish according to *halakhah*. The author laments that although the Reform movement has not made his brother's decisions more difficult, they have made his own "unconscionable." *See* C. Derek Fields, *When Brothers Differ*, SH'MA J. 8 (Mar. 1994).

Return and the control exerted by the Orthodox rabbinate in Israel concerning life cycle matters such as marriage, divorce, burial within a Jewish cemetery,[44] and—significantly for purposes of this discussion—conversion. The Law of Return, initially enacted in 1950, two years after the formal establishment of the state of Israel, provides that every Jew has the right to immigrate to Israel. In 1970, the law was amended to elaborate upon its application. Significantly, it defined a Jew as someone who "was born of a Jewish mother or has become converted to Judaism and who is not a member of another religion."[45] The amended Law of Return further provides that its rights of citizenship extend not only to Jews as defined according to the law, but also to the "child and grandchild of a Jew, the spouse of a Jew, the spouse of a child of a Jew and the spouse of a grandchild of a Jew, except for a person who has been a Jew and has voluntarily changed his religion."[46]

Therefore, as applied, the Law of Return would not bar citizenship for Jews who are considered Jews according to the patrilineal principle (or to their children and even Gentile spouses). According to its terms, the Law of Return applies to the Gentile spouse of a Jewish man's grandchild that is the offspring of a Gentile grandmother and mother. For purposes of citizenship, the Law of Return can more properly be understood as embodying a definition of Jewish peoplehood, especially as it pertains to those individuals who have never formally converted but who consider themselves Jewish and want to be part of the Jewish community of Israel.

Despite the broad application of the Law of Return, complications result from the Orthodox rabbinical control over life cycle matters, including conversion. According to the prevailing position of the Orthodox Israeli Rabbinate, conversions in Israel require the convert to adhere to Orthodox

---

44. According to *halakhah*, non-Jews are not allowed to be buried in Jewish cemeteries. The Orthodox rabbinate in Israel maintained total control over burial until secular cemeteries were created in the mid-1990s. *See* ASHER COHEN & BERNARD SUSSER, ISRAEL AND THE POLITICS OF JEWISH IDENTITY 114–15 (2000).

45. ISR., ISRAEL'S BASIC LAWS: THE LAW OF RETURN (1950), http://www.jewishvirtuallibrary.org/jsource/Politics/Other_Law_Law_of_Return.html (Amendment No. 2, 1970) (last visited July 8, 2014). *See also* COHEN & SUSSER, *supra* note 44, at 33 (noting that the "'Who is a Jew?' controversy is probably the most salient and familiar of secular-religious issues in Israel").

46. LAW OF RETURN, *supra* note 45. *See also* COHEN & SUSSER, *supra* note 44, at 112–13 for a discussion of the history and impact of this law.

theology and ritual observance as preconditions.[47] The state of Israel refuses to recognize as *halakhically* legitimate conversions performed by Reform and Conservative clergy. Until 2011, not even all Israeli Orthodox conversions were recognized.[48] In essence, the Orthodox rabbinate in Israel uses the religious definition of "who is a Jew" for purposes of determining eligibility for marriage, divorce, and burial, whereas the state of Israel uses the "peoplehood" definition for citizenship as embodied in the Law of Return.[49]

---

47. Donniel Hartman, *Who Is a Jew? Membership and Admission Policies in the Jewish Community, in* JUDAISM AND THE CHALLENGES OF MODERN LIFE 114, 129 (Moshe Halbertal & Donniel Hartman eds., 2007).

48. *See Israeli Chief Rabbinate to Accept All Domestic Orthodox Conversions,* HUFFINGTON POST (May 5, 2011), http://www.huffingtonpost.com/2011/05/05/israel-chief-rabbinate-to_n_858251.html. In 2013, an issue surfaced regarding the *halakhic* decisions made by a prominent American Orthodox rabbi in connection with issues of Jewish personal status in Israel pertaining to members of his community. Subsequently, an agreement was reached between the Rabbinical Council of America ("RCA") and the Israeli rabbinate pursuant to which the RCA would take responsibility for verifying the Jewish status of the congregants of any of its rabbinical members, including the rabbi in question, and such decisions would be accepted in Israel. As of this writing, however, the Israeli Chief Rabbinate has not signed the agreement. *See* Yair Ettinger, *Israeli's Chief Rabbinate Postpones Signing Conversion Treaty with U.S. Rabbis,* HAARETZ (June 16, 2014), http://www.haaretz.com/jewish-world/jewish-world-news/.premium-1.572699.

49. In 2002 the Israeli Supreme Court ruled that non-Orthodox conversions of Israeli citizens, regardless of whether they were performed inside Israel or abroad, were sufficient for purposes of allowing these individuals to be registered as Jews by the governmental body operating under the Population Registration Act of 1965, which invokes the same definition of a Jew as the Law of Return (the Court's decision did not address the Law of Return, but dealt only with the Registration question). Significantly, however, the Court did not rule on whether such conversions were valid from a *halakhic* standpoint.

Legally speaking, the Court held that the definition of the term "converted" as used in the Population Registration Act is ambiguous and capable of multiple understandings. Therefore, judicial precedent mandated registration of Jews who had been converted according to Reform or Conservative conversions if these conversions are recognized as valid in the community in which they were performed. The state of Israel argued against this position on the ground that court precedent requires all conversions to be recognized in the community in which they were performed, and that in Israel, the Chief Rabbinate recognizes only Orthodox conversions. In rejecting this view, the majority opinion held that Israel is not the country of the Jewish community but rather the country of the Jewish people, which is comprised of many different denominations. For an English summary of the Court's opinion, see *Israel Supreme Court: Ruling on Reform & Conservative Conversions,* http://www.jewishvirtuallibrary.org/jsource/Society_&_Culture/convert.html (last visited July 8, 2014)

In 2005, the Israeli Supreme Court approved Reform and Conservative conversions under the Law of Return for fifteen non-Israeli residents of the state. *Israel Supreme Court: Ruling on Conversions to Judaism Done Abroad,* http://www.jewishvirtuallibrary.org/jsource/Society_&_Culture/convert1.html (last visited July 8, 2014). In this case, the application of the Law of Return was squarely in play rather than the registration issue. The Israeli Supreme Court approved these conversions performed outside of Israel after year-long non-Orthodox programs of study within Israel.

The large number of Soviet Jews currently living in Israel who are the off-spring of mixed marriages exacerbates the difficulties inherent in this situation. The intensified influx of Soviet Jews in the early 1990s, many of whom are the offspring of Jewish fathers and Gentile mothers, made this issue a real concern for Israel for the first time.[50] Although these Russian immigrants and their offspring may consider themselves fully Jewish and part of the Israeli Jewish community (including service in the Israeli Amy), the Israeli rabbinate says otherwise with respect to those individuals who have a Jewish father but a Gentile mother. With control over conversions lodged in the Israeli rabbinate, such individuals will never be considered Jewish from a religious standpoint unless they are willing to commit to an Orthodox Jewish faith and lifestyle. Israeli parents who adopt a non-Jewish baby face this same conversion problem; such infants cannot be converted in Israel unless the entire family is willing to adhere to Orthodox tenets and practices. If conversion takes place under Reform or Conservative auspices (either within Israel or abroad), the adopted children are not regarded as Jewish for religious purposes in Israel. As a result of these circumstances, there are many Jews living in Israel who are not entitled to full recognition in religious—as opposed to citizenship—terms.

Of course, the Patrilineal Resolution is not responsible for the existence of these political difficulties in Israel. Nevertheless, Reform's adoption of the patrilineal principle complicates the situation not only for Jews in the United States and the rest of the Diaspora, but also for Jews in Israel, who face a distinct set of political issues. The foregoing discussion illustrates why the 1983 Patrilineal Resolution spurred such conflict and how the difficulties created by its departure from the tradition, and adoption of a murkier standard for membership, has impacted the Jewish community worldwide. It has created the need for non-Reform clergy to address sticky and uncomfortable situations and caused difficulties for individual Jews and their families. In Israel, the patrilineal principle adds an additional layer of complexity to a situation that is already fraught with political difficulties and power struggles. Although advocates of Reform's position support the movement's Resolution on both ideological and practical grounds, opponents vehemently disagree.

---

50. *See* Daniel J. Elazar, *How Do the Issues in the Conversion Controversy Relate to Israel?*, Jerusalem Center for Public Affairs (1999), http://jcpa.org/dje/articles2/conversion.htm.

Ritual Conflict: Sabbath Laws on Driving and Electricity

Throughout the ages, observance of the Sabbath (known in Hebrew as *Shabbat*) has been the hallmark of the Jewish tradition. References to *Shabbat* appear numerous times throughout the Written Torah, including the two recitations of the Decalogue that incorporate the injunction to observe *Shabbat*, found in the Fourth Commandment.[51] In fact, observance of *Shabbat* is the only ritual included in the Decalogue.[52] The founder of the Cultural Zionist movement, writer Ahad Ha'am, once remarked that "more than Jews have kept the Sabbath, the Sabbath has kept the Jews."[53] Although Ahad Ha'am was a secular Jew whose life spanned the second half of the nineteenth and early twentieth centuries, his observation still is widely quoted precisely because it evinces a reality for many Jews, not just those who are traditionally observant.[54]

In order to facilitate an appreciation for the legal determinations concerning *Shabbat* that have been made historically and are continually required by modern technology,[55] it is vital to understand the theological underpinnings of *Shabbat*. Several theologically based reasons underlie *Shabbat* observance. Starting with the Creation narrative in Genesis, the seventh day is depicted as the culmination of God's creation, thus differentiating Divine creativity from *cessation* of Divine creativity. The text of Genesis states:

> On the seventh day God finished the work that He had been doing, and He ceased on the seventh day from all the work that he had done.

---

51. *See* Exodus 20:8–11; Deuteronomy 5:12.

52. Daniel S. Nevins, *The Use of Electrical and Electronic Devices on Shabbat*, 7 (2012), http://www.rabbinicalassembly.org/sites/default/files/public/halakhah/teshuvot/2011-2020/electrical-electronic-devices-shabbat.pdf.

53. Ahad Ha'am was the Hebrew and pen name of Asher Zvi Hirsch Ginsberg, who died in 1927. In Hebrew, his name means "One of the People." *See* Hillel Halkin, *You Don't Have to Be Orthodox to Cherish the Sabbath*, JEWISH WORLD REV. (Dec. 13, 2002), http://www.jewishworldreview.com/hillel/halkin121303.asp.

54. *See id.*

55. In discussing *Shabbat* specifically, two Orthodox scholars have remarked that throughout the centuries, technological advances have posed "practical challenges to decisors" of Jewish law, but the advances of modern technology have brought these challenges to an entirely different level. Rabbi Michael Broyde & Rabbi Howard Jachter, *The Use of Electricity on* Shabbat *and* Yom Tov, J. HALACHA & CONTEMP. SOC'Y, Spring 1991, at 5.

And God blessed the seventh day and declared it holy, because on it God ceased from all the work of creation that He had done.[56]

The first recitation of the Decalogue in the Book of Exodus echoes this rationale for *Shabbat* by focusing on the element of holiness. God created the world in six days and hallowed the seventh day by designating it as a day of rest.[57]

Moreover, the Jewish tradition sees man as obligated to mirror God, both with respect to the command to create, and to cease creating on *Shabbat*. The text of Genesis also states, "God created man in His image, in the image of God He created him."[58] God commanded man to "fill the earth and master it."[59] According to Rabbi Joseph Soloveitchik, a leading modern Jewish philosopher and theologian, "the term 'image of God' in the first account" of the Creation underscores "man's striving and ability to become a creator."[60] The Jewish tradition maintains that man is obligated to create to mirror the Divine,[61] and the same is true of resting on *Shabbat*. This interpretation not only emphasizes man's mirroring God, but also the holiness of *Shabbat* because man sanctifies *Shabbat* and in doing so mirrors God's hallowing the day of rest. From this perspective, any activity that evidences man's mastery

---

56. Genesis 2:2–3 (translation from Etz Hayim: Torah and Commentary 11–12 (David L. Leiber et al. eds., 2001) [hereinafter Etz Hayim]).

57. *See* Exodus 20:11.

58. Genesis 1:27 (translation from Etz Hayim, *supra* note 56, at 10).

59. Genesis 1:28 (translation from Etz Hayim, *supra* note 56, at 10).

60. Joseph B. Soloveitchik, The Lonely Man of Faith 12 (1965). Jewish theology teaches that man's capacity for speech mirrors God's, and that man's speech is reflective of his creative capacity in the same way that God's speech reveals His creative capacity. In describing the Divine act of creation, the Torah does not say that God *made* a world, but that He *spoke* the world into existence by preceding every creative act by saying what He will do. "God said, 'Let there be light,' and there was light." The Chumash: The Stone Edition 3 (Nosson Scherman et al. eds., 1st edition, 1993). These "speakings" are referred to as the "Ten Utterances" with which, according to the text, God created the world. *See* Berel Wein, Pirkei Avos—Teaching for Our Times 184–85 (2003).

Even historians who are not writing about the Bible from a theological perspective view this language as furnishing a path leading man to regard himself as a potential creator, thus underscoring an unprecedented parallel between God and humanity. *See* Daniel Boorstin, The Creators 41 (1992). For further discussion and development of these themes, see Roberta Rosenthal Kwall, The Soul of Creativity 11–22 (2010).

61. Rabbi Soloveitchik claims that the Torah chose to relate to man "the tale of creation" so that man could derive the law that humans are obligated to create. Joseph B. Soloveitchik, *Halakhic* Man 101 (1983).

over nature would be prohibited on *Shabbat*.[62] Talmud professor Joel Roth has observed that "if Creation establishes God's supremacy over space, *Shabbat* establishes God's supremacy over time."[63] He adds that these two markers establish "the essence of biblical theology." Roth writes that "God is entirely free from any constraints of nature. God is the sovereign of space and time, and *Shabbat* is the symbol of that divine transcendence."[64]

Another theological basis for *Shabbat* derives from the second recitation of the Decalogue appearing in the Book of Deuteronomy. This text also emphasizes as a basis for observing *Shabbat* God freeing the Israelite people from slavery.[65] Daniel Nevins, the current Dean of the Rabbinical School at the JTS, has written that although the precise connection between observing *Shabbat* and Israel's liberation from slavery is not discussed in the Torah, perhaps "the point of resting is ... to inspire gratitude to God for our freedom."[66] The view in Deuteronomy highlights the social value of *Shabbat* in addition to the holiness of the day.[67]

In addition, Nevins notes another theological basis for *Shabbat*. Drawing from the narrative in Exodus in which the Israelites are instructed to collect a double portion of manna on the sixth day so they can refrain from gathering food on the day of rest,[68] Nevins asserts that "the purpose of *Shabbat* here seems to be an amplification of the lesson of *manna*—to foster a sense of trust in God's reliability as a provider for the people's physical sustenance."[69] According to this view, *Shabbat* represents the ultimate sense of Israel's trust in and reliance on God: "Into a world whose landscape is dominated by visible and massive monuments to human ingenuity and power, the Sabbath

---

62. *See* Joel Roth, Shabbat *and the Holidays, in* ETZ HAYIM, *supra* note 56, at 1456 (noting that modern scholars are virtually agreed on this point).

63. *Id.* at 1455.

64. *Id. See also* ABRAHAM JOSHUA HESCHEL, THE SABBATH: ITS MEANING FOR MODERN MAN (1951) (articulating a theory of *Shabbat* emphasizing its focus on sacred time).

65. *See* Deuteronomy 5:12–15.

66. Nevins, *supra* note 52, at 7–8 (noting also that this explanation has been both approved and rejected by the traditional sources).

67. Roth, *supra* note 62, at 1455. Roth notes that "the two emphases are not mutually exclusive." *Id.*

68. *See* Exodus 16:22–30. The Israelites named the food God provided in the wilderness *manna*. The Torah describes it as "like coriander seed, white, and it tasted like wafers in honey." Exodus 16:31 (translation from ETZ HAYIM, *supra* note 56, at 418–19).

69. Nevins, *supra* note 52, at 8.

quietly but firmly brings the humbling and saving message of man's dependence on God."[70]

Moving from the theological to the legal, the Torah explicitly prohibits burning wood, or any other combustible material, on *Shabbat*.[71] This prohibition of creating fire "is the Torah's most clearly prohibited labor."[72] Still, from a *halakhic* standpoint, the rabbinic tradition rather than the Written Torah determines the particulars of how *Shabbat* is to be observed. As discussed in Chapter 2, during the Talmudic period (the first few centuries of the Common Era), the sages looked to the Oral Law to clarify the biblical commands concerning *Shabbat*. Although the Torah generally prohibits performing labor on *Shabbat* and even specifies certain prohibited activities, the Mishnah enumerates "forty less one" specific labors that are proscribed on *Shabbat*. The sages derived these thirty-nine prohibited tasks, known in Hebrew as *avot m'lakhah*, from the principal categories of work necessary to construct the Tabernacle.[73]

In addition, the sages added a long list of derivations (called *toledot*, meaning "offspring") that they believed to "issue, like descendants" from these thirty-nine more general categories. These *toledot* are biblically forbidden because they accomplish a forbidden purpose via a mechanism distinct from that of the primary labor.[74] For example, planting is one of the prohibited *avot m'lakhah*, and watering a plant is considered a prohibited derivative.[75] Further, the sages enacted additional prohibitions called *sh'vut* that

---

70. Morris Adler, Jacob Agus & Theodore Friedman, Responsum *on the Sabbath* [hereinafter Sabbath *Responsum*], *in* 3 PROCEEDINGS OF THE COMMITTEE ON JEWISH LAW AND STANDARDS OF THE CONSERVATIVE MOVEMENT, 1927–1970 [hereinafter PROCEEDINGS], at 1112 (David Golinkin ed., 1997).

71. Exodus 35:3 ("You shall kindle no fire throughout your settlements on the sabbath day") (translation from ETZ HAYIM, *supra* note 56, at 553).

72. Nevins, *supra* note 52, at 22.

73. *See* Shabbat 7:2 (Mishnah); *supra* Chapter 2, notes 35–41 and accompanying text. The Hebrew term *m'lakhah* used by the sages in their discussion of activities prohibited on *Shabbat* is especially significant because it is the same term used in Genesis 2:2–3 translated as "work" in the narrative discussing God's creating the world in six days and resting on the seventh day. *See supra* note 56 and accompanying text.

74. Nevins, *supra* note 52, at 27.

75. Michael Katz & Gershon Schwartz, *Shabbat, in* THE OBSERVANT LIFE, *supra* note 36, at 127. Both planting (or sowing seeds) and watering "have the purpose of making a plant grow in the soil, but the mechanisms are physically distinct"; watering therefore is a "derivative labor sharing the same goal of causing plants to grow." Nevins, *supra* note 52, at 13.

are "designed to protect the special atmosphere of *Shabbat*"[76] and to prevent people from committing inadvertent violations of the *Shabbat* rules.[77]

As discussed in Chapter 4, the CJLS ruled in 1949 to permit reliance on extralegal factors in its *halakhic* decisions.[78] This development paved the way for the issuance in 1950 of a controversial opinion entitled *Responsum on the Sabbath* ("Sabbath *Responsum*") that allowed driving to the synagogue on *Shabbat* in order to attend services, and also permitted the use of electricity to enhance the Sabbath's enjoyment.[79] Prior to this opinion, the Conservative movement adhered to the traditional position that turning on lights on *Shabbat* constitutes a violation of a biblical law because it is analogous to creating a fire.[80] In addition, the traditional view is that turning lights off is biblically prohibited as extinguishing fire.[81] Similarly, the tradition prohibits driving an automobile on *Shabbat* because starting the engine entails combustion of gasoline to produce power, thereby constituting a prohibited derivative of the biblical prohibition of creating fire.[82] The 1950 opinion by the CJLS concerning driving to synagogue and the use of electricity spurred a significant degree of controversy that continued for decades. In fact, the movement's rabbinic leadership continues to engage in active discourse and write *responsa* on these matters.

With respect to turning on electric lights on *Shabbat*, the Sabbath *Responsum* asserts that this activity does not constitute a violation of a biblical law but rather involves a *sh'vut* and therefore can be set aside for the sake of observing *Shabbat*. The Sabbath *Responsum* relies on the rationale that *halakhah* is designed to be "an instrument of the people" and states:

> In the spirit of a living and developing *halakhah* responsive to the changing needs of our people, we declared it to be permitted to use

---

76. Nevins, *supra* note 52, at 6.

77. Roth, *supra* note 62, at 1456.

78. *See supra* Chapter 4, notes 209–10 and accompanying text.

79. Sabbath *Responsum, supra* note 70, at 1109–34.

80. For a more detailed treatment of a traditional perspective on this and related issues involving electricity, see Broyde & Jachter, *supra* note 55 and sources cited therein. The authors conclude that the overwhelming consensus of authority maintains that turning on an incandescent electric light is a biblical violation, and the majority of these authorities maintain the precise prohibition is that of lighting a flame. *Id.* at 8.

81. Nevins, *supra* note 52, at 22.

82. David Novak, *Riding on the Sabbath, in* LAW AND THEOLOGY IN JUDAISM 24, 29 (1974). For a more detailed explanation of this theory, and a discussion of the other *halakhic* difficulties with driving an automobile and automobile travel on *Shabbat*, see *id.*

electric lights on the Sabbath for the purpose of enhancing the enjoyment of the Sabbath, or reducing personal discomfort or of helping in
the performance of a *mitzvah* [commandment].[83]

Regarding use of an automobile, the Sabbath *Responsum* states that burning
for the sake of producing power is not a violation of the biblical prohibition
of burning because it does not involve burning for the sake of a specifically
proscribed purpose.[84] For this reason, the Sabbath *Responsum* argues that
igniting the engine involves the violation of a rabbinically prohibited activity
and therefore can be excused for the purpose of observing *Shabbat* (as is the
case with using electricity).[85]

Significantly, the Sabbath *Responsum* was issued as part of an overall plan
to revitalize *Shabbat* observance among Conservative Jews, and it intended to
reintroduce *Shabbat* in a way the authors of the *responsum* believed was possible for Conservative Jews to observe in mid-twentieth-century America.[86]
For example, the Sabbath *Responsum* highlights the social reality that most
Jews in the United States do not live in walking distance to a synagogue,
and embodies the value judgment that "the positive values involved in the
participation in public worship on the Sabbath outweigh the negative values of refraining from riding in an automobile."[87] Equally significant, the
articulated theory of the Sabbath *Responsum* emphasizes that, although it
considers social realities, it also attempts to derive its conclusions from the
received Talmudic and subsequent Jewish tradition.[88] It justifies its leniencies

---

83. Sabbath *Responsum, supra* note 70, at 1127 (also stating "[g]reat stress was laid in our
tradition on the duty of having one's home brightly illuminated in honor of the Sabbath").
A minority opinion issued by Rabbi Neulander extended permission to use electricity
to all activities that do not involve *avot m'lakhah* even if such activities are not necessarily connected with the performance of a commandment. *See* Arthur Neulander, *The Use of
Electricity on the Sabbath, in* Proceedings, *supra* note 70, at 1162–68 (Section C of the
1950 *Responsum*). *See also infra* note 102 and accompanying text.

84. Sabbath *Responsum, supra* note 70, at 1127.

85. *Id.* at 1128.

86. *Id.* at 1118 ("The program that we propose…is not to be regarded as the full and complete regimen of Sabbath observance, valid for all Jews for all times and for all places. On
the contrary, it is aimed to meet the particular situation that confronts us, a situation without parallel in the long annals of Judaism."). The Sabbath *Responsum*'s position on driving
to synagogue on *Shabbat* has been rejected by the *Masorti* movement in Israel. *See* Rabbi
David Golinkin, *Riding to the Synagogue on* Shabbat, Responsa for Today, http://www.
responsafortoday.com/engsums/4_3.htm (last visited July 8, 2014).

87. Sabbath *Responsum, supra* note 70, at 1118, 1120, 1129.

88. *Id.* at 1126–29 (discussing these aspects of the tradition).

on both driving and the use of electricity "by applying *halakhic* precedents to the scientific processes by which electricity is produced and automobiles operate."[89] This balancing of current realities with conclusions alleged to be derived from the tradition is characteristic of many of the legal opinions issued by the CJLS.[90]

A minority opinion authored by Rabbi Ben Zion Bokser repudiates the Sabbath *Responsum* and urges a continuation of the movement's long-standing position on these issues.[91] Bokser emphasizes the importance of a *Shabbat* experience grounded in the home and quality family time: "There can be no Sabbath atmosphere, none of its sanctifying or relaxing elements, without the rejection of the things that undermine the home's fixity, and threaten the stability of the family as an integrated unit of human life."[92] He also speaks of the nervous tension that travel imposes and the value of *Shabbat* as "an emancipation from the machines and the complexities" of modern life.[93] Interestingly, Bokser's opinion is "not based on a legalistic interpretation but rather on sociological and psychological argument concerning the spirit and function of the Sabbath."[94] Although Bokser advocates against a change in the law by his colleagues, his rationale generally manifests a cultural analysis and positive historical (rather than Orthodox) orientation.[95] Moreover, toward the end of his opinion, he expressly recognizes that if "[g]iven a choice between travel on the Sabbath or the total denial of the opportunities of worship on Sabbaths and festivals, we would regard traveling as the less objectionable alternative."[96]

In 1961, a question was raised concerning whether the Sabbath *Responsum* could be extended to permit riding on *Shabbat* to a synagogue other than a person's regular place of worship, in order to attend a Bar Mitzvah. In response,

---

89. DORFF, *supra* note 1, at 486 (commenting on Sabbath *Responsum*).

90. *Id.*

91. Ben Zion Bokser, *The Sabbath Halakhah—Travel, and the Use of Electricity, in* PROCEEDINGS, *supra* note 70, at 1153 (Section B of Sabbath *Responsum*).

92. *Id.* at 1157 ("If we want to preserve the Sabbath, then we must create fixed home experience and limit movement away from home, in order that the family be kept together.").

93. *Id.* at 1158.

94. David Aronson, *Discussion, in* PROCEEDINGS, *supra* note 70, at 1169, 1171.

95. *See supra* Chapter 4, notes 205–18 and accompanying text.

96. Bokser, *supra* note 91, at 1160.

the CJLS issued a statement stipulating that its ruling permitting travel on *Shabbat* is limited just to travel for attendance at a synagogue for purposes of worship. Therefore, the statement explained that the reach of its ruling does not extend to "travel for social purposes or…travel to the synagogue in order to attend a Bar Mitzvah ceremony or reception, for the motivation here is not the service of God but the honor of man."[97]

The Sabbath *Responsum* produced a firestorm of protest, both at the time it was issued and for decades afterward.[98] One opponent claimed that the *responsum* was indeed revolutionary in that the Rabbinical Assembly "decided that it was a competent authority to challenge the decisions of other groups in the American rabbinate" and affirm that it has the right to choose leniency in this regard.[99] Over fifty years after the Sabbath *Responsum* appeared, it was still spurring commentary and controversy.[100]

In 2012, Nevins authored a *responsum* for the CJLS in which he attempted to grapple in greater detail with the legal technicalities as well as the extralegal issues involved in the use of electricity.[101] Although his analysis and conclusion with respect to the permissibility of turning on incandescent light bulbs draws from a separately issued opinion to the 1950 *responsum* by Rabbi Arthur Neulander,[102] the responsum by Nevins is far more extensive and addresses newer forms of technology.[103] So whereas he does not believe the use of electricity per se is a violation of the biblical prohibition of burning, he reasons that the use of many electrical appliances are prohibited on the ground that they violate other

---

97. A Statement Adopted by the Committee on Jewish Law and Standards, *Travel on the Sabbath, in* PROCEEDINGS, *supra* note 70, at 1188.

98. *See, e.g.,* PROCEEDINGS, *supra* note 70, at 1169–85 (Discussion); Novak, *supra* note 82.

99. *See* PROCEEDINGS, *supra* note 70, at 1173–74 (Discussion, comments by Rabbi William Greenfield).

100. *See Reflections on the Driving Teshuvah,* 56 CONSERVATIVE JUDAISM 21–50 (2004) [hereinafter *Reflections*].

101. *See* Nevins, *supra* note 52.

102. Nevins reaffirms Section C of the 1950 *Responsum* entitled *The Use of Electricity on the Sabbath,* authored by Rabbi Arthur Neulander. *See* Neulander, *supra* note 83. Section C rejects the argument that the use of electric lights on *Shabbat* constitutes a violation of the biblical prohibition of burning. For a detailed discussion of the differences between the 1950 *Responsum* and Rabbi Neulander's position, see David J. Fine, *in Reflections, supra* note 100, at 33, 37.

103. Specifically, Nevins argues that electric lights are not considered fire, and therefore their use should not be considered biblically prohibited as burning. Nevins, *supra* note 52, at 22. Nevins maintains that "the process, the purpose and the result of using an electrical lighting fixture are all dissimilar to the process, purpose and result of burning wood, gas or any other

prohibited labors on *Shabbat*.[104] For example, the use of cell or smart phones that record information is prohibited as a functional equivalent of conventional writing and therefore constitutes a derivative of the biblically prohibited labor of writing.[105] Similarly, he would prohibit the use of electrical microwave ovens as well as dishwashers (absent a delay timing function) on the basis that they constitute a derivative of the biblically prohibited labor of cooking because they heat food and water.[106] On the other hand, his *responsum* reveals an interesting sensitivity to modern environmental concerns. Nevins asserts that because he does not understand turning electrical appliances off to involve prohibited labor, the principal of "conserving natural resources indicates that we should indeed turn off unneeded appliances on *Shabbat*."[107]

Within the ranks of the Conservative movement's CJLS, it seems as though the views of Nevins are widely accepted, as his *responsum* generated a vote of 17 acceptances, 2 rejections, and 2 abstentions. This vote suggests that at least with respect to Conservative Judaism's lawmaking body, a consensus has developed over the past sixty years concerning the permissibility of using electricity on a limited basis on *Shabbat*. With respect to the driving issue, however, the existence of a consensus seems more difficult to determine. Nevins does not discuss the issue of driving except in a footnote in his opinion, which suggests that he personally does not accept the 1950 opinion permitting driving to synagogue in a gas-powered car.[108] Interestingly, JTS prohibits its rabbinical and cantorial

---

fuel." *Id.* at 28. In supporting his argument, Nevins further emphasizes that the thirty-nine categories of labor the Talmudic sages prohibited "were concerned with *making permanent, or at least durable, changes to one's physical environment.*" *Id.* at 38.

104. *See id.* at 54–55.

105. *Id.* at 34.

106. *Id.* at 21. "Any device which directly heats food or water to a scalding temperature may not be operated on *Shabbat.*" *Id.* at 55. The sages considered "cooking" to be prohibited regardless of the substance in question and regardless of whether the substance came into direct contact with fire. *Id.* at 20. Under this line of reasoning, the use of an electric flat iron to straighten one's hair on *Shabbat* would be considered "cooking" the hair, and thus prohibited as a derivative of cooking.

107. *Id.* at 50. Nevins argues, "If we are commanded to remember the majesty of God's creation on Shabbat, then surely we should not observe it in a way which wastes the resources which God has so graciously provided." *Id.* at 49. It is important to understand, however, that Nevins reaches this conclusion only as a corollary to his conclusion that turning off an electrical appliance is not prohibited labor because were his conclusion otherwise, he acknowledges that "the principle of not wasting resources does not supersede the prohibition" of labor. *Id.* at 49.

108. *Id.* at 77 n.191 (expressing concerns about driving to synagogue in an electric car but indicating that those who accept the 1950 CJLS opinion permitting driving "in a gas-powered car would be justified extending this permission to electric cars").

students from traveling on *Shabbat* but allows more latitude with respect to electricity in accordance with the 1950 *responsum* and the more recent one authored by Nevins.[109]

The Conservative movement's approach to the issues of driving and use of electricity on *Shabbat* also presents a distinct theological perspective. First and foremost, the Sabbath *Responsum* and the subsequent written discussions do not explicitly acknowledge that traveling on *Shabbat* (as well as the use of electricity) is a sin.[110] Perhaps this omission reflects the more fluid nature of legal interpretation characteristic of the Conservative movement, a quality that arguably stems from its emphasis on the human element of the legal sources. This emphasis on human input tends to favor legal interpretations that are more forward-looking rather than backward.[111] When the law is framed in this manner, it also changes the circumstances under which repentance—a fundamental precept of the Jewish tradition—is required. In other words, if the law is not being interpreted to say that a particular activity, such as traveling on *Shabbat*, is a sin, there is no need for repentance for those who engage in this activity. In criticizing the traveling aspect of the Sabbath *Responsum*, David Novak (an ordained Conservative rabbi) states that allowing riding to the synagogue presents a "fundamental spiritual problem": "The assumption underlying this dispensation ignores the possibility of repentance (*teshuvah*). To tell people who are not living according to the law of the Torah that what they are doing is correct is to close the door of return in their faces. It places a 'stumbling block before the blind.'"[112]

We also see this more fluid perspective concerning lawmaking, and its connection to the theological realm, in the discussions concerning whether the use of electricity constitutes "mastery over nature," a theologically based explanation of prohibited activity on *Shabbat*. Whereas Rabbi Joel Roth concludes that operating electric lights should be prohibited for

---

109. *See* Jewish Theological Seminary, *Religious Policies, in* NORMS OF RELIGIOUS IDENTITY AND PRACTICE, http://www.jtsa.edu/Documents/Norms%20of%20Religious%20 Identity%20and%20Practice.pdf (last visited July 8, 2014). With respect to electricity, the JTS Policy recognizes the "significant variety of practice within" the community and briefly outlines some parameters, followed by asking the students to "study and debate these issues." *Id.*

110. *See* PROCEEDINGS, *supra* note 70, at 1182 (Discussion, comments by Rabbi Gordis on the Sabbath *Responsum* pertaining to the issue of travel).

111. See *supra* Chapter 4 discussing *halakhic* theory in Conservative and Orthodox Judaism.

112. Novak, *supra* note 82, at 29 (quoting Pesahim 22b (Babylonian Talmud), interpreting Leviticus 19:14).

this reason, Rabbi Daniel Nevins disagrees.[113] Nevins does not understand using electricity in and of itself to constitute mastery over nature and posits that other permitted activities—even rest itself—can be seen "as an assertion of mastery."[114] As discussed earlier, Nevins supports his theological—or non-formalistic—perspective on this point by invoking an environmentally sensitive theme: "Using available resources and leaving the minimum impact on our environment during the holy hours of *Shabbat* is a way of focusing the mind on the divine creation and on the twin gifts of life and liberty which are mentioned in the Torah and in our liturgy."[115]

From a cultural analysis standpoint, it is important to emphasize that the approach of the Conservative movement's Sabbath *Responsum*, including the opinions of those rabbis who opposed change, is consistent with an overall focus on law as a product of historical context. As discussed, when the law is seen in this manner, it becomes more malleable in both theory and practice. Still, the tradition always is given a vote according to this perspective, and there are boundaries that cannot be crossed despite the law's purported flexibility. Whereas Conservative authorities may disagree as to whether, as a matter of Jewish law, turning on an electric light violates the biblical prohibition of creating a fire[116] or using a microwave oven to warm (rather than cook) food is prohibited as a derivative of cooking,[117] no Conservative authority would approve lighting a bonfire on *Shabbat*. Similarly, although Conservative authorities disagree as to whether driving to the synagogue on *Shabbat* for purposes of attending a prayer service should be permissible, there is unanimity that driving to the dry cleaner after the service clearly is beyond the boundaries of the tradition. Admittedly, this approach is messier than one that draws more hard and fast lines, but the same can be said for cultural analysis in academic terms and for real-life situations in practice.

---

113. Nevins, *supra* note 52, at 37–38.

114. *Id.* at 38.

115. *Id.* at 38–39.

116. *See* Avram Israel Reisner, *A Dissent Justified to Rabbi Daniel S. Nevins' The Use of Electrical and Electronic Devices on* Shabbat (2012), http://www.rabbinicalassembly.org/sites/default/files/public/halakhah/teshuvot/2011-2020/reisner-dissent-nevins.pdf (arguing that creating light on *Shabbat* is prohibited, regardless of how the light is created).

117. *See* Elliot N. Dorff, *Concurring Opinion with Rabbi Daniel Nevins' Reponsum* (2012), http://www.rabbinicalassembly.org/sites/default/files/public/halakhah/teshuvot/2011-2020/MicrowaveOvensOnShabbat.pdf (arguing that microwave ovens may be used on *Shabbat* for warming solid foods and even liquids).

The legal process adopted by the CJLS is significant because it manifests an explicit acknowledgment of the role of culture and sociology in lawmaking. As discussed in Chapter 4, lawmaking in the Orthodox sector is far less inclined to allow these extralegal factors to play a significant role in its decision-making. Although advocates of both the Orthodox and Conservative approaches would claim that certain things are simply beyond the boundaries of Jewish law, their distinct theories of law result in differences as to how these boundaries are drawn. Not surprisingly, there is a spectrum of thought within each camp, but the lines are clearly drawn between the camps. Those in the historical camp accuse the Orthodox of ignoring historical realities and fostering stagnation in the law's development.[118] On the other hand, in the view of most Orthodox authorities, the Conservative movement itself violates *halakhah* because it allows for changes in laws that have been settled by the sealing of the Talmud and by decades of Jewish observance.[119] In the context of the laws concerning *Shabbat*, for example, Orthodox authorities maintain there is no possibility that the received tradition can justify the use of an automobile or electricity on *Shabbat*, and these activities are seen as a desecration of the day of rest.[120] Further, according to biblical law, violation of *Shabbat* is a capital offense.[121] Although Judaism has not practiced capital punishment for two millennia,[122] the seriousness of this matter to some Jews who are observers of *Shabbat* cannot be overstated.

---

118. *See* LOUIS JACOBS, A TREE OF LIFE: DIVERSITY, FLEXIBILITY, AND CREATIVITY IN JEWISH LAW 223–31 (2d edition, 2000); PROCEEDINGS, *supra* note 70, at 1182–83 (noting how the Conservative movement disagrees with the Orthodox view to the extent that it rejects the idea "that the law is unchanging") (Discussion, comments by Rabbi Gordis). Compare the "accumulative approach" to the *halakhic* process, articulated by an Orthodox scholar, which maintains that Revelation is ongoing and therefore the rabbis of each generation have the responsibility to "make Torah law." *See* Aaron Kirschenbaum, *Subjectivity in Rabbinic Decision-Making, in* RABBINIC AUTHORITY AND PERSONAL AUTONOMY 61, 66–67 (Moshe Z. Sokol ed., 1992) [hereinafter RABBINIC AUTHORITY]. Some traditional authorities question the validity of the accumulative approach as articulated by Kirschenbaum. *See* Steven H. Resnicoff, UNDERSTANDING JEWISH LAW 104 (2012); Alan J. Yuter, *Review Essay: Rabbinic Authority and Personal Autonomy*, 27 TRADITION 140, 141–44 (1993).

119. *See* Jonathan Sacks, *Creativity and Innovation in* Halakhah, *in* RABBINIC AUTHORITY, *supra* note 118, at 123, 126–27, 132–33 & n.15. Sacks asserts that it is impossible to combine "historical consciousness with *halakhah*." *Id.* at 141.

120. *See, e.g.*, Broyde & Jachter, *supra* note 55; L.Y. HALPERIN, *SHABBAT* AND ELECTRICITY (1993).

121. Nevins, *supra* note 52, at 4 (citing Exodus 31:14).

122. *Id.*

The Reform movement's adoption of the patrilineal principle and the Conservative movement's permission to use electricity on *Shabbat* and drive to the synagogue for *Shabbat* services are responses to modern social realities such as escalating intermarriage, assimilation, and changing demographics. These topics provide excellent examples of the relationship between the evolution of Jewish law and cultural norms. The following two chapters continue to probe the relationship between *halakhah* and culture in the context of even more culturally laden issues that involve rules impacting specific groups of people based on characteristics such as sexual orientation and gender. Indeed, from a cultural analysis standpoint, the very existence of sexual taboos, such as homosexuality and certain restrictions on women, often can be explained as the result of viewpoints that were once prevalent in society but that are now increasingly seen as outmoded and discriminatory in secular culture. In these contexts, the dilemma of using a cultural analysis paradigm with respect to *halakhah* clearly surfaces. Specifically, although cultural analysis places a value on preservation of the tradition, it also seeks to embrace a more democratic approach to lawmaking that endorses a multiplicity of perspectives. Further, cultural analysis emphasizes the relationship between age-old legal positions (as well as more modern ones) and the cultural norms that helped shape them. The following chapters illuminate these tensions.

6 HOMOSEXUALITY

Two verses in the Torah compose the starting point for this discussion. Chapter 18 of Leviticus begins by instructing the Israelites to refrain from copying the practices of both the lands of Egypt and Canaan and instead to follow only God's laws. This chapter enumerates a list of various prohibited sexual activities, including the following: "Do not lie with a male as one lies with a woman; it is an abhorrence."[1] Shortly afterward, chapter twenty contains a somewhat similar verse in a similar context, with the addition of a stipulated punishment: "If a man lies with a male as one lies with a woman, the two of them have done an abhorrent thing; they shall be put to death—their bloodguilt is upon them."[2] These verses are the only two explicit references to homosexual activity in the Hebrew Bible. They refer exclusively to male homosexuality, but the sages in Talmudic times also prohibited lesbian activity.[3] In sum, the Jewish tradition historically has viewed intercourse between individuals of the same sex as forbidden.

It cannot be denied that across all the movements, homosexuality is seen differently from other types of Jewish law violations. This reality is illustrated by the remarks of one of the most respected Modern Orthodox leaders arguing against the prevalent pattern of treating homosexuals differently from all other violators of *halakhah* (Jewish law).[4] Even for the more liberal sectors of Judaism that do not

---

1. Leviticus 18:22 (translation from ETZ HAYIM: TORAH AND COMMENTARY 691 (David L. Leiber et al. eds., 2001) [hereinafter ETZ HAYIM]).

2. Leviticus 20:13 (translation from ETZ HAYIM, *supra* note 1, at 702).

3. *See* Joel Roth, *Homosexuality*, 616–17 (1992), http://www.rabbinicalassembly. org/sites/default/files/public/halakhah/teshuvot/19912000/roth_homosexual. pdf [hereinafter Roth, *Homosexuality*].

4. *See infra* notes 28–29 and accompanying text.

necessarily understand the Torah to be the direct word of God, the issue of how to respond to homosexuality has been difficult, and the responses have been inconsistent. For example, as late as 1973 the Reform movement apparently understood homosexuality as a sin,[5] despite the fact that during its formative years the movement jettisoned the family purity laws also contained in the same sections of the Torah.[6] Conservative Judaism also has struggled with this same problem, although it has grappled with the *mesorah* (Jewish tradition) directly in attempting to address whether and to what extent *halakhah* can accommodate a homosexual lifestyle.

Homosexuality can be compared to another sexual taboo contained in the Torah—sexual intercourse with a menstruating woman. Even though this prohibition appears in three distinct passages in the Book of Leviticus,[7] it is much less familiar to non-Jews, and even to many Jews. Although the biblical texts treat these two sexual taboos similarly in their explicit prohibition,[8] there are important differences from the standpoint of analyzing these laws in cultural analysis terms. These differences are worth noting as a prelude to this treatment of homosexuality.

---

5. *See infra* note 13 and accompanying text.

6. *See infra* notes 7–10 and accompanying text.

7. Chapter 15 contains the first prohibition, and the text's overall context concerns discharges from sexual organs that render an individual ritually impure, meaning being in a state that would prohibit approaching the Tabernacle, the place of the Divine presence. *See, e.g.,* RACHEL BIALE, WOMEN AND JEWISH LAW 148 (1984). This chapter contains several verses that address female bloody discharge and the appropriate protocol. Although these verses are complicated, they contain an explicit statement that menstruating women are considered impure for seven days, and if a man "lies with her, her menstrual impurity is communicated to him; he shall be impure seven days." Leviticus 15:23 (translation from ETZ HAYIM, *supra* note 1, at 668–69). Chapter 18 of Leviticus, the same chapter that contains the prohibition of homosexuality and other sexual transgressions, states, "Do not come near a woman during her period of impurity to uncover her nakedness," (meaning to have intercourse). Leviticus 18:19 (translation from ETZ HAYIM, *supra* note 1, at 690). Further, Chapter 20, the same chapter that specifies the punishment for homosexual intercourse between men, similarly issues another prohibition against sex with a menstruating woman and details the punishment: "If a man lies with a woman in her infirmity and uncovers her nakedness, he has laid bare her flow and she has exposed her blood flow; both of them shall be cut off from among their people." Leviticus 20:18 (translation from ETZ HAYIM, *supra* note 1, at 703).

8. *See also* Martin S. Cohen, *The Biblical Prohibition of Male Homosexual Intercourse,* 19 (4) J. HOMOSEXUALITY 3, 9 (1990) (noting that in the ancient world of the Israelites, both menstrual flow and semen, the "twin fluids of life," were regarded as possessing special qualities that necessitated particular care and regulation).

The laws concerning menstruation are of *practical* relevance today mainly to Orthodox Jews.[9] These laws are very complex and beyond the scope of this treatment[10] but for purposes of this discussion, it is important to note that their observance is privately negotiated between husbands and wives. If a woman does not comply with the laws, or partially complies, no one (even her husband) will necessarily know. Thus, this taboo has a very private feel on an individual level, is confined in the scope of its practical application, and does not give rise to opportunities for general public debate.

In contrast, in recent years the topic of homosexuality has taken center stage in secular culture. This development has impacted the discourse in many religious traditions, including Judaism. Further, within Judaism, the most visible disputes about homosexuality relate to matters that are very public in nature, such as the performance of same-sex commitment ceremonies and the rabbinic ordination of openly gay individuals.

The first three parts of this chapter discuss interdenominational rabbinic responses to homosexuality; the fourth part relates these responses to the norms of the people to whom they are addressed. The discussion therefore combines a top-down and bottom-up perspective that is consistent with cultural analysis methodology. The goal is to illustrate how all of the major movements of Judaism negotiate the intersection between law and culture when it comes to homosexuality.

---

9. The Committee on Jewish Law and Standards ("CJLS") issued three *responsa* on the observance of the laws concerning menstruation in 2006, the same year it issued the opinions on homosexuality. *See infra* notes 64–70 and accompanying text. All three *responsa* reaffirm the *halakhic* requirement of the observance of these laws, requiring women to immerse in a *mikveh* (ritual bath) following the conclusion of their menstrual periods, although the specifics and rationales differ somewhat in the opinions. Rabbis Miriam Berkowitz, Susan Grossman, and Avram Reisner, the respective authors of the three *responsa*, also issued a joint statement entitled Mikveh *and the Sanctity of Family Relations* (Dec. 5, 2006), http://www.rabbinicalassembly.org/sites/default/files/public/halakhah/teshuvot/20052010/mikveh_introduction.pdf. All three opinions can also be found on the Rabbinical Assembly website at http://www.rabbinicalassembly.org.

From a *halakhic* standpoint, none of these opinions depart from the tradition to the same extent as even the middle ground opinion on homosexuality, discussed in *infra* notes 110–41 and accompanying text. Significantly, however, although the CJLS explicitly reaffirmed the requirements of the laws concerning menstruation, anecdotal evidence suggests that these laws are observed in Conservative communities relatively infrequently and are seldom the focus of explicit discussion.

10. For an insightful case study of Orthodox practice in the observance of these laws from the standpoint of the women who follow them, see Tova Hartman, Feminism Encounters Traditional Judaism 81–98 (2007).

Rather than provide a comprehensive history of the subject within each movement, this chapter highlights the progression and nature of the discourse, particularly in recent decades. This analysis also reaffirms the main thesis of this book. Specifically, *halakhah* and the culture from which it has been derived are inextricably intertwined. When *halakhah* is not directly considered in the decision-making process on any given issue, the result may not represent an authentic Jewish response. In other words, when law and culture are seen as separate domains, it becomes impossible to maintain a shared language and continuity of the tradition. On the other hand, when there is a complete resistance to incorporating a consideration of current cultural norms in *halakhic* interpretation, the tradition may suffer from paralysis. Most important, this chapter demonstrates that a cultural analysis methodology does not necessarily dictate a particular resolution with respect to any given issue.

Reform Judaism

As discussed in Chapter 4, the *responsa* (Jewish legal opinions) issued by the Central Conference of American Rabbis ("CCAR") are considered advisory in nature. Therefore, Reform rabbis, in keeping with the autonomous nature of Reform Judaism, enjoy tremendous individual discretion on matters, particularly those that are highly contested. In 1973, the CCAR issued a *responsum* (singular form of *responsa*) concluding that it is not in accord with the Jewish tradition to encourage the establishment of gay synagogues.[11] The language of this *responsum* is not in keeping with today's social discourse in liberal circles to the extent the language reflects caution about isolating homosexuals and increasing their "mutual availability" to one another.[12] The *responsum* also explicitly reaffirmed that homosexuality is "deemed a sin in Jewish tradition" as well as "in Jewish life practice" but highlighted that the Jewish tradition historically has embraced within the midst of the community those who sin.[13] Thus, despite the particular view of homosexuality articulated in the *responsum*, the paper made clear that homosexuals are not to be excluded from the community of worshippers.

---

11. Cent. Conference of Am. Rabbis *Responsa*, Judaism and Homosexuality (1973), http://ccarnet.org/responsa/arr-49-52/.

12. *Id.*

13. *Id.*

Yet, as early as 1977, the CCAR actively supported the civil liberties of homosexuals and called for the decriminalization of homosexual acts between consenting adults as well as the eradication of discriminatory measures against homosexuals.[14] In 1990, the CCAR adopted the position that homosexuality is not a basis for automatic denial of admission to its rabbinical school,[15] thus seemingly departing from the theoretical premise of a 1981 *responsum* addressing whether a synagogue should hire a known homosexual as a religious school teacher at the high school level.[16] The 1981 *responsum* concluded that heterosexuals and homosexuals whose overt behavior "is considered objectionable by the community disqualifies the person involved from leadership positions in the Jewish community."[17]

In 1985, a very terse *responsum* was issued that squarely addressed the issue of homosexual marriage, concluding that "we cannot accommodate the relationship of two homosexuals as a 'marriage' within the context of Judaism" and therefore, a rabbi cannot participate in such a "marriage."[18] In 1996, the CCAR issued, by its own admission, "an uncommonly long *responsum*" on the same subject, with the majority reaffirming that "Reform rabbis should not officiate at ceremonies of marriage or 'commitment' for same-sex couples."[19] Four years later, however, a large majority of the voting members of the CCAR passed a resolution supporting the decision of individual rabbis to officiate at Jewish same-sex ceremonies.[20] The resolution recognized the diversity of opinion among the organization's membership on this issue and

---

14. Cent. Conference of Am. Rabbis, Yearbook 87 (1977).

15. Cent. Conference of Am. Rabbis, Yearbook 90 (1990).

16. Cent. Conference of Am. Rabbis Responsa, Homosexuals in Leadership Positions (1981), http://ccarnet.org/responsa/arr-52-54/.

17. *Id.*

18. Cent. Conference of Am. Rabbis Responsa, Homosexual Marriage (1985), http://ccarnet.org/responsa/carr-297-298/. The *responsum* also states that "Judaism places great emphasis on family, children and the future, which is assured by a family."

19. Cent. Conference of Am. Rabbis Responsa, On Homosexual Marriage (1996), http://ccarnet.org/responsa/rr21-no-5756-8/.

20. Cent. Conference of Am. Rabbis, Resolution on Same Gender Officiation (2000), http://ccarnet.org/rabbis-speak/resolutions/all/same-gender-officiation/. *See also Reform Rabbis Vote to Allow Same-Sex Marriage*, Beliefnet (Mar. 29, 2000), http://www.beliefnet.com/News/2000/04/Reform-Rabbis-Vote-To-Allow-Same-Sex-Marriage.aspx.

explicitly stated that it supported the decisions of those who choose to officiate at same-sex marriages as well as those who choose not to.[21]

From a cultural analysis standpoint, perhaps the most interesting aspect of the Reform movement's opinions on this issue is the manner in which the 1996 *responsum* addresses the nature and degree of conflict among those who deliberated on this matter. The articulated reason for the length of the *responsum* was that the nature of the discussion fostered "profound disagreements, not only over the specific question of homosexual marriage but also over the nature of Reform Jewish religious discourse."[22] The *responsum*'s explicit acknowledgment that those who were involved in the deliberation "had ceased to share the most elemental kinds of assumptions necessary for a common religious conversation" is especially significant.[23] The *responsum* elaborates upon this difficulty in language that is relevant not just to the resolution of this specific issue, but to any discussion concerning how tradition negotiates between preservation and change:

> In order for an argument to occur at even the most elementary level, its opposing sides must be able to express themselves in a language which both can speak fluently.... In the absence of a language common to all members of the community...argument no longer makes sense, true conversation can no longer take place, and the continued existence of the community as a community, a collective whose members are united by a shared language with which to imagine and describe their deepest commitments, is imperiled.[24]

With respect to the Jewish tradition, the *halakhah*, including its conceptual framework, content, and the process through which it has developed over the centuries, furnishes the shared language of discourse. When this fails to be the case, cultural and religious community disintegrates. This remains true despite considerable disagreement as to how this language ought to be interpreted and applied. Although the Jewish tradition encompasses more

---

21. *See* Cent. Conference of Am. Rabbis, Resolution on Same Gender Officiation, *supra* note 20.

22. Cent. Conference of Am. Rabbis *Responsa*, On Homosexual Marriage, *supra* note 19.

23. *Id.*

24. *Id.*

than the *halakhah*, the law and its interpretation furnishes the foundation for negotiating between the tradition's preservation and change.

Interestingly, the 1996 *responsum* acknowledges that under normal circumstances, CCAR *responsa* authors do look to the tradition—defined as "the resources of the Jewish past, its sacred texts and the history of their interpretation"—when they discuss the questions submitted to them.[25] They state that in this case, however, the "tradition" provides "but the most uncertain guidance."[26] The *responsum* reveals that the committee was even "unable to reach a consensus as to whether Jewish tradition is at all relevant to our discussion."[27] When the *halakhah* is seen as a voluntary component of the tradition rather than an aspirational element, it is easier to label the tradition as either unhelpful or simply irrelevant, as opposed to using creativity to work through the *halakhic* process. This *responsum* reveals the pain of its deliberators, a pain caused not as much by their failure to agree, but more so by their inability to achieve a viable process of deliberation. It serves as a poignant reminder of the cultural analysis insight that in the context of the Jewish tradition, culture without the *halakhic* foundation lacks the necessary grounding to facilitate a shared worldview that is necessary to create community.

Orthodox Judaism

Within Orthodox Judaism, a discussion concerning the parameters of appropriate communal response to homosexuality also has emerged in recent years. This discussion was partially fostered by the popular 2001 documentary *Trembling before God*, which illuminates the struggle of gay Orthodox Jews from a variety of backgrounds. In 2012, one of the most prominent and well-respected Modern Orthodox rabbis, Dr. Aharon Lichtenstein, acknowledged the very public nature of the discourse on this issue. He argued for a greater level of honesty on the part of the Orthodox community in dealing with the homosexual community.[28] He seemed to be saying that homosexuals

---

25. *Id.*

26. *Id.*

27. *Id.*

28. Aharon Lichtenstein, *Perspective on Homosexuals*, PAGES OF FAITH (Dec. 2, 2012), http://pagesoffaith.wordpress.com/2012/12/02/perspective-on-homosexuals/ (posted by Dov Karoll).

should not be singled out for different treatment than other violators of *halakhah*, such as those who do not observe *Shabbat*.[29]

As would be expected, the issues that are being seriously debated in the Orthodox community differ from those getting traction in the more liberal movements. Specifically, it is unlikely that any subgroup of Orthodox Judaism will give its blessing to any version of same-sex marriage anytime soon (if ever), and this topic has not been the subject of a serious debate in academic or popular Orthodox literature. On the other hand, recent discussion has surfaced about whether Orthodox Jews can support gay rights in the secular political arena, an issue that has triggered mixed responses.[30] More significant for this discussion, however, is the current debate on the extent to which Orthodox synagogues should be welcoming to individuals living overt and active homosexual lifestyles, as well as to homosexuals who are less open about their sexual orientation.

Within traditional Judaism, there has been an historic debate concerning how "the community" should respond to transgressors. In other words, should traditional communities be closed to those who do not maintain Orthodox standards of practice or welcome them into their midst?[31] The current dispute within Orthodoxy concerning homosexuality essentially is an illustration of this more profound issue. At one end of the spectrum are those who feel that an Orthodox community does not have to be welcoming to Jews with homosexual orientations or same-sex attractions. At the other end of the spectrum are those who feel that an Orthodox community should be welcoming even to individuals who are openly practicing homosexuality. A middle ground position is that Orthodox synagogues should be welcoming to homosexuals who are not openly gay.

A Torah Declaration signed by over two hundred rabbis, mental health professionals, and other religious community leaders representing the right

---

29. *Id.*

30. *See* Michael Broyde & Shlomo Brody, *Homosexuality and* Halakhah: *Five Critical Points*, TEXT AND TEXTURE (Aug. 1, 2010), http://text.rcarabbis.org/homosexuality-and-halakha-in-tradition-and-beyond/. These authors support "workplace policies of non-discrimination based on sexual orientation," and also argue that one should not feel a need to "combat gay marriage." They currently do not support the civil legalization of gay marriage but arguably leave a window open to this possibility by saying "as this debate develops it will remain important not to overly conflate our religious views with our political stands." *Id.* Some of the comments to this blog post take a position to the right of these authors, and others warmly embrace their perspective.

31. *See id.*

end of the Orthodox spectrum explicitly rejects "the notion that a homosexually inclined person cannot overcome his or her inclination and desire."[32] This Declaration affirms that the "only viable course of action that is consistent with the Torah is therapy" and repentance.[33] It states that the "key point to remember is that these individuals are primarily innocent victims of childhood emotional wounds" who "deserve our full love, support and encouragement in their striving towards healing."[34]

Veering more toward the middle approach is a blog entitled Jew in the City, which features a self-denominated "centrist Orthodox" woman named Allison answering questions from correspondents.[35] Much of her material is geared for popular consumption, and Allison does not claim authority as an expert on *halakhah*. In a post from 2010 entitled "How Can You Be an Orthodox Jew Considering Its Position on Homosexuality?" a correspondent asked Allison, among other things, "When will the Orthodox world offer a sincerely empathetic response to the suffering of its gay members (not one that denies their existence or condemns them to misery)?"[36] Allison's response leaves a reader with the impression that she is somewhere between the middle and right end of the spectrum:

> Now when you mention that the Orthodox community needs to come to a point where they don't "deny the existence of gays," I assume you mean that you hope there'll be a day when gay couples can be openly gay and welcomed in Orthodox *shuls* [synagogues].
>
> I don't think this will ever happen and I don't think this *should* ever happen, but not because I want to "condemn gays to misery" but

---

32. DECLARATION ON THE TORAH APPROACH TO HOMOSEXUALITY, http://www.torahdec.org/ (last visited July 8, 2014).

33. *Id*. The Declaration further provides, "The therapy consists of reinforcing the natural gender-identity of the individual by helping him or her understand and repair the emotional wounds that led to its disorientation and weakening, thus enabling the resumption and completion of the individual's emotional development. *Teshuvah* [repentance] is a Torah-mandated, self-motivated process of turning away from any transgression or sin and returning to God and one's spiritual essence. This includes refining and reintegrating the personality and allowing it to grow in a healthy and wholesome manner." *Id*.

34. *Id*.

35. *See* Allison Josephs, *Do Orthodox Men Wear Suits 24/7?*, JEW IN THE CITY (Mar. 10, 2010), http://www.jewinthecity.com/2010/03/do-orthodox-men-wear-suits-247/.

36. Allison Josephs, *How Can You Be an Orthodox Jew Considering Its Position on Homosexuality?*, JEW IN THE CITY (Apr. 28, 2010), http://www.jewinthecity.com/2010/04/how-can-you-be-an-orthodox-considering-its-position-on-homosexuality/.

rather because being part of the Orthodox community means striving towards keeping the Torah in its entirety. Torah observance doesn't have to be an all-or-nothing deal and no one, in reality, is keeping every single law; but the attitude of a Torah committed Jew is to be working on it all. That means that whatever part of a person's life is at odds with *halakhah* (and we all have something) it should be kept as a private struggle and not highlighted.[37]

In 2010, a Statement of Principles on the topic of homosexuality was issued by a group of Modern Orthodox rabbis and educators, and the number of signatories as of this writing is over two hundred.[38] This position paper, which adopts twelve principles, reflects a middle-ground approach. One of these principles states that regardless of the etiology of sexual orientation, "*halakhic* Judaism" prohibits all same-sex sexual interactions.[39] On the other hand, the paper does "affirm the religious right of those with a homosexual orientation to reject therapeutic approaches they reasonably see as useless or dangerous."[40] The paper also calls for sensitivity on the part of religious leaders to those with a homosexual orientation who live in an Orthodox community. Although the paper explicitly states that "Jews with homosexual orientations and same-sex attractions should be welcomed as full members of the synagogue and school community" and should enjoy full participation "as appropriate with regard to gender," it does not seek to "address what synagogues should do about accepting members who are openly practicing homosexuals and/or living with a same-sex partner."[41] Thus, it leaves this decision to the synagogues and their rabbis on an individual basis, calling only for the standards that are applied for "open violators of *halakhah*" to "be applied fairly and objectively."[42]

The paper also leaves it up to individual communities to decide upon eligibility for particular religious roles, such as the prayer leader.[43] Although

---

37. *Id.*

38. *Statement of Principles on the Place of Jews with a Homosexual Orientation in Our Community*, STATEMENTOFPRINCIPLESNYA (July 28, 2010), http://statementofprinciples nya.blogspot.com/.

39. *Id.* at Principle 4.

40. *Id.* at Principle 5.

41. *Id.* at Principle 8.

42. *Id.*

43. *Id.* at Principle 9.

the language of this particular principle does not specifically refer to homosexuality, it does speak of *halakhah*'s "very exacting criteria and standards for eligibility" and the need for "the entire congregation" to be "fully comfortable" with any given person serving "as its representative."[44] Other principles call for Jews with a homosexual orientation, even those who engage in sexual interactions, to fulfill the commandments to the best of their ability because a majority of *halakhic* thinkers historically have rejected the "all or nothing" approach.[45] Finally, although the paper explicitly proscribes "individuals and communities from encouraging practices that grant religious legitimacy to gay marriage and couplehood," it encourages communities to "display sensitivity, acceptance and full embrace of the adopted or biological children of homosexually active Jews in the synagogue and school setting."[46]

For some rabbis, this Statement of Principles is unacceptable because the "language is too nuanced and in places could be mistaken to mean Orthodox approval of alternative life style and choices."[47] For other rabbis, however, the paper does not go far enough because it fails to advocate for welcoming sexually active homosexuals into the community.[48] For this latter group, there is an articulated sense that Orthodox communities should welcome and embrace active homosexuals, and perhaps celebrate "the fact that two people commit to living with each other forever, raising Jewish observant children together, keeping Shabbos [the Sabbath] as a family, keeping kosher,…and learning Torah."[49]

The most outspoken self-denominated Orthodox advocate for the left end of the spectrum is Rabbi Steven Greenberg, who holds an Orthodox ordination from Yeshiva University and is the first Orthodox gay rabbi to be open about his sexual orientation. In his book, *Wrestling with God and*

---

44. *Id.*

45. *Id.* at Principle 10.

46. *Id.* at Principle 11. The Statement also discourages those with an exclusively homosexual orientation from marrying someone of the opposite gender. *Id.* at Principle 12.

47. *See* Heshie Billet, *Comment to Yosef Kanefsky, An Orthodox Gay Wedding?*, Morethodoxy (Nov. 21, 2011), http://morethodoxy.org/2011/11/18/an-orthodox-gay-wedding/.

48. *See* Zev Farber, *Homosexuals in the Orthodox Community*, Morethodoxy (Jan. 11, 2012), http://morethodoxy.org/2012/01/11/homosexuals-in-the-orthodox-community-by-rabbi-zev-farber/. *See also* Hyim Shafner, *Welcoming Gay Jews in the Orthodox Community*, Morethodoxy (June 26, 2009), http://morethodoxy.org/2009/06/26/welcoming-gay-jews-in-the-orthodox-community-by-rabbi-hyim-shafner/#more-130.

49. Shafner, *supra* note 48. Shafner does recognize, however, that "Orthodox rabbis and communities can't celebrate same gender weddings." *Id.*

Men,[50] Greenberg argues that welcoming synagogues do not require homo-sexuals to lie about their sexual orientations and claims that "this stipulation is really the crux of the matter."[51] In November 2011, Greenberg officiated at what he called a "*halakhi*cally meaningful"[52] same-sex wedding ceremony, incorporating some Jewish prayers and rituals, that was performed accord-ing to the laws of the District of Columbia. He maintains, however, that this ceremony differed, and appropriately so in his view, from the traditional Jewish wedding ceremony known as *kiddushin*.[53] Still, the ceremony sparked heated reactions from even liberal-minded Modern Orthodox leaders,[54] as well as some homosexual lay Jews identifying as Orthodox.[55] According to one report, when asked why he performed such a ceremony if he does not expect any other Orthodox rabbis to do so, Greenberg replied, "Because I am gay. Because I bear a unique responsibility that comes from a personal under-standing of the conflict."[56]

One of the most interesting facets of the discussion of homosexuality within the Orthodox world can be found in a book review of *Wrestling with God and Men* authored by Rabbi Asher Lopatin, the president of the Open Orthodox Seminary Yeshivat Chovevei Torah. In this review, Lopatin criti-cizes Greenberg for failing to play sufficiently with the *halakhah* in a creative way in order to arrive at solutions to the problems being discussed. Lopatin faults Greenberg for not plunging "into the great pool of our tradition, cer-tain that he will be received by water rather than a dry cement bottom."[57]

---

50. Steven Greenberg, Wrestling with God and Men: Homosexuality in the Jewish Tradition (2004).

51. *Id.* at 264.

52. *See* Steven Greenberg, *Comment to Yosef Kanefsky, An Orthodox Gay Wedding?*, More-thodoxy (Nov. 18, 2011), http://morethodoxy.org/2011/11/18/an-orthodox-gay-wedding/.

53. *Id.*

54. *See* Yosef Kanefsky, *An Orthodox Gay Wedding?*, Morethodoxy (Nov. 18, 2011), http://morethodoxy.org/2011/11/18/an-orthodox-gay-wedding/ (but concluding that a nuanced discussion of this issue must be continued, and observing that "the central idea that gays and lesbians who desire to *daven* [pray] and perform *mitzvot* [commandments] should be welcomed into the community of *davening* and *mitzvot*, still makes sound religious sense").

55. See the responses to Rabbi Kanefsky's post on the Morethodoxy blog. *See id.*

56. Steven Greenberg, *A Place for Gays in Orthodoxy*, Jewish Daily Forward (Jan. 11, 2012), http://forward.com/articles/149114/a-place-for-gays-in-orthodoxy/?p=all.

57. Asher Lopatin, *What Makes a Book Orthodox?* Wrestling with God and Men *by Steven Greenberg*, 4(2) Edah J. 1, 9 (2004), http://www.edah.org/backend/JournalArticle/4_2_Lopatin.pdf.

From a cultural analysis standpoint, Lopatin's critique is insightful because it offers the hope that the *halakhah* can take Greenberg where he wants to go when a sufficiently creative analysis is performed. Indeed, Lopatin's point is as much about affirming the creative power of *halakhah* as it is about critiquing Greenberg when Lopatin asserts that "only an Orthodox thinker, who truly has the confidence that *halakhah* can and must work for our world, will work with *halakhah* in the creative and innovative way necessary to derive the true meaning of the sources and Orthodox tradition."[58] The global point here—one that is vital for a cultural analysis understanding of the *halakhah*—is that the "pool" of the tradition furnishes the basis for the shared understanding of how Jews are to arrive at their understanding of the world. Ironically, Lopatin's critique of Greenberg is reminiscent of some language contained in the 1996 Reform *Responsum* on homosexual marriage discussed above. In discussing the importance of tradition, the *Responsum* states that traditions "are inescapably particular; they are the record of a *particular* community's thought, experience, and struggle with circumstance and change."[59] Both Lopatin and the CCAR *Responsum* are affirming that ignoring this "pool of tradition" endangers its preservation; working with it creatively reaffirms its relevance to our current environment. This theme will be explored again in the following section that focuses on the range of responses to homosexuality within the Conservative movement.

Conservative Judaism

As discussed in earlier chapters, the Conservative movement's approach to *halakhic* decision-making permits a greater degree of flexibility than that which is considered acceptable under even a fairly liberal Orthodox perspective. The issue of how homosexuality should be addressed today within the context of a Jewish law framework is very much in the front and center of the discussion among both the leaders and laity of the Conservative movement.[60]

---

58. *Id.*

59. Cent. Conference of Am. Rabbis *Responsa*, On Homosexual Marriage, *supra* note 19.

60. Elliot Dorff has observed, "It is only in the Conservative movement that the issues involved in same-sex relationships are still being actively discussed on an official level." Elliot N. Dorff, *Same-Sex Relationships, in* The Observant Life 657, 659 (Martin S. Cohen & Michael Katz eds., 2012). Although Dorff may understate the degree to which there is discourse about these matters in Orthodoxy, particularly in the Open Orthodox end of the spectrum, he certainly is correct about homosexuality being the subject of intense discourse in Conservative Judaism.

Based on several *responsa* issued in 1992, the Committee of Jewish Law and Standards ("CJLS") issued a resolution concluding that Conservative clergy should not perform commitment ceremonies for gay individuals and that "sexually active gay people should not be admitted to the movement's rabbinical and cantorial schools."[61] Since the 1992 deliberations of the CJLS, the secular legal and cultural landscapes have changed considerably.[62] In December 2003, the CJLS was asked "to revisit the issues of commitment ceremonies and ordination."[63] They deliberated for three years, rendering numerous *responsa* in 2006.

A reading of the multiple *responsa* that were issued in 2006 by the CJLS reveals that they are not responding to a unified issue. Indeed, the specific questions presented for discussion in the beginning of each opinion vary. Although some of the opinions discuss the permissibility of commitment ceremonies and ordination for openly gay individuals, the overriding issue seems to be whether homosexuality is a *halakhically* valid lifestyle choice. In total, the CJLS issued three opinions and two dissents to their decisions. One opinion, written by Jewish Theological Seminary ("JTS") professor Joel Roth, argued that the tradition's view of same-sex sexual relations should be maintained.[64] Another opinion, which passed the CJLS without a majority vote, took the same *halakhic* position but also focused on the possibility of changing sexual orientations with therapy.[65] A third opinion, coauthored by

---

61. *Id.* at 661. Interestingly, "according to the rules of the Rabbinical Assembly, individual rabbis were free to perform commitment ceremonies for gays and lesbians on their own authority; they simply could not claim that they were acting with the endorsement of the CJLS in doing so." *Id.* In 1992, the Rabbinical Assembly passed a resolution calling for the creation of a "Commission on Human Sexuality to study how the Jewish tradition should be applied to all aspects of sexuality, both heterosexual and homosexual." *Id.* at 662.

62. For further discussion of the legal and cultural changes since 1992, see Myron S. Geller, Robert E. Fine & David J. Fine, *The* Halakhah *of Same-Sex Relations in a New Context*, 14, 15 (2006), http://www.rabbinicalassembly.org/sites/default/files/public/halakhah/teshuvot/20052010/geller_fine_fine_dissent.pdf.

63. Dorff, *supra* note 60, at 663.

64. Joel Roth, *Homosexuality Revisited* (2006), http://www.rabbinicalassembly.org/sites/default/files/public/halakhah/teshuvot/20052010/roth_revisited.pdf [hereinafter Roth, *Homosexuality Revisited*]. *See also* Roth, *Homosexuality, supra* note 3. Despite these opinions being separated by fourteen years, the votes were fairly comparable. *Homosexuality* passed with a vote of fourteen in favor, seven opposed, and three abstentions. *Homosexuality Revisited* passed with a vote of thirteen in favor, eight opposed, and four abstentions.

65. *See* Leonard Levy, *Same-Sex Attraction and* Halakhah (2006), http://www.rabbinicalassembly.org/sites/default/files/public/halakhah/teshuvot/20052010/levy_ssa.pdf. This paper passed because it received six affirmative votes, but it also resulted in eight opposing votes and eleven abstentions. *See supra* Chapter 4, text following note 216.

Elliot Dorff (the current head of the CJLS), Daniel Nevins (the current dean of the Rabbinical School at the JTS), and Rabbi Avram Reisner, affirmed the permissibility of ordaining openly gay rabbis and permitting Conservative clergy to perform commitment ceremonies for homosexuals. This opinion refrained, however, from ruling on the *halakhic* status of gay relationships and instructed gay men, based on the biblical prohibition, to avoid anal sex.[66] Essentially, the three opinions that passed reveal two distinct views: one approach understands homosexuality as completely prohibited and the other reflects a more nuanced perspective. Significantly, one member of the twenty-five person CJLS voted for both the Roth and the coauthored *responsa*, insuring that each would receive the requisite thirteen votes for passing with a majority of the CJLS.[67]

The two dissents were considered *takkanot* (legislative *halakhic* changes) rather than judicial ones, and therefore required a majority of thirteen rather than six votes for approval.[68] Neither received the requisite number to pass under these circumstances. One of these dissents, written by Rabbi Gordon Tucker, called for the adoption of an "enhanced *halakhic* method" to override the biblical prohibition.[69] The other dissent was coauthored and focused on contemporary sensibilities to reach similar conclusions.[70]

Despite the multiple and varying opinions issued by the CJLS, those who participated in the deliberations have publicly and privately acknowledged "the high degree of mutual respect and civility" that characterized the CJLS's discourse on this controversial topic.[71] Both the nature of the CJLS's

---

66. *See* Elliot N. Dorff, Daniel S. Nevins & Avram I. Reisner, *Homosexuality, Human Dignity & Halakhah: A Combined Responsum for the Committee on Jewish Law and Standards*, 19 (2006), http://www.rabbinicalassembly.org/sites/default/files/public/halakhah/teshuvot/20052010/dorff_nevins_reisner_dignity.pdf.

67. See *supra* note 64 for a breakdown of the vote on Roth's more recent *Homosexuality responsum*. The vote on the coauthored Dorff *responsum* was thirteen in favor and twelve opposed.

68. Dorff, *supra* note 60, at 666.

69. Gordon Tucker, Halakhic *and* Metahalakhic *Arguments concerning Judaism and Homosexuality* (2006), http://www.rabbinicalassembly.org/sites/default/files/public/halakhah/teshuvot/20052010/tucker_homosexuality.pdf. The vote on this *responsum* was seven in favor, fourteen opposed, and four abstentions.

70. *See* Geller et. al., *supra* note 62. The vote on this *responsum* was six in favor, seventeen opposed, and two abstentions.

71. *See* Dorff, *supra* note 60, at 659. Another participant in the CJLS deliberations, Rabbi Vernon Kurtz, has expressed this same sentiment to the author privately on numerous occasions.

discussions and the diverse content produced by the *responsa* illustrate the Conservative movement's commitment to *halakhic* pluralism. Such a commitment to pluralism is consistent with a cultural analysis perspective of the law.

The following discussion features a comparative analysis of three of these *responsa* (as well as some other material) that represent the spectrum of the CJLS's thinking on this topic. These *responsa* are analyzed to illuminate the role that cultural analysis plays in the development of Jewish law, particularly under the Conservative movement's approach. Therefore, the focus of this discussion is not on the Talmudic discourse contained in these *responsa*. Rather, the discussion emphasizes that despite different results and reasoning, all three *responsa* manifest a cultural analysis perspective to varying degrees. They are a testament to the relationship that exists between law and the culture that produces the law. All three *responsa* explicitly recognize that extralegal factors can and should play a role in the *halakhic* process, and all resort to outside sources and to social realities to inform their *halakhic* analyses. Moreover, these three *responsa* demonstrate that the application of cultural analysis to a hotly disputed subject can entail a wide spectrum when it comes to application of the law. As a methodology, cultural analysis can be used to affirm the status quo, to reinterpret norms, or even to displace the existing systematic process as well as its norms. Regardless of the particular result reached in a given opinion, however, the invocation of the cultural analysis model makes for a richer, and more intellectually honest, discourse.

Cultural Analysis and Affirmation of the Status Quo

Joel Roth's initial *responsum* on this topic, *Homosexuality*, was approved by the CJLS in 1992, and he incorporated this paper into his 2006 *responsum, Homosexuality Revisited*. Roth, who teaches Talmud at JTS and is a former chair of the CJLS, is a prolific writer and a complex thinker. He is particularly known for providing a *halakhic* justification for women being ordained as rabbis in the Conservative movement, a paper that formed the basis of the JTS faculty's vote to admit women to the seminary in 1983.[72] Throughout his career, Roth has substantially documented his legal theory of *halakhah*,

---

72. *See* ELLIOTT N. DORFF, UNFOLDING TRADITION 491 (2005); Joel Roth, *On the Ordination of Women as Rabbis* (1984), http://www.rabbinicalassembly.org/sites/default/files/public/halakhah/teshuvot/19861990/ordinationofwomen2.pdf.

and more recently, he has articulated his theological perspective.[73] An initial consideration of both will be helpful to understanding his position on homosexuality and why it furnishes an example of a cultural analysis perspective being used to affirm the status quo.

From a theological standpoint, Roth distinguishes himself from traditional Orthodox thinkers in that he does not maintain that it is necessary to espouse direct, verbal Revelation of God's word or even an historical event at Sinai as the sole means of the Torah's authorship.[74] Rather, he posits that God can also work through the process of editing, or redacting, the Torah so that the text we have is the result of Divine Providence, thus rendering it the infallible word of God and an accurate representation of His will.[75] In light of Roth's articulated theology, he is able to claim that he is embracing the insights of modern biblical critical theory without compromising his fidelity to the concept that the Torah is infallible.[76]

Notwithstanding Roth's recent articulation of his theology, he regards himself principally as someone involved in the study and activity of *halakhic* decision-making, rather than as a theologian. Roth firmly believes that "since normative Judaism is *halakhic*, the Conservative movement must be *halakhic* if it is to have any claim to authenticity."[77] In light of his membership on the CJLS from 1978 to 2006,[78] he has had frequent opportunities to draft *responsa* for the Conservative movement and to participate in its *halakhic* discourse. Further, in 1986, he published *The Halakhic Process*, a comprehensive work that details his theory of *halakhah* with precision and substantial support.[79]

To a degree, Roth understands the *halakhic* system as one that is circular and insular, and thus he has been labeled a legal positivist by some of his colleagues.[80] Roth maintains, however, that it is "open to question" whether

73. *See* Joel Roth, *Musings toward a Personal Theology of Revelation*, CONSERVATIVE JUDAISM 22, Fall 2012.

74. *Id.* at 25, 32.

75. *Id.* at 30, 32.

76. *See supra* Chapter 4, notes 166–73 and accompanying text.

77. Roth, *supra* note 73, at 28.

78. *See infra* note 131.

79. JOEL ROTH, THE *HALAKHIC* PROCESS (1986).

80. Regarding Roth's description of the *halakhic* process, his colleague Elliot Dorff remarked that "Roth seeks to understand Jewish law as a deductive system, much like geometry, with foundational definitions and axioms, and everything else—or almost everything

he is "correctly characterized as a positivist,"[81] and the discussion that follows illuminates the validity of Roth's point in this regard. Although from a theological standpoint he maintains that the Torah represents the will of God, he also recognizes that the sages' interpretation of the Torah validates their interpretative authority.[82] The result of this posture is that the sages' interpretation also represents God's will.[83] Of course, this perspective raises the issue of whether the interpreters (and for that matter the redactors) of the Torah are objectively determining the will of God outside of their historical and personal situations. Cultural analysis suggests that an affirmative answer to this question is impossible, and therefore, this methodology takes into account the personal subjectivity of the interpreter.

Although Roth's articulated theology does not specifically address the possible subjectivity of the human redactors of the Torah, he discusses this issue at length regarding the Talmudic and other interpreters of the biblical text. Indeed, Roth adopts a bold cultural analysis insight when he recognizes that the great sages of the Talmudic era "cannot be faulted" for failing "to understand how the unconscious attitudes" resulting from personal circumstances "can distort one's outlook, but a modern *posek* [legal decision-maker] who deliberately refuses to make use of such knowledge and such insights as are available to him can, indeed, be faulted."[84] Therefore, a modern *posek* must look not only to the legal sources of the *halakhah*, but also to the "data available to him as a result of the advancement of human knowledge."[85] Both of these sources of data ultimately may be rejected, but "neither can be prejudged as irrelevant and requiring no analysis whatsoever."[86]

As will be discussed more below, Roth's explicit willingness to consider extralegal sources in any *halakhic* analysis allows him to be considered a proponent of cultural analysis methodology, although perhaps not to the same extent as some of his other Conservative colleagues. In *The Halakhic Process*, Roth devotes an entire chapter—over seventy pages—to the relevance of

---

else—following deductively from those." DORFF, *supra* note 72, at 212. *See also* Gordon Tucker, *God, the Good, and* Halakhah, JUDAISM 365, 370, Summer 1989.

81. Roth, *supra* note 73, at 26.

82. ROTH, *supra* note 79, at 122.

83. *Id.* at 151–52.

84. *Id.* at 314.

85. *Id.*

86. *Id.*

extralegal sources in *halakhic* decision-making, and he examines this topic from the standpoint of medical, sociological, economic, and psychological categories of information.[87] By virtue of Roth's candid admission that "extralegal considerations influence not only the abrogation or modification of norms but their original promulgation as well,"[88] he explicitly acknowledges the interconnection between law and culture and even acknowledges how the borrowings from other legal systems "consciously or unconsciously" impact the development of *halakhah* and infuse it with "sociological reality."[89]

In his view, however, extralegal sources do not automatically possess legal significance. Instead, legal significance occurs when "the historical source is affirmed to be the sole rationale for the continued observance of the norm," and the determination of this matter is a subjective one dependent upon the judgment of a particular *posek*.[90] Again, Roth's explicit recognition of the subjectivity involved in creating *halakhah* reveals a sensitivity to the cultural analysis methodology.[91]

Still, the unchecked potential for subjectivity in the legal process always is a concern, particularly for thinkers such as Roth, whose theory of law also contains elements of legal positivism.[92] Roth's embrace of extralegal factors is tempered by his caution concerning the *legal significance* of extralegal sources in any particular case. He claims explicitly that extralegal factors do not "play a part in every legal decision; there are many decisions reached on the basis of legal sources alone."[93] This admission, and the manner in which it

---

87. *See id.* at 231–304.

88. *Id.* at 279.

89. *Id.* at 303. Roth also emphasizes the importance of *halakhic* discourse using the vocabulary of outside sources of knowledge such as the social sciences. *Id.* at 306, 314. This admission constitutes yet another manifestation of his cultural analysis perspective.

90. *Id.* at 265. Roth's caution concerning the invocation of extralegal sources is further illuminated in the following observation: "[I]t is frequently the case that legal sources that were themselves formulated on the basis of extralegal considerations are cited again and again without any reconsideration of those extralegal sources; the possibility of a nexus between the extralegal and the legal sources in these cases remain precisely that, a possibility, no more. If there is no impetus motivating the *posek* to elevate the historical sources to legal significance, they remain legally insignificant." *Id.* at 302.

91. *See also id.* at 304, 314 (noting the difficulty of defining many terms objectively).

92. In concluding his chapter on extralegal factors, Roth reconciles this conflict with his observation that "the only guarantee of the integrity of the *halakhic* system is the integrity of its recognized authorities." *Id.* at 304. Elsewhere in his book, he discusses the importance of legal decision-makers possessing *yirat shamayim* (fear of Heaven), which functions as an essential safeguard for maintaining *halakhic* integrity. *Id.* at 148, 203–04.

93. *Id.* at 302.

factors into his legal applications, reveals his leanings toward legal positivism. Significantly for purposes of this discussion, he believes the use of extralegal material requires "the greatest degree of caution" when a recognized precedent is at stake, particularly when that precedent is understood as a matter that is biblical (*de-oraita*) rather than rabbinic *(de-rabbanan)*.[94]

As a result of his theology and *halakhic* theory and interpretation, Roth believes that the conduct of sexually active homosexuals cannot be squared with *halakhah*. Thus, he believes it violates *halakhah* for clergy to perform commitment ceremonies for homosexuals and for the movement's rabbinic and cantorial schools and associations to knowingly admit sexually active homosexuals. On the other hand, throughout his *responsa* he affirms that homosexuals should be welcome in Conservative synagogues and not denied worship honors or leadership positions.[95]

Despite his affirmation of the *halakhic* status quo on these matters, Roth invokes a cultural analysis methodology throughout both of his *responsa*. His 1992 *responsum* begins with two sections that discuss, respectively, the Torah and Talmud's treatment of homosexuality and the possible reasons for the texts' views. He opens the third section of this *responsum* by "enthusiastically" affirming that "knowledge unavailable to earlier ages has potential *halakhic* relevance today" and therefore, he claims that his first two sections "are insufficient."[96] He examines modern theories of the etiology of homosexuality for nearly thirty pages in order to determine whether they should have "actual *halakhic* significance."[97] Roth's analysis of the modern sources is comprehensive. This discussion does not attempt to summarize fully his findings or reasoning, but instead highlights the cultural analysis methodology that permeates his treatment.

---

94. *Id.* at 304. See also *supra* Chapter 4, notes 137–40 and accompanying text, for a discussion of this distinction.

Roth well understands the theological problem presented here. Specifically, if the power of humans extends to amendments and abrogations of the Torah, their judgment essentially is being substituted for that of God's. ROTH, *supra* note 79, at 201. This problem raises the issue of whether the human action pertaining to *de-oraita* norms should be seen as ultra vires. *Id.* at 201, 203. Roth discusses the systematic justification for allowing such amendments when *halakhic* authorities are properly motivated (e.g., possessing *yirat shamayim, see supra* note 92) and conscious of maintaining the integrity of the *halakhic* system. *Id.* at 201, 203.

95. See Roth, *Homosexuality Revisited, supra* note 64, at 34, for a summary of his conclusions.

96. Roth, *Homosexuality, supra* note 3, at 635.

97. *Id.* at 635; *see also id.* at 635–63 for this analysis.

Initially, Roth discusses psychoanalytic theory first proposed by Freud and frames his response to the argument articulated by others—that new knowledge supporting the non-voluntary nature of homosexuality militates in favor of overturning the biblical precedent because "the moral God would not demand the avoidance of a behavior of one whose attraction to that behavior was not a matter of pure volition."[98] Manifesting a cultural analysis orientation, Roth observes that this argument must be "either answered or accepted" but "cannot be ignored."[99] Although Roth embraces the opportunity to discuss psychological and other areas of modern knowledge,[100] ultimately he concludes that modern findings do not warrant a change in the precedent.[101] He believes that the research supports the possibility for change, at least for some homosexuals. Moreover, even with respect to those homosexuals for whom change is not possible, he concludes that the classical explanations for the Torah's prohibition, which are that homosexuality is "disruptive to family structure and life, unnatural, and nonprocreative," remain defensible and justify the *halakhic* prohibition even today.[102] Roth places reliance on these explanations, which he also discusses in modern terms,[103] in concluding that a moral God can require homosexuals to suppress an essential element of their being in order to further the values embodied in the prohibition.[104] Notwithstanding Roth's ultimate conclusion, his implicit adoption of a cultural analysis methodology is revealed by his inclination to go beyond the texts of the classical sources in his reliance on "the values and principles" embodied in the prohibition as a justification for the law.[105]

More globally, Roth's cultural analysis inclination is revealed by his position that "modern knowledge might well have an impact upon *halakhic* decision-making by providing data which might impel *poskim* [plural of *posek*] to reinterpret or overturn accepted precedents and norms, even ones that are

---

98. *Id.* at 641.

99. *Id.*

100. Roth also analyzes modern sources examining biochemical and sociobiological theories.

101. Roth states that if knowledge of the etiology "holds out the possibility that one who is homosexual can be changed from homosexuality to heterosexuality, the precedent can and ought to be retained, and therapy urged." *Id.*, at 641.

102. *Id.* at 644, 672.

103. *See id.* at 623–35.

104. *Id.* at 644, 652.

105. *Id.* at 644.

de-oraita."[106] He acknowledges that in certain cases modern knowledge that can be proved definitively can furnish the basis for significant changes even in biblical precedents. This admission is a telling sign that he appreciates the interconnectedness between law and culture. Roth's willingness to consider the possible relevance of the externalities of modern knowledge even in cases involving certain biblical mandates places him within the cultural analysis spectrum, even if in this particular case, he feels the modern knowledge simply does not "offer any compelling reasons to overturn the normative *halakhic* precedents."[107]

In Roth's 2006 *responsum*, he attempts to address the arguments of some of his Conservative colleagues who are advocating a *halakhic* and policy change concerning homosexuality. For purposes of this discussion, the most relevant aspect of his second *responsum* is his reaffirmation that it is "critically important for the *halakhist* to study the prevalent theories of the etiology of homosexual orientation precisely because only that investigation can help them determine whether a moral God could demand celibacy of homosexuals."[108] Thus, in both of his *responsa*, Roth articulates the view that a study of the etiology must inform an examination of the issue of morality, a perspective that is representative of a cultural analysis mode of discourse.[109]

Recall also that cultural analysis is very much concerned with loss of value and dilution of a tradition's authenticity. These concerns often prompt cultural analysis thinkers to embrace a degree of selectivity with respect to implementing changes in the tradition. Roth's position is very much representative of this perspective.

Cultural Analysis and Innovation within the Traditional Process

The provocative *responsum* of Rabbis Dorff, Nevins, and Reisner was intended by its authors to work "within the limits of traditional *halakhic* discourse."[110] In other words, these authors desire to work within the system in order to

---

106. *Id.* at 663.

107. *Id.*

108. Roth, *Homosexuality Revisited, supra* note 64, at 32.

109. *See id.* at 27, 32. *See also supra* notes 97–107 and accompanying text.

110. Dorff et al., *supra* note 66, at 1. Despite his strong disagreement with this *responsum*, Roth has acknowledged "for the record" that it does "not undermine the foundational premise of the *halakhic* system." Roth, *supra* note 73, at 34 n.15. *See also infra* note 131 and accompanying text.

arrive at *halakhic* accommodations for homosexuals. Their rationale for this undertaking is made explicit early on in their opinion: "the permanent social and sexual loneliness mandated by *halakhic* precedent for homosexuals undermines their human dignity."[111]

Initially, the authors engage in a *halakhic* discussion on the meaning of the passages in the Torah, and conclude that "the Torah forbids anal sex between men, nothing more, and nothing less."[112] Following this discussion, they examine the rabbinic prohibitions on homosexuality and lesbianism and acknowledge that "the established *halakhah* presents a complete ban on all acts of homosexual intimacy."[113] That said, they also read the precedent as including some legitimate *halakhic* authority from which can be derived accommodations for homosexuals outside of the biblical prohibition that they construe as limited to anal sex.[114]

Moving on from the *halakhic* discussion concerning homosexuality, the authors continue with an examination of what they see as the core issue today—"whether the demand of celibacy that has been made of observant homosexuals is practically or morally feasible."[115] It is clear from the tone and content of the *responsum* that their concern for resolving this issue is driven not only by the questionable practicality of celibacy, but also by their view of the questionable morality of such a demand given their perspective that the current *halakhic* position devalues gay and lesbian individuals and undermines their human dignity.[116] That said, the authors fully acknowledge that this concern for safeguarding human dignity manifested in the tradition generally "is not considered capable of overturning an explicit biblical rule."[117] Nevertheless, they provide a detailed analysis of the Talmudic discourse on

---

111. Dorff et al., *supra* note 66, at 3. In a subsequent *responsum* on rituals for same-sex marriage and divorce, Rabbis Dorff, Nevins, and Reisner observe that "current discriminatory attitudes toward gay men and lesbians do indeed undermine their dignity," citing to empirical evidence of higher suicide rates among gay teens than heterosexuals. *See* Elliot N. Dorff, Daniel S. Nevins & Avram I. Reisner, *Rituals and Documents of Marriage and Divorce for Same-Sex Couples*, 1, 2 n.4 (2012), http://www.rabbinicalassembly.org/sites/default/files/public/halakhah/teshuvot/2011-2020/same-sex-marriage-and-divorce-appendix.pdf [hereinafter *Rituals and Documents*]. *See also infra* notes 133–41 and accompanying text.

112. Dorff et. al., *supra* note 66, at 5.

113. *Id.* at 8.

114. *Id.*

115. *Id.* at 9.

116. *Id.* at 10.

117. *Id.*

this point and conclude that the sages applied the value of human dignity even in cases involving overriding certain biblical requirements.[118] They also furnish a discussion of human dignity in medieval and modern *halakhic* sources, although they acknowledge that human dignity is "seldom cited as sweepingly in later sources as in the Talmud."[119]

Further, the authors underscore how disgrace, the very opposite of dignity, is considered a major offense in Jewish law. They argue that the Jewish community's general refusal to recognize and celebrate families established by homosexuals is shameful and "demands the attention of the larger community."[120] The authors also explicitly recognize that the values of both dignity and shame are not objectively measured; both are "relative" phenomena.[121] Moreover, they explicitly observe that "dignity is a social phenomenon," which suggests that a relationship exists "between the dignity of the actor and the dignity of his neighbors."[122]

Ultimately, the authors conclude that gay and lesbian Jews cannot be assured "an internal state of dignity as long as their social status is one of utter humiliation."[123] Further, given that dignity is a social construct, the humiliation of homosexual Jews also reflects upon the entire Jewish community and constitutes humiliation for all concerned.[124] Given that modern research has established that sexual orientation is not a voluntary choice, the contemporary *halakhic* decision-maker must use this information to alleviate the distress of gay and lesbian Jews who wish to be Torah observant. A failure to do so ignores the *halakhic* principle of human dignity.[125]

The ultimate *halakhic* prescriptions set forth in this *responsum* extend far beyond anything that the Conservative movement had previously endorsed. Specifically, although the ruling reaffirms that "heterosexual marriage between two Jews remains the *halakhic* ideal" and instructs gay men to refrain from anal sex, it applies the Talmudic principle of human dignity

---

118. *Id.* at 12.

119. *Id.* at 13.

120. *Id.* at 12.

121. *Id.*

122. *Id.* at 16.

123. *Id.* at 15.

124. *Id.* at 16.

125. *Id.* at 17.

to supersede the rabbinic prohibitions associated with "gay and lesbian intimate acts."[126] The ruling also welcomes gay and lesbian individuals who are interested in becoming rabbis, cantors, and educators to apply to the movement's professional schools.[127] The authors stipulate, however, that they are "not prepared at this juncture to rule upon the *halakhic* status of gay and lesbian relationships"[128] (as discussed below, six years later the CJLS addressed aspects of this issue).

The authors of this *responsum* argue that they are working entirely within the *halakhic* system in that they not only affirm biblical law, but also depend upon *halakhic* precedent for their conclusions.[129] Moreover, they believe that their *halakhic* rulings will actually foster a greater observance of *halakhah* by enabling Jewish communities to fulfill the Talmudic precept of human dignity. Still, they are aware of how the "concepts and policies" articulated in their *responsum* alter established precedent and thus represent "a sea change in attitude within traditional Judaism."[130]

This *responsum* manifests an even bolder cultural analysis perspective than the one authored by Roth because the authors are adopting a cultural analysis methodology to reinterpret, at least in part, legal norms. Significantly, however, their reinterpretation is conducted within the confines of the existing *halakhic* structure. Even Joel Roth, who disagrees strongly with their position and resigned from the CJLS following its adoption of this opinion, has explicitly stated that this *responsum* "did not undermine the foundational premise of the *halakhic* system."[131] The argument these authors seem to be making is that it is *against* the *halakhah* to read the Torah in any way other than what they propose because a contrary reading diminishes the dignity of homosexual individuals. Thus, they claim that their *responsum* "brings the light of Torah to the regulation of homosexual relations."[132]

---

126. *Id.* at 19.

127. *Id.*

128. *Id.*

129. *Id.* at 18.

130. *Id.* at 19.

131. Roth, *supra* note 73, at 34 n.15. Roth resigned because he believed that the authors of this *responsum* "were so blinded by their predisposition...that they had recourse to exceptionally questionable legal reasoning, should have known better, and undermined the *halakhic* legitimacy of the Law Committee by what they wrote." *Id.*

132. Dorff et al., *supra* note 66, at 18.

Six years later, these authors issued an appendix to their earlier *respon-sum* entitled *Rituals and Documents of Marriage and Divorce for Same-Sex Couples*.[133] In this paper, they substantially extend their original *responsum* by furnishing concrete "ceremonies for gay marriage and divorce."[134] At the outset, the authors reveal their thinking concerning the nomenclature for these rituals and clarify that what is being contemplated here "is still a Jewish marriage" despite a distinct *halakhic* mechanism for achieving this result.[135] The paper offers two model ceremonies: one that closely tracks the traditional liturgy for a Jewish wedding and a second that is innovative. The authors emphasize, however, that they do not employ the term *kiddushin*, the term used for heterosexual Jewish marriage, to designate these ceremonies.[136] Instead, the authors prefer to "create a new *halakhic* structure for same-sex unions and separations that is fully egalitarian," unlike the traditional rituals for both marriage and divorce.[137] The reasons provided by the authors seem to suggest that they are interested in avoiding some of the non-egalitarian and gender-specific aspects of the heterosexual model. For example, according to Jewish law, a married Jewish woman requires a Jewish writ of divorce (known as a *get*) in order to enter into another religious marriage.[138] A woman whose husband refuses to provide her with a *get* is known as an *agunah* and is considered chained to her husband.[139] This law has been the source of tremendous pain and suffering for women whose husbands cannot, or will not, comply with the *get* requirement. The authors of this paper avoid the *get* issue by virtue of their suggested models, but they still recognize that same-sex couples who wish to separate should "have a proper dissolution of their union," and they provide a document of dissolution and suggested protocol for its delivery.[140]

---

133. *See Rituals and Documents, supra* note 111.

134. *Id.* at 2.

135. *Id.* at 3.

136. *Id.* at 4. The term *kiddushin* can be translated as either "sanctification" or "designation."

137. *Id.* at 5.

138. This law derives from Deuteronomy 24:1 (providing that when a woman fails to please her husband "he writes her a bill of divorcement, hands it to her, and sends her away from his house") (translation from ETZ HAYIM, *supra* note 1, at 1127–28).

139. *See infra* Chapter 8, notes 45–47 and accompanying text.

140. *Rituals and Documents, supra* note 111, at 17–19.

The *Rituals and Documents* addendum was put to a vote by the CJLS and passed with fifteen affirmative votes and one abstention. Although the original *responsum* and addendum represent a marked departure from the traditional *halakhic* perspective on homosexuality, for some Conservative Jews it does not go far enough. For example, a letter to the editor of the Conservative movement's lay-focused magazine responding to an article on the subject by Avram Reisner objected to the fact that the two proposed commitment ceremonies cannot be considered *kiddushin*, or "sanctification." The author of this letter laments, "In other words, a same-sex union is not really *holy*. A same-sex partnership still retains its second-class unholy status."[141] Regardless of whether one agrees with the approach of the *responsum* and addendum, this letter identifies a salient difficulty with an approach that seeks innovation within a traditional paradigm. For some, such innovation simply is not sufficient because it takes place within a traditional framework.

Cultural Analysis and Innovative Process

A third *responsum* represents the most radical use of cultural analysis because it advocates not only a partial revision of the *halakhic* system as a practical matter, but also a departure from the foundational premise of the system on a theological level. The author of this *responsum*, Gordon Tucker, is an occasional adjunct professor at the JTS, a pulpit rabbi, and the former dean of the Rabbinical School at the JTS. As noted earlier, his opinion was submitted as a dissent from those decisions that were approved.[142]

Tucker begins his *responsum* by suggesting that the Torah is fallible: "We have not shunned or feared the notion that the texts of the Torah itself, and of the Talmud, were the products of historically unfolding processes involving human hands, and not infallible, self-authenticating formulations of the transcendent divine will in human language."[143] In essence, he is saying that given the Conservative movement's belief that there was human involvement in producing the texts of the tradition, including the Torah, the resulting lawmaking should evidence a greater latitude than that which is found "only by appeal to rules set forth within the proverbial four cubits of *halakhah*

---

141. David M. Cohen, *Letters*, VOICES OF CONSERVATIVE/MASORTI JUDAISM 54, Winter 2012–13.

142. *See supra* note 69 and accompanying text.

143. Tucker, *supra* note 69, at 1.

itself, and to the transformations that they explicitly authorize."[144] Indeed, Tucker laments "the artificial bounds that we have placed on ourselves in terms of *halakhic* method, bounds that have been at odds with our intellectual and theological commitments."[145] At the outset of his *responsum*, therefore, Tucker distinguishes his theology from that of his colleague, Joel Roth.

In light of Tucker's theological position,[146] it is not a stretch for him to conclude that the movement's current *halakhic* position concerning homosexuality is in need of revision. Tucker believes that God's will is represented in the Torah "only imperfectly, in a form that awaits the engagement and honest searching of religious communities that connect to one another."[147] Therefore, in his view it does not make sense to deny homosexuals their need for "love, companionship and family life."[148] His theology provides the basis for his articulation of a new "*Halakhic*[149] methodology" that would "include the more conventional *halakhic* methods but would also appeal to *aggadic* (narrative) texts that have withstood the tests of time to become normative Jewish theology and ethics."[150] Specifically, Tucker believes the "*halakhic* method needs to be opened up to a receptivity to the potential normative force of *aggadah*."[151]

Tucker relies on legal scholar Robert Cover as support for embracing *aggadic* narrative as part of the texts that should be given "legal standing."[152] Tucker identifies certain powerful motifs in the classic Jewish law *aggadic* sources, as well as "the more recent compelling personal narratives of Jewish gays and lesbians" that can be combined "to provide an authentic reading of

---

144. *Id.* at 2.

145. *Id.*

146. The reader should not be left with the impression that Tucker does not believe in God or in Revelation. He understands the Torah as "our first (and...most sacred) expression of God's will in human language." *Id.* at 6.

147. *Id.* at 7.

148. *Id.*

149. *See infra* note 161 and accompanying text.

150. Tucker, *supra* note 69, at 20. See *supra* Chapter 1, notes 125–29 and *infra* Chapter 10, notes 31–58 and accompanying text for a further discussion of *aggadah*.

151. Tucker, *supra* note 69, at 29.

152. *Id.* at 19–20 (citing Robert Cover, *Nomos and Narrative*, 97 HARV. L. REV. 4 (1983)). Also see *supra* Chapter 1, notes 120–24 and accompanying text for a discussion of Cover's influence in the legal academy concerning the incorporation of narrative into the lawmaking process.

the Torah" and the Jewish tradition.[153] In short, Tucker recommends that the strictly legal components of *halakhah* should be "enhanced" by certain types of narratives, both classic and modern, in order to fashion more appropriate results in "relatively infrequent, yet vexing" cases that require additional types of guidance other than the strictly legal.[154]

Tucker's reliance on narrative methodology as part of the *halakhic* process clearly reflects the insights of cultural analysis. Cultural analysis embraces a view of law that is non-hierarchical and democratic. For several decades, legal scholars working in "outside" areas have adopted the narrative methodology as a response to law's hegemonic character.[155] In order to foster a more balanced legal discourse and result, these scholars have emphasized stories from a variety of perspectives, especially those whose views historically have been excluded from the decision-making process.[156] Tucker explicitly embraces this approach by claiming that "if we want to measure *halakhic* precedent against Jewish gay and lesbian reality" perhaps we should "simply…listen to [their] voices and stories."[157] Further, he critiques the existing system on the grounds that its logic "and its precedents do not fit well with the personal experiences and narratives of gay and lesbian Jews, and with the growing moral senses of the community."[158]

Further, Tucker is explicitly critical of what he terms a "positivist precedent-controlled legal method"[159] precisely because it fails to incorporate "moral senses" in the lawmaking process.[160] It is telling that his methodology specifically calls for *halakhah* "with a capital 'H'" in order to distinguish his approach from the current *halakhah* that he sees as exclusively legally based.[161] In this respect, Tucker evidences his view that the legalistic *halakhah* is inappropriately divorced from the more culturally nuanced *aggadic* tradition. Interestingly, although Tucker is the most extreme cultural analysis thinker of the group discussed in this section, he does not appear to embrace the

---

153. Tucker, *supra* note 69, at 29.

154. *Id.* at 19.

155. *See supra* Chapter 1, note 31 and accompanying text.

156. *See supra* Chapter 1, notes 44–47 and accompanying text.

157. Tucker, *supra* note 69, at 13.

158. *Id.* at 12.

159. *Id.* at 19.

160. *Id.* at 12, n.27.

161. *Id.* at 20.

idea that the legal *actually incorporates* the cultural, probably because at least on this issue, he does not feel the *halakhah* itself can be read to support his position.[162] He generally equates the *halakhic* process with "legal positivism" and claims that it provides "objectivity, predictability, and independence of fad that law seems to require."[163] Ironically, this view of the law is inconsistent with a cultural analysis perspective, which recognizes that no law, even one whose root source is Divine, is objectively neutral. In other words, the *halakhic* process itself is the product of cultural elements, a point that earlier chapters have addressed in various contexts.[164]

Cultural Analysis and *Halakhic* Pluralism

The divergent views discussed in this chapter provide an opportunity to examine the intersection between Jewish law and culture more generally. Cultural analysis begins with the premise that law is a product of cultural production. This is true for any type of law, including *halakhah*, whose root source of authority is Divine. As such, cultural analysis is respectful of cultural tradition, which includes legal tradition, given that tradition is a product of cultural particularity. Therefore, tradition is seen as a desirable

---

162. In an implicit response to the position taken by the coauthors of the *Human Dignity and Halakhah responsum, see supra* note 66, Tucker observes that there is no way to read into sources available to us on the positivist methodology the "story of how there is more than one human sexuality, and that loving attachment to a partner of the same sex can, for those constituted this way, be as fulfilling and as redemptive to the human soul as heterosexual marriage can be." Tucker, *supra* note 69, at 27.

163. *Id.* at 8. Moreover, although Tucker explicitly says that law is a "critical element of human culture," he does not seem to believe that law *is* culture and culture *is* law. *Id.* at 26.

164. Tucker claims Roth is a legal positivist. *See* Tucker, *supra* note 80, at 365, 370. Yet, a careful reading of Roth's theory of *halakhah* reveals that he possesses a more nuanced view of the relationship between culture and law in the *halakhic* process than Tucker seems to maintain. Perhaps this is not surprising as Tucker's main point in his 2006 *responsum* on homosexuality is that the *halakhah* as it has been defined and applied is by itself simply inadequate to deal with this issue appropriately:

> The delicate and fruitful interplay between religious law (*halakhah*) and sacred narrative (*aggadah*) is summarily set aside as being irrelevant when it comes to deciding matters of legal practice even though it is a real community and real people that are expected to integrate those rules of practice into their religious lives.

Tucker, *supra* note 69, at 2. *See also id.* at 19–20 for further examples of his view that as it is currently constituted, *halakhah* is divorced from "a more expansive repertoire of legally relevant materials, which include the accretions over time of theological and moral underpinnings of the community of faith."

means of reaffirming group and individual identity. On the other hand, cultural analysis understands tradition as deeply contextualized and historically specific. It also maintains an open view toward the development, or evolution, of tradition as culture changes. This perspective inevitably welcomes the push-pull, or conflict, that is created when those seeking change in the cultural tradition argue for new and different interpretations of the law, and even modifications of the tradition. Indeed, cultural analysis embraces such conflict as it seeks to democratize the formation of the tradition. This democratization can take the form of recognizing a ground-up narrative, a change in the top-down perspective, or both as the top-down process inevitably takes the ground-up narrative into account.

This chapter illustrates how all of the above cultural analysis themes play out in various sectors of the Jewish community when it comes to the issue of homosexuality. Initially, it is important to underscore that all of the perspectives discussed in this chapter place a value on the tradition, even if according to some views, the *halakhah* is not the driving force behind the decisional process. All of the perspectives discussed in this chapter are attempting to wrestle with the tradition to some degree, in one way or another.

In the context of the Jewish tradition, a cultural analysis methodology should affirm *halakhah* as the fundamental starting point because it is the source of the tradition's particularity. Therefore, discounting or ignoring the *halakhah* places the continuity of the tradition in jeopardy. That said, the importance of *halakhah* does not detract from the struggle that can result in some sectors that are engaged in determining the ongoing application of the *halakhah*. Cultural analysis embraces this struggle and thus reaffirms engaging with the *halakhah* on a deep and meaningful level.

The history of Reform and Conservative Judaism's institutional religious response to homosexuality at the rabbinic level shares some similarities, but there are also important differences. Both movements initially issued opinions by their respective rabbinic committees rejecting the possibility of same-sex marriage within the religious tradition and disfavoring, or outright rejecting, the possibility of open homosexuals being admitted to rabbinical school. Yet, once the secular cultural view of homosexuality changed, groups within both movements moved away from their earlier views on homosexuality. Eventually, openly gay individuals were admitted to the movements' rabbinical and other professional schools, and statements and *responsa* were written giving rabbis the choice whether to officiate at same-sex religious commitment ceremonies.

Nevertheless, the processes by which these developments occurred in each movement were quite distinct. When the Reform movement ultimately issued its resolution in 2000, there was little visible attempt to engage with the *halakhic* process in rendering its final resolution. As it was virtually impossible for the movement's leaders to communicate in a shared language in 1996, the year in which the CCAR issued its lengthy *responsum* on the subject, in 2000 it simply issued a statement giving rabbis a choice. This development, when seen through a cultural analysis lens, is problematic because while it embraces conflict, it does so at the cost of failing to invoke the tradition's shared language of communal discourse.

In contrast to Reform, the Conservative movement's deliberations on this issue were completely rooted in the *halakhic* process, even though some have suggested that the results reached in both the coauthored and the Tucker *responsa* were completely beyond the bounds of the *halakhah*. Significantly, the coauthored *responsum* can be seen as a very bold attempt to do what Orthodox thinker Rabbi Lopatin advocates: "leap into the great pool" of the tradition.[165] This *responsum* endeavors to maintain the integrity of the *halakhic* system despite its very nontraditional, and controversial, interpretation of the biblical text. This process enables the authors to maintain the external structure of *halakhah* while tinkering with its internal contents. Moreover, given these authors' belief that it is *not halakhic* to deny gay individuals a viable outlet for their sexual satisfaction, this *responsum* can be seen as a reaffirmation of the *halakhah*'s role in the tradition despite its substantial departure from the tradition's interpretation.

Tucker's approach also differs from that of the Reform movement. Essentially, Tucker can be understood as saying that with respect to some types of issues, *halakhah* by itself is insufficient. Still, he is not maintaining that the tradition is irrelevant to his position. On the contrary, he seeks to redefine the *halakhah* by expanding it to include not just the strictly legal content, but also its *aggadic* or narrative components. Regardless of whether one agrees or disagrees with his proposal, Tucker cannot be accused of abandoning the tradition. On the contrary, he too is attempting to "leap into the great pool" but in a different way from that which is invoked in the coauthored *responsum* and also from the path taken by his colleague, Joel Roth. In contrast, Roth's *responsum* has more in common with Orthodox positions although his methodology also is distinctly Conservative. He displays a

---

165. *See supra* note 57 and accompanying text.

sensitivity to cultural concerns by invoking extralegal factors even if he does not find them compelling in this particular area.

On a theoretical level, cultural analysis suggests that the strength of the Conservative movement lies in its embrace of pluralism. Recall that one rabbi on the CJLS voted affirmatively for both the coauthored and the Roth *responsa* because he wanted to support *halakhic* pluralism within the movement.[166] Still, some are concerned that the movement's pluralistic character will be compromised by a slow creep to the left on this issue within the ranks of the Conservative movement's leadership that will result in delegitimizing the position articulated by Roth.[167] With respect to homosexuality and other divisive issues, it remains to be seen where the "center" of the movement's leadership will coalesce.

Despite the theoretical appeal of pluralism, the opinions of the CJLS can be criticized on the ground that they send mixed messages to the movement's laity, who typically are not concerned with *halakhic* technicalities or the nuance of cultural analysis. One might legitimately ask, therefore, how those Conservative Jews who are paying attention to the deliberations of the CJLS on this issue are processing these opinions. There is, of course, no uniform answer to this question, but a good starting point would be to ask what matters to the typical Conservative Jew, gay and straight alike. As a general matter, Conservative, as well as Reform and other liberal Jews, exercise a significant degree of autonomy in their ritualistic and other *halakhic* observances. They do not see the *halakhah* as binding in the same way as most Orthodox Jews do, and they do not necessarily understand themselves to be "sinning" when they fail to follow *halakhic* norms, such as the dietary laws and Sabbath observance.[168] Given this reality, it seems likely that what matters to most Conservative gay Jews, their families, and members of the movement at large is not so much *halakhic* permission but rather the sociological validation that

---

166. See *supra* note 67 and accompanying text. *See also* Dorff, *supra* note 60, at 666 (discussing the vote of Rabbi Adam Kligfeld).

167. Roth makes a veiled reference to this concern in Joel Roth, *Gufei Torah: The Limit to Halakhic Pluralism, in* TIFERET LEYISRAEL: JUBILEE VOLUME IN HONOR OF ISRAEL FRANCUS 207, 220 (Joel Roth, Menahem Schmelzer & Yaacov Francus eds., 2010). Other Conservative rabbis also have voiced this concern in private conversations.

168. *See* Roth, *Homosexuality, supra* note 3, at 633 (noting that the percentage of Conservative Jews who keep kosher and observe the Sabbath is "not very high"). Given that younger non-Orthodox Jews are even less likely to adhere to these rituals than their parents, his observation in 1992 seems even more relevant today. According to a comprehensive survey of American Jewry conducted in 2013, 31 percent of Conservative Jews keep a kosher home, 34 percent regularly light Sabbath candles, and 13 percent refrain from handling money on the Sabbath. *See* A Portrait of Jewish Americans–Pew Research

is gained from the movement's recognition of same-sex marriage ceremonies and admission to rabbinic and other professional schools of the movement. If this is correct, it is possible to understand the coauthored *responsum* and even the Tucker *responsum* as using *halakhah* for sociological validation, an approach that further underscores the link between law and culture that is emphasized in cultural analysis. Moreover, both of these *responsa* pay tribute to a cultural analysis methodology by advocating an inclusive approach, one that is sure to be welcomed by many Conservative Jews.[169]

On the other hand, it is reasonable to posit that the theoretical benefits of *halakhic* engagement evidenced in these *responsa* may well be lost on the movement's lay membership. Lay Jews do not necessarily have in the forefront of their minds an understanding of how the shared language of *halakhah* facilitates the perpetuation of the tradition. Therefore, although many Conservative Jews welcome the perceived liberal stance of these *responsa*, they need more help from their leadership in order to appreciate the *halakhah's* role in maintaining the tradition's cultural particularity and continuity. In other words, at the lay level, more education may be needed before the movement's membership can appreciate the theoretical advantages of this approach beyond what is perceived as the immediate practical benefit.

The Orthodox responses to homosexuality triggered by the current cultural climate are also interesting and somewhat more varied than one might expect given the explicit biblical prohibition and the uniformity of the tradition. For many Orthodox thinkers, and even some Conservative thinkers such as Joel Roth, there is virtually no wiggle room in the tradition given the theological position that the Divine will has been clearly revealed in the Torah. Homosexuality is seen as a sin. According to this view, it is virtually impossible to overturn the prohibition even if some might desire to do so. As discussed earlier, Roth's theological perspective is reinforced by a cultural analysis methodology to the extent he takes extralegal factors into account in reaffirming his position from a policy perspective. On the other hand, certain Orthodox thinkers might embrace an even stronger cultural analysis approach than Roth to the extent they are willing to "leap into the great

---

Religion & Public Life Project (Oct. 1, 2013), http://www.pewforum.org/2013/10/01/jewish-american-beliefs-attitudes-culture-survey/ [hereinafter Pew Report] (follow "Chapter 4: Religious Beliefs and Practices" hyperlink).

169. *See* Pew Report, *supra* note 168 (follow "Chapter 6: Social and Political Views" hyperlink) (showing that among Conservative Jews, 80 percent believe homosexuality should be accepted by society).

pool" of *halakhah* and attempt to strongly engage the tradition in search of some different answers.[170] In general, however, Orthodoxy manifests a reluctance to engage *halakhah* on this issue given the belief that the prohibition is explicit and absolute. Still, Orthodox communities, both the laity and the leadership, differ on the propriety of whether, and to what extent, Orthodox synagogues should be welcoming of those living an open, and even not-so-open, homosexual lifestyle.

Another interesting facet of the analysis of the Orthodox community concerns the response of gay Jews who self-denominate as Orthodox. Here, we see a split between those who approve of and welcome the efforts of Steven Greenberg and those who vehemently disagree with his agenda. Many gay Jews who identify as Orthodox understand, and affirm, the boundaries of the tradition on this issue and even feel conflicted about more liberal interpretations of the law that can be seen as inviting a slippery slope to other issues that will undermine the integrity of the *halakhic* system. For this reason, many seriously observant gay individuals belong to Modern Orthodox communities rather than Conservative ones, despite Conservative Judaism's willingness to embrace a *halakhic* viewpoint that reaffirms their ability to engage in some types of homosexual sexual relations. This reality gives rise to a rather ironic question: Does the type of *halakhic* permission granted by some of the Conservative movement's *responsa* actually engender negativity on the part of a segment of seriously observant gay Jews because they believe that such permission simply cannot be given *halakhically*?[171]

This question relates to a much larger discussion concerning the relationship between law and culture and how this relationship will play out in the decades ahead given the escalating assimilation and acculturation on the part of the Jewish community globally. A cultural analysis methodology understands law and culture as intertwined on an integral level. For non-Orthodox

---

170. *See supra* note 57 and accompanying text. Asher Lopatin, who is quoted in the text, notes that Joel Roth "ignores any possibility of such *halakhic* play" and observes that "only an Orthodox thinker, who truly has the confidence that *halakhah* can and must work for our world, will work with *halakhah* in the creative and innovative way necessary to derive the true meaning of the sources and Orthodox tradition." Lopatin, *supra* note 57, at 9. As Chapter 7 demonstrates, Lopatin's confidence in the possibility of Orthodox "*halakhic* play" may be somewhat overstated when it comes to issues concerning women and ritual. *See infra* Chapter 7. Interestingly, Roth authored a groundbreaking paper advocating the ordination of female rabbis that was filled with "*halakhic* play." *See* Roth, *supra* note 72.

171. Recall that some Orthodox gay Jews reacted negatively to the ceremony performed by Rabbi Steven Greenberg. *See supra* notes 52–56 and accompanying text.

laity, the culture often is given priority; for Orthodox Jews (clergy and laity alike), the opposite is true. In Conservative Judaism, there is an attempt at the level of the leadership to integrate the law and culture so as to formulate *halakhic* responses that take cultural developments into account.

As the discussion in this chapter illustrates, a cultural analysis methodology does not compel a particular conclusion even with respect to a hotly contested topic that many believe involves an explicit biblical prohibition that conflicts with modern sensibilities. The following chapter tackles an application of cultural analysis in a context that presents a different set of challenges from both a process and substantive standpoint. Surprisingly to some, the question of female participation in synagogue ritual is not nearly as clear-cut as many believe it to be, as a matter of strict *halakhah*. Unlike the issue examined in this chapter, there is no biblical or even Talmudic prohibition on some types of female participation. Yet, over the centuries, a consensus developed in favor of an exclusionary perspective. This type of situation presents an ideal opportunity for applying cultural analysis to support a change in willing traditional communities.

7 WOMEN AND SYNAGOGUE RITUAL

The particular application of the cultural analysis paradigm developed in this chapter concerns female participation in public Torah reading—the first area in the realm of gender and synagogue ritual to be subjected to a serious academic discourse among observant Jews.[1] According to the *mesorah* (the Jewish tradition), a young man of thirteen is eligible to become a Bar Mitzvah. Typically, the Bar Mitzvah rite involves an adolescent being called to read from the Torah, which as a general matter is read publicly from a scroll during certain Jewish services by either knowledgeable male congregants or a trained professional. The Bar Mitzvah rite marks the transition from childhood to adulthood and therefore can be seen as a sign of dignity and personhood. Traditionally, the Torah can only be read in the presence of at least ten Jewish males above the age of thirteen (this service is known in Hebrew as a *minyan* or *minyanim* in the plural). Upon being called to read from the Torah, the Bar Mitzvah also recites, often for the first time in his life, a specific blessing before and after sections of the Torah are read.[2] The tradition of reciting these blessings is known as receiving an *aliyah* (*aliyyot* in the plural).[3] In short, the ability to receive

---

1. Chaim Trachtman, *Editor's Preface* to DANIEL SPERBER ET AL., WOMEN AND MEN IN COMMUNAL PRAYER: *HALAKHIC* PERSPECTIVES (Chaim Trachtman ed., 2010) [hereinafter COMMUNAL PRAYER].

2. The Bar Mitzvah ceremony traces its origins to Germany in the Middle Ages. *See* IVAN G. MARCUS, THE JEWISH LIFE CYCLE 40 (2004) (noting that this ceremony "reached a recognizable shape no earlier than the sixteenth century, and even then, only in central Europe").

3. A Bar Mitzvah ceremony typically occurs on the Sabbath morning (Saturday), but it can take place anytime the Torah is publicly read. According to the *mesorah*, the Torah also is read publicly every Monday and Thursday morning and every Saturday afternoon, *see* Bava Kamma 82a (Babylonian Talmud), as well as on numerous festivals and holidays throughout the year. As a general matter,

an *aliyah* and read from the Torah represents a vital aspect of traditional synagogue observance. The act of reading from the Torah can be extremely spiritually satisfying because it enables the reader to connect with the narratives and history of his people in a visceral, compelling manner as the ancient text comes alive through the Hebrew words and the traditional accompanying musical tropes.

Significantly, according to the normative *halakhah* (Jewish law), women are not eligible to receive an *aliyah* or to read publicly from the Torah during a *minyan*. This is the practice in virtually every Orthodox synagogue today throughout the world. In contrast, non-Orthodox synagogues do not adhere to the traditional practice and allow greater female participation in the service to varying degrees. Thus, in 2002, the Conservative movement's Committee on Jewish Law and Standards ("CJLS") voted that women may count in a *minyan* and lead the prayer service.[4] Although not all Conservative synagogues allow women to participate in these ways, the majority do allow women to read publicly from the Torah and to receive an *aliyah*.[5]

The story of women and public Torah reading provides an ideal subject for exploring the synergies among law, culture, and tradition and how a cultural analysis perspective can illuminate these synergies. This chapter argues that Orthodoxy's exclusion of women in this regard is more the result of cultural sensibilities rather than unalterable law, a point that is not widely acknowledged in most Orthodox circles. The analysis demonstrates that unanimity within Orthodoxy concerning women's inability to participate in public Torah reading exists despite significant ambiguity in the strictly legal realm of the tradition up until the Middle Ages. Given this ambiguity, and the process of how change comes about within *halakhah*, the current legal reality is best understood as a response to cultural influences. Thus, the introduction of greater female participation in synagogue ritual can be understood as a natural development in *halakhah* based on current understandings of the role and character of women in today's cultural milieu rather than as a

---

various male members of the congregation are customarily granted the honor of saying the *aliyah* blessings accompanying the readings. The number of *aliyyot* varies according to the particular type of service, and ranges from three to seven. *See* Megillah 4:1–2 (Mishnah).

4. *See* David J. Fine, Comm. on Jewish Law and Standards of the Rabbinical Assembly, Women and the *Minyan* (2002), https://www.rabbinicalassembly.org/sites/default/files/public/halakhah/teshuvot/19912000/oh_55_1_2002.pdf.

5. E-mail from Rabbi Vernon Kurtz, former member of the lawmaking body of the Conservative movement and past president of the movement's Rabbinical Assembly, to author (Jan. 1, 2012, 9:42 p.m. CST).

"major reform" necessitating a substantial departure from the tradition. In other words, from a strictly *halakhic* standpoint, there is a basis in the tradition to enable women to receive *aliyyot* and to read publicly from the Torah.

Notwithstanding the resistance to greater female participation in synagogue ritual, the academic literature in certain Orthodox circles is manifesting an increasing awareness of, and interest in, allowing more ritualistic participation for women in public Torah reading. In recent years, much literature has been generated that examines both sides of this issue.[6] The emergence of this discourse within Orthodoxy is significant not only because of its substance and growing impact in academic and certain lay circles, but also because of the identity of those who are arguing in favor of a more inclusive, culturally based *halakhic* position. These proponents of change are not marginally committed to the *halakhic* system but are, instead, serious Orthodox Jews whose Orthodox self-identity and pedigree are not in question.[7] One proponent, Professor Daniel Sperber, is an internationally renowned Jewish law scholar and rabbi whose reputation and erudite learning is readily acknowledged in the Orthodox world.[8] Equally significant, some who oppose such changes in the system are highly respected Orthodox scholars who are taking the arguments of the other side seriously and engaging in respectful, honest discourse.[9]

---

6. Several articles arguing both sides have appeared in *Tradition*, a premier Orthodox journal in the United States. *See* Yosef Kanefsky, Letter to the Editor, *Communications: Women's* Aliyyot *in Contemporary Synagogues*, 40 TRADITION 116, Spring 2007; Aharon Lichtenstein, *The Human and Social Factor in* Halakha, 36 TRADITION 1, Spring 2002; Gideon Rothstein, *Women's* Aliyyot *in Contemporary Synagogues*, 39 TRADITION 36, Summer 2005; Mendel Shapiro, Letter to the Editor, *Communications: Women's* Aliyyot *in Contemporary Synagogues*, 40 TRADITION 107, Spring 2007. In 2010, an entire book was devoted to the topic, with essays also advocating diverse perspectives. *See generally* COMMUNAL PRAYER, *supra* note 1. In 2013, *Tradition* published an extensive *halakhic* analysis of this issue advocating the normative position. *See* Aryeh A. Frimer & Dov I. Frimer, *Women*, Kri'at haTorah *and* Aliyyot, 46 TRADITION 67, Winter 2013.

7. *See* Tamar Ross, *Balancing Tradition and Modernity: The Case for Women's Participation in Synagogue Ritual, in* COMMUNAL PRAYER, *supra* note 1, at 1, 2 (noting that "finding a… legal basis for such an innovation" is the "prime concern" among a group of these proponents).

8. Daniel Sperber is a chaired professor emeritus in the Talmud Department at Bar Ilan University and currently serves as president of its Higher Institute of Torah Study. He also serves as the rabbi of Congregation Menachem Zion in the Old City of Jerusalem.

9. *See* Shlomo Riskin, *Torah* Aliyyot *for Women, in* COMMUNAL PRAYER, *supra* note 1, at 359; Eliav Shochetman, Aliyyot *for Women, in* COMMUNAL PRAYER, *supra* note 1, at 291; *see also* Daniel Sperber, *Congregational Dignity and Human Dignity: Women and Public Torah Reading, in* COMMUNAL PRAYER, *supra* note 1, at 37 n.7 (acknowledging the thorough, detailed commentary of Professor Eliav Shochetman, whom he calls a good friend, appearing in the same volume).

Orthodox scholars who advocate for increased participation by women in public Torah reading interpret the traditional Jewish sources in light of historical and sociological sensibilities.[10] Thus, the proponents of increased participation for women in public Torah reading are invoking a cultural analysis approach to Jewish law, although this approach is not explicitly acknowledged in the *halakhic* discourse.[11] Equally significant, even some scholars who disagree with the conclusion that women should be allowed greater opportunities for participation are now couching their arguments, at least to some extent, in culturally based reasons, presumably in response to a mode of discourse that is beginning to take cultural considerations into account.[12]

This chapter initially discusses some of the classical Jewish law sources governing public Torah reading and *aliyyot* for women in a *minyan* of ten males. It then applies the cultural analysis paradigm to the issue of female participation in public Torah reading. In addressing how cultural analysis can be applied to shape the discourse of Jewish law in this area, the discussion explores the cultural underpinnings of the *mesorah's* perspective on women and the historical resistance of *halakhah* to feminism. It then examines competing arguments and recent developments that may bring more inclusivity to willing Orthodox communities.

---

10. *See* Sperber, *supra* note 9, at 123. Interestingly, Mendel Shapiro, who authored the seminal article on this issue, took a much more traditional, textual approach to the subject. Mendel Shapiro, Qeri'at ha-Torah *by Women: A* Halakhic *Analysis, in* COMMUNAL PRAYER, *supra* note 1, at 207, 209 [hereinafter Shapiro, Qeri'at ha-Torah] (with new afterword) (originally published without Afterword in 1 EDAH J., no. 2, 2002). Subsequently, Shapiro explained his original approach as the "editorial means that was called for to drive a wedge into accepted and received *halakhic* interpretation and to make room for innovative *halakhic* possibility." Mendel Shapiro, *Afterword* to Qeri'at ha-Torah *by Women: A* Halakhic *Analysis, in* COMMUNAL PRAYER, *supra* note 1, at 289 [hereinafter Shapiro, *Afterword*].

11. *Cf.* Ross, *supra* note 7, at 8–9 (comparing *halakhic* discourse and feminist jurisprudence).

12. *See* Shapiro, *Afterword, supra* note 10, at 290 (commending the counterarguments by Rabbi Henkin and Professor Shochetman as "compelling" for their sociological focus). On the dust cover of COMMUNAL PRAYER, Samuel C. Heilman, a professor of sociology, wrote that the issue examined in this chapter "serves *as the key to discovering how Jewish law and changing social and cultural norms interact in important ways....*" Samuel C. Heilman, *Comment on Book Cover* of COMMUNAL PRAYER, *supra* note 1 (emphasis added).

The Classical Jewish Law Sources Governing Torah Reading and *Aliyyot* for Women

The following discussion of the Jewish law sources begins with the oldest sources addressing female participation in the Torah service and then examines subsequent interpretations of these sources by ancient and modern commentators. The oldest sources date back to the Talmudic period and thus serve as the foundation for all subsequent Jewish law discussions.

Talmudic Sources

The issue of women and public Torah reading is one area in which the Babylonian Talmud lacks clarity. The relevant Talmudic text derives from an even earlier rabbinic source called a *baraita*. It states

> Our Rabbis taught: All may be included among the seven [called to the Torah on *Shabbat*], even a minor and a woman, but the Sages said that a woman should not read in the Torah because of the dignity of the congregation [*kevod ha-tsibbur*].[13]

Even a cursory reading of this language shows that it furnishes conflicting messages. The first clause indicates that women may be called to the Torah on the Sabbath (*Shabbat*), but the second clause cautions against women reading from the Torah, based on the more vague concept of the "dignity of the congregation" (*kevod ha-tsibbur*). According to one commentator, the Talmud contains "almost no further discussion of this point," and he therefore asks whether the Talmud's position concerning women in this regard is "a rabbinic decree, good advice, or something else?"[14]

Some argue that the overall language of the Talmudic text exhibits ambiguity as a result of the conflicting clauses concerning women's participation. Others conclude the Talmud's language that women should not read publicly from the Torah is unambiguous, but the text still leaves open the question

---

13. Megillah 23a (Babylonian Talmud), as translated in Shapiro, Qeri'at ha-Torah, *supra* note 10, at 211.

14. Michael Broyde, *Women Receiving* Aliyyot: *A Short* Halakhic *Analysis, in* Jewish L. Ass'n, "Wisdom and Understanding": Studies in Honour of Bernard S. Jackson 2 (2011).

whether the sages' statement that women cannot read from the Torah is an immutable ruling or whether its prescription is changeable if the underlying reason for its position changes. In other words, is the "dignity of the community" a relevant concept based on local *minhag* (custom) or "a durable, timeless perception that withstands shifting cultural sensibilities"?[15]

Had the Talmud conclusively decided that females are not categorically eligible to be called to the Torah for an *aliyah* or to read publicly from the Torah during a *minyan*, it would be more difficult to challenge this conclusion under a traditional *halakhic* perspective. According to Sperber, however, as the language in the Talmud stands, it displays "an uncertainty regarding a matter of rabbinic law."[16] In contrast, Professor Eliav Shochetman writes that even if the beginning of the *baraita* represents a minority opinion, the Talmud did not codify the *halakhah* according to this view, and therefore, "post-Talmudic rabbis lack the authority to rule according to the logically sound minority opinion."[17]

There is a parallel, but separate, early rabbinic text addressing this same matter in a distinct compilation called the Tosefta. This text provides

All may be included among the seven [called to the Torah on *Shabbat*], even a woman, even a minor. We do not bring a woman to read to the public.[18]

The text in the Tosefta dates from the same period as the text in the Talmud,[19] and it also exhibits an internal contradiction. Rabbi Mendel Shapiro, a committed Orthodox Jew living in Israel and a lawyer who wrote the first extensive legal analysis advocating increased participation for women in public Torah reading, notes that the Tosefta's language leaves "open the possibility that there may be circumstances where a woman might read."[20]

Significantly, whether women may engage in these activities was never addressed directly until very recently. Therefore, it is reasonable to argue that this is one of those historically gray areas lacking specific prohibitions

---

15. Shapiro, Qeri'at ha-Torah, *supra* note 10, at 241. For a further discussion of communal dignity, see *infra* notes 43–61 and accompanying text.

16. Sperber, *supra* note 9, at 53.

17. Shochetman, *supra* note 9, at 329.

18. Megillah 3:5 (Tosefta).

19. Sperber, *supra* note 9, at 49.

20. Shapiro, Qeri'at ha-Torah, *supra* note 10, at 234.

or instructions delineating a clear-cut mandatory legal position. The classic legal discourse on the issues of women publicly reading from the Torah and receiving *aliyyot* centers around two basic questions: (1) are women obligated to hear the Torah being read, and (2) can the "dignity of the congregation" be waived and, if so, under what circumstances?

The Obligation Issue

According to the *mesorah*, the performance of *mitzvot* (the commandments) is binding rather than voluntary.[21] The *mitzvot* entail human obligations to other humans, as well as human obligations to the Divine.[22] Some of the *mitzvot* apply especially to women,[23] and others to men.[24] There is also a rule announced in the early rabbinic literature that "one who is not himself under obligation to perform a religious duty cannot perform it on behalf of a congregation."[25] Based on this rule, the argument has been advanced that because women are excluded from the requisite *minyan* of ten males needed for a public Torah reading,[26] and also because women are not obligated to study Torah,[27] they cannot fulfill the obligations for men in connection with a public Torah reading.[28] This reasoning, although adopted by the majority

---

21. *See generally supra* Chapter 4.

22. *See* MOSES MAIMONIDES, THE GUIDE FOR THE PERPLEXED 129 (M. Friedlander trans., E.P. Dutton & Co. 2d edition, 1904) (translated from the original Arabic text).

23. *See* Shabbat 20a (Jerusalem Talmud) (discussing the commandments of ritual immersion prior to resuming sexual relations after menstruation, separating challah, and lighting candles for the Sabbath). The command to light candles for the Sabbath applies to both men and women, but according to the tradition, women should satisfy this obligation on behalf of their households.

24. The commandments of marrying and procreating apply to men rather than women. *See* Shulhan Arukh Even Haezer 1:13; Yevamot 65b (Babylonian Talmud); Yevamot 6:6 (Mishnah)

25. Rosh Hashanah 3:8 (Mishnah), as translated in Shapiro, Qeri'at ha-Torah, *supra* note 10, at 212.

26. Riskin, *supra* note 9, at 366; Shochetman, *supra* note 9, at 300.

27. Kiddushin 29a–b (Babylonian Talmud).

28. The Mishnah states that women are exempt from affirmative precepts that are time-bound. Kiddushin 1:7 (Mishnah). Yet, commentators have noted that the Talmud's discussion of this point is considerably more nuanced. Saul Berman has observed that it is "impossible to explain women's exemptions exclusively in terms of the absence of need for time conditional commandments." Saul Berman, *The Status of Women in* Halakhic *Judaism, in* THE JEWISH WOMAN: NEW PERSPECTIVES 114, 119 (Elizabeth Koltun ed., 1987). *See also* RACHEL BIALE, WOMEN AND JEWISH LAW 10–17 (1984) (discussing this point); JUDITH

of Orthodox authorities, does seem to contradict the explicit language of both the *baraita* and the Tosefta[29] quoted above allowing women to be called to the Torah.

With respect to the issues of publicly reading from the Torah and receiving an *aliyah*, the determinative question is whether these are areas that fall under the general realm of Torah study (from which women are exempt), or something else. As discussed, according to the Talmud, women are not prohibited from being called to the Torah, but they are seemingly barred from reading the Torah publicly, based on "the dignity of the congregation" rationale rather than one concerned with the nature of the obligation. Given that the sages could have barred women from publicly reading the Torah on the basis that this act involves Torah study, from which women are exempt,[30] but instead chose to support their decision with the dignity rationale, Shapiro has concluded that "no primary objection to women's reading can be adduced."[31] Moreover, Shapiro argues that the model for public Torah reading is not the commandment of Torah study, but rather the commandment of gathering the community to hear the law, in which women and men participated together.[32] According to this perspective, the public Torah reading is a community obligation "revolving around the religious life of the synagogue"[33] rather than an individual responsibility pertaining only to men. The logical conclusion under this perspective is that women should be allowed to read the Torah on behalf of men because they are not discharging an obligation applicable only to men.[34] Once the obligation issue is placed in its proper perspective, the issue of women publicly reading from the Torah must be addressed from the standpoint of the "dignity of the congregation" concern specifically articulated in the text of the Talmud.

HAUPTMAN, REREADING THE RABBIS 233 (1998) ("In the ancient world women were on a lower social rung than men and for that reason could not assist them in discharging their ritual obligations").

29. For a summary of attempts to reconcile the obligation argument with the language of the Tosefta, see Riskin, *supra* note 9, at 369–72.

30. The sages also could have relied on the rationale that reading the Torah is a time-bound obligation. *See* Shapiro, Qeri'at ha-Torah, *supra* note 10, at 212.

31. *Id.*

32. *See id.* at 213–14. This command is known as *hakel*, and it derives from Deuteronomy. *See* Deuteronomy 31:12 (directing that all the Israelite people be gathered to hear and learn to revere God).

33. Shapiro, Qeri'at ha-Torah, *supra* note 10, at 215.

34. *Id.* at 217.

Before moving to the "dignity" discussion, however, it is worth addressing briefly the issue of *aliyyot* apart from that of reading from the Torah. At
the time that the text of the *baraita* originated, those who were called to
the Torah for an *aliyah* also read the corresponding Torah portion itself.[35]
Moreover, according to the earliest tradition, only the first and last *aliyah*
recipients actually recited the special blessings before and after reading their
assigned sections of the Torah.[36] Sometime before the year 1000 CE, however, the rabbis switched to a practice in which one person read the entire
Torah portion for the week, and those receiving an *aliyah* read along silently
or just listened.[37] Also, the current practice that each person who receives an
aliyah recites the introductory and concluding blessings was instituted during the Talmudic period to protect the honor of the Torah.[38] Because not
everyone who received *aliyyot* before this time recited the introductory and
concluding blessings (although they did read a portion from the Torah), the
weight of authority understands these *aliyah* prayers as blessings of thanksgiving to God for giving us the Torah, rather than as part of the commandment of studying Torah.[39] Significantly, if the *aliyah* prayers were viewed as
part of the command to study Torah, every person called to the Torah would
have been required to say these blessings from the outset. As a result of this
logic, Shapiro argues that women who are not commanded to study Torah
can say these blessings of thanksgiving without being seen as discharging a
male's obligation to study Torah.[40] Under this view, the concern that women

---

35. Today, the people receiving *aliyyot* generally are not the same individuals as the actual
Torah readers. *See id.* at 229–30.

36. Megillah 4:1 (Mishnah). *See also supra* notes 2–3 and accompanying text.

37. *See* Shapiro, Qeri'at ha-Torah, *supra* note 10, at 230. Some synagogues still maintain this
practice, although in many others the Torah is read by several different people during a particular service.

38. The sages believed that the honor of the Torah would be damaged under the earlier practice because those who left the service early—or arrived late—and were not present to hear
the requisite blessings might falsely assume that the Torah reading did not require an introductory or concluding blessing. *Id.* at 220.

39. See *id.* note 10, at 218–29 for a discussion of rabbinic authority on this point.

40. *Id.* at 221–22. Another *halakhic* argument that is often asserted in support of the view
that women should not publicly read from the Torah or recite the *aliyah* blessings has a
basis in the laws of modesty. *See* Shochetman, *supra* note 9, at 306–10 (discussing the view
that the presence of women among men in synagogue can disrupt the men's concentration).
Moreover, a woman's singing voice is regarded as "nakedness," which presumably can cause
sexual arousal in men. *See* Berakhot 24a (Babylonian Talmud). Shapiro notes that he is
not aware of a direct opinion on whether a woman chanting the words of the Torah or the
accompanying blessings in accordance with the prescribed musical tropes violates the laws

should be barred because they cannot recite these blessings on behalf of the men in the community is not relevant.[41] In contrast, some authorities understand the *aliyah* blessings to involve "matters of sanctity" requiring a *minyan* of men, and therefore women cannot fulfill men's obligations in this regard.[42]

Dignity of the Congregation and Waiver

The pivotal issue concerning whether women are permitted to read publicly from the Torah and to receive *aliyyot* centers on the concept of the "dignity of the congregation" *(kevod ha-tsibbur)* as mentioned in the *baraita* in the Talmud. Specifically, if "dignity of the congregation" is a fixed *halakhic* concept that does not change with place and time, then it might be appropriate to conclude that the *halakhic* system bars women from these ritual activities for all time. On the other hand, if "dignity of the congregation" is understood to reflect social sensitivity of the times, then the rationale provided in the *baraita* may not seem to be applicable in modern times, at least for all Orthodox communities. The significance of this distinction is critical: those who oppose allowing women to participate in public Torah reading tend to believe that "dignity of the congregation" is an objective, independent, and "scientific" *halakhic* category divorced from place and time, whereas those favoring such participation understand the concept as "a context-related principle indicating a recommendation of policy to the community under certain circumstances."[43]

Shapiro takes issue with those who treat "dignity of the congregation" as a restatement of the obligation argument against female participation because this view "leads naturally to the conclusion that [dignity of the congregation], at least in the case of women's *aliyyot*, is an objective, nonwaivable standard."[44] Based on the other examples of "dignity of the congregation" enumerated in

---

of modesty on this ground. Shapiro, Qeri'at ha-Torah, *supra* note 10, at 269–70. He notes, however, that the issue of women publicly chanting other religious texts has been raised, and the majority of Jewish law authorities conclude that no violation exists. *Id.* at 270.

41. Shapiro, Qeri'at ha-Torah, *supra* note 10, at 221–22.

42. *See* Riskin, *supra* note 9, at 387.

43. Ross, *supra* note 7, at 6; *see also id.* at 11–12.

44. Mendel Shapiro, *A Response to Shlomo Riskin, in* COMMUNAL PRAYER, *supra* note 1, at 391, 403. Shapiro critiques Riskin's definition of this concept as being "so specific to the case of women's *aliyyot* that it bears no similarity to the meaning of *kevod ha-tsibbur* as it is generally used." *Id.*

the Talmud, Shapiro concludes that "it appears that *kevod ha-tsibbur* generally covers a range of related but distinct concepts, whose common purpose is to prohibit conduct that imposes unnecessary bother on the congregation…or that disturbs the seriousness and propriety of the synagogue service."[45] Indeed, the general approach to illuminating the meaning of the congregation's dignity appears to depend on situational relativity.[46] For example, "dignity of the congregation" requires "that the Torah not be read publicly from a printed book, yet if there is no [Torah] scroll available, the book may—indeed, must—be used."[47]

If women's participation in public Torah reading is considered as an absolute prohibition, it would be very difficult to make an argument that the tradition allows a congregation to relinquish its dignity so as to permit women to participate. This is the view of many authorities in the Orthodox world today.[48] On the other hand, if the congregation's dignity is not considered as a fixed *halakhic* category applicable for all time, the question arises as to whether the congregation may waive its dignity or may consider its dignity unimpaired by allowing women to participate in public Torah reading. This issue actually generated significant discussion in the Middle Ages. Not surprisingly, however, when the issue surfaced at this time, it was in the context of a discussion that did not focus directly on the question of whether women could receive an *aliyah*.

The precise question that occupied the rabbinic scholars of this period concerned whether, in a hypothetical city in which all the men were *kohanim* (the descendants of the biblical High Priests), a woman could be called to the Torah in lieu of a man. According to the Talmud, the first *aliyah* of a Torah reading is given to a *kohen* (a priestly descendant), but it is not permitted to give one *kohen* an *aliyah* after another in succession.[49] The reason for this prohibition is to avoid generating doubt as to whether any of the *kohanim* receiving an *aliyah* in these circumstances are truly valid *kohanim*. This possibility of doubt as to the validity of a *kohen's* pedigree is known as the stigma of the *kohen*.[50] Thus, the hypothetical problem that generated

---

45. Shapiro, Qeri'at ha-Torah, *supra* note 10, at 242.

46. *Id.* at 242–43 (discussing examples in both the Talmudic literature and the later commentaries).

47. Sperber, *supra* note 9, at 59–60.

48. *See, e.g.,* Shochetman, *supra* note 9, at 351–52.

49. Gittin 59b (Babylonian Talmud).

50. Broyde, *supra* note 14, at 4 (explaining that in Hebrew the stigma is known as *pegam kohen*).

the critical discussion in medieval times regarding the propriety of women receiving *aliyyot* concerned how to have a successful Torah reading in a city in which all the men were *kohanim*.

In the thirteenth century, Rabbi Meir ben Baruch of Rothenburg, commonly known by the acronym *Maharam* of Rothenburg, proposed the following solution: the same *kohen* receives the first two *aliyyot*[51] and women receive the remaining five. The *Maharam's* reasoning in this regard was that because the Talmud does permit women to count toward the obligation of Torah reading, the sages' concern with violating congregational dignity if women were allowed to read should be discarded in situations in which there is no other choice.[52] In other words, "[a]ccording to *Maharam*, there is no objective rabbinic decree flatly prohibiting women from receiving *aliyyot* in all circumstances."[53] In evaluating the significance of the *Maharam's* ruling, it is important to understand that overall the *Maharam* was not liberal concerning women and synagogue ritual. On the contrary, in some instances, his decisions can be read as trying to exclude women from the synagogue.[54] Yet, the *Maharam* clearly interpreted the law to be sufficiently flexible to allow women to receive *aliyyot* where necessary. Law professor Michael Broyde, who is also an Orthodox rabbi, has observed that "[t]he intellectual predicate of *Maharam's* view is that women may receive aliyot in certain cases."[55]

Although a number of rabbis at the time agreed with the *Maharam* on this issue, a different position was articulated by Shlomo ben Aderet,

51. According to the Talmud, the first *aliyah* goes to a *kohen*, the second goes to a descendant of the Levite tribe, and the remaining five *aliyyot* to descendants of the general population (known as *yisraelim* in Hebrew). Gittin 59a–b (Babylonian Talmud). Significantly, under traditional Jewish law, these lines of descent are relevant only for males given that women had no part in the rituals to which they pertained. In some Conservative synagogues today, however, female descendants of the *kohanim* and the Levite tribe are allowed to have the first and second *aliyyot* during a Torah reading. *See* Joel Roth, *The Status of Daughters of* Kohanim *and* Leviyim *for* Aliyot, *in* PROCEEDINGS OF THE COMMITTEE ON JEWISH LAW AND STANDARDS, 1986–1990, at 419 (2001), https://www.rabbinicalassembly.org/sites/default/files/public/halakhah/teshuvot/19861990/roth_daughtersaliyot.pdf.

52. *See* Broyde, *supra* note 14, at 3 (quoting the original position of the *Maharam* in English).

53. *Id.; see also* Sperber, *supra* note 9, at 58 n.24 (observing that if the *Maharam* had understood women receiving *aliyyot* as absolutely prohibited, he "would not have been able to permit it").

54. Sperber, *supra* note 9, at 56–58 (citing authority on this point).

55. Broyde, *supra* note 14, at 5. Significantly, however, Broyde is not a proponent of increased participation by women in public Torah reading. For a contrary opinion on this particular point in the text, see Shochetman, *supra* note 9, at 331–34.

known as the *Rashba*, who lived in Spain during the thirteenth and early fourteenth centuries. The *Rashba's* solution to the situation presented by the hypothetical city containing only *kohanim* was to allow successive *kohanim* to read from the Torah because everyone knows that only *kohanim* are present, and therefore no doubt exists in the community as to the validity of any given *kohen*.[56] According to the *Rashba*, no stigma exists because the women could not be relied upon to save them from the stigma.[57] Further, the *Rashba* seems to suggest that the issue of a particular *kohen's* perceived pedigree is a socially subjective matter given the *Rashba's* view that in a community in which everyone knows that all the men are *kohanim*, no doubt or stigma is created by successive *kohanim* receiving an *aliyah*.

Broyde notes that many of the rabbis of this time also adopted the *Rashba's* view and the matter remained in dispute during this period of *halakhah's* development.[58] Further, Broyde emphasizes the completely contradictory nature of these two views. On the one hand, the *Maharam* maintains that women may receive *aliyyot* in certain situations. In contrast, the *Rashba's* view is based on the concept that women receiving *aliyyot* is prohibited by the *halakhah* by virtue of a rabbinic decree.[59]

Even if the *Maharam* is correct as a matter of *halakhah* with respect to the specific issue involving a town containing all *kohanim*, one might argue that it is a leap to conclude that women may generally receive *aliyyot*. Nevertheless, as Broyde observes, "it must be conceded—*it is a leap that is within the range of possibility*."[60] Despite the initial existence of the dispute between the *Maharam* and the *Rashba*, as time passed, a consensus eventually developed

---

56. *See* Broyde, *supra* note 14, at 4 (quoting the original position of the *Rashba*, in English translation).

57. *Id.* at 14.

58. *Id.* at 5.

59. *See id.* at 6 and n.15. Based on these two distinct positions, Broyde has observed

[O]ne can say with some *halachic* confidence that seven hundred years ago, a person living in Northern France or Southern Germany (those areas where the intellectual school of thought of the *Maharam* dominated) would not be considered a sinner if he or she lived in a village where all the adult men were *kohanim* and women received *aliyyot* after them, as this school of thought was certainly a reasonable one for a [religious leader] to choose at that time.

Id. at 8.

60. *Id.* at 3 (emphasis added).

in favor of the *Rashba's* position.[61] The fact that such a consensus exists in the mainstream Orthodox discourse is clear, but the nature of the legal process that gave rise to this consensus leaves ample room for a different legal conclusion on the part of willing Orthodox communities.

The Jewish Law Codes

On its face, the sixteenth-century Code of Jewish law[62] acknowledges the possibility of women receiving *aliyyot* with the following text:

> All are included in the count of seven, even a woman and a minor who knows to Whom one recites blessings. But the Sages said: A woman ought not to read in public because of [the dignity of the congregation]. [Moses Isserles]: These may indeed be included among those called up, but not all those called up may be women or children.[63]

Modern commentators disagree with one another regarding exactly what this language means. Sperber understands this language to mean that even when women and children are permitted to have *aliyyot*, it is improper for them to receive all of them. He sees this formulation as "clear, lending itself to no alternative understanding."[64] Similarly, Shapiro, providing an extensive analysis, interprets this language as permitting women to receive *aliyyot* (as long as all who receive *aliyyot* are not women or minors) but prohibiting them from reading from the Torah publicly due to the situationally related concept of "communal dignity."[65] In contrast, Rabbi Yehuda Herzl Henkin, a noted authority on Jewish law, questions Shapiro's conclusions, writing that it lacks credibility to assert that the Code would allow for "such an innovation in practical *halakhah* without openly calling attention to it."[66]

---

61. *Id.* at 15–17. But see Sperber, *supra* note 9, at 59, for an interesting story of a prominent and learned woman in Baghdad reading from the Torah in 1901, presumably with the knowledge of the rabbinic authority there.

62. *See supra* Chapter 4, note 143 and accompanying text.

63. Shulhan Arukh Orach Chayim 282:3, as translated in Sperber, *supra* note 9, at 56.

64. Sperber, *supra* note 9, at 56.

65. Shapiro, Qeri'at ha-Torah, *supra* note 10, at 251–59. *See also supra* notes 43–47 and accompanying text.

66. Yehuda Herzl Henkin, Qeri-at Ha-Torah *by Women: Where We Stand Today*, 1(2) EDAH J. 1, 4 (2001), http://www.edah.org/backend/JournalArticle/1_2_henkin.pdf; *see also* Shochetman, *supra* note 9, at 325 (disputing Shapiro's interpretation of the Code).

Broyde acknowledges that, from his perspective, Isserles's "formulation is more troubling" but explains it away with the assertion that because Isserles does not quote the *Maharam* in this particular passage, he is indicating that he does not believe the *halakhah* follows the *Maharam's* view on this point.[67]

Consensus and Ability to Revisit

Overall, then, the foregoing discussion illustrates that the classical Jewish sources concerning the issues of women reading from the Torah and receiving *aliyyot* contain contradictory strands and are capable of supporting different conclusions. From a strictly *halakhic* perspective, in the thirteenth and early fourteenth centuries respectable authorities differed on the issue of whether it is objectively prohibited for women to receive *aliyyot*. The dispute eventually closed, with the consensus being that women cannot ritually participate in this way.[68] Further, this consensus is still the norm followed today.[69] In other words, apparently a rabbinic decree can result from an after-the-fact interpretation of the Talmud by subsequent generations, and once such a consensus has been reached regarding the existence of this rabbinic decree, it is nearly impossible to override.[70]

In instances where the Babylonian Talmud reaches a clear consensus, this consensus arguably controls, at least according to the strictest interpretations of the tradition.[71] In the case of women reading from the Torah in a public forum and receiving *aliyyot*, no clear Talmudic consensus exists. Therefore, a reasonable *halakhic* argument can be made that the issue is not beyond

---

67. Broyde, *supra* note 14, at 9–10.

68. *Id.* at 13.

69. *Id.* at 14.

70. It is especially interesting to compare Broyde's position on women reading publicly from the Torah and receiving *aliyyot* with his position on ordination for Orthodox women rabbis. In another article, Broyde outlines his thinking in this regard. Although he does not recommend that the Orthodox movement begin ordaining female rabbis at this point in time, because such a consensus has yet to develop, his entire discussion of this issue, unlike his work concerning the issue of public Torah reading, is steeped in a culturally nuanced perspective. Significantly, in the only mention of *aliyyot* for women in his article on ordination, he groups this possibility with other reforms advocated by more liberal sectors of Orthodoxy that manifest "various degrees of radicalism and *halakhic* plausibility…and…have the potential to recklessly break the bounds of Orthodoxy." Michael J. Broyde & Shlomo B. Brody, *Orthodox Women Rabbis? Tentative Thoughts That Distinguish between the Timely and the Timeless*, 11 HAKIRAH 25, 52–53 (2011).

71. *See supra* Chapter 1, note 101 and accompanying text.

revisiting according to the *halakhic* process as it has been developed and applied throughout history.[72]

The issue raised by the Talmud's language, and its subsequent interpretation, centers on whether the Talmud provides a categorical prohibition concerning women publicly reading Torah and receiving *aliyyot*. The discussion here illustrates that there is room for concluding that the Talmud's prohibition should not be understood as one that is fixed for all time. Even the language in the Code may be interpreted as consistent with the view that no categorical prohibition exists. It is telling that in arguing against Shapiro's conclusion that women should be afforded greater opportunities for participation in synagogue ritual surrounding Torah reading, Henkin acknowledges that he agrees with "much of Rabbi Mendel Shapiro's comprehensive and thoughtful article."[73] In Henkin's view, however, the bottom-line issue is that permitting women to receive *aliyyot* today is simply "outside the consensus."[74] Significantly, Henkin, who would not permit women to receive *aliyyot* (or read from the Torah), bases his ultimate conclusion on a sociological or culturally based analysis. He writes that synagogues that permit women to receive *aliyyot* are "not Orthodox in name and will not long remain Orthodox in practice."[75] Thus, Henkin manifests a nuanced approach to the relationship between law and culture but nonetheless rejects the possibility that the law can move in a more inclusive direction based on his assessment of the current cultural realities.

For purposes of this discussion, it is not necessary to move beyond the theoretical parameters of *halakhah* as invoked in the most traditionally observant circles. In this respect, the issue of women participating in public Torah reading arguably presents a different situation from the issue of homosexuality discussed in Chapter 6. Mainstream Orthodox scholars have argued that there is no fixed, categorical prohibition to women receiving *aliyyot* or reading publicly from the Torah. Had the Babylonian Talmud

---

72. Even Broyde implicitly acknowledges this point in a footnote toward the end of his paper. *See* Broyde, *supra* note 14, at 15 n.53.

73. Henkin, *supra* note 66, at 1.

74. *Id.* at 6. Henkin claims this is the case now and for "the foreseeable future," and thus sees "no point in arguing about it." *Id.*

75. *Id.* This approach is distinct from that of Michael Broyde, whose analysis of "minimal *halakhah* of Torah reading, independent of any other issues" seemingly rejects the essential insight of cultural analysis that law both reflects and is constituted by culture. Broyde, *supra* note 14, at 1.

clearly maintained a categorical prohibition on women participating in public Torah reading, there would be less room in the tradition to argue otherwise, despite the fact that a cultural analysis framework might question the neutral objectivity of even conclusive Talmudic rulings. On the other hand, cultural analysis also is concerned with maintaining authenticity and therefore justifies selectivity regarding changes to the tradition.

The subject of women's participation in public Torah reading exemplifies the utility of the cultural analysis framework because arguably no substantial *halakhic* barrier prevents a re-examination and change of the tradition as it developed in the Middle Ages and beyond. Indeed, based on the authority of the *Maharam*, and the language of Moses Isserles in the Code, a *halakhic* basis exists upon which to predicate the development of the law in this regard. In other words, the rabbinic prohibition advocated by the *Rashba* was not seen as a fixed reality at the time of the Talmud, given the fact that the tradition was conflicted on this point for centuries following the Talmud's redaction. Instead, this rabbinic prohibition was the result of reinterpretation by later generations who were responding to their own cultural realities. This approach acknowledges that even if the *Rashba's* view of what was forbidden in the thirteenth or fourteenth centuries was appropriate in its cultural context, the cultural context has changed substantially since then.

In sum, a candid assessment of this topic compels the conclusion that the tradition contains a basis for the adoption of a practice that would be more inclusive, at least for those Orthodox communities willing to adopt this approach. Sperber fittingly captured the state of the law in this regard:

> [W]hen we attempt to reconstruct the issue of women's participation in the synagogue and in various rituals in retrospect, we find that the stream does not follow a uniform course; rather, it is multidirectional, moving in different directions, reflecting different aspects at different times and places.[76]

In situations such as this, where the *halakhah* itself is "multi-directional," the cultural analysis methodology provides an especially useful tool for facilitating a change in the stream's directional course without compromising the authenticity of the tradition. Yet, as the next section demonstrates, changes

---

76. Sperber, *supra* note 9, at 36.

that are steeped in feminist thought by and large have not been embraced warmly by the Jewish tradition.

The Nature of Past and Present Resistance to Feminist Claims

The primary insight of cultural analysis is that because the law cannot be understood without reference to the culture from which it emerged, it is important to examine the influence culture has had upon the development of the law. Therefore, it is impossible to evaluate the considerations that militate for or against change in this context without understanding the overall attitude of the traditional Jewish culture concerning matters involving claims perceived as feminist in nature. This section addresses this alignment more fully by focusing on reasons for past and current resistance. It illustrates that the development of the *halakhah* concerning women and synagogue ritual has been influenced from the outset by a strong cultural bias concerning women and their place in religious society. This bias continues into the present in Orthodox circles, even in the Modern Orthodox sector.

A modern person easily can understand the Talmudic, and also the medieval, hesitancy to involve women in the business of ritual, which would explain the original "dignity of the congregation" rationale as to why women could not read from the Torah in public.[77] Throughout history, the rabbis sought to establish their authority and power so that they could execute their role as lawmakers. The female voice is noticeably absent not only in the biblical texts, but also in the texts produced in the Talmudic period and later. As a result, women did not have a voice in the development or outcome of Jewish ritualistic law (and this is essentially still the case in the Orthodox world). The primary domain of women was that of the home and family.[78] Although women had virtually no opportunity to directly influence the

---

77. Indeed, Shapiro has observed that "[i]n light of women's cultural situation and status at the time, no explanation was required" concerning why reading by women violated the "dignity of the congregation." Shapiro, Qeri'at ha-Torah, *supra* note 10, at 247.

78. Interestingly, as late as 1916, a religious census in the United States showed that whereas 60.7 percent of synagogue members were male, women constituted only 39.3 percent of the members. In contrast, the survey showed that more women than men belonged to churches. Professor Jonathan Sarna explains these statistics as consistent with Eastern European practice in which the women concentrated on maintaining Judaism in the home, whereas the men focused their religious energies within the synagogue. JONATHAN D. SARNA, AMERICAN JUDAISM 164 (2004).

development of the law concerning synagogue ritual or any other matter, it is important to recognize that Jewish law in some areas concerning women was very pro-female. For example, the Talmudic sages elaborated upon the biblical requirement of conjugal rights, mandating that men were obligated to have sex regularly with their wives for the sole purpose of providing their wives with sexual gratification.[79] This recognition of female personhood is quite remarkable not only for the early centuries of the Common Era, but even by today's standards. The point, then, is that the sages were not necessarily sexist or anti-female. On the contrary, many of the laws they instituted tried to ameliorate the overall social and economic status of women.[80] Still, on the issue of synagogue ritual, it is clear that their views were limited by their historic context, and undoubtedly the majority of women themselves may not even have been inclined to press for reforms given that they were also a product of this same cultural milieu.

Although the Jewish tradition's historic resistance to feminist religious claims can be explained by the greater social culture of bygone eras, the present-day situation is more complex. Today, the Modern Orthodox community in particular appears to maintain a dualistic stance on gender equality—one for secular areas in which different rules for the genders are simply unacceptable and one for the religious realm where separation and distinction are perpetuated.[81] Israeli professor and social activist Tova Hartman

---

79. The Torah refers to the man's obligation to provide his wife with regular sexual relations, *see* Exodus 21:10, but the sages of the Talmudic period expanded upon this concept. The sages required that men perform their conjugal duties with intimate bodily contact. They even specified how often a husband was required to satisfy his wife, which depended on the nature of the husband's occupation (occupations that did not require the husbands to be away from home obligated the man to have a greater amount of sex with his wife). *See* Ketuvot 61b (Babylonian Talmud); Ketuvot 5:6 (Mishnah). The wife's conjugal rights apply even during pregnancy when she is incapable of conceiving. *See* Niddah 31a (Babylonian Talmud) (discussing times when sex is beneficial or injurious for the woman or fetus).

80. For example, rabbinic rules were developed during the early centuries of the Common Era attempting to ameliorate women's social and economic vulnerabilities due to the ability of their husbands to secure a divorce without their consent. The *ketubah*, or marriage contract, a device developed by the rabbis during this time and still in use today, was instituted to delineate a man's financial obligations to his wife in the event of divorce. *See* BIALE, *supra* note 28, at 80.

81. TOVA HARTMAN, FEMINISM ENCOUNTERS TRADITIONAL JUDAISM 11 (2007) ("Any Modern Orthodox parents whose daughter was denied the right to pursue the career of her choosing, or was accorded second-class status in any way, would fight the case tirelessly, to the highest court in the land, and be lauded as heroes by their Modern Orthodox compatriots."); *see also* Shochetman, *supra* note 9, at 357 ("The incorporation of women in professional and communal life has no *halakhic* relevance to the laws of conduct during public prayer, nor to the specific issue of women's *aliyyot*.").

has done groundbreaking work on this topic, particularly with respect to the Modern Orthodox community in Israel. After years of frustration and anguish, Hartman founded the first "semi-egalitarian" Orthodox *minyan*, Shira Hadasha, in 2001. This grass roots congregation, known as a partnership *minyan*, allows women to read publicly from the Torah, receive *aliyyot*, and even lead certain parts of the prayer service. Much discussion and thought went into the process of how to effectuate a more egalitarian model within the parameters of Orthodox Judaism, although the *minyan* lacks official approval from any Orthodox authority or institution.[82] Since its inception, Shira Hadasha has become enormously popular among certain circles of Israelis and American visitors and has spawned several spin-off partnership *minyanim* in both Israel and some cities in the United States.[83]

Although Hartman lives and works in Israel, little difference exists across the globe with respect to the issues about which she writes. For example, Modern Orthodox synagogues in the United States exhibit virtually no movement toward incorporating greater participation by women in public Torah readings, and the same is true for Jewish communities elsewhere. Interestingly, to date almost all of the scholarship written on this topic by those scholars who self-denominate as Orthodox has been published by Israeli academics rather than by those affiliated with Yeshiva University, the premier Modern Orthodox institution in the United States.[84]

Modern Orthodoxy sets itself apart from the more centrist and even right-wing versions of Orthodoxy by its explicit prescriptive adoption of modern sources of knowledge and values that are not derived directly from Jewish sources.[85] The problem, according to Hartman, is that only some

---

82. Women and men sit separately at Shira Hadasha, as is the norm in Orthodox synagogues. Still, the space is configured in such a way that women are able to be called to the *bimah* (the place where the prayers are led) and to read publicly from the Torah. *See also* Shapiro, Qeri'at ha-Torah, *supra* note 10 at 271–72 (arguing that the presence of a small number of women in the men's section is not *halakhically* invalid and therefore cannot be used as a basis to prohibit women's participation in public Torah readings).

83. A partnership *minyan* was started several years ago in Skokie, Illinois, and others exist in New York.

84. Mendel Shapiro and Daniel Sperber, discussed throughout this chapter, are the primary Israeli examples, although Benjamin Lau, another important Israeli scholar and practicing rabbi, also has briefly mentioned these issues as examples concerning the status of women "requiring comprehensive rethinking." *See* Benjamin Lau, *The Challenge of Halakhic Innovation*, 8 MEOROT 1, at 9–10 (2010).

85. *See supra* Chapter 4, note 107 and accompanying text. *See also* HARTMAN, *supra* note 81, at 7; JONATHAN SACKS, ORTHODOXY CONFRONTS MODERNITY 10 (1991); Saul Berman, *The Ideology of Modern Orthodoxy*, SH'MA, Feb. 1, 2001, at 6.

"foreign" values make the cut. For example, Modern Orthodoxy is extremely comfortable incorporating and compartmentalizing certain types of scientific knowledge into its overall framework.[86] Feminism, on the other hand, has been relegated to the "back alley" as seemingly inconsistent with the values of the tradition.[87] Hartman argues that in order to move beyond the currently set boundaries the tradition maintains with respect to feminism, it is important to understand why Modern Orthodoxy is comfortable incorporating certain areas of knowledge or value systems, but not feminism.[88]

Of course, Modern Orthodoxy's views on this score are shared with the more centrist and right-wing sectors of Orthodoxy. In the majority of the current Orthodox world, feminism is categorically dismissed as a dangerous, Westernizing influence, one that threatens the entire fabric of the tradition.[89] Hartman acknowledges that the work of Third-World feminists have helped her to better understand the importance of the "Western label" in the overall process of delegitimizing feminism.[90] At base, however, the overarching issue is one of power relationships, one of the critical themes of cultural analysis.

Tamar Ross, a committed Orthodox Jew and professor emerita of Jewish philosophy at Bar Ilan University, has observed that "the gender-based distribution of power has prevented women from active participation in the process of *halakhic* interpretation, by deliberately distancing them from the type of education that might have suited them to such activities, in the name of an

---

86. This integration is epitomized by Modern Orthodoxy's umbrella slogan, "Torah and *Madda.*" *Madda* is generally interpreted as secular, particularly scientific, knowledge. *See* HARTMAN, *supra* note 81, at 8. *See generally* NORMAN LAMM, TORAH *UMADDA* (1990).

87. HARTMAN, *supra* note 81, at 8.

88. *Id.* at 7.

89. The observation in the text was reinforced by Yosef Kanefsky, a Modern Orthodox rabbi in the United States, who wrote to the author the following:

> The Orthodox community has adopted a consciously reactionary position relative to modernity and all of the trends it has spawned. I have heard that *poskim* [Jewish law authorities] speak of "*hilchos* feminism," which is the mechanism of *halachik* decision-making that actively seeks to disqualify and delegitimize *halachik* arguments offered in favor of innovation.

E-mail from Rabbi Yosef Kanefsky to Roberta Kwall (Aug. 28, 2013, 10:41 a.m. CST). *See also* Yosef Kanefsky, *Partnership* Minyanim: *Let's Live and Let Live*, MORETHODOXY (Dec. 24, 2013), http://morethodoxy.org/2013/12/24/partnership-minyanim-lets-live-and-let-live-by-r-yosef-kanefsky/ (arguing that these *minyanim* are viable from a *halakhic* standpoint and should not be considered beyond the pale of Orthodoxy).

90. HARTMAN, *supra* note 81, at 6 (quoting Uma Narayan).

'objective' understanding of their role in Jewish life."[91] Hartman's work also has repeatedly emphasized the power of religious authorities in framing feminism for the Modern Orthodox world and "the extremely conscientious way" they exercise this power.[92] Moreover, the "framing" about which Hartman writes is performed not only by Modern Orthodox authorities, but also by their more centrist Orthodox colleagues, who teach in Modern Orthodox schools and serve as local rabbis for Modern Orthodox communities.[93]

This last point concerning the synergy between the modern and more centrist Orthodox camps is extremely significant beyond the issue of framing, as Chapter 4's discussion of the swing to the right in Orthodoxy illustrates.[94] In addition, an Orthodox approach stresses the importance of consensus in lawmaking.[95] Thus, more open-minded Orthodox rabbis who might be inclined to institute a practice in their own synagogues in which women are permitted to participate in public Torah reading fail to do so because they require the approval of an official *poseq*, a Jewish law authority highly regarded by all segments of the Orthodox community. Approval by such an authority has not yet emerged.[96] Also, because it is fairly certain that the more centrist and right-wing segments of the Orthodox movement will never endorse a change in this area, more open-minded leaders may conclude that it is not prudent or useful to spend their political capital on this issue.

Saul Berman's essay, "The Status of Women in Halakhic Judaism," furnishes yet another pertinent example. Berman, who is a prominent Modern Orthodox rabbi and scholar with a law degree, opens his essay with rhetoric that could easily appear in an article embracing a cultural analysis perspective: "Our apologetics have relegated women to the service role; all forces of the male dominated society were brought to bear to make women see themselves in the way most advantageous to men."[97] Moreover, Berman forcefully argues that "Jewish women have been culturally and religiously colonized

---

91. Ross, *supra* note 7, at 18.

92. HARTMAN, *supra* note 81, at 6.

93. *Id.* at 139 n.1.

94. *See supra* Chapter 4, notes 109–18 and accompanying text.

95. *See supra* Chapter 4, notes 160–61 and accompanying text.

96. Ross, *supra* note 7, at 3 (recounting the story of a rabbi in Teaneck, New Jersey, who found Mendel Shapiro's arguments convincing and would institute this practice if a reputable *poseq* would approve it).

97. Berman, *supra* note 28, at 116. For confirmation of this point, see Riskin, *supra* note 9, at 387 (discussing the "broader perspective" illustrating how the sages "assigned to women the

into acceptance of their identities as 'enablers.'"[98] His solution is that "we must encourage women to develop in a creative fashion whatever additional forms they find necessary for their religious growth."[99] Despite the promise of these words, Berman's ultimate recommendations, although written before the issue of women reading publicly from the Torah was a topic of serious debate in Orthodox circles, include designing synagogue space in a way that is more welcoming for women and asking rabbis to encourage their female congregants to come earlier to synagogue services and refrain from talking during the services.[100]

Thus, the "framing" and filtering processes that are responsible for rejecting many of the insights feminist theory offers are very deeply ingrained in all sectors of the Orthodox community. Part of the reason for this deeply ingrained perspective is explained by the yeshiva (school of Jewish learning) education system, which not only maintains gender separation, but also treats Jewish law as a closed legal system not admitting of social, cultural, or historical factors.[101] This resistance to understanding the cultural context of Jewish law exists not just with respect to current issues, but also regarding the laws as they developed over time, including the Talmudic era. The failure to incorporate the cultural dimension of law results in a tendency to freeze the law, especially in matters involving gender issues that are highly culturally sensitive. Thus, in responding to Sperber's argument that denying women the ability to participate in public Torah reading violates their human dignity,[102] Shochetman has queried, "Is it possible to say of a rabbinic law—which no doubt was based on careful deliberation, after all relevant factors were taken into account—that it is harmful to one's esteem and therefore he may treat it with disregard?"[103]

The ingrained nature of the status quo concerning female participation in public Torah reading gives rise to the related issue of whether this practice should be considered *minhag* (custom) that has now been elevated to the status of *halakhah*. Sperber also addressed this argument when he observed that

---

primary obligations related to purity and sanctity of the household" and that this "division of responsibility is grounded in historical, sociological, and biological factors").

98. Berman, *supra* note 28, at 116.

99. *Id.* at 124.

100. *Id.* at 123–24.

101. *See* Sperber, *supra* note 9, at 123 (Appendix I: On *Halakhic* Methodology).

102. *See infra* notes 125–27 and accompanying text.

103. Shochetman, *supra* note 9, at 343.

the current resistance to increased female participation in public Torah readings derives from the "underlying idea...[that] 'Your ancestors didn't do so; your parents didn't do so; and therefore your children are forbidden to do so as well.'"[104] Interestingly, in an e-mail response to the question whether his synagogue in the Old City in Jerusalem has adopted his suggested views in this regard, Sperber wrote, "[it] suffers my views but does not apply them."[105]

The perpetuation of the status quo in this area also can be explained by the role "negative identity" plays in the Orthodox world. Each of the Jewish movements has its respective identity, and greater participation for women in ritual matters is a hallmark of Reform and now even most Conservative synagogues. Orthodox leaders of all sectors fear that responding to feminist claims in ritual matters will result in a detrimental blurring with these more liberal movements and ultimately, even a weakening of practice across the board among Orthodox Jews ("the slippery slope").[106] The heart of this concern is not just that it might lead to increased assimilation among those who are currently Orthodox, but also that Orthodoxy's adoption of practices more supportive of female participation would be perceived by the more liberal movements as signs of their own merit, and Orthodoxy's respective failings.[107]

Further, although education on the part of a disenfranchised group is generally believed to lead to changes in the sociolegal structure, this result is not necessarily expected in the Orthodox culture with respect to this particular matter. In other words, the increased educational opportunities available today for Orthodox women probably will not have an immediate impact on increasing the role of women in synagogue ritual. Today, more Orthodox women are learning Talmud (once thought to be off limits for women) than ever before. Also, programs exist to train women to become advocates

---

104. Sperber, *supra* note 9, at 63.

105. E-mail from Professor Daniel Sperber to author (Feb. 13, 2011, 4:10 a.m. CST).

106. HARTMAN, *supra* note 81, at 15; *see also* Shapiro, Qeri'at ha-Torah, *supra* note 10, at 259–60, 272–73; Shochetman, *supra* note 9, at 326 (quoting Ovadiah Yosef, the former Sephardic Chief Rabbi of Israel). The slippery slope argument was made in connection with prohibiting women from saying the Mourner's prayer (*Kaddish*) for a deceased parent, but in the end, it was not accepted in this context. Sperber, *supra* note 9, at 178 (Appendix VIII: Women and *Kaddish*).

107. *See* Shapiro, Qeri'at ha-Torah, *supra* note 10, at 260 (noting the argument that "tampering with [the status quo] would encourage the 'assimilationists,' presumably the Conservative and Reform movements"). Interestingly, Broyde dismisses this argument as a legitimate basis for decision with respect to the issue of female ordination. *See* Broyde & Brody, *supra* note 70, at 51–52; *see also* Sperber, *supra* note 9, at 131 ("[T]he fear of seeming to emulate non-Orthodox movements is not realistic so long as there are normative *halakhic* sources upon which to rely").

before rabbinic courts in Israel,[108] as well as Jewish law consultants.[109] Esti Rosenberg, the daughter of the renowned Modern Orthodox authority Rabbi Aharon Lichtenstein and the granddaughter of Rabbi Joseph Soloveitchik, published an illuminating article in *Tradition Magazine* providing a candid examination and assessment of the more recent opportunities for women in Israel with respect to advanced Torah learning.[110] Rosenberg reports many positive, and even extraordinary, developments on this topic, although one of her concluding observations is that to date, no female "Torah scholars in the true sense of the term" have been produced, and "there is still a long way to go" before this possibility becomes a reality.[111] She also acknowledges that as a result, these developments still have not impacted "the world of men's Torah learning."[112] The absence of this influence is a major obstacle for progress on the topic of increased participation for women with respect to public Torah reading because the legal realm still lacks a legitimate, authoritative female voice.

As Hartman's saga illustrates, widespread resistance exists to increasing the role of female participation in ritual matters. Hartman questions whether

> it is precisely the rabbis' awareness of their powerful agency in shaping tradition that has generated their adamant rejection of feminism; not only because their awareness of their power is what makes them so reluctant to share it, but because their selective faculties caused them to question, very reasonably, the potential impact on their values and culture of feminism's sweeping claims about the need to create the world anew.[113]

---

108. Rabbi Riskin is the founder of such programs in Israel. *See* Riskin, *supra* note 9, at 361 n.2. See *infra* Chapter 8, notes 38–59 and accompanying text for a discussion of the rabbinical court system.

109. One area in which women serve as Jewish law consultants is the complex subject of the family purity laws governing sexual relations between spouses. HARTMAN, *supra* note 81, at 17; *see also* Broyde & Brody, *supra* note 70, at 48 (noting that consultant positions, existing in both Israel and the United States, have been created with the support of prominent *halakhic* authorities and are growing in their acceptance).

110. Esti Rosenberg, *The World of Women's Torah Learning—Developments, Directions and Objectives: A Report from the Field,* 45:1 TRADITION 13 (2012).

111. *Id.* at 34.

112. *Id.*

113. HARTMAN, *supra* note 81, at 17.

Hartman's observations describe not only the status of the Orthodox world in Israel, but also the current reality in the United States and the rest of the Diaspora.

Significantly, some of the resistance also can be attributed to women who self-denominate as Orthodox. A process of acculturation exists in these communities that can result in women being reluctant to question or push the boundaries of the status quo for fear of being marginalized or isolated. This reality exists for women on both a social and a professional level. Women who do have ambitions of becoming spiritual leaders may refrain from activism in this area for fear of being seen in a negative light by the male authority figures. Additionally, many women also buy into the existing system, either consciously or unconsciously. With respect to the conscious choice explanation, the norms of the Orthodox community—and especially the realities of the "matchmaking" marriage system under which women in general have increasingly fewer opportunities—cannot be underestimated.[114] Women, fearing negative consequences for either themselves or their daughters, may simply find it easier to stay silent. As for the unconscious choice explanation, it also stands to reason that many women who grow up not knowing of any other ritual possibility do not necessarily miss something to which they have never been exposed. Tamar Ross, whose specialty is gender studies, writes about her own experience as originally somewhat indifferent to the issue of women participating in public Torah reading. Only after she had learned more about the arguments made by Shapiro and others advocating for a more inclusive approach did she come to realize that if she were nearing Bat Mitzvah age she "would be most eager to mark the event by reading the Torah" and that she would regard "any other form of celebration as a pale second best."[115] Yet, even now Ross prefers a conventional Orthodox *minyan* in which women do not publicly read.[116]

Moreover, many women who are raised and educated in Orthodox environments actively agree with the parameters to which they have been exposed. Some who do not agree with the mainstream Orthodox ritual norms leave Orthodoxy and find spiritual homes in more inclusive movements (or even

---

114. Tamar Snyder, *Houses of Worship: Single Jewish Female Seeks Stress Relief,* WALL ST. J., July 11, 2008, at W11 (discussing the problems for young women presented by the *shidduch* (matchmaking) system).

115. Ross, *supra* note 7, at 3.

116. *Id.* at 3–4.

leave the world of organized Jewish religion completely). Tova Hartman is unique in that her father was David Hartman, an Orthodox rabbinic leader and scholar who educated her himself;[117] most women do not have the education, pedigree, or contacts to undertake grass roots initiatives such as Shira Hadasha and provide the necessary leadership to ensure its success.

A Basis for Change

Currently, most Orthodox communities probably would not be willing to make even some changes concerning women reading publicly from the Torah and receiving *aliyyot*, despite the possibility of doing so within certain articulated boundaries.[118] Nevertheless, although certain laws within the tradition such as refraining from eating pork are immutable, other practices can be re-evaluated when religious authorities feel that circumstances have changed, even if such practices have never been allowed within a given Orthodox community.[119] As discussed earlier, the Talmud does not categorically preclude this type of female participation, and a dispute among the *halakhic* authorities subsequently developed. The fact that the dispute eventually was resolved organically would not—under a cultural analysis paradigm—foreclose its reconsideration. Thus, cultural analysis views the norms of female ritualistic participation concerning being called to, and reading from, the Torah as the result of environment, conditioning, history, and context, rather than as an unalterable mandate. This methodology understands law in its historical context and as the product of power relationships.

Jewish law reflects the multiplicity of values characteristic of cultural analysis by incorporating both a top-down and a bottom-up approach. In other words, in certain instances the bottom-up practices of the people can eventually acquire the force of law. Shapiro also notes that there are "aspects of *halakhic* practice that are shaped by social circumstances of time and place"[120] and therefore "originate in entirely casual circumstances and only after time

---

117. See *infra* Chapter 8, notes 96–99 and accompanying text for a discussion of Rabbi David Hartman.

118. Shapiro, *supra* note 44, at 400–01 (recommending, in accordance with traditional authority, that at least some of the *aliyyot* during a service should be reserved for men).

119. Broyde & Brody, *supra* note 70, at 46. As discussed, Broyde does not believe this logic extends to females publicly reading from the Torah or receiving *aliyyot*, presumably because in his view this practice violates Jewish law. *See supra* note 70.

120. Shapiro, Qeri'at ha-Torah, *supra* note 10, at 277–78.

are invested with *halakhic* cachet."[121] He posits that perhaps the *minhag* of excluding women from participation in public Torah readings began in this way because there are only so many synagogue honors to go around.[122] Shapiro argues that if a *minhag* of denying women *aliyyot* does indeed exist, its origins must be examined and its authority carefully evaluated.[123] In his view, there is no real support for the position that female participation in public Torah reading should be universally prohibited based on *minhag*.[124]

A culturally based approach to the issue of whether women ought to be permitted to read from the Torah and receive *aliyyot* in today's times would consider the reasons for the current practice and weigh them against arguments that militate in favor of a more inclusive practice. Resort to this type of balancing approach is, in and of itself, a characteristic of cultural analysis, which rejects the idea that the law is autonomous and nonresponsive to cultural realities. This section discusses some philosophically based considerations that favor allowing women to read from the Torah in public and to receive *aliyyot*. These considerations offer a counterpoint to the arguments raised in the prior section discussing resistance to change.

The first consideration focuses on human dignity. This argument posits that denying women the ability to participate in public Torah reading is problematic from a human dignity standpoint with respect to those women who have a spiritual yearning to participate in synagogue ritual in this way.[125] Sperber has been a primary proponent of this position and laments that the current discourse on this topic does not include a discussion of human

---

121. *Id.* at 278.

122. *Id.*

123. *Id.*

124. *Id.* at 279–85. He asserts, however, that this *minhag* can be respected for communities that genuinely believe the synagogue experience is enhanced by this practice. *Id.* at 284. Of course, on a practical level, this position does beg the filtering and framing issues Hartman raises concerning whose voices are allowed into the discourse in any given community. *See supra* notes 92–93 and accompanying text.

125. *See* Sperber, *supra* note 9, at 85. Sperber's points are amply illustrated by the following sentiments of a female Modern Orthodox teenager:

> As the time for Torah reading approaches, someone takes the Torah around the boys' side. I must jump if I wish to reach over the *mechitza* [partition separating the men and women] and kiss the Torah. The [Torah reading] is a bitter point for me. The boys assist, compliment and teach each other—laughing, joking and living the rituals. They literally own the room. I am a nothing.

Eden Farber, *Through the Looking Glass of the* Mechitza, FRESH INK FOR TEENS (Apr. 27, 2013), http://www.freshinkforteens.com/articles/through-looking-glass-mechitza.

dignity. To him, it is clear that "the dignity of the congregation" is of doubtful validity in these times, but even it if exists, "human dignity outweighs communal dignity."[126] Sperber believes that calling women to the Torah to receive *aliyyot* is "within the normative *halakhic* framework," and therefore, the absence of such a change "will constitute a source of pain and anguish to an important segment of the community."[127] In essence, Sperber's argument is based on the cultural analysis insight that the law should reflect a multiplicity of values and be applied in a manner that is as inclusive as possible. Therefore, denying women who very much want to participate in public Torah reading the ability to do so causes them unnecessary distress, because the tradition includes evidence of flexibility on this score.

It is important to emphasize once again that this view does not call for violating the norms of the *mesorah*. Shapiro has observed that the "dignity of the congregation" is "a social sensitivity, and the fact that it must be interpreted to us shows how far removed we are from the social culture of the Talmud."[128] Given the lack of a clear consensus in the tradition early on, a cultural analysis approach leaves the door open for reform even under a traditional perspective.[129]

From the standpoint of cultural analysis, Sperber's human dignity position is extraordinary, not only because of the more inclusive position he endorses, but also because of the nature of his *halakhic* theory given his understanding of the constraints presented by the traditional Jewish sources.[130] He sees the changes for which he advocates as reflective of the overall advancement in the ethical development of humanity—a development the *halakhah* is bound to embrace.[131] Whereas many of those who lobby for retaining the status quo resort to an objectified, rational *halakhic* standard,[132] Sperber's mode of analysis boldly embraces a cultural analysis perspective.

---

126. Sperber, *supra* note 9, at 84.

127. *Id.* at 106.

128. Shapiro, Qeri'at ha-Torah, *supra* note 10, at 247.

129. *See* Sperber, *supra* note 9, at 88.

130. *See id.* at 124 (calling for a "renewed reading of the sources, taking into account the contemporary reality"). *See also* Ross, *supra* note 7, at 23–24.

131. Sperber, *supra* note 9, at 126 (observing that *halakhah* must change in the face of this ethical advancement and "also must encourage such ethical sensitivity").

132. *See* Shapiro, *supra* note 44, at 405–06; Shochetman, *supra* note 9, at 339, 341.

Such an approach to the issues concerning gender and Jewish law requires an important shift in the discourse more generally. As Shapiro has observed, the "formal, categorical basis for opposing women's *aliyyot*" does not necessitate exposing "stressful aspects of Orthodox attitudes toward gender and contemporary culture."[133] Shapiro feels that these formalistic arguments are problematic because they not only "disregard broader issues" but also place an "unfair burden" on the classic Jewish sources.[134] Ross agrees that "[s]hifting the weight of *halakhic* deliberation regarding women's *aliyyot* from the limited vocabulary of legal technicalities to a richer lexicon of principles and policies can contribute much to the honesty of the discussion, revealing the true stakes involved."[135]

Tova Hartman's work emphasizes a second consideration that also is grounded in a philosophical framework. Hartman's central insight in this regard is that the cultivation of a positive collective Jewish identity depends upon reclaiming aspects of the tradition that prioritize "the cultivation of relationships with various different 'others' as integral to one's own sense of self."[136] Although the focus on relationship building clearly is drawn from feminist theory,[137] her insight moves well beyond this discipline. In essence, Hartman is saying that Modern Orthodoxy in particular has done such a good job of incorporating the ideals of Kantian autonomy into its intellectual framework "that it has assimilated too deeply into an extremely Western vision of what modernity means."[138] The result of this assimilation, in her view, is that positive values of relationship building and connection have been lost. Hartman thus sees feminism as an important way to "reaccess the relational ethos of traditional Judaism" so that it can reintroduce these lost values.[139]

The sensibilities about which Hartman writes are very much present in a cultural analysis paradigm that seeks to introduce a multiplicity of values into any discourse. Her argument is that traditional Judaism's very essence would benefit from incorporating the relational ethos of feminism into its discourse, and that such an ethos was present at one point in time. In other

---

133. Shapiro, *supra* note 44, at 406.

134. *Id.*

135. Ross, *supra* note 7, at 16.

136. HARTMAN, *supra* note 81, at 16.

137. *See* CAROL GILLIGAN, IN A DIFFERENT VOICE: PSYCHOLOGICAL THEORY AND WOMEN'S DEVELOPMENT 146–48 (2003).

138. HARTMAN, *supra* note 81, at 13.

139. *Id.* at 14.

words, this perspective is valuable for traditional Judaism's very identity, beyond its application to any specific area of law or the *halakhic* process as a whole.

In the context of increased female participation in public Torah readings, cultural analysis can be used as the basis for re-examining the tradition as well as for modifying the current practice, at least with respect to willing Orthodox communities. As discussed earlier, we are now witnessing some movement in certain Orthodox circles concerning women's involvement in aspects of the religion from which they were previously completely excluded. Women are becoming increasingly educated from a Jewish law standpoint and are even taking on leadership roles in certain areas of decision-making.[140] One Orthodox rabbi has already ordained a female rabbi (despite his subsequent agreement not to do this in the future).[141] Other respected Orthodox scholars are taking the issue of female ordination seriously by exploring the *halakhic* parameters of this possibility.[142] An especially significant development occurred in 2009 with the opening of a privately funded Modern Orthodox yeshiva dedicated to training Orthodox women to be *halakhic* and spiritual leaders.[143] Yeshivat Maharat in New York graduated its first class of three women in the spring of 2013, investing them with the title *maharat*, which means "spiritual leader" in Hebrew.[144] One of its graduates, Rachel Finegold, became the first Orthodox woman to be hired in the capacity of a full clergy member by an unaffiliated synagogue adhering to Orthodox practice. Although Modern Orthodoxy's Rabbinical Council of America currently does not recognize the ordination of females, this development represents an especially important milestone for those seeking a more inclusive approach to the issue of women and synagogue ritual within a traditional context.

The negotiation between preservation and change confronts virtually all cultural traditions in modernity. The past three chapters have examined

---

140. *See supra* notes 108–10 and accompanying text.

141. *See supra* Chapter 1, note 109 and accompanying text.

142. *See, e.g., supra* note 70.

143. *See generally* Sara Hurwitz, *From behind the Veil of* Tzniyut: *Using Modesty to Block Women as Ritual Leaders*, MORETHODOXY (Feb. 7, 2012), http://morethodoxy. org/2012/02/07.

144. *See* Manya A. Brachear, *Chicagoan's Jewish Faith Helps Her Blaze New Spiritual Trail* (Apr. 27, 2013), http://articles.chicagotribune.com/2013-04-27/news/ ct-met-female-orthodox-clergy-20130418_1_modern-orthodox-synagogue-orthodox-wo men-jewish-law.

this global issue in the context of particularly contested areas of Jewish law. Together, they illustrate how a cultural analysis perspective animates a view of Jewish law and *halakhic* process that is dynamic, relational, and culturally driven, regardless of the ultimate outcomes reached on particular issues. Until this point, the role of the state of Israel in applying cultural analysis to Jewish law has not been addressed explicitly. As the following chapter demonstrates, any discussion of Israel from a cultural analysis standpoint raises extraordinarily complicated questions concerning the relationship among Israeli law, Jewish law, and Jewish identity in both Israel and the Diaspora.

8 THE STATE OF ISRAEL'S ROLE IN FORGING JEWISH LAW AND CULTURE IN THE POST-HOLOCAUST ERA

This chapter examines two complex sets of relationships. The first relationship is that which exists between secular Israeli law and *halakhah*, Jewish law. The second relationship is between the *mesorah* (the Jewish tradition, including *halakhah*) and Jewish identity in the state of Israel. Because either one of these issues could be the subject of an entire book, the goal of this discussion is to explore these critical issues in the context of the cultural analysis paradigm developed throughout this book. The first part of this discussion looks specifically at the development of Israeli law as a cultural product and therefore seeks to unbundle not only the historical origins of Israel's secular law, but also how the Israeli legal system negotiates the relationship between its secular law and its rabbinical judicial system. Given the vastly different secular legal model in the United States, the material introduced in this part may be unfamiliar and perhaps even surprising to some readers.

The second part of this chapter focuses primarily on current rather than historical concerns and addresses matters that are at the heart of this book's exploration of Jewish law from a cultural analysis standpoint. Cultural analysis is interested in the role that law plays in forming Jewish culture and identity. Thus, this section examines the unique relationship between *halakhah* specifically, the *mesorah* generally, and the formation of Jewish identity among Israeli Jews.

Halakhah and Israeli Law

The development of Israeli law reflects two particular themes of cultural analysis: marked dispute and the relationship between law and culture. Professor Menachem Mautner observes that Israeli law manifests "the struggle over the shaping of Jewish culture and identity" that has been waged in modernity.[1] Israeli law also serves as an important window into the history of Israel's major cultural processes and furnishes a basis for studying how "Israeli culture and identity in the coming decades will be shaped."[2] Prior to 1948, the existing culture in the *Yishuv*, the term used to designate the Jewish community in the land now called the state of Israel, was largely reflected by an emphasis on Hebrew language and Hebrew culture rather than the Jewish tradition. Those who shaped this culture emphasized the biblical roots of the Israelites rather than the rabbinic *halakhah* that was developed in exile.[3] This emphasis on Hebrew culture peaked in 1948 with the creation of the state but began a slow decline in the 1950s as a rise in traditional Jewish culture, and most recently Israeli culture, has emerged.[4]

In an analysis that is rich with cultural analysis terminology and methodology, Mautner explains that the post-1948 Israeli culture manifested significant cultural borrowing and blended four distinct cultures: traditional Jewish culture, European culture, English culture, and the local secular culture. From a practical perspective, the Jewish tradition provided a "key reservoir" of cultural categories from which the new Israeli culture borrowed, although these elements were revamped with a new, nationalistic perspective.[5] The link to European culture resulted from the mental and behavioral framework that many immigrants from Europe retained once they arrived in Israel.[6] Not surprisingly, the English cultural influence was the product of Britain's governance of the land for the three decades of the British Mandate prior to the establishment of the state of Israel.[7] Finally, the local secular

---

1. Menachem Mautner, Law & The Culture of Israel 1 (2011).

2. *Id.*

3. *Id.* at 23. *See also* David Hartman, *The Significance of Israel for the Future of Judaism, in* Judaism and the Challenges of Modern Life 141, 142 (Moshe Halbertal & Donniel Hartman eds., 2007) (noting that the early Zionists "treated the Bible not only as the greatest literary treasure of the revived Hebrew language, but also as a major source of the ethical norms that would guide Jews in rebuilding their ancient homeland") [hereinafter Judaism and Challenges].

4. Mautner, *supra* note 1, at 24.

5. *Id.* at 25.

6. *Id.* at 26.

7. *Id.* The British Mandate spanned the years 1918–1948.

culture that began to develop in Israel after its establishment influenced the general tone and nature of the emerging Israeli culture.[8] In time, the introduction of a fifth cultural source emerged as American culture began to displace the influence of both the European and English cultures.[9] It is also important to note that the presence of a substantial Arab minority culture from the state's inception has resulted in the existence of two national cultures from the outset.[10]

In more recent decades, the influx of immigrants into Israel has continued to shape considerably the country's rich but heavily contested culture. Well-publicized rescue efforts in the latter part of the twentieth century resulted in the transport of over twenty thousand Ethiopian Jews to Israel between 1984 and 1991.[11] The arrival of Russian-speaking Jews, which intensified in the early 1990s, is even more significant from a numerical standpoint. Today, this group constitutes almost one-sixth of the state's population.[12] Many of these individuals have Jewish roots but are not necessarily Jewish according to *halakhic* standards.[13]

In the early years, the developing Israeli culture was detached from religious Jewish culture, causing some to observe that the new culture created in the state suffered from "cultural thinness and a depletion of meaning."[14] Meanwhile, the secular sector of Israeli society was developing a decidedly liberal stance due to its ties to Western traditions and values. Mautner has observed that as a result of these Western influences, secular Jewish Israelis were able to tap into the raw material they needed to maintain their struggle

---

8. *Id.*

9. *Id.* at 27. *See also* Fania Oz-Salzberger, *What America Means to Israel*, NEWSWEEK (Apr. 22, 2013), http://www.thedailybeast.com/newsweek/2013/04/22/fania-oz-salzberger-what-america-means-to-israel.html. *See also* ASHER COHEN & BERNARD SUSSER, ISRAEL AND THE POLITICS OF JEWISH IDENTITY 107 (2000).

10. MAUTNER, *supra* note 1, at 27.

11. *See The History of Ethiopian Jews*, http://www.jewishvirtuallibrary.org/jsource/Judaism/ejhist.html (last visited July 8, 2014) (noting that the authentic Jewish identity of the Ethiopian Jews has been confirmed by both the Sephardic and Ashkenazic Chief Rabbinate in Israel). They have been accepted officially under the Israeli Law of Return. *See Timeline of Ethiopian Jewish History*, http://www.jewishvirtuallibrary.org/jsource/Judaism/ejtime.html (last visited July 8, 2014). For a further discussion of the Israeli Law of Return, see *supra* Chapter 5, notes 44–49 and accompanying text.

12. Philip Reeves, *On Multiple Fronts, Russian Jews Reshape Israel*, NPR (Jan. 2, 2013), http://www.npr.org/2013/01/02/168457444/on-multiple-fronts-russian-jews-reshape-israel.

13. *See supra* Chapter 5, note 50 and accompanying text.

14. MAUTNER, *supra* note 1, at 28.

against the Jewish religious culture that began to emerge in the later decades of the twentieth century. Whereas the religious groups tapped into a vibrant religious tradition, the secular culture relied on Western values such as "humanism, natural law, natural rights and liberalism" that became the backbone of the law created and applied by Israeli courts.[15] In turn, this legal trend facilitated an emphasis among the greater secular Israeli society on individualism, hedonism, consumerism, and other hallmarks of a "neo-liberal" worldview.[16] This situation increased the perception of "cultural shallowness," which in turn strengthened the "anti-Western and anti-liberal" sentiment of Jewish religious fundamentalists.[17] The "slide to the right" among the American Orthodox communities discussed in Chapter 4 became even more pronounced among many Orthodox communities in Israel.[18]

Since the state of Israel's inception, there were voices favoring *halakhah* as the basis for Israeli law. In 1947, David Ben Gurion, the first prime minister of Israel, sent a letter to the representative of the Orthodox Agudah party seeking to ensure Agudah's part in signing the state's Declaration of Independence. He promised "that marriage in Israel would be in accordance with Torah law, that *Shabbat* [the Sabbath] would be the day of rest, and that kosher food would be served in the military."[19] This letter established the status quo that subsequently "served as the general guideline for questions of religion and state."[20] Nevertheless, in the early years of Israel's existence, most of the voices looking to *halakhah* were secular and therefore urged the adoption of a *halakhic* approach that was revamped with a focus on Jewish nationalism rather than binding religious obligation.[21] Given the influence of British law in Israel's early years, however, those urging this approach as the basis for the state's law found little traction initially.

---

15. *Id.* at 30.

16. *Id.*

17. *Id.*

18. *See supra* Chapter 4, notes 109–18 and accompanying text.

19. Menachem Lorberbaum, *Religion and State in Israel, in* JUDAISM AND CHALLENGES, *supra* note 3, at 152. The struggle between the religious and the secular sectors in Israel is manifested even in the language of the Declaration of Independence, which reflects a linguistic compromise using the term "Rock of Israel" rather than a direct reference to God. *See* COHEN & SUSSER, *supra* note 9, at xi.

20. Lorberbaum, *supra* note 19, at 152. Thus, the state of affairs on these matters that "had prevailed in the *Yishuv* would prevail in the state." COHEN & SUSSER, *supra* note 9, at 18.

21. MAUTNER, *supra* note 1, at 32. According to Mautner, this movement declined in the late 1940s.

With respect to the issue of a constitution for the state, the influence of the religious groups on the outcome was, and remains, substantial. The religious groups opposed the drafting of a constitution, on the ground that any constitution acceptable to the secular camp would be incapable of adequately expressing the essential character of a Jewish state (namely, as one that complies with the laws of the Torah). Partly as a result of this opposition, no constitution ever was drafted.[22] Instead, a compromise plan was implemented for the Knesset (Israel's legislature) to pass a series of Basic Laws that would eventually become the basis for a constitutional document.[23] Moreover, Israeli politics came to be characterized by a compromise-oriented style manifesting mutual accommodation. This style has been termed "consociational" by Professors Asher Cohen and Bernard Susser.[24]

In the latter part of the twentieth century, Israel passed several laws that partially opened the door to a greater sphere of *halakhic* influence in the operation of the state's secular laws. In 1980, the Knesset passed the Foundations of Law statute that called for the following sources as grounds for decision in situations where the existing law does not furnish an answer: "the principles of freedom, justice, equity and *peace of Israel's heritage*."[25] Significantly, this statute also revoked the law dictating that English law should be the basis for amplification of Israeli law.[26] Although in practice, the courts are too deeply attached to Anglo-American law for this statute to make a meaningful difference, in theory it "has compelled the Israeli legal community to confront fundamental questions about Israeli identity in general, and about the identity of Israeli law in particular."[27]

In 1992, the Knesset enacted the following two Basic Laws that can be understood "as part of the general drive toward constitutionalism" that was renewed in the second half of the 1980s: Basic Law: Human Dignity, and

---

22. COHEN & SUSSER, *supra* note 9, at 21. *See also id.* at 87 (discussing Ben-Gurion's fear "that a constitution would limit his political maneuvering room").

23. *Id.* at 87. The authors also discuss the reasons the Basic Laws prior to the 1990s were not "constitutional" documents "in the familiar Western sense" given their ability to be easily repealed and modified. *Id.* at 87–88.

24. *Id.* at xii.

25. Foundations of Law, 5740–1980, 34 LSI 181, § 1 (1948–1989) (emphasis added). *See* MAUTNER, *supra* note 1, at 41.

26. MAUTNER, *supra* note 1, at 41.

27. *Id.*

Liberty and Basic Law: Freedom of Occupation.[28] Both of these Basic Laws provide that their purpose is "to entrench in a Basic Law the values of the state of Israel as a Jewish and democratic state."[29] The legislative enactment process, impact, and aftermath of these two laws is complex and beyond the scope of this treatment.[30] Significant for purposes of this discussion, however, is the point that the invocation of the "Jewish and democratic" terminology again required Israeli jurists to contend with the fundamental issues of the nation's cultural identity and that of its legal system.[31] Further, some believe this language marked a shift in the balance of power between liberalism and Judaism in Israeli law, with the latter encroaching upon the former's position as the main source of inspiration in the development of the state's secular law.[32] This development required, however, a definition of what it means to be a "Jewish" state, a topic that was hotly contested by Aharon Barak and Menachem Elon, two of the especially influential justices of the Israeli Supreme Court during this time.

Originally Justice Barak sought to define Jewishness through a rather abstract perspective as opposed to one that called for the introduction of actual *halakhah* into the creation of Israeli secular law. Justice Elon, in contrast, endorsed a direct application of *halakhah* as part of what it means to be a Jewish state.[33] Elon also believed that the contents of Judaism should be learned through the traditional sources of the religion and its heritage. By the end of their contested discourse on this topic, however, there was not as significant a difference in their respective approaches. Justice Barak moved more toward the position of Justice Elon, so that both appeared willing to accord *halakhah* a central position in the law's development and to learn about Judaism's values from the "inside" sources.[34] Although these justices may have reached a level of theoretical agreement, the real-world application of what it means to be a Jewish state, and how this identity meshes with that of a democratic state, remains difficult. Professor Menachem Lorberbaum

---

28. COHEN & SUSSER, *supra* note 9, at 86, 88.

29. MAUTNER, *supra* note 1, at 44.

30. For a more detailed discussion, see COHEN & SUSSER, *supra* note 9, at 88–95.

31. MAUTNER, *supra* note 1, at 44.

32. *See id.* at 45.

33. *Id.* at 50.

34. *Id.* at 52. In practice, many judges on various courts in Israel refer to *halakhah* in their opinions. I thank Tal Zarsky for bringing this point to my attention with specific examples

has observed that "the state of Israel has not succeeded in adequately address-ing the place of religion in its political society"[35] and therefore, "both secular and religious Israelis have come to the point that they do not understand what a 'Jewish and democratic state' might even mean."[36]

In 2013, the Israeli Supreme Court grappled with a lawsuit that clearly implicated this central question of the meaning of a Jewish democratic state. The suit was filed by twenty-one Israelis, most of whom are officially regis-tered as Jews but who were requesting to be listed as Israeli in the registry. The group had argued that without a secular Israeli identity, Israeli policies would favor Jews and discriminate against minorities. The Court refused to allow the category of "secular Israeli" on the nation's population regis-try. According to Anita Shapira, professor emerita of Jewish history at Tel Aviv University, "the attempt to claim that there is a Jewish nationality in the state of Israel that is separate from the Jewish religion is something very revolutionary."[37]

In addition to the foregoing complexities, the Israeli judicial system's dualistic regime is relatively unusual with respect to family law. The rabbini-cal court system predated the establishment of the state of Israel by hundreds of years by virtue of the Ottoman Empire's imposition of the *millet* system under which distinct groups resorted to their own religious tribunals in mat-ters relating to personal status.[38] Although the original jurisdiction of the rabbinical courts included a variety of family and estate matters of law, at this point rabbinical courts retain "sole authority to issue and validate divorce decrees and parallel authority in all matters related to divorce"[39] such as child custody and division of property.[40] Moreover, both civil family courts and rab-binical courts decide divorce according to *halakhah*, "unless an overriding norm

---

of judges who quote and rely on *halakhah*. E-mail from Tal Zarsky to author, Sept. 25, 2013 (3:00 a.m. CST).

35. Lorberbaum, *supra* note 19, at 153.

36. *Id.* at 154.

37. Tia Goldenberg, *Israeli Court Rejects Israeli Nationality Status*, ASSOCIATED PRESS (Oct. 4, 2013), http://news.yahoo.com/israeli-court-rejects-israeli-nationality-status-062621938.html.

38. Daphna Hacker, *Religious Tribunals in Democratic States: Lessons from the Israeli Rabbinical Courts*, XXVII J. L. & RELIGION 59, 62 (2012). This reality also illustrates the influence of Turkish law on the Israeli legal system.

39. *Id.* at 78. *See also* Rabbinical Court Jurisdiction (Marriage and Divorce) Law, 5713–1953, 7 LSI 139, § 1 (1953) (Isr.).

40. Hacker, *supra* note 38, at 63.

is set in a specific civil law provision."[41] In this respect, then, religious law governs even those who are not observant Jews. With respect to matters such as adoption and inheritance, civil courts have juristic priority but rabbinical courts may have jurisdiction if all parties consent.[42] Thus, the current situation allows certain family law matters to be governed exclusively by religious law while other matters are governed by "a complicated system of overlapping jurisdiction."[43]

The 1995 Sanctions Law furnishes an interesting example of the intersection between the mandate of *halakhah* and the operation of secular law that is unique to Israel.[44] According to *halakhah*, a legal divorce requires the husband to grant the wife a Jewish decree of divorce, known as a *get*.[45] The Knesset passed the Sanctions Law to allow the imposition of a variety of sanctions against husbands who refuse to grant their wives a *get*. This law now also applies to wives who refuse to *receive* a get, but in practice, this rarely occurs.[46] Wives, by virtue of Jewish law, are more vulnerable than husbands because women, but not men, are clearly prohibited from remarrying without a valid *get*.[47] Among other things, the stipulated sanctions prevent recalcitrant spouses from traveling outside of Israel; from obtaining, maintaining, or renewing a driver's license; and from working in a profession regulated by the law. The sanctions also limit the freedoms of spouses who are serving prison sentences.[48] According to a study conducted by Bar-Ilan University's Rackman Center for the Advancement of the Status of Women, these sanctions are used only in 1.5 percent of the cases in

---

41. *Id.*

42. *See id. See also* Succession Law, 5725–1965, SH No. 446 p. 63; Adoption of Children Law, 5741–1981, 35 LSI 365, §§ 26–27 (1980–1981) (Isr.).

43. Hacker, *supra* note 38, at 64.

44. Rabbinical Courts Law (Enforcement of Divorce Judgments), 5755–1995, SH No. 1507 p. 139 (Isr.).

45. The basis for this law is Deuteronomy 24:1, which speaks of a husband handing his wife a bill of divorcement and sending her away from his home.

46. *See* Yehiel S. Kaplan, *Enforcement of Divorce Judgments in Jewish Courts in Israel: The Interaction between Religious and Constitutional Law, in* MIDDLE EAST LAW AND GOVERNANCE 1, 37 (2012), http://weblaw.haifa.ac.il/he/Faculty/Kaplan/Publications/MELG_article-Kaplan-divorce%20judgments.pdf.

47. *See* Hacker, *supra* note 38, at 71. Further, should a woman have children with a man who is not her husband, the offspring are considered *mamzerim* (bastards), who are only allowed to marry other people of a similar status.

48. *See* Kaplan, *supra* note 46, at 31. In 2000, the law was amended to allow further sanctions upon spouses serving prison sentences. Rabbinical Courts Law (Enforcement of Divorce Judgments), (Amendment no. 4) 5760–2000, 1732 LSI 133 (2000) (Isr.).

which they are applicable.[49] The reluctance on the part of the rabbinical courts to utilize this law to impose sanctions derives from Jewish law's view that inappropriate coercive sanctions may potentially invalidate the *get* because, according to *halakhah*, it must be granted and received consensually.[50]

The draft bill preceding the Sanctions Law explained that it was designed to rely upon Jewish law's acceptance of isolating measures in order to afford a means of relieving the plight of those married to recalcitrant spouses.[51] In this respect, then, Israel essentially codified *halakhah* in its secular law when it adopted the Sanctions Law. According to some observers of family law practice in Israel, there is a stark dichotomy between the rabbinical courts' internal perception of their own authority as compared with the perception of their authority by the secular courts. Specifically, the judges of the rabbinical courts (known as *dayanim*) see their authority as deriving from *halakhah*, and therefore, they evaluate any secular legislation from the standpoint of whether it facilitates the implementation of *halakhah*. In contrast, the secular courts believe the jurisdiction of rabbinical courts is created by the law of the state, and therefore, limited in scope.[52]

Additional problems are reflected in legal scholar Daphna Hacker's comparative empirical study of rabbinical and civil court adjudications of both divorce and inheritance matters that, taken together, spanned the period 1997–2004. Hacker noted the existence of a striking discrepancy in the behavior of the rabbinical courts with respect to these two types of disputes. Specifically, she concluded that the rabbinical courts zealously guarded their jurisdiction in matters of divorce but often refrained from asserting their jurisdiction and authority in inheritance matters. Hacker explains this divergence largely as the result of the institutional freedom enjoyed by rabbinical courts given their sole jurisdiction with respect to the issuance and validation of divorce decrees.[53]

---

49. Jeremy Sharon, *Bar-On Urges Sanctions on Men Who Refuse Divorce*, JERUSALEM POST (Jan. 18, 2012), http://www.jpost.com/Diplomacy-and-Politics/Bar-On-urges-sanctions-on-men-who-refuse-divorce.

50. Kaplan, *supra* note 46, at 4, 52.

51. *Id.* at 57.

52. I thank Rabbi Jeremy Stern, a practicing family law attorney in Israel, for this observation. *See also* Kaplan, *supra* note 46, at 42–49.

53. Hacker, *supra* note 38, at 78–79. *See also supra* note 40 and accompanying text. Hacker claims that "the grant of sole jurisdiction over a particular subset of legal matters to the rabbinical courts is easily followed by resistance to liberal values." *Id.* at 78. With respect to the topic of divorce, however, both Hacker's work and other studies demonstrate that the civil system also is problematic for women. *Id.*

In the 1990s, the Religious-Zionist contingent[54] augmented the difficulties stemming from the dual system of jurisdiction by establishing a system of arbitration tribunals in competition with the state court system. The objective of these tribunals is the resolution of private civil disputes according to *halakhah*.[55] Additionally, there is a movement by the state's rabbinical courts to expand their current jurisdiction over family law matters to provide arbitration services in private civil law matters.[56] These two developments have "contributed to furthering the claim that the *halakhah* should be made the prevailing law in the state."[57] These developments also illustrate how in Israel, "private law has become a site for waging the war of cultures!"[58] Observers believe that the "coalitional politics of religion in Israel are indicative of a much deeper cultural rift."[59]

In analyzing the unique legal landscape in Israel, Mautner has observed that the real problem in connection with Israel's multiculturalism is the lack of definition with respect to the composition of the state's "center"—"the character of the regime, political culture and law of the country."[60] A further consequence of this lack of definition is that despite Israel's status as a liberal democracy, the institutions of the ultra-Orthodox and Religious Zionist groups receive substantial funding and are enshrined with the religious power of the nation.[61] Indeed, a recent article appearing in the American Modern Orthodox journal *Tradition Magazine* actually reveals the rich irony embedded in the relationship between Israel's liberal ideology and multicultural religious accommodation. In "The Practice of Gender Separation on Buses in the Ultra-Orthodox Community in Israel: A View from the Liberal Cathedral," Rabbi Yehuda Warburg makes the argument that gender separation on public transportation can be viewed as consistent with the values of liberal multiculturalism.[62] Specifically, because the practice of gender separation

---

54. The Religious Zionists embrace the state of Israel as "a prelude to the coming of the Messiah." Hartman, *supra* note 3, at 144. In contrast, most ultra-Orthodox Jews do not have any ideological identification with the state. *See infra* notes 77–84 and accompanying text.

55. MAUTNER, *supra* note 1, at 189.

56. *Id.* at 53, 189.

57. *Id.* at 53.

58. *Id.* at 190.

59. Lorberbaum, *supra* note 19, at 152.

60. MAUTNER, *supra* note 1, at 191. In this respect, he equates Israel to countries in the Middle East.

61. *Id.*

62. A Yehuda Warburg, 44 TRADITION 19, 28, Spring 2011.

on Israeli buses has a valid *halakhic* basis, and because those engaged in this practice find it meaningful and morally significant, this practice manifests a "liberal multicultural accommodation agenda."[63] Although the Supreme Court ruled in 2011 that state enforcement of gender segregation on public transportation is illegal, passengers may elect gender separation, and therefore, those segregated bus lines in existence can continue to operate. Thus, the critical element of Warburg's contribution for purposes of this discussion is that the type of neutrality manifested by this decision—and by the approach he endorses—is nonetheless consistent with a liberal state order.[64] As of this writing, others would vehemently disagree, including the current Minister of Justice, Tzipi Livni, who has pledged to push through legislation outlawing any such segregated service.[65]

Although there are signs of change in Israel, historically the "liberals" were content to abdicate matters of religion in favor of all else. From a cultural analysis standpoint, the problem with this approach is that religion is a part of the entire cultural fabric and cannot be confined to a separate sphere. The integration of law and culture prompts the question of how to define Jewish identity. This complex issue must be unbundled given the importance of Jewish identity to the perpetuation of the tradition, a central concern of cultural analysis. Specifically, although adherence to *halakhah* is one measure of Jewish identity, cultural analysis methodology suggests there are other important markers given the inevitable intersection of law and culture. In light of the distinct cultural conditions and challenges facing Israeli and Diaspora Jews, the subject of identity formation is best addressed separately for these groups. The following section concentrates on Israeli Jewish identity, and Chapter 9 examines the formation of Jewish identity in the Diaspora.

An Examination of Israeli Jewish Identity

The relationship between *halakhah* and Jewish identity is a foundational element of this book's examination of Jewish law through a cultural analysis paradigm. Therefore, it is important to examine what it means for Israel to

---

63. *Id.* at 28 (discussing and embracing the view of law professor Alon Harel).

64. *Id.* at 23.

65. Jeffrey Heller, *Israel Seeks to End Back-of-the-Bus Gender Segregation*, REUTERS (May 9, 2013), http://www.reuters.com/article/2013/05/09/us-israel-women-idUSBRE9480FH20130509.

be considered a Jewish state when the majority of Jews in the country do not observe Jewish law. If a cultural analysis of Jewish law suggests that observance of the *halakhah* promotes Jewish particularity and survival, what are the implications for Israel, and for world-Jewry, in light of the reality that most Israelis are not religious in a traditional sense?

The discussion of the history of Israel and its culture in the first part of this chapter furnishes an important backdrop for this discussion. Recall that the early secular Zionists did not reject the Jewish tradition but instead reformulated it, particularly its biblical roots, with a nationalistic emphasis.[66] Rabbi David Hartman has noted that in doing so, these secular Zionists could not help but invoke the Jewish heritage "as a major source of the ethical norms that would guide Jews in rebuilding their ancient homeland."[67] He also observed that the "concern for the survival of the Jewish people and commitment to the state of Israel" substituted for traditional Judaism.[68] Nonetheless, these early secularists "rejected the traditional view that the covenant with God at Sinai was constitutive of Jewish self-understanding."[69]

Recall that unanimity never has existed on the subject of what it means for Israel to be a Jewish state, as evidenced by the debate between Justices Elon and Barak discussed earlier in this chapter. Observers of Israeli culture believe that since the mid 1980s the situation has worsened "to a crisis-dominated relationship between secular and religious Jews" that has become "progressively more strident" as these groups have lost a common political language.[70] Writing in the late 1990s, Cohen and Susser refer to this struggle as "the politics of identity" that embodies "the very identity of the Jewish collectivity in Israel."[71] They argue that both the secular and the religious camps have lost interest in the "consociational" model, which embodied "the adaptive, unity-preserving political style of the first decades of Israel's existence."[72]

---

66. *See supra* notes 3–5 and accompanying text.

67. Hartman, *supra* note 3, at 141, 142.

68. *Id.* at 143.

69. *Id.*

70. COHEN & SUSSER, *supra* note 9, at xiii.

71. *Id.* at x. The authors emphasize that this struggle is not about "distributory justice" but instead embodies a much more fundamental type of conflict involving "the very nature of the Jewish state." *Id.* at 20–21.

72. *Id.* at xii–xiii. The authors note that institutions in the *Yishuv* also manifested a consociational style of operation. *Id.* at 5. In their view, the legal and authoritative status of the rabbinic courts constitutes "one of the central arrangements hammered out during the formative period of Israel's consociationalism." *Id.* at 77.

Instead, both sides are now "playing to win."[73] The political and cultural climate in Israel today continues to mirror this reality.

Political theorist Michael Walzer has observed that Jewish identity is anomalous because it is composed of two collectives, nationhood and religion, which do not typically coincide.[74] Although throughout the centuries of exile the Jews may have been a "stateless nation,"[75] the biblical narrative combined both of these collectives into a singular whole, and it is through this narrative that Jewish identity was defined historically. The co-existence of these two collectives produced an uncomfortable fit for those Orthodox Jews who initially denied any religious significance to the establishment of the state of Israel. The basis for this view is the idea that "the establishment of a Jewish state represents a serious infringement on the role of God and Torah in Jewish history."[76] In other words, for this group of Jews, God's direct intervention rather than the secular world's political processes must provide the path to redemption. This view continues to be the party line for the majority of Israel's *haredim* (ultra-Orthodox) community despite their participation since 1977 in government coalitions in order to ensure continued support for their institutions.[77] Thus, these Jews do not celebrate Israel's Independence Day or offer the traditional prayers of thanksgiving for the re-establishment of the state.[78] More fundamentally, they believe the current type of identity Israel offers Jews poses a dangerous threat to the traditional Jewish worldview to the extent it is a proactive model based on elements such as Hebrew language, nationalism, Zionist history, and folklore rather than *halakhah*, spirituality, patience, and obedience to Divine command.[79] In essence, the ultra-Orthodox are opposed to the idea of Israel as a Western, liberal democracy.[80] In terms of numbers, this group represents about 8 percent of the

---

73. *Id.* at xiii–xiv.

74. Michael Walzer, *The Anomalies of Jewish Political Identity*, *in* JUDAISM AND CHALLENGES, *supra* note 3, at 134.

75. *Id.*

76. Hartman, *supra* note 3, at 143. *See also supra* Chapter 4, note 188 and accompanying text.

77. MAUTNER, *supra* note 1, at 122–23.

78. Hartman, *supra* note 3, at 144.

79. *Id.*

80. *See* COHEN & SUSSER, *supra* note 9, at 92 (also noting "that the very dispute over constitutional principles has become integral to the general confrontation over collective Jewish identity in the Jewish state").

Jewish population in Israel,[81] although the number is growing due to high birth rates.

In contrast to the *haredim*, the Religious Zionists (comprising between 12 to 15 percent of the state's Jewish population)[82] strongly embrace the state of Israel as a prelude to the establishment of the messianic kingdom on earth. Rabbi Abraham Isaac Kook, the first Ashkenazic Chief Rabbi of the *Yishuv*, initially espoused this perspective prior to the state's creation, and his teachings still influence the movement.[83] Today, Religious Zionists "assign religious value to nation building activities such as settlement, military service, economic development, and even the cultivation of national Hebrew culture."[84]

Thus, among traditionally observant groups in Israel, both the state and the physical land are topics of dispute. For many *haredim* today, the state of Israel and the land itself are not essential to their worldview and to their Jewish identity. In contrast, for the Religious Zionists, both the state and the tangible land furnish an opportunity for messianic redemption and are of vital importance to their mission and ideology

With respect to Israel's non-Orthodox Jewish population, at least three distinct types of nationalistic identity have been identified. For a significant group of secular Israelis, including a large number of Russian immigrants who may not even be *halakhically* Jewish,[85] the state of Israel essentially constitutes the sole content of their Jewish identity. According to Professors Shlomo Fischer and Suzanne Last Stone, the primary meaning of Israeli Jewishness to this group "seems to be that one identifies with the Jewish state and values the state's well-being."[86] This identification necessitates "partaking in the effort and responsibility to maintain and cultivate the state, and to share in the trust and social capital necessary for this effort."[87] Fischer

---

81. Shlomo Fischer & Suzanne Last Stone, *Jewish Identity and Identification: New Patterns, Meanings, and Networks* 12 (Jewish People Policy Inst., Working Paper, 2012), http://ejewishphilanthropy.com/wordpress/wp-content/uploads/2012/11/Jewish_Identity_and_Identification-New_Paterns_Meanings_and_Networks.pdf.

82. *Id.* at 13.

83. *See* Hartman, *supra* note 3, at 144–45.

84. Fischer & Stone, *supra* note 81, at 13 (noting that "for many Religious Zionists, the primary instrument for the explicit sacralization of Jewish nationalism is the project of settling and annexing 'Greater Israel' (Judea and Samaria and the Golan)").

85. *See supra* note 12–13 and accompanying text.

86. Fischer & Stone, *supra* note 81, at 12.

87. *Id.*

and Stone note, however, that this "context-bound" Jewish identity results in a problem when such Israeli Jews move abroad. Specifically, they suggest that these Israelis resist developing contacts with their respective local Jewish communities in their new environments. Instead, they form communities of expatriate Israeli Jews with whom they share a cultural affiliation.[88]

For this group of Israeli Jews, the religious component of Israeli Jewish identity is completely overshadowed by the nationalistic aspect. Hartman also has observed that "in contrast to the Diaspora, there is a much sharper repudiation of traditional Judaism in Israeli Jewish society than in many other Jewish communities."[89] Undoubtedly, the tensions between the *haredim* and other Israeli Jews have been fueled by the state's historically favorable treatment of the *haredim* with respect to educational funding, exemption from military service,[90] and the perpetuation of a legal system that places control of marriage and divorce in the hands of this group.[91]

It is also possible, however, that these observations do not tell the whole story of Jewish identity for secular Israelis, especially when they move to large urban centers in the United States where they cannot help but interact with other Jews on a regular basis. Despite the findings of Fischer and Stone concerning how these Jews manifest Jewish identity when they move away from Israel, other evidence suggests that Israelis often manage to find a greater religious Jewish identity outside of Israel. In *The Case for Jewish Peoplehood*, Doctors Erica Brown and Misha Galperin have noted that when secular Israeli Jews are liberated from the politics and the perceived religiously coercive characteristics of life in Israel, they often allow themselves to embrace a more traditional Jewish identity.[92] Their findings are supported by anecdotal evidence based on the experience of Israeli Jews living in the United States, particularly those who gravitate to Reform and Conservative synagogues.

Brown and Galperin note a second type of Israeli Jewish identity that is perhaps less focused on nationalistic concerns and more focused on

---

88. *Id.*

89. Hartman, *supra* note 3, at 146.

90. In March 2014, a draft bill was passed requiring military national service for ultra-Orthodox Jews, with enforcement scheduled to begin in mid-2017. *See* Haviv Rettig Gur, *New Ultra-Orthodox Draft Law Seen as Ineffective, Insulting*, TIMES OF ISRAEL (Mar. 19, 2014), http://www.timesofisrael.com/after-passage-criticism-of-haredi-draft-law-abounds.

91. *See supra* notes 38–43 and accompanying text.

92. ERICA BROWN & MISHA GALPERIN, THE CASE FOR JEWISH PEOPLEHOOD 137 (2009).

familism.[93] These authors note that Israeli Jews have embraced "familism as a component of peoplehood with greater intensity than American Jews have."[94] Their explanation of this phenomenon is not surprising: "Being part of a small and progressive nation often under siege and the only democracy in the Middle East has created a degree of isolation from Israel's geographic neighbors that mimics the ties that exist in families."[95] As is the case with the first type of nationalistic identity, however, this identity embodies a cultural thinness given its lack of a relationship to the religious tradition.

A third, and still emerging, type of Israeli Jewish identity derives from the work of David Hartman and other scholars. Hartman, an Orthodox rabbi and the founder of the Shalom Hartman Institute dedicated to pluralistic Jewish research and education, believed that Israel furnishes the laboratory where Jewish life and values can be actualized. He observed that by "returning to the land, we have created the conditions through which everyday life can mediate the biblical foundations of our covenantal destiny."[96] His philosophy differs from that of some Religious Zionists because he wants to avoid treating "the rise of Israel as a divine ruse leading towards the messianic kingdom."[97] Instead, his vision for the state is a proactive one focused on the here and now, which sees Israel as providing an opportunity to redefine the meaning of the covenant between God and the Jews. This redefinition requires the covenantal community to take upon "itself responsibility for what the word of God means."[98] According to Hartman, therefore, "rebuilding and renewing the community's national life extended and developed further the rabbinic tradition's understanding of the role assigned to human beings in the covenant."[99]

Hartman's vision thus depends upon the proactive utilization of Judaism's values, which are essentially seen as part of the "public domain" of the country. According to this vision, the return of the Jews to the land furnishes the opportunity to put Jewish values into action. Israel is, in other words, the laboratory of Judaism today. Fischer and Stone, working in conjunction

---

93. *Id.* at 143.

94. *Id.* at 144.

95. *Id.*

96. Hartman, *supra* note 3, at 145.

97. *Id.*

98. *Id.* at 150.

99. *Id.* at 149.

with Israel's Jewish People Policy Institute, are in the process of articulating a compatible vision of Israeli Jewish identity that understands "Judaism as a civilization." Their vision calls for utilization of the texts and traditions of Judaism as a "present-day resource"[100] to create "a renewed Jewish culture."[101] Like Hartman, they differentiate their version of Israeli Jewish identity from that of the more militant Religious Zionist movement. Their "Judaism as a civilization" model posits "the social message of Judaism and the ordering of interpersonal relations" as central components of the cultural constitution.[102]

The viability of visions such as that of Hartman, Fischer, and Stone depends upon providing a greater definitional content to the social message of Judaism and the core Jewish values upon which these formulations depend.[103] The *mesorah*, with its long-standing concern for social justice, provides much content from which to draw. Recall from Chapter 4 the discussion of Rabbi Samson Raphael Hirsch's view that Judaism requires the Jews to provide their non-Jewish neighbors with love and support, as well as economic and spiritual sustenance.[104] In 1977, the first act of Menachem Begin after he became prime minister was to take in and give citizenship to sixty-six Vietnamese refugees fleeing on a small, leaky boat from the communist takeover of their homeland.[105] More recently, this philosophy has been actualized in Israel through the work of organizations such as Israel Flying Aid, the Israeli global humanitarian organization that was first to land in Haiti following the 2010 earthquake. Such organizations *literally deliver* Judaism's message of social justice to victims of natural disasters and devastation worldwide.[106] Another prime example of such "literal delivery" occurred

---

100. Fischer & Stone, *supra* note 81, at 6.

101. *Id.* at 16.

102. *Id.* at 14.

103. To the extent these visions can be seen as utopian models, they can be compared with Theodor Herzl's depiction of the perfect Jewish state in the Land of Israel in his novel *Altneuland* (The Old New Land), published in 1902. In this seminal Zionist text, he illustrates a utopian, liberal-egalitarian society. Herzl was the founder of political Zionism.

104. *See supra* Chapter 4, note 91 and accompanying text.

105. Shoshana Bryen, *Israel and the Boat People*, TIMES OF ISRAEL (June 6, 2012), http://blogs.timesofisrael.com/israel-and-the-boat-people/. At the time, Begin told President Carter that it was "natural" for Israel to provide a "haven in the land of Israel" for these refugees as he recalled the refusal of any countries to take in the nine hundred Jews who tried to flee Germany on a boat in the weeks before World War II.

106. *See* Karen Levy, *Israel Flying Aid Gives Food, Generators, Gas to Hurricane Sandy Victims*, NEW MEDIA J. (Nov. 4, 2012), http://newmediajournal.us/indx.php/item/7468.

in the wake of Typhoon Haiyan in November 2013. The Israeli Defense Forces set up a makeshift hospital in the Philippines following this natural disaster, in which Israeli army medics delivered a baby boy whose parents named him "Israel" as a showing of gratitude.[107] The state of Israel also has officially implemented Judaism's social message on a national level through MASHAV, Israel's Agency for International Development Cooperation. This agency is a division of the Ministry of Foreign Affairs, and it was created in 1958 when Israel was very much a fledgling nation. Its purpose is to provide training to people from other developing countries in areas of Israel's expertise, such as water management. Since its inception, over 140 nations have sent representatives to Israel to learn relevant skills and techniques that are designed to alleviate poverty, enhance education and health services, and provide greater food security.[108]

A fair understanding of both the Hartman approach and the "Judaism as a civilization" conception of Israeli Jewish identity acknowledges that although they are not necessarily tied to strict *halakhic* observance, they are very much influenced by the values of both *halakhah* specifically and the *mesorah* in general. Thus, these visions of Israeli Jewish identity are steeped in a cultural analysis methodology given their implicit recognition that law and culture are inseparable. The successful implementation of these models prioritizes knowledge of the Jewish tradition as well as a general commitment to the importance of *halakhah* in shaping Jewish values. They are premised on the theoretical foundation that Israeli Jewish identity can, and must, be defined more broadly than simply adhering to a *halakhic* lifestyle. Additionally, they place a premium on the knowledge that can be culled from the *mesorah* in furnishing a present-day laboratory for Judaism's values to be actualized. From a practical perspective, they emphasize proactive measures designed to improve life in the here and now by utilizing the core values of the *mesorah*.

In the wake of Hurricane Sandy, Israel Flying Aid also supplied large quantities of gas to hospitals, as well as food, batteries, and generators. *See also* Rachel Avraham, *IsraAID Is Helping Hurricane Sandy Victims*, UNITED WITH ISRAEL (Nov. 14, 2012), http://unitedwithisrael. org/israaid-hurricane-sandy/#.UbjrE-DR1FI\ (discussing IsraeAID's disaster relief efforts in New York as well as Japan, Haiti, and the South Sudan).

107. *See* ASSOCIATED PRESS, *Cebu—Israeli Army Deliver Baby in Typhoon-Hit Philippines, Mother Names Him Israel*, VOSIZNEIAS (Nov. 16, 2013), http://www.vosizneias.com/ 146640/2013/11/16/2139-cebu-israeli-army-deliver-baby-in-typhoon-hit-philippines -mother-names-him-israel/.

108. *See* ISRAEL DIPLOMATIC NETWORK: EMBASSY OF ISRAEL IN INDIA, MASHAV– ISRAEL'S AGENCY FOR INTERNATIONAL DEVELOPMENT COOPERATION (2014), http:// embassies.gov.il/delhi/Departments/Pages/MASHAV.aspx.

For those concerned with greater religious pluralism in Israel as well as the perpetuation of democracy, this type of Israeli Jewish identity is likely to be very appealing. Thus, Lorberbaum has eloquently explained the connection between religious pluralism and democracy in articulating his vision of Israeli Jewish identity. He asserts that "Jewish politics must be worldly in character while always seeking to negotiate the place of the holy in human life."[109] A proponent of Jewish religious pluralism and "affirming the value of freedom of religion," Lorberbaum argues that "the democratic debate in Israel should allow the differences in society to surface in the parliamentary deliberation as to the Jewish cultural and religious character of public space."[110]

With respect to top-down action by the state, historically Israel's track record in encouraging religious pluralism clearly is problematic. Despite calls for change,[111] both the Ashkenazic and Sephardic chief rabbis of the state, as well as the more than 150 state-employed neighborhood rabbis, all are Orthodox. Moreover, non-Orthodox movements typically do not receive state funding for their rabbinic leaders or communal activities.[112] This situation is believed by some to be inconsistent with Israel's status as a democracy.[113] The status quo also is troubling to those who believe that "Israel

---

109. Lorberbaum, *supra* note 19, at 152, 160.

110. *Id.* at 161.

111. *Id.* at 162 ("The state should actively help to fund the whole variety of religious forms of life as a means of encouraging individual freedom of religion and freedom of religious association."). *See also* Donniel Hartman, *Only Multiple Chief Rabbis Will Guarantee Religious Freedom in Israel*, SHALOM HARTMAN INSTITUTE (May 5, 2013), http://www.hartman. org.il/Blogs_View.asp?Article_Id=1131&Cat_Id=273&Cat_Type=Blogs; David Golinkin, *Abolish the Chief Rabbinate*, JERUSALEM REPORT (Nov. 28, 2013), http://www.jpost.com/ Jerusalem-Report/Israel/Abolish-the-Chief-Rabbinate-333324; Avi Weiss, *End the Chief Rabbinate's Monopoly*, TIMES OF ISRAEL (Oct. 24, 2013), http://blogs.timesofisrael.com/ end-the-chief-rabbinates-monopoly/; Bernard Avishai, *A Hebrew Democratic State for All Its Citizens*, DAILY BEAST (Oct. 3, 2013), http://www.thedailybeast.com/articles/2013/10/0 3/a-hebrew-democratic-state-for-all-its-citizens.html.

112. *But see* Sam Sokol, Greer Fay Cashman & Jeremy Sharon, *Recognition of Non-Orthodox Streams "in Progress,"* JERUSALEM POST (June 26, 2013), http://www.jpost.com/National-News/Recognition-of-non-orthodox-streams-in-progress-317831; Jeremy Sharon, *Israel to Fund Non-Orthodox Rabbis in Reform Victory*, JERUSALEM POST (May 30, 2013), http:// www.jpost.com/Diplomacy-and-Politics/Israel-to-fund-non-Orthodox-rabbis-in-reform-victory-314968. Cohen and Susser note that the current budgeting of religious institutions—particularly those of the *haredim*—"is one of the most fundamental sources of Orthodox hegemony and autonomy." COHEN & SUSSER, *supra* note 9, at 109.

113. *See* Sokol et al., *supra* note 112 ("In a democratic country everyone is equal before the law, so there should be equal funding and freedom for people to practice religion in ways their conscience dictates.") (quoting the Conservative movement's Rabbinical Assembly Executive Vice President Julie Schonfeld).

should not be considered a Jewish state simply for adopting and validating only *one* component out of so many that make up the entire Jewish cultural heritage."[114] As Mautner argues in classic cultural analysis terms:

> Israel should be seen as "the state of the Jews" rather than a "Jewish state," ie, as the state meant to enable various groups of Jews to develop to the fullest their different Jewish cultures—each group with its own cultural components, each group with its own unique mix of cultural elements.[115]

Mautner thus does not believe Israel should single out *halakhah* as the *only* element of Jewish culture. Instead, he feels Israel should be a place where "the various groups of Jews living in it are simultaneously developing different versions of Jewish culture using different cultural components."[116]

To the extent the definition of the Jewish people ultimately becomes one and the same with ultra-Orthodox philosophies and practices, the continued existence of the Jewish people may be assured but their creative abilities to exist in a modern world may be debatable. Throughout history, elements of both the *halakhah* as well as Jewish cultural identity were constructed creatively by virtue of the Jews' deep engagement with their surrounding cultures.[117] In other words, both Jewish law and Jewish culture reflected and were shaped by the reality of assimilation and acculturation.

Cultural analysis suggests that the Israeli world of both the ultra-Orthodox and strongly secular extremes needs a stronger and more cohesive middle ground.[118] Such a middle ground could well be shaped by the conception of Israeli Jewish identity articulated by those who understand the importance of *halakhah* in forging Jewish culture, but who also see Jewish culture as

---

114. MAUTNER, *supra* note 1, at 209.

115. *Id.*

116. *Id.* at 210 (providing a cogent cultural analysis-oriented rationale for his position).

117. *See supra* Chapter 2, notes 127–31 and accompanying text.

118. *See* interview of Dr. Micah Cohen of Ein Prat Institute with Dr. Steven Cohen, *Dr. Micah Cohen: Israel Needs a More Passionate Middle Ground* (May 5, 2011), http://www.youtube.com/watch?v=hTpfgrhxNv0 (discussing the need for more learned and passionate secular Israelis and more open-minded observant Israelis). *Cf.* MAUTNER, *supra* note 1, at 208 (discussing the "traditionalists" in Israel as an important potentially mediating voice in the continuing struggle between the extremes in the nation); COHEN & SUSSER, *supra* note 9, at 130–32 (discussing the importance of the "traditionalist" center as a positive presence). *See infra* notes 143–49 and accompanying text.

deriving from a more expansive variety of sources. From a cultural analysis perspective, there is much appeal in this vision of Israeli Jewish identity because it recognizes that culture is the product of dispute "over the status of various cultural elements" and their interpretation.[119]

The fundamental issue, however, is whether this vision of Israeli Jewish identity is practical given the sociological makeup of Israeli society. Even those who advocate for this conception of Israeli Jewish identity acknowledge that its proponents represent "a small but growing and important group of academic and social elites."[120] Yet, there are signs that this conception has the potential for having a wider impact on Israeli society as opposed to being confined to "think-tank" environments.[121] Recently, bottom-up initiatives have emerged that are helping to strengthen Jewish, including religious, identity in Israel. One notable example of such a bottom-up initiative is a grass roots prayer community in Tel Aviv. *Beit Tefilah* Israeli (Israeli House of Prayer), a unique community affording opportunities for prayer, socialization, and social action,[122] embraces a cultural analysis model by combining traditional and *halakhic* elements in its prayer services with modern music, poetry, and literature characteristic of Israeli culture. The leaders of this community request Israeli artists and musicians to create texts and music that can be integrated into the prayers. Most of the participants are secular Jews searching for some type of spiritual middle ground that is inspired by the tradition but adapted to the urban Israeli experience. Friday evening services, known as *Kabbalat Shabbat* (welcoming of the Sabbath), are held on the beach and attract hundreds of worshippers each week.

The appeal of *Beit Tefilah* Israeli illustrates that secular Israelis living in Israel have particular needs and face distinct challenges with respect to spirituality and religious involvement. The community's founder, Esteban Gottfried, drew his inspiration from a liberal Conservative synagogue on the Upper West Side in New York City that pioneered the "Friday Night Live" concept of live music accompanying the Friday evening service welcoming the Sabbath.[123] Gottfried,

---

119. MAUTNER, *supra* note 1, at 210.

120. Fischer & Stone, *supra* note 81, at 14.

121. *See* COHEN & SUSSER, *supra* note 9, at 130–32.

122. *See* Abigail Pickus, *Prayers by the Sea,* WORLD JEWISH DIGEST, Oct. 2008, at 19; KBY CONGREGATIONS TOGETHER, http://www.kbyonline.org/Beit-Tefilah/ (last visited July 8, 2014).

123. Normative traditional Jewish practice disallows the playing of instruments on the Sabbath (*Shabbat*). According to the Talmud, repairing a musical instrument is prohibited

who was born in Argentina, has received rabbinic ordination from the Reform seminary in Jerusalem since starting the community, but neither he nor any of the community's other founders were rabbis at the time of its inception.[124] Thus, *Beit Tefilah* Israeli constitutes a true bottom-up approach to prayer that is innovative in Israeli society. In this respect, it represents an interesting parallel to the partnership *minyanim* (prayer services) discussed in Chapter 7 where some Orthodox women (and men) are able to find an increased sense of spirituality through a more egalitarian approach to prayer despite a lack of endorsement by the Orthodox establishment.[125] Significantly, though, although *Beit Tefilah* Israeli began as a bottom-up initiative, the municipality of Tel Aviv has begun to fund this prayer community.[126]

Another notable bottom-up initiative began in Jerusalem in the spring of 2013, when hundreds of Jews representing all religious spectrums began to gather together prior to the onset of *Shabbat* at the First Train Station for an unofficial *Kabbalat Shabbat* service. This particular *Kabbalat Shabbat* service features mixed seating, beer, dancing, and musical instruments and thus would violate normative *halakhah* if it were to be conducted after sundown. A local nonprofit group organized this *Kabbalat Shabbat* in order to foster a much-needed "sense of unity in Jerusalem."[127] Like *Beit Tefilah* Israeli, this initiative also is successful in attracting secular Jews who might not attend any *Shabbat* services under other circumstances.

Although many secular Israelis do observe certain Jewish practices and customs, they often regard "the synagogue" as an "Orthodox" institution. Given the political situation in Israel, this reaction typically drives secular Israelis in the opposite direction. Yet, the popularity among secular Israelis of the Jerusalem First Train Station *Kabbalat Shabbat*, *Beit Tifilah* Israeli, and

---

on *Shabbat*. *See* Beitzah 36b (Babylonian Talmud). Based on this authority, normative *halakhic* practice disallows instrumental music on *Shabbat* and the holy festivals. Some Conservative communities are more lenient on this matter, although many Conservative synagogues still follow the traditional practice.

124. *See* Pickus, *supra* note 122, at 20.

125. *See supra* Chapter 7, notes 82–84 and accompanying text and *infra* note 141.

126. *See also* Yossi Klein Halevi, *I Have No Chief Rabbi*, SHALOM HARTMAN INSTITUTE (Apr. 8, 2013), http://www.hartman.org.il/Blogs_View.asp?Article_Id=1183&Cat_Id=275& Cat_Type=Blogs (noting that other municipalities are also beginning to fund liberal synagogues).

127. Nathan Jeffay, *Jerusalem Gets Very Different Kind of Kabbalat Shabbat*, JEWISH DAILY FORWARD (July 22, 2013), http://forward.com/articles/180899/jerusalem-gets-very-different-kind-of-kabbalat-sha/?p=all. The organizer is the interdenominational Ginot Ha'Ir Community Council.

a growing number of similar prayer groups attests to the need among secular Israelis to create a spiritual space that imbeds Israeli culture with traditional Jewish sources. In discussing this phenomenon, journalist Yossi Klein Halevi has described these Israelis as "post secular" and applauds their creation of new "expressions of Judaism" through prayer experiences "drawing on Israeli poetry and song, as well as on traditional prayer."[128]

In some ways, secular Israelis operate on a daily basis very much like Reform and liberal Conservative Jews in the United States. In other words, they exercise significant autonomy with respect to when and how they practice Judaism, rather than adhering to the view that *halakhah* represents binding religious obligation. Still, secular Israelis tend to avoid affiliation with the non-Orthodox denominations that do exist in Israel because they see them as "American constructs" and therefore are not perceived as the right fit for Israeli Jews who are more accustomed to seeing Judaism in black and white terms (meaning Orthodox versus everything else).[129] For this reason, the bottom-up initiatives discussed in this section have much potential for forging a distinct Israeli Jewish identity with meaningful content.

Moreover, today an increasing number of secular Israelis are manifesting a desire to satisfy their spiritual needs by embracing their heritage and history through study. Thus, in addition to emerging nontraditional venues for prayer, Israel now boasts a growing number of self-described "secular" institutions of classical Jewish learning.[130] Two such initiatives devoted to the pluralistic study of Jewish culture and texts are ALMA Home for Hebrew Culture, and Elul, Israel's first house of Jewish learning geared to men and women, religious and secular.[131] Both ventures were started by Dr. Ruth Calderon, who was a student of Rabbi Hartman. The story of Dr. Calderon, a secular Israeli who was elected to the Knesset in 2013, exemplifies the spirituality of secular

---

128. Halevi, *supra* note 126.

129. *See* Pickus, *supra* note 122, at 21; KBY CONGREGATIONS TOGETHER, http://www. kbyonline.org/Beit-Tefilah (last visited July 8, 2014). *See also* COHEN & SUSSER, *supra* note 9, at 121 (noting that the Conservative and Reform movements in Israel have a small presence numerically and historically "were never a part of the consociational arrangements that regulated religious-secular relations in Israel").

130. Such organizations include Ein Prat—The Academy for Leadership, which maintains a "pluralistic Beit Midrash" serving young adults. *See* http://midrasha.einprat.org/en/ ידלל-כ-דומע/about-us (last visited July 8, 2014). Another secular yeshiva (school of Jewish learning) is maintained by BINA, an organization concerned with Jewish pluralism and social action. *See* http://www.bina.org.il/en/about (last visited July 8, 2014).

131. *See* http://alma.org.il/content.asp?lang=en&pageid=8; http://www.elul.org.il/content. asp?lang=en&pageid=11 (both last visited July 8, 2014).

Israelis and the potential for the development of a distinct Israeli Jewish identity steeped in the *mesorah*. Calderon used her introductory speech to the
Knesset as a vehicle for teaching Talmud and for expressing her love of, and
devotion to, the text.[132] The most fascinating aspect of her talk was how she
captured the approval of Chairman Yitzhak Vaknin, an ultra-Orthodox Jew
from the *Shas* party, who stated during her discourse, "I think the idea she is
saying is wonderful."[133] At that moment, "two members of the Knesset from
diametrically opposed worldviews on the future of Israel and how to get there
found a mutual language from" their shared tradition.[134] Yosef Kanefsky, an
American Modern Orthodox rabbi, has written that Calderon's address to
the Knesset "created more buzz around the Jewish world than any speech
like it in the history of the state of Israel."[135] A week after her speech, her
party, *Yesh Atid*, initiated a weekly Torah study in the Knesset featuring a
rotating group of male and female teachers from secular to ultra-Orthodox
backgrounds.[136]

Although Dr. Calderon is considered a member of Israel's intellectual
elite, her spiritual search is typical of many secular Israelis. As one respon-
dent to Rabbi Kanefsky's post about her Knesset speech declared, "Many
of us 'orthodox folks' here in Israel understand what you folks out there [in
the Diaspora] have so much trouble grasping. The vast majority of Jews in
Israel ARE 'religious' in ways you simply can't fathom."[137] Another respon-
dent agreed: "Vast numbers of people who are not part of the religious Jewish
establishment are profoundly spiritual, and act in a manner that affirms the
existence of the Divine."[138] Such sentiments seem to recognize the potential
for the third model of Israeli Jewish identity discussed in this chapter that
understands Israel's existence as a laboratory for putting Jewish values into

---

132. An English translation of Calderon's speech appears in THE JEWISH WEEK (Feb. 14,
2013), http://www.thejewishweek.com/editorial-opinion/opinion/heritage-all-israel.

133. *Id.*

134. Rabbi Yehoshua Look, *The Knesset as* Beit Midrash: *A Model of Hope for a Better
Israel*, HAARETZ (Feb. 25, 2013), http://www.haaretz.com/jewish-world/rabbis-round-
table/the-knesset-as-beit-midrash-a-model-of-hope-for-a-better-israel-1.505685.

135. Yosef Kanefsky, *Ruth Calderon—Mother of Redemption?*, MORETHODOXY (Feb. 26,
2013), http://www.jewishjournal.com/morethodoxy/item/ruth_calderon_mother_of_
redemption [hereinafter *Mother of Redemption*].

136. *Id.*

137. *Id.* (reply by Menachem Lipkin).

138. *Id.* (reply by Michael Stein).

action. This potential is not surprising given that this model also derives from the pluralistic religious perspective of scholars such as Hartman and others. In Rabbi Kanefsky's post about Dr. Calderon's speech, he also recognized the value of pluralism when he affirmed the potential partnership Orthodox Judaism can have with secular Israelis and secular institutions of Jewish learning seeking to engage in a "dynamic intellectual and spiritual interchange... weaving a net of Jewish life that will capture so many who might otherwise fall through the cracks."[139]

From a cultural analysis perspective, progress in creating greater religious pluralism in Israel should be possible through a combination of state-supported initiatives and grass roots efforts. This combination reflects a cultural analysis methodology that embraces both a top-down and bottom-up approach to creating culture. With respect to the top-down political front, there seems to be some movement toward state support for religious pluralism that could result in the creation of indigenous, non-Orthodox Jewish religious expression in Israel.[140] As for bottom-up initiatives, the Jerusalem *Kabbalat Shabbat, Beit Tifilah* Israeli, partnership *minyanim*, secular institutions of Jewish learning, and academic centers such as the Shalom Hartman Institute represent successful ventures that seem to be having an impact not only in Israel, but also in the Diaspora.[141] These initiatives are grounded in the reality that bringing secular Israelis back to Judaism necessitates instilling in them a deep awareness of, and love for, their "cultural roots and heritage."[142]

---

139. Kanefsky, *supra* note 135.

140. *See* Sokol et al., *supra* note 112 (quoting Conservative movement Rabbi Julie Schonfeld stating this is the goal for her movement in Israel); Halevi, *supra* note 126 (noting that the state's apparent commitment to implementing a plan to create "a space for egalitarian prayer along a stretch of the Western Wall... would mark the first time that the state of Israel officially sponsors a liberal synagogue—and at the religious site most beloved by Jews today").

141. Many non-Orthodox Diaspora Jews believe greater religious pluralism in Israel is vital. Both the Conservative and Reform movements have lobbied the state of Israel for greater recognition of their movements. *See* Sokol et al., *supra* note 112. Moreover, given the frequent travel between the United States and Israel on the part of sectors of American Jews, bottom-up initiatives begun in Israel can easily make their way to the United States. One such example discussed in Chapter 7 is the spin-off partnership *minyanim. See supra* note 125 and accompanying text and *supra* Chapter 7, notes 82–84 and accompanying text. Of course, the Jewish cultural climate in the United States differs significantly from that in Israel, and therefore, the success of any Israeli grass roots venture in America, or any other part of the Diaspora, cannot be assumed. *See generally infra* Chapter 9.

142. This language is taken from the "About Us" text of Yachad Amiel, an initiative dedicated to making "Jewish culture significant" by encouraging secular Israelis to "reclaim and cherish their heritage in warm and non-coercive environments." This initiative trains Cultural Facilitators and places them in community centers throughout Israel. The program

The potential for the success of this third model of Israeli Jewish identity also is enhanced to the extent that a large number of Israelis purport to self-identify as traditional, but not Orthodox, Jews.[143] These Israelis focus on "history, culture and ethnicity rather than upon religion per se," and as a group, the traditionalist center represents "a variety of secular identity, even though many of its sources and practices may overlap with those of Judaism."[144] According to Cohen and Susser, this group "observes religious rites without being concerned with their theological import or the *halakhic* consistency of their actions."[145] Through this group, "religion is transmuted into folkways, theology into cohesiveness-enhancing family observances, and Orthodox devotion into communal solidarity."[146]

Writing in 2000, Cohen and Susser call this large group "the forgotten center" because traditionalists tend to be overlooked in popular perceptions of Israeli public discourse that are dominated by the religious and secular camps.[147] Moreover, unlike the Reform and Conservative movements in the Diaspora and even in Israel, this traditional group does not articulate a principled existence distinct from that of Orthodoxy and therefore is not perceived as "a combative alternative to Judaism in its dominant Orthodox mode."[148] As a result of their "inarticulate character," their status as "forgotten" makes sense.

Significantly, the Israeli traditionalists essentially embody the insights of cultural analysis and seek to combine *halakhah* and culture in a proactive manner that is potentially relevant to the lives of Jews living in the state. They are "inspired by the desire to preserve meaningful ties to the Jewish people and to Jewish history," and they "turn to the Jewish heritage, to the practices contained in the Jewish religious tradition, and adopt them as their own."[149] The adoption

---

is under the supervision of the Joseph and Gwendolyn Straus Rabbinical Seminary in Israel, founded and led by Modern Orthodox Rabbi Shlomo Riskin. *See* http://www.ots-amiel.org. il/english/yachad/ (last visited July 8, 2014).

143. COHEN & SUSSER, *supra* note 9, at 153 n.3 (noting that about 25 percent of Israeli Jews self-identify as "traditional," but the number substantially increases when reported practices of observance are considered).

144. *Id.* at 131.

145. *Id.*

146. *Id.*

147. *Id.* at 130. *See also* Charles Liebman & Bernard Susser, *The Forgotten Center: Traditional Jewishness in Israel*, 17 MOD. JUDAISM 211 (1997).

148. COHEN & SUSSER, *supra* note 9, at 131.

149. *Id.*

of this mindset and lifestyle furnishes an excellent example of cultural analysis methodology at work "on the ground."

It is also fair to wonder whether this approach also could provide a model for enhancing Jewish identity outside of Israel where the Jewish culture is not the majority one. Historically, the United States displays a larger degree of Jewish religious pluralism than Israel and has sustained a greater number of religious models than have been available in the state. That said, it is fair to question whether these models maintain an authentically Jewish connection given that they are spawned in a culture in which Jews are, and always have been, a cultural minority. Unlike in Israel, Reform and Conservative Jews together comprise the majority of affiliated Jews in the United States.[150] These movements, in contrast to the Israeli traditionalist group, articulate coherent ideologies that distinguish themselves from mainstream Orthodoxy. This reality not only exacerbates the tensions between the movements, but also makes the issue of what constitutes Jewish identity much more complex.

Further, notwithstanding Israel's many problems, Jewish identity in Israel is far easier to create and maintain than in the Diaspora. Even Israeli Jews who are not highly educated from a Jewish standpoint have a basic familiarity with Jewish texts, customs, and traditions that is more extensive than the norm in the Diaspora. They also speak Hebrew, which affords them a significant advantage with respect to being able to access rabbinic texts absent the need for translation. Moreover, Israel operates according to "Jewish time," as Jewish holidays are an important part of the state's cultural capital. On Yom Kippur, for example, the roads tend to be clear, businesses are closed, and most public transportation ceases to operate.[151] Jewish history, music, art, and literature create a tangible environment that is largely culturally Jewish. The situation is completely different in the Diaspora where the majority culture is not based on Hebrew or Jewish roots and the land on which the Jews live is not their historic homeland.

The following chapter addresses Jewish identity in the Diaspora, particularly the United States, where the majority of Jews outside of Israel live. This discussion examines numerous models that have been proposed for cementing Jewish identity in the Diaspora, including the Zionist model. It analyzes these models as a prelude to a concluding discussion of lessons and future directions.

---

150. *See supra* Chapter 4, notes 221–22 and accompanying text.

151. *See* Ian Deitch, *Israel Marks Solemn, Silent Day of Atonement,* TIMES OF ISRAEL (Sept. 13, 2013), http://www.timesofisrael.com/israel-prepares-for-solemn-silent-day-of-atonement/.

9 JEWISH IDENTITY IN THE UNITED STATES

Jewish Geography is a very popular game, particularly among American Jews. Typically this game is played when two or more Jews meet for the first time, either in their home area or while traveling. The game involves asking fellow Jews about possible common acquaintances. The popularity of Jewish Geography by far predates the advent of electronic media, although the social media craze has facilitated the ability of Jews to connect with other Jews in a more formalized fashion.

The urge to locate common acquaintances certainly is not unique to Jews. People from all different backgrounds often feel a strong connection to strangers from their same background and try to find common connections. What is unique about Jewish Geography is that it is a well-known phenomenon of Jewish culture. For example, a Google search for "Chinese geography" or "Polish geography" yields results on the physical geography of these places. In contrast, a search for "Jewish geography" initially reveals numerous items, including a Wikipedia entry[1] describing the game and its popular status among Jews.

One self-described "tongue-in-cheek" piece from a website catering to Generation Y defines Jewish Geography and then observes, "Because Jewish Geography isn't exclusively just for Jews—like kosher meat, it can be enjoyed by everyone!"[2] In truth, the Jewish affinity for bagels and lox is the more accurate culinary

---

1. *See Jewish Geography* (Apr. 17, 2014), http://en.wikipedia.org/wiki/Jewish_geography.

2. Laura Argintar, *Oh, You Know ___ Cohen? The Step-by-Step Guide to Playing Jewish Geography*, ELITE DAILY (Oct. 2, 2013), http://elitedaily.com/women/oh-you-know-cohen-the-step-by-step-guide-to-playing-jewish-geography/.

analogy to Jewish Geography because these markers of Jewish identity exist independently of a basis in *halakhah* (Jewish law).[3] In contrast, when a Jew does consume meat, it is *halakhically* required that the meat be kosher.

Historically, much of what makes Jewish culture "Jewish" has a basis in *halakhah*, even if today that basis is not generally recognized as such by the majority of American Jews. *Halakhah* has played a central role in shaping the particularity of Jewish practices, culture, and identity throughout time and space. Yet, to the extent American non-Orthodox Jews have become increasingly incapable of recognizing and appreciating the *halakhic* roots of Jewish culture, the "Jewish" content of American-Jewish culture is becoming increasingly less apparent and important to these Jews. This problem is exacerbated by growing degrees of assimilation and intermarriage. These developments are of concern to most clergy and lay leaders in the American Jewish community from a range of religious backgrounds. Paradoxically, although the religious commitment of non-Orthodox American Jews is not strong, the same cannot be said for their Jewish identity and pride of peoplehood.[4] From a cultural analysis perspective, this reality is perplexing because cultural analysis maintains that law and culture cannot be separated from one another and that both are necessary in formulating Jewish identity.

This chapter grapples with these issues. It begins with a discussion of the 2013 Pew Research Religion & Public Life Project (the Pew Report), the most extensive national survey of the Jewish population since 2000.[5] By examining Pew's data concerning current Jewish observance, identity, culture, and beliefs, it is possible to obtain a reasonable snapshot of the current Jewish community in the United States despite the presence of some surprising and even questionable findings.[6] To augment this empirical picture of American Judaism, this chapter next examines various philosophical and ideological markers of American Jewish identity and culture that are not dependent on

---

3. If there is a basis in the *halakhah* for the popularity of bagels and lox, it is not one that is commonly known or recognized. The same is true for Jewish Geography.

4. *See* A Portrait of Jewish Americans—Pew Research Religion & Public Life Project (2013), http://www.pewforum.org/2013/10/01/jewish-american-beliefs-attitudes-culture-survey/ [hereinafter Pew Report] (follow "Chapter 3: Jewish Identity" hyperlink).

5. *See generally id.*

6. For example, skepticism is justified with respect to Pew's findings that as high as 16 percent of Orthodox respondents attend "non-Jewish religious services at least a few times a year," and that as many as 24 percent of that same group attend Jewish services only a few times a year or "seldom." *See id.* (follow "Chapter 4: Religious Beliefs and Practices" hyperlink).

halakhic content. The final part examines the existing social forces the tate against a more expansive role for *halakhah* in forming American identity among non-Orthodox American Jews.

The Empirical Picture of American Judaism

Prior to the Enlightenment, Jews did not separate their religion from their ethnic identity. Throughout the centuries, the ethno-religious communal existence of the Jews provided them with sustenance and support during frequent persecutions and ordeals.[7] Even from the post-Enlightenment inception of the Reform movement, its proponents embraced Judaism as both a religion and a culture although they did not look to the particularities of *halakhah* as a measure of their identity.[8]

In contrast, today Jewish ethnicity as an entity separate from religiosity is thriving across the United States as demonstrated by the results of the recent Pew Report.[9] Statistics demonstrate that Jewish identity, even if not adherence to *halakhah*, has retained a strong foothold among American Jews.[10] The difficult issue, however, is defining the content of this identity. This discussion highlights the most significant data from the Pew Report from a cultural analysis standpoint in order to give some content to the present nature of American Jewish identity.

The Pew Report is based on protracted interviews conducted in 2013 with 3,475 Jews from every state.[11] Based on these interviews, Pew estimates that the Jewish population is roughly 6.7 million people of all ages.[12] Pew also estimates that there are 5.3 million Jewish adults in the United States, and uses the term "NET Jewish population" to designate this group. The Pew data divides this group into 4.2 million people who self-denominate as "Jews

---

7. BERNARD SUSSER & CHARLES LIEBMAN, CHOOSING SURVIVAL 29–30 (1999).

8. *See supra* Chapter 4, notes 26–32 and accompanying text.

9. Although the 2013 findings of Pew provide ample evidence for this observation, Bernard Susser and Charles Liebman noted this same phenomenon in 1999. *See* SUSSER & LIEBMAN, *supra* note 7, at 29–30.

10. *See generally* Pew Report, *supra* note 4 (follow "Chapter 3: Jewish Identity" hyperlink).

11. More than 70,000 screening interviews were conducted to identify Jewish respondents in all fifty states and the District of Columbia. Longer interviews were completed with 3,475 Jews, including 2,786 Jews by religion and 689 Jews of no religion. The Pew survey was conducted between February 20 and June 13, 2013. *See id.* (follow "Overview" hyperlink).

12. *Id.* (follow "Chapter 1: Population Estimates" hyperlink).

by religion" and 1.2 million people whom the study calls "secular or cultural Jews—those who say they have no religion but who were raised Jewish or have a Jewish parent and who still consider themselves Jewish *aside* from religion."[13] Pew also claims that the percentage of adults in the United States who claim to be "Jews by religion" has declined since the late 1950s while the number of people with Jewish upbringing who consider themselves Jewish but describe themselves as atheist, agnostic, or having no particular religion appears to be rising.[14]

According to the Pew Report, a majority of Jews in the United States "see being Jewish as more a matter of ancestry, culture and values than of religious observance."[15] For example, six out of ten Jews reported that "being Jewish is mainly a matter of culture or ancestry."[16] Pew also revealed that less than a quarter of the respondents said that being Jewish is "a matter of religion as well as ancestry and/or culture,"[17] thus demonstrating the relatively small number of Jews who appreciate the fundamental insight of cultural analysis that Jewish law and Jewish culture are intertwined.[18]

---

13. *Id.*

14. According to the findings of the Pew Report, the percentage of American adults who say they are Jewish when asked about their religion has declined by about half since the late 1950s and currently is about 1.8 percent of the U.S. adult population, representing 4.2 million people. *Id.* (follow "Overview" hyperlink; follow "Chapter 1: Population Estimates" hyperlink). Meanwhile, the number of Americans with direct Jewish ancestry or upbringing who consider themselves Jewish, yet describe themselves as atheist, agnostic, or having no particular religion, appears to be rising and is now about 0.5 percent of the U.S. adult population, representing 1.2 million people. *Id.* The Pew Report also finds that by a two-to-one margin, former Jews by religion outnumber those who have become Jewish by religion after not having been raised Jewish. *Id.* (follow "Chapter 1: Population Overview" hyperlink).

15. *Id.* (follow "Chapter 3: Jewish Identity" hyperlink).

16. *Id.* By comparison, Pew reports that 15 percent of the respondents believe that "being Jewish...is mainly a matter of religion." *Id.*

17. *Id.*

18. Specifically, 23 percent of the respondents affirmed that being Jewish involves both religion and culture. The Pew Report breaks this religion-versus-culture data down further by separating out Jews by religion from Jews of no religion, although the percentages do not change significantly. More than half of Jews by religion (55 percent) responded that being Jewish is "mainly a matter of ancestry or culture," 17 percent said "mainly a matter of religion," and 26 percent said being Jewish "is a combination of religion and ancestry/culture." The Pew Report also furnishes statistics for Orthodox Jews (separated into categories of Modern and ultra-Orthodox). Within the combined Orthodox group, 15 percent said being Jewish is "mainly a matter of ancestry and culture," 46 percent said "mainly a matter of religion," and 38 percent said being Jewish means both religion and culture. Among ultra-Orthodox Jews, 53 percent said being Jewish is "mainly a matter of religion" and 35 percent said both religion and culture. *Id.*

With respect to the extent of their religious commitment, American Jews exhibit lower levels than the American public in general.[19] As would be expected, the Pew Report offers much evidence that there is greater commitment to the religious aspects of Judaism among individuals who are affiliated with denominations, and that commitment increases from Reform to Orthodox.[20] Further, the Pew Report also notes that most of the switching between the denominations "is in the direction of less-traditional Judaism."[21]

Nevertheless, although religious commitment may be comparatively unimportant to most Jews, *being Jewish* appears to be very important to them. Among the NET Jewish population, nearly half reported that "being Jewish" is a "very important part of their lives," and at least one-third said it is "somewhat important."[22] As might be expected, the percentage of Jews saying that being Jewish is "very important" to them is highest among the Orthodox group, although a strong majority of Conservative Jews feel similarly.[23] Significantly, among the NET Jewish population, 94 percent said they

---

19. A "slim majority" of Jews surveyed responded that religion is "very important" (26 percent) or "somewhat important" (29 percent) in their lives compared to 56 percent of the general public saying religion is very important and an additional 23 percent saying "somewhat important." *Id.* (follow "Chapter 4: Religious Beliefs and Practices" hyperlink). Pew notes that Orthodox Jews "stand out sharply on this measure as compared with other Jews." *See infra* note 20 and accompanying text.

20. With respect to Orthodox Jews, 83 percent say religion is "very important" in their lives. This number is lower than might be expected, especially with respect to the figure for Modern Orthodox (77 percent for Modern Orthodox as compared to 89 percent for ultra-Orthodox Jews). The percentage among Conservative Jews is 43 percent and Reform Jews 16 percent. By way of comparison, 86 percent of white evangelical Protestants said religion is very important in their lives. *See* Pew Report, *supra* note 4 (follow "Chapter 4: Religious Beliefs and Practices" hyperlink).

21. According to the Pew Report, "approximately one-quarter of people who were raised Orthodox have since become Conservative or Reform Jews, while 30% of those raised Conservative have become Reform Jews, and 28% of those raised Reform have left the ranks of religion entirely." The survey also notes that there is much less switching "in the opposite direction." *Id.* (follow "Overview" hyperlink). It should be noted, however, that among Orthodox Jews, the "falloff" seems "to be declining and is significantly lower among 18 to 29 year-olds (17%) than among older people." In contrast, "roughly half of the survey respondents who were raised as Orthodox say they are no longer Orthodox." *Id.* This data suggests that the issue of declining affiliation impacts all of the denominations in some way, although the median age of Orthodox Jews is significantly lower than for the other denominations (forty for Orthodox, fifty-five for Conservative, fifty-four for Reform). *Id.* (follow "Chapter 2: Intermarriage and Other Demographics" hyperlink).

22. *See id.* (follow "Chapter 3: Jewish Identity" hyperlink) (showing that 46 percent reported "very important" and 34 percent "somewhat important.").

23. *See id.* (the specific figures are 87 percent for Orthodox, 69 percent for Conservative, and 43 percent for Reform).

are proud to be Jewish,[24] and 75 percent of Jews reported they have a "strong sense of belonging to the Jewish people."[25]

The significance of cultural tradition also is demonstrated by the fact that although Jews say religion is not important in their lives, participation in certain Jewish traditions is not uncommon, particularly those that are performed infrequently, such as the Passover seder and even fasting on Yom Kippur. Seven out of ten Jews reported that they participated in a seder within the past year, and over half of Jews, including about one in five Jews of no religion, said "they fasted for all or part of Yom Kippur in 2012."[26]

Not surprisingly, the Pew Report devotes an entire chapter to the topic of intermarriage and other related demographics. The survey documents the escalation of intermarriage over the past five decades. Among Jewish respondents who have gotten married since 2000, 58 percent have a non-Jewish spouse.[27] Not surprisingly, among the various denominations, the percentage of Jewish individuals marrying Jews increases with the observance level of the denomination.[28] Also, married Jews by religion are much more likely than married Jews of no religion to have Jewish spouses.[29] There is also some

---

24. This percentage includes 83 percent of Jews of no religion and 97 percent of Jews by religion. *Id.*

25. This figure includes 42 percent of Jews of no religion and 85 percent of Jews by religion. *Id.*

The Pew Report also shows that denominational attachment goes hand in hand with a sense of belonging to the Jewish people, a sense of "special responsibility to care for Jews in need," and to a much lesser extent, with Jewish pride. The Pew Report shows that whereas 87 percent of Jews who are not affiliated with a denomination are proud to be Jewish, only 53 percent have a strong sense of belonging to the Jewish people, and 39 percent feel a special responsibility to care for Jews. These numbers contrast sharply with much higher percentages among all the denominations. *Id.*

26. *Id.* (follow "Chapter 4: Religious Beliefs and Practices" hyperlink). Some scholars would explain these results as evidence that certain rituals, such as fasting, "lose their status as God prescribed observances and become symbols exemplifying human ethical imperatives" such as "vindicating the capacity for human control over pressing creaturely urges." Susser & Liebman, *supra* note 7, at 77.

27. Among Jews who were married before 1970, only 17 percent have a non-Jewish spouse. The percentages have been steadily rising. *See* Pew Report, *supra* note 4 (follow "Chapter 2: Intermarriage and Other Demographics" hyperlink).

28. With respect to Jews marrying other Jews, the percentages are as follows: Orthodox (98 percent); Conservative (73 percent); Reform (50 percent); and "no denomination" (31 percent). *Id.*

29. Pew reports: "Among Jews by religion who are married, 64% have a Jewish spouse and 36% have a non-Jewish spouse." In contrast, "just 21% of married Jews of no religion are married to a Jewish spouse, while 79% are married to a non-Jewish spouse." *Id.*

evidence provided by sources other than the Pew Report that the rates of intermarriage are lower in major cities such as Chicago that have larger concentrations of Jews.[30]

The Pew Report also reveals that intermarriage has a substantial impact on whether children are being raised as Jews. Jews who have non-Jewish spouses are significantly less likely than those married to Jews to be raising children as Jewish by religion, and much more likely to be raising children as partially Jewish, Jewish not by religion, or not Jewish at all. Among Jews with a non-Jewish spouse, only 20 percent say they are raising their children Jewish by religion.[31] In contrast, Pew shows that nearly all Jews who have a Jewish spouse say they are raising their children as Jewish by religion.[32] Further, Jews who are the offspring of intermarriages appear to be more likely to intermarry than Jews with two Jewish parents.[33]

In addition, the Pew Report contains some potentially significant information on how Millennials view their connection to Judaism. These individuals, also known as Generation Y, were born between the early 1980s and the

---

30. In Chicago, the overall intermarriage rate is 37 percent, compared to the Pew Report's finding of 58 percent, and the percentage of intermarried Jews raising their children as "Jewish only" is 49 percent compared to Pew's finding of 20 percent. These statistics are from the 2010 Jewish Federation of Metropolitan Chicago Population Study. E-mail from Rose Jagust, Jewish Federation of Metropolitan, Chicago (Oct. 9, 2012, 5:11 p.m. CST). *See also infra* notes 31–33 and accompanying text.

31. Pew Report, *supra* note 4 (follow "Chapter 3: Jewish Identity" hyperlink). Further, more than one-third (37 percent) of intermarried Jews who are raising children say they are not raising those children as Jewish at all. *Id.*

Not surprisingly, the statistics also show more commitment generally among Jews who marry other Jews. *See id.* (follow "Chapter 4: Religious Beliefs and Practices" hyperlink). For example, married Jewish respondents who have a Jewish spouse attend Jewish religious services much more frequently than do intermarried Jews. Four-in-ten respondents with a Jewish spouse (41 percent) reported they attend religious services at least monthly, and only 7 percent said they never attend religious services. Among Jews married to a non-Jew, these figures are essentially reversed (9 percent attend at least monthly; 37 percent never attend). Further, although 32 percent of Jews reported having had a Christmas tree last year (including 27 percent of Jews by religion and 51 percent of Jews of no religion), the percentage of intermarried Jews having a Christmas tree is 71 percent. *Id.*

32. According to the Pew Report, "among Jewish parents who are married to a Jewish spouse…96% say they are raising their children Jewish by religion, and just 1% say that are not raising their children Jewish." *Id.* (follow "Chapter 3: Jewish Identity" hyperlink). In addition, "Jewish parents who are married to a Jewish spouse are roughly four times as likely to have enrolled their children" in a Jewish youth program such as a youth group, camp, or day care, compared to Jews who are married to non-Jews. *Id.*

33. Among married Jews with only one Jewish parent, 83 percent are married to a non-Jewish spouse. Among married Jews with two Jewish parents, only 37 percent have a non-Jewish spouse. *Id.* (follow "Chapter 2: Intermarriage and Other Demographics" hyperlink).

late 1990s or early 2000s. According to Pew, a significantly smaller percentage of Jewish Millennials identify as Jewish by religion than is the case with prior generations.[34] This sense of religious disaffiliation is typical of all American adults in the age range of eighteen to twenty-nine years.[35] In addition, younger Jews are more likely to have no denominational attachment.[36]

On the salient issue of the role of *halakhah* in constructing American Jewish identity, the Pew Report strongly suggests that as a way of life, *halakhah* is largely irrelevant to the majority of Jews in the United States, aside from those living an Orthodox lifestyle. Specifically, only 19 percent of the NET Jewish population reported that observing Jewish law is essential to what being Jewish means to them.[37] As would be expected, the statistics also show that for a strong majority of Orthodox Jews, observing Jewish law is critical.[38] Although the relative lack of importance non-Orthodox Jews ascribe to *halakhah* seems to be clear, much less clarity exists with respect to those elements that are essential for Jewish identity among the NET Jewish population. In other words, based on the survey's data, it is difficult to determine what "being Jewish" means to the majority of Jews, despite the fact that a large majority of Jews reported that "being Jewish" is either "very important" or "somewhat important" to them.[39]

The Pew data shows that in general, American Jews have "a broad view of their identities."[40] Pew identified nine potential elements of Jewish identity

---

34. According to Pew, with respect to Millennials, "68% identify as Jews by religion while 32% describe themselves as having no religion and identify as Jewish on the basis of ancestry, ethnicity, or culture." The Pew Report also demonstrates that the percentages of Jews who identify as Jewish by religion have been decreasing with successive generations. *See id.* (follow "Overview" hyperlink). For example, 81 percent of baby boomers claimed to be Jews by religion. *Id.*

35. The Pew Report demonstrates that the percentage of those who are religiously disaffiliated among Jews between the ages of eighteen and twenty-nine is 32 percent, the same as among the general public. *Id.*

36. For Jews under the age of thirty, 41 percent lack a denominational affiliation. In contrast, 33 percent of Jews in their thirties and forties lack a denominational attachment, and the number drops to 24 percent for Jews between the ages of fifty and sixty-four. *Id.* (follow "Chapter 3: Jewish Identity" hyperlink).

37. *Id.* For Jews by religion, 23 percent responded that observing Jewish law is essential to what Judaism means to them; for Jews of no religion the response for this factor is 7 percent. *Id.*

38. Among Orthodox respondents, 79 percent said observing Jewish law is essential for Jewish identity. In contrast, 24 percent of Conservative Jews and 11 percent of Reform Jews responded similarly. *Id.*

39. *See supra* note 22 and accompanying text.

40. *See* Pew Report, *supra* note 4 (follow "Chapter 4: Religious Beliefs and Practices" hyperlink).

and asked the respondents whether each one is "essential to what being Jewish means to them."[41] Among the nine areas identified by the survey, remembering the Holocaust drew the largest number of affirmative responses, with nearly three-quarters of the NET Jewish population responding that such remembrance is essential to being Jewish.[42] The next largest categories are "leading an ethical life" and "working for justice and equality." Perhaps the biggest surprise is that only 28 percent of the NET Jewish population reported that being part of a Jewish community is essential for Jewish identity.[43] This statistic also is lower than one would expect among Orthodox respondents.[44] In general, these findings suggest that the importance of community seems underappreciated across the Jewish spectrum.

Given the incomplete nature of the empirical evidence with respect to Jewish identity in the United States, it is helpful to augment this picture by focusing on other markers for identity that have been proposed in the scholarly literature. The following discussion examines four such possibilities: Jewish civil religion, Israel, anti-Semitism and anti-Zionism, and Jewish liberalism. To the extent the Pew Report contains interesting evidence about these markers, this discussion also incorporates relevant information concerning the survey's findings.

Jewish Federations as Civil Religion

The Jewish federation system fosters Jewish identity by promoting philanthropy that is largely, although not exclusively, directed toward the global Jewish community, and by furnishing opportunities for developing Jewish community outside of a synagogue or other religious structure. The current extensive system has its roots in Europe and other places in which Jews lived.

---

41. *See id.* (follow "Chapter 3: Jewish Identity" hyperlink). The survey also asked whether these elements are "important but *not* essential" or not important.

42. The percentage of Jews responding that remembering the Holocaust is an essential element of Jewish identity is 73 percent. The remaining eight elements and percentages of Jews responding that they constitute an essential element of Jewish identity are as follows: "leading an ethical and moral life" (69 percent), "working for justice/equality" (56 percent), "being intellectually curious" (49 percent), "caring about Israel" (43 percent), "having a good sense of humor" (42 percent), "being part of a Jewish community" (28 percent), "observing Jewish law" (19 percent), and "eating traditional Jewish foods" (14 percent). *Id.*

43. *Id.* For Jews by religion, the figure is 33 percent and for Jews of no religion, 10 percent.

44. *See id.* (showing only 69 percent of Orthodox respondents affirming that Jewish community is essential for Jewish identity).

In these locations, the Jews developed a uniquely Jewish communal infra-structure that allowed anonymous donations to the *kuppah*, the community collection box, and communal leaders distributed the money to a multitude of local welfare providers.[45] In 1895, the Jews of Boston created a centralized Jewish organization that brought together all of the previously distinct Jewish charitable organizations. This "one stop" model of philanthropy promoted efficiencies in both fundraising and distribution and eventually became the backbone of the Jewish federation system of North America. Today, there is a Jewish federation in virtually every North American city with a Jewish popu-lation of more than one thousand people.[46] Although the local Jewish com-munities were the initial focus of these federations, today their help extends to Jews, and also non-Jews, across the world.[47]

Jewish education advocate Jonathan Woocher has written extensively about the Jewish federation system.[48] Drawing from sociologist Robert Bellah's seminal work on American "civil religion,"[49] Woocher posited the Jewish federation system, with its core mission of Jewish survival,[50] as a means through which Jews in the United States could forge Jewish identity. This system offered Jews a way to enhance Jewish culture, community, and ethical behavior within an American milieu. Woocher explained that the particular contribution of this Jewish civil religion was the carving out of a unique sphere of Jewish activity he termed "the public agenda of the Jewish polity."[51] He claimed that within this sphere American Jews could pursue their "particularist/survivalist goals" and validate them in American terms

---

45. *Helping Others in Need: A Brief History of the Federation System*, THE JEWISH FEDERA-TIONS OF NORTH AMERICA, http://www.jewishfederations.org/page.aspx?ID=1039 (last visited July 8, 2014). In these communities, a different organization existed to meet every need of the members of the community.

46. *Id.* at 2.

47. *Id.* Special federation campaigns are conducted regularly to benefit the victims of natural and other disasters, regardless of race or religion.

48. *See* JONATHAN WOOCHER, SACRED SURVIVAL (1986).

49. Bellah's essay on this topic was originally published in 1967. *See* Robert N. Bellah, *Civil Religion in America, in* Dædalus, 96(1) J. AM. ACADEMY OF ARTS & SCIS. 1–21, Winter 1967.

50. *See* Byron L. Sherwin, *Thinking Judaism Through, in* THE CAMBRIDGE COMPANION TO AMERICAN JUDAISM 117, 118 (2005) ("[p]articularly in the last decades of the twenti-eth century, the doctrine of Jewish survival became the prime directive and basic dogma of Jewish communal life.").

51. WOOCHER, *supra* note 48, at 99.

while simultaneously pursuing "universalist/integrative programs" that could be "legitimated in terms of Jewish values."[52]

The primary directives of Jewish federations involve philanthropy and social action. Through this model, American Jews were, and still are, able to synthesize their individual and communal Jewish identities and also to meld their Jewish and American identities.[53] This model of Jewish identity also furnished an appropriate complement to the preoccupation of American Jews with building synagogues that occurred between 1945 and 1965. Both federation involvement and synagogue building absorbed time, energy, and money, but these activities did not require particular religious theologies or adherence to *halakhah*.[54]

Significantly, therefore, civil Judaism at its core is not a model concerned with *halakhic* observance, although there are ways in which it has manifested a "growing appreciation of and commitment" to Jewish tradition.[55] Over time, federations have developed an increasing sensitivity to certain religious observance. Thus, it is not uncommon for federation functions to serve kosher food and to avoid holding public events that conflict with the observance of the Sabbath and other Jewish holidays.[56] Generally speaking, however, civil Judaism as expressed through the current federations and their mission concentrates on Judaism as an expression of Jewish identity "through identification with the Jewish people as a corporate entity, its history, culture and tradition, but without necessarily accepting the authoritative character of *halakhah* or the centrality of *halakhah* in defining Jewishness."[57]

Writing in 1986, Woocher observed, "The future of the civil religion as an integrating and mobilizing ideology for American Jewry seems relatively

---

52. *Id.*

53. *Id.*

54. *See* Jonathan Woocher, *Sacred Survival Revisited, in* THE CAMBRIDGE COMPANION TO AMERICAN JUDAISM, *supra* note 50, at 283, 287 (noting that synagogue building allowed Jews to align with their "church-building Christian neighbors" but because Jews "were uncertain about the content with which to fill these synagogues," Jewish civil religion provided the content); JONATHAN D. SARNA, AMERICAN JUDAISM 279 (2004) (observing that synagogue building "constituted the 'central religious activity' of many American Jews" during this period).

55. WOOCHER, *supra* note 48, at 147.

56. *Id.*

57. *Id.* at 159 (quoting Daniel Elazar's characterization of "neo-Sadducean Judaism" as a model through which Jews manifest their identity through culture, history, and peoplehood rather than *halakhah*).

secure."[58] By the early part of the twenty-first century, however, Woocher explicitly recognized that the nature of the Jewish polity upon which civil Judaism depended had substantially changed, rendering many of his earlier theories about the composition and constitution of civil Judaism no longer applicable in the same way.[59] Several of these reasons will be examined more fully throughout this chapter, but for purposes of this discussion, his ongoing faith in the continuing importance of civil Judaism is noteworthy. Specifically, he maintains that civil Judaism "is *not* simply a species of Jewish secularism" but rather a phenomenon that is "very much about finding genuine, life-shaping meaning in one's Jewishness."[60] When framed in this way, he sees the "civil Jewish message of solidarity," mutual responsibility, and obligation to one another as core, enduring expressions of an authentic Judaism.[61]

Israel

The idea of Jewish empowerment, exemplified by the rebirth of the Jewish people with the founding of the state of Israel, resonates strongly with many Jews. Following the Holocaust, many American Jews began to believe that Israel was living proof "that Jews need not be victims of history any longer, that with vigilance and dedication they can be its masters."[62] In a world that has witnessed the uprising of Islamic terrorism not only against Israel but also against the United States, and most recently, other countries in the Middle East, there seems to be a strong, increased solidarity on the part of Jewish Americans concerning Israel.

Recent evidence reveals steady support for Israel on the part of American Jews, despite areas of actual and potential disagreement on aspects of Israeli policy concerning the peace process.[63] The frequent public demonstrations of

---

58. *Id.* at 161.

59. *See generally* Woocher, *supra* note 54.

60. *Id.* at 293.

61. *Id.* at 294.

62. WOOCHER, *supra* note 48, at 134.

63. *See infra* notes 65–69 and accompanying text. The Pew Report also shows that 38 percent of American Jews believe "that the current Israeli government is making sincere efforts to effectuate a peaceful settlement with the Palestinians." This percentage is significantly higher among Orthodox Jews (61 percent) and Conservative Jews (52 percent). *See* Pew Report, *supra* note 4 (follow "Chapter 5: Connection with and Attitudes toward Israel" hyperlink).

support for Israel and the generous donations often spearheaded by federation emergency campaigns[64] suggest that Israel advocacy still has the potential for providing a powerful source of Jewish identity among American Jews. According to the Pew Report, which devotes an entire chapter to Israel, about seven out of ten Jews feel either very or somewhat attached to Israel.[65] These results closely resemble the 2000–2001 National Jewish Population Survey and therefore demonstrate that emotional attachment to Israel on the part of American Jews has not declined considerably over the past decade.[66] Only 12 percent of the NET Jewish population said that caring about Israel is not an important part of being Jewish.[67] Yet, compared to other markers of "essential" Jewish identity, "caring about Israel" ranks behind "remembering the Holocaust," "leading an ethical life," "working for justice and equality," and "being intellectually curious."[68] Perhaps somewhat surprisingly, 40 percent of American Jews reported they believe that God gave to the Jewish people the land that now constitutes Israel.[69] This number is arguably higher than would be expected given the relatively low importance American Jews attach to religion as a general matter.

Based on this evidence, it does seem as though Israel still functions as an important component of positive Jewish identity among American Jews.[70]

---

64. Woocher, *supra* note 54, at 290. *See also* SUSSER & LIEBMAN, *supra* note 7, at 58 (quoting observation by Arthur Hertzberg that the ingrained response of the American Jewish soul to danger is to give money).

65. *See* Pew Report, *supra* note 4 (follow "Chapter 5: Connection with and Attitudes toward Israel" hyperlink). According to Pew, 30 percent of American Jews feel "very attached" and 39 percent feel "somewhat attached" to Israel. Also, 43 percent of American Jews have been to Israel, and 23 percent have visited more than one time. *Id.*

66. *See id.* Although emotional attachment to Israel is still high, it is markedly stronger among Jews by religion than Jews of no religion. *Id.*

67. Together, a vast majority of the NET Jewish population said that caring about Israel is either an "essential part of being Jewish" (43 percent) or "important but not essential" (44 percent). *Id.*

68. *See supra* note 42.

69. *See* Pew Report, *supra* note 4 (follow "Chapter 5: Connection with and Attitudes toward Israel" hyperlink). The Pew Report also notes that 27 percent of those surveyed do not believe this is literally true, and 28 percent were not asked this question because they do not believe in God. Among Jews by religion, 47 percent believe "Israel was given by God to the Jews" compared with 16 percent of Jews of no religion. *Id.*

70. Woocher's later work on civil Judaism published in 2005 also explicitly acknowledges the increased solidarity on the part of Jewish Americans concerning Israel. He raises, but seemingly rejects, the possibility that Israel's change in circumstances resulting from the inception of the Second Intifada in 2000 may furnish the basis for a reinvigorated civil Judaism. Woocher, *supra* note 54, at 290.

As will be discussed more fully below, however, the positive nature of Israel's influence on American Jewish identity is becoming somewhat more contested in light of the political realities facing the state. This conflict is particularly noticeable among Millennials, for whom Israel is not as strong a marker of positive Jewish identity. According to the Pew Report, only 32 percent of Jews under the age of thirty said "caring about Israel" is an "essential part of being Jewish" compared to 43 percent of the NET population.[71] Pew concludes that it is difficult to interpret these statistics to mean that the attachment of American Jews to Israel will weaken over time. Specifically, if Jews become more attached to Israel as they get older, then attachment to Israel overall could hold steady or even grow.[72] Still, given the availability and popularity of free, sponsored trips to Israel provided by Taglit-Birthright,[73] these numbers are a bit puzzling. They can, however, perhaps be explained by the more pronounced anti-Israel sentiment that has taken hold of many college campuses in recent years.

Anti-Semitism and Anti-Zionism

Political science professors Bernard Susser and Charles Liebman have written extensively about the "ideology of affliction" as a catalyst for Jewish identity and survival throughout the ages.[74] Historically, much of this affliction has been the result of anti-Semitism in one form or another. Susser and Liebman note that beginning with the Torah and continuing throughout the normative Jewish texts, the Jewish religion "both explained *and* predicted affliction as an integral part of the Divine plan."[75] Specifically, when the Jews sin, God punishes them through the agency of non-Jews; when they repent and return, God ameliorates the punishment.[76] Susser and Liebman also discuss how this

---

71. *See* Pew Report, *supra* note 4 (follow "Chapter 5: Connection with and Attitudes toward Israel" hyperlink). *See also supra* note 67 and accompanying text.

72. *See* Pew Report, *supra* note 4 (follow "Chapter 5: Connection with and Attitudes toward Israel" hyperlink). The percentage of Jews who say caring about Israel is an essential part of their identity increases with age, despite the fact that the statistics regarding visiting Israel are essentially similar among all the ages. *See id.*

73. Among those younger than thirty who have visited Israel, 48 percent participated in a Taglit-Birthright Israel trip. *Id.*

74. SUSSER & LIEBMAN, *supra* note 7, at 15–37.

75. *Id.* at 30.

76. *Id.*

ideology of affliction has become ingrained in the consciousness of the Jews and suggest that it has become one of the hallmarks of Jewish ethnicity and identity throughout the centuries. According to this theory, "Jews survived because anti-Semitism defined them and preserved them as a people apart."[77] When confronted with persecution, Jews looked to their tradition and to one another for solace and sustenance.

Conceivably, no topic concerning anti-Semitism has the potential to unify Jews more than the Holocaust. Susser and Liebman have observed that "'the vicarious memory of the Holocaust' is perhaps the single uniting experience that consolidates the 'fractious' American Jewish community."[78] The recent Pew findings substantiate this perspective. As discussed earlier, of the nine factors for "essential" Jewish identity, remembering the Holocaust garnered the largest percentage of affirmative responses among the NET Jewish population.[79]

Susser and Liebman published their book in 1999, well after the period of history in the United States when Jews faced active discrimination,[80] but just before the beginning of the Second Intifada that commenced in 2000. Thus, they worry that "having incorporated Gentile hostility deep into Jewish religious and popular perceptions there is great difficulty in reconstructing a plausible and relevant worldview when it is absent."[81] They further observe that Jewish existence in the United States and Israel has "become reasonably secure and promises to become only more so."[82] Unfortunately, subsequent events in the twenty-first century have called their assumptions of future security into question with respect to the situation of Israel, Jews in Europe, and elsewhere.

Professor Robert Wistrich, the director of Hebrew University's Vidal Sassoon International Center for the Study of Anti-Semitism, is one of the world's leading academic authorities on anti-Semitism. In his view, the

---

77. *Id.* at 20.

78. *Id.* at 56. The authors also observe that "despite its unifying power, the fact that there is room for creative interpretation of the Holocaust, that all 'may draw different conclusions' from it only reinforces its position as a central focus of American Jewish identity." *Id.*

79. *See supra* note 42 and accompanying text.

80. Susser and Liebman document examples of employment and other types of discrimination against Jews in the United States as recently as the period following World War II. SUSSER & LIEBMAN, *supra* note 7, at 42–43.

81. *Id.* at 28.

82. *Id.* at 35.

return of anti-Semitism confirms "its near-ubiquity and perennial nature."[83] Wistrich and others have been trying to combat anti-Semitism by raising awareness of Holocaust revisionism, increased toleration of neo-Nazi sympathizers, and other forms of hatred toward the Jews in Europe and elsewhere.[84] According to some scholars and observers, much of the current version of anti-Semitism appears in the guise of anti-Israel sentiment.[85] According to Wistrich, "anti-Zionism and anti-Semitism are two distinct ideologies that over time (especially since 1948) have tended to converge, generally without undergoing a full merger."[86]

In 2005, the Palestinian Civil Society called for boycott, divestment, and sanctions against Israel, thus formally commencing the BDS movement.[87] This movement has been steadily gaining ground. In 2014, Malcolm Hoenlein, the executive vice chairman of the Conference of Presidents of Major American Jewish Organizations, called this growing international boycott campaign a "politically correct" form of anti-Semitism.[88]

Anti-Israel sentiment, including support for the BDS movement, is particularly strong on college campuses in the United States. These views have gained a foothold not only among many college students but also among the professors who teach them. For example, in 2013, 66 percent of the members of the American Studies Association voted to support a boycott of Israeli academic institutions, which was unanimously passed by the association's

---

83. *See* Scott Johnson, *An Interview with Robert Wistrich*, POWERLINE (Jan. 3, 2013), http://www.powerlineblog.com/archives/2013/01/an-interview-with-robert-wistrich.php.

84. *See* Robert Wistrich, *How Not to Fight Anti-Semitism*, JERUSALEM POST (May 21, 2013), http://www.jpost.com/Opinion/Op-Ed-Contributors/How-not-to-fight-anti-Semitism-313906; Daniella Peled, *French Hatred of Jews Goes Far beyond Muslim Anti-Semitism, Says U.K. Author*, HAARETZ (Feb. 18, 2014), http://www.haaretz.com/jewish-world/jewish-world-features/.premium-1.574909. *See also* Naftali Bendavid, *Poll Says Anti-Semitism Is Global Matter*, WALL ST. J., May 13, 2014, at A8. (discussing the results of a new global survey sponsored by the Anti-Defamation League).

85. *See, e.g.*, Robert Wistrich, *Anti-Zionism and Anti-Semitism*, JEWISH POLITICAL STUDIES REV. 16(3–4) (Fall 2004), http://www.jcpa.org/phas/phas-wistrich-f04.htm; Johnson, *supra* note 83; Ian Black, *Israel Boycott Movement Is Antisemitic, Says Binyamin Netanyahu*, GUARDIAN (Feb. 18, 2014), http://www.theguardian.com/world/2014/feb/18/israel-boycott-movement-antisemitic-netanyahu.

86. Wistrich, *supra* note 85.

87. *See Palestinian Civil Society Call for BDS*, BDS MOVEMENT (July 9, 2005), http://www.bdsmovement.net/call.

88. *Malcolm Hoenlein Calls on Western Governments to Combat Anti-Israel Boycotts*, ALGEMEINER (Feb. 7, 2014), http://www.algemeiner.com/2014/02/07/malcolm-hoenlein-calls-on-western-governments-to-combat-anti-israel-boycotts/.

national council.[89] Numerous college presidents as well as the president of the American Council on Education condemned this resolution, and several universities announced resignations from the American Studies Association. Still, there has been pushback on the part of faculty and students to such condemnations of the resolution.[90]

As for the perceived prevalence of current anti-Semitism in the United States, the Pew Report shows that actual concern exists. According to the survey, 43 percent of American Jews believe there is still significant discrimination against Jews today, with 54 percent saying the opposite.[91] With respect to instances of personal experience with discrimination, however, only 15 percent of Jews reported having been the victim of particular discrimination during the past year, such as being called offensive names or feeling snubbed in a social setting. Interestingly, Jews between the ages of eighteen and twenty-nine have reported a somewhat higher incidence of being called offensive names because they are Jewish.[92] Although the survey does not posit a reason for these findings, it is plausible that the increasingly prevalent anti-Israel sentiment on college campuses in the United States may account for the difference between younger Jews and those over the age of thirty with respect to their experiences in this regard.

Overall, by promoting a certain type of unity against persecution, it seems as though guarding against anti-Semitism still has a role in forging Jewish identity among American Jews. Ironically, however, a different version of Jewish solidarity is emerging in some quarters of the Jewish community; it centers on opposition to Israel or, perhaps more accurately, on opposition to Israel's policies. For Jews who do not share these views, the essence of this solidarity is seen as a delegitimization of Israel.

---

89. Jonathan Marks, *A Vote against Israel and Academic Freedom*, WALL ST. J., Dec. 16, 2013, at A15. *See also Council Resolution on Boycott of Israeli Academic Institutions*, AMERICAN STUDIES ASSOCIATION (Dec. 4, 2013), http://www.theasa.net/american_studies_association_resolution_on_academic_boycott_of_israel.

90. For a discussion of these matters, see Elizabeth Redden, *Boycott Battles*, INSIDE HIGHER ED (Jan. 2, 2014), http://m.insidehighered.com/news/2014/01/02/presidents-denounce-academic-boycott-israel-some-campuses-faculty-and-presidents#sthash.T8Qx18YB.dpbs. *See also* William A. Jacobson, *List of Universities Rejecting Academic Boycott of Israel*, LEGAL INSURRECTION (Dec. 22, 2013), http://legalin-surrection.com/2013/12/list-of-universities-rejecting-academic-boycott-of-israel/.

91. *See* Pew Report, *supra* note 4 (follow "Chapter 6: Social and Political Views" hyperlink).

92. *See id.* (22 percent between the ages of eighteen and twenty-nine as opposed to 16 percent of Jews between thirty and forty-nine, and 6 percent of Jews between fifty and sixty-four.

An opinion letter appearing in the *New York Times* in 2014 states the "BDS movement has nothing to do with animus toward Jews," that many American Jews such as the letter's author "are vigorously working" to support BDS, and that "there are more and more of us with every passing month."[93] These Jews join BDS based on their perceived view of Israel's treatment of Palestinians and their objection to the support provided by the United States to Israel. Young Jewish college students are particularly susceptible to this perspective. For example, many young Jews are attracted to Jewish Voices for Peace, a highly controversial grass roots organization that provides active support for the BDS movement.[94] In 2014, *Wall Street Journal* correspondent Lucette Lagnado wrote an article lamenting the anti-Israel sentiment at Vassar, her alma mater, and discussing the open support of the American Studies Association's boycott on the part of the president of the Vassar Jewish Union and the head of the school's Jewish Studies Program.[95] Whereas anti-Israel sentiment previously functioned to encourage solidarity among Jewish students as part of their response, today anti-Israel sentiment is providing a basis for unity among some Jewish students in their opposition to Israel.[96]

Jewish Liberalism

It is clear that a strong concern for social justice is deeply embedded in the text of the Torah. For example, in the book of Leviticus, God commands the Israelites to refrain from reaping the harvest to the edges of the land and to leave the "gleanings" for the poor and the stranger.[97] This theme is repeated in verses in the book of Deuteronomy, the final chapter of the Torah, as the Jews are commanded to preserve portions of their harvest, olive trees, and

---

93. Hannah Schwarzschild, The Opinion Pages Letters, *Is a Boycott of Israel Just?*, N.Y. TIMES (Feb. 18, 2014), http://www.nytimes.com/2014/02/19/opinion/the-case-for-the-israel-boycott.html?_r=0_.

94. *See* Miriam Berger, *The Jews behind BDS*, NEW VOICES (Sept. 27, 2010), http://newvoices.org/2010/09/27/0100-2/; Dan Pine, *Report Rips Jewish Voices for Peace and Its Tactics*, JWEEKLY.COM (July 18, 2013), http://www.jweekly.com/article/full/69058/report-rips-jewish-voice-for-peace-and-its-tactics/.

95. Lucette Lagnado, *Anti-Israel Jews and the Vassar Blues*, WALL ST. J., Feb. 24, 2014, at A15.

96. *See id.*

97. Leviticus 19:9–10 (translation from ETZ HAYIM: TORAH AND COMMENTARY 695 (David L. Leiber et al. eds., 2001) [hereinafter ETZ HAYIM]). *See also* Leviticus 23:22.

vineyards for strangers, orphans, and widows.[98] Steeped in these and other texts, the Jewish psyche warmly embraced the ethical and moral dimensions of the Enlightenment.

An authentic Jewish quest for social justice also derives from the concept of *tikkun olam* (repairing the world). Significantly, the earliest appearance of *tikkun olam* in the rabbinic literature is in the Mishnah's tractate Gittin, where it is used in connection with various precepts of Jewish law that are termed as precautions "for the general good."[99] Over time, however, the development of *tikkun olam* shifted in focus from an exclusive concern with the Jewish community as a means of preserving *halakhah* and caring for the most vulnerable in Jewish society to a more universal application.[100] The ideals of the Enlightenment and the emancipation of the Jews facilitated this process: "When the boundaries sealing off Jewish life from society at large were breached by the Enlightenment and emancipation, the drive for social justice, so long an internal concern, was propelled outward."[101] Since this time, the mission for social justice "has served as an all-purpose catalyst for progressive causes," especially among Jews who are less traditional from a religious standpoint.[102]

Since the inception of the Enlightenment, Jews were strongly drawn to the idea of modernity and the abandonment of tradition that modernity often encouraged. In this regard, Susser and Liebman have observed that Jews not only joined "the bandwagon of secularism and modernization" but also "in many important ways they led it."[103] Their suggestion that Jews

---

98. *See* Deuteronomy 24:19–21.

99. Gittin 4:1–5:3 (Mishnah) at 310–12 (Herbert Danby trans., 1933).

100. *See generally* Byron L. Sherwin, Tikkun Olam: *A Case of Semantic Displacement*, 25 (3–4) Jewish Political Studies Rev., Fall 2014. Sherwin is critical of contemporary understandings of *tikkun olam* on the ground that they depart from the original understanding of the concept.

101. Susser & Liebman, *supra* note 7, at 66.

102. Susser and Liebman have observed, "In much the same way that Jewish intellectualism turned from Talmud and *halakhic* law to philosophy and literature, so the Jewish emphasis on the mutual responsibility of community members for one another became, in the 'emancipated' version, a universalist pursuit of fraternity and mutuality—often with the older religious-messianic dreams recycled and secularized." *Id.*

103. *Id.* at 18 (positing that Marx, Freud, and Einstein formed "the central triad of modern consciousness"). In a recent book, Robert Wistrich has documented how "anti-Semitism has been an important feature of left-wing thought ever since its beginnings in the 1840s." *See* Robert Wistrich, From Ambivalence to Betrayal: The Left, the Jews and Israel (2012)

gravitated toward Enlightenment ideals because these concepts represented a particularly authentic Jewish worldview is especially interesting. Initially, the Enlightenment was understood as an attempt to recast Jewish life and culture in modern terms, and as such, it presented a strong case for Jewish survival and identity. This early message of the *maskilim*, the Hebrew term for the "enlightened ones," sought to broaden Jewish consciousness to make room for modern scholarship and Western philosophies rather than to displace the core traditional beliefs. Gradually, the "'emancipatory' message" became "stridently antitraditional," but even when "Jewishness was detached from Judaism entirely—the Enlightenment agenda understood itself as a legitimate and necessary step in the evolution of Jewish history."[104] As Susser and Liebman observed, the Jews were "psychologically posed to sympathize" with the message of the Enlightenment: "[t]here is something exceptionally beguiling to a persecuted minority about a vision of democratic equality and universal human fellowship."[105]

Additional factors round out an explanation of the positive response on the part of Jews to the Enlightenment and its universal ideals. By and large, Jews lived in urban centers in Europe, which afforded them geographic proximity to those espousing Enlightenment philosophies. Also, the attraction of the Enlightenment for many Jews derived from their historically deep regard for educational accomplishment and their familiarity with rigorous analytical thought as developed in the prevalent yeshiva (school of Jewish education) culture.[106] This culture thrives on questioning, critical thinking, and systematic analysis, all of which meshed well with "the Enlightenment's emphasis on reasoning and inquiry."[107] This respect for education also rendered many Jews especially receptive to exciting new intellectual challenges.[108]

In the aftermath of the Enlightenment, anti-Semitism emerged "as a problem to be solved rather than as a divinely ordained fate to be endured."[109] Part of the explanation for this phenomenon was that the justifications for Jewish suffering that were grounded in the traditional Jewish worldview and

---

104. SUSSER & LIEBMAN, *supra* note 7, at 21.

105. *Id.* at 22.

106. *Id.*

107. *Id.*

108. *Id. See supra* note 42 (noting that according to the Pew Report, 49 percent of Jews reported that being intellectually curious is essential to their Jewish identity).

109. SUSSER & LIEBMAN, *supra* note 7, at 20.

texts were no longer as persuasive to many Jews. Thus, they affirmatively sought a proactive solution to their affliction.

When Jews settled in the United States, this "socio-cultural reformation"[110] fostered a liberal Jewish identity that centered on aligning with other oppressed groups, notably African Americans.[111] In the 1960s, Rabbi Abraham Joshua Heschel, a professor at the Jewish Theological Seminary, "emerged as the central prophet of civil rights activism within the Jewish community."[112] In 1965, Heschel was photographed marching arm in arm with Dr. Martin Luther King Jr. and other African-American civil rights activists in a march through Selma, Alabama. According to Professor Jonathan Sarna, this photograph has become an "icon of American Jewish life, and of black-Jewish relations."[113]

Today, American Judaism and political liberalism seem to go hand in hand, along with a strong concern for social justice, human rights, and caring for those who are disadvantaged in our society.[114] The recent findings of the Pew Report substantiate these connections. According to the study, "working for justice and equality" is the third most popular quality essential for Jewish identity, with 56 percent of American Jews responding positively on this point.[115] Further, the Pew Report demonstrates that outside of those who denominate as Orthodox, "Jews are among the most strongly liberal, Democratic groups" in American politics.[116] Among American Jews, there are "more than twice as many self-identified Jewish liberals as conservatives, while among the general public, this balance is nearly reversed."[117] Also,

---

110. *Id.* at 36.

111. With respect to liberalism, Susser and Liebman note that although this ideology does "draw upon an authentic Jewish proclivity for social justice, it fails as a strategy for Jewish survival because it lacks the resources to justify Jewish cohesion and particularism." *Id.* at 69.

112. SARNA, *supra* note 54, at 310.

113. *Id.* at 311.

114. Writing more than a decade ago, Susser and Liebman note that "for many American Jews, the non-Orthodox in particular, political liberalism is constitutive of what it means to be a good and caring Jew." SUSSER & LIEBMAN, *supra* note 7, at 63.

115. *See supra* note 42.

116. *See* Pew Report, *supra* note 4 (follow "Chapter 6: Social and Political Views" hyperlink). Pew also reveals that 54 percent of Orthodox Jews describe themselves as political conservatives, and 57 percent "identify with or lean toward" the Republican Party. *Id.*

117. *See id.* (showing that 49 percent of American Jews "describe themselves as political liberals" in contrast to 19 percent political conservatives; among the general public, 21 percent identify as liberal as opposed to 38 percent conservative). For a

the Pew Report shows that 70 percent of American Jews "identify with or lean toward" the Democratic Party in contrast to 49 percent of the general public.[118]

The foregoing discussion demonstrates that generally speaking, the identity of the American Jewish community is difficult to unbundle given its multilayered complexity. One matter that is rather clear, however, is that by and large American Jewish identity does not depend upon traditional observance of *halakhah*, at least for the majority of American Jews. The next part probes social forces that currently drive this non-*halakhic* dimension of Jewish identity in the United States.

Social Forces Militating against Tradition

In recent decades, American society as a whole has become characterized by the concepts of "custom-made" and individual choice as reflected by the Internet generation's more generalized obsession with personalized experiences across the board—from clothing to media.[119] This trend has had important consequences for American Judaism. Toward the end of the twentieth century, scholars of American Judaism Steven Cohen and Arnold Eisen produced a portrait of "religious personalism" among American Jews that emphasized the centrality of "the sovereign self" in defining the role of authority with respect to their Jewishness.[120] Based on their interviews with moderately affiliated Jewish individuals mostly between the ages of thirty and fifty, Cohen and Eisen concluded that, from a ritualistic standpoint, even committed Jews decide when, how, and what they will observe.[121] Autonomy is prized, and consequently, these Jews fail to see Jewish norms, and certainly *halakhah*, as binding in its entirety.[122] Jonathan Woocher also has observed that American Jews "manifest a growing disenchantment with

---

critical and controversial indictment of this trend among American Jews, see NORMAN PODHORETZ, WHY ARE JEWS LIBERALS? (2009).

118. *See* Pew Report, *supra* note 4 (follow "Chapter 6: Social and Political Views" hyperlink).

119. Nick Bilton, *A Tech World That Centers on the User*, N.Y. TIMES, Sept. 13, 2010, at B1.

120. STEVEN M. COHEN & ARNOLD M. EISEN, THE JEW WITHIN: SELF, FAMILY AND COMMUNITY IN AMERICA 1–2 (2000).

121. *See, e.g., id.* at 4, 7, 10, 184.

122. *See, e.g., id.* at 37, 75–76, 91 (discussing the prevalence of personal selectivity in religious observance).

or indifference to any formalized version of Judaism that impinges on their autonomy in choosing when, how, and even whether to 'be Jewish.'"[123] In this regard, Woocher has noted that the traditional appreciation for Jewish history as an operative factor in the Jewish experience has been replaced by a biography of self and family.[124] Cohen and Eisen provide an example of this phenomenon in discussing how the Passover seder is observed among the individuals they interviewed. They write that the ritual framework of the seder, including the text of the prayers and the consumption of required foods, such as parsley, matzah, and horseradish, no longer constitute the meaning of the seder. Instead, these elements have become merely the script to transmit what is perceived as the most important meaning of the seder, which is "particular, unique to each family."[125]

In light of the increasing level of autonomy desired by American Jews, Judaism has become privatized.[126] In discussing this phenomenon, Susser and Liebman have written that pursuant to a privatized or "personalized" view of Judaism, individuals are detached "from the larger social collectives of which they are a part" and released "from the binding duties these collectives impose."[127] This leads, in their view, "toward self-directed lives that pursue rare moments of meaning and growth."[128] Rabbi Byron Sherwin worries that the "sovereign self" phenomenon is particularly dangerous because it is responsible for the increasingly prevalent idea among American Jews that they can decide for themselves what is meaningful with respect to Jewish belief, ethics, and ritual.[129]

---

123. See Woocher, *supra* note 54, at 284. Woocher also noted the emergence of a trend toward "inwardness" among American Jews in his earlier work. See WOOCHER, *supra* note 48, at 166–67. *See also* SUSSER & LIEBMAN, *supra* note 7, at 86.

124. Woocher, *supra* note 54, at 283–84. Woocher also observes that this lack of appreciation for historical (and ethnic) sensibilities results in a weakening of "the Jewish polity to which the civil religion is so closely linked." *Id.* at 289.

125. COHEN & EISEN, *supra* note 120, at 84.

126. *See, e.g., id.* at 84, 86, 91, 93.

127. SUSSER & LIEBMAN, *supra* note 7, at 79.

128. *Id. See also* Bruce Phillips, *American Judaism in the 21st Century, in* THE CAMBRIDGE COMPANION TO AMERICAN JUDAISM (2005), *supra* note 50, at 397 (discussing Robert Bella's notion of "religious privatization").

129. Sherwin, *supra* note 50, at 130. At the 2005 Lay Leaders Retreat at the Shalom Hartman Institute in Jerusalem, founder Rabbi David Hartman observed that Judaism now is viewed as a matter of choice and must compete with other alternatives that are viewed as equally appealing. *See also* AKIVA TATZ & DAVID GOTTLIEB, LETTERS TO A BUDDHIST JEW (2004) (discussing the appeal of Buddhism for many Western Jews).

In commenting on "the privatization of Jewishness," Susser and Liebman have lamented that "de-theologizing religious observances, that is, replacing human for Divine content...takes precedence over self-standing, objective religious obligations."[130] The reality they describe seems to be an accurate assessment because most American Jews do not believe they are commanded to observe *halakhah*. Therefore, to preserve its relevance, *halakhah* must be justified in some other way. Also, for Jews who self-denominate as liberal or progressive, the category of "tradition" is largely an inactive one.[131]

In addition to this trend of religious personalism, the process of "coalescence" presents another social trend potentially threatening the survival of Judaism in the United States. Sociologist Sylvia Fishman describes the process of "coalescence" as one in which, for most American Jews, the boundaries between what is Jewish and what is American have disappeared, resulting in a merger of the two belief systems "into one coalesced whole widely known as 'Judaism.'"[132] In other words, "coalescence" exists because American and Jewish values have become so blended that even knowledgeable American Jews no longer recognize the distinct origins of these value systems.[133] In his work revisiting the American Jewish civil religion, Woocher also acknowledged the "coalescence problem,"[134] as have Susser and Liebman.[135] From a cultural analysis standpoint, the particular danger "coalescence" presents for Jewish survival is that this blended Jewish-American perspective will result in the eradication of Jewish particularity for a large number of American Jews who may not even realize this is happening.

---

130. SUSSER & LIEBMAN, *supra* note 7, at 78 (noting that this scenario is at the heart of "personalism" with "individual experience situated at the very center of religions life").

131. *See* Menachem Martner, *A Dialogue between a Liberal and an Ultra-Orthodox on the Exclusion of Women from Torah Study*, in RELIGOUS REVIVAL IN A POST-MULTICULTURAL AGE 33 (Shai Lavi and Rene Provost eds., 2013). *See also* COHEN & EISEN, *supra* note 120, at 91 ("the rules of tradition...exist as guidelines or opportunities, but exercise little compulsion or authority in and of themselves.").

132. SYLVIA BARACK FISHMAN, NEGOTIATING BOTH SIDES OF THE HYPHEN 40 (1996).

133. Byron L. Sherwin, *The Assimilation of Judaism: Heschel and the "Category Mistake,"* JUDAISM 40, 45, Fall/Winter 2006, http://www.ajcongress.org/site/DocServer/Assimilationofjudaism.pdf?docID=2124.

134. "For large numbers of Jews, the boundaries separating them from the larger American society and culture have collapsed to the point where their Jewishness and Americanness are not only compatible but virtually indistinguishable (at least in their minds)." Woocher, *supra* note 54, at 284.

135. SUSSER & LIEBMAN, *supra* note 7, at 87 (noting that in the Jewish "'civil religion,' Judaism is represented as a facsimile of Americana, America read from right to left").

These trends of customization and privatization have become increasingly pronounced among the millennial generation. Doctors Erica Brown and Misha Galperin have written about American Jewish identity generally being "layered," meaning that "being Jewish does not represent only one aspect of identity"[136] but rather "is based on layers of personal choice."[137] With respect to Millennials in particular, they note that the level of experimentation with Jewish identity "is astounding."[138] A relatively recent research paper produced by the Hillel Foundation quoted by the authors notes the complexities inherent in the expression of Jewish identity among Millennials. According to this paper: "What pulls [Millennials] to Jewishness, finally, is not guilt, fear or inherent obligation but Jewish meaning and the opportunity to celebrate that meaning with their Jewish and non-Jewish friends."[139]

The multifaceted quality of Jewish identity among American Millennials is illustrated in many ways. Thus, although they may take great pride in their Jewishness, it "does not demand more commitment from them than any of the multiple identities that have shaped a complex generation weaned on technology and multiculturalism."[140] Moreover, many of the ways in which they express their connection to Judaism actually can be seen as subversive, as is exemplified by the play *Jewtopia* and the subsequent book and movie based on the play.[141] The storyline centers on two thirty-year-old men, one Jewish and the other Gentile. The Jew wants to escape his roots by dating and marrying a Gentile woman, and the Gentile wants to date a Jewish woman

---

136. Erica Brown & Misha Galperin, The Case for Jewish Peoplehood 110 (2009).

137. *Id.* at 71.

138. *Id.* at 150.

139. *Id.* at 151 (quoting Beth Cousens, *Hillel's Journey: Distinctively Jewish, Universally Human* 7 (Hillel: The Foundation for Jewish Campus Life, 2007)).

140. *Id.* at 151–52.

141. The play, authored by Bryan Fogel and Sam Wolfson, was first produced in Los Angeles in 2003 and then went to off-Broadway where it ran for three years with 1,100 performances. In 2007, the authors released a coffee table book based on the play, which has been labeled the "ultimate book of Jewish humour." Bryan Fogel & Sam Wolfson, Jewtopia: The Chosen Book for the Chosen People (2007). The above-quoted language describing the book appears on Amazon.com at http://www.amazon.com/Jewtopia-Chosen-Book-People/dp/0446579548/ref=la_B001H6IG70_1_1?s=books&ie=UTF8&qid=13947 22348&sr=1-1. The movie version appeared in 2012, and although it is based on the play, apart from the main theme there are significant differences. *See* J Space Staff, *Catching Up with "Jewtopia" Director Bryan Fogel*, J Space (Apr. 25, 2012), http://www.jspace.com/news/articles/catching-up-with-jewtopia-director-bryan-fogel/8691 [hereinafter *Catching Up with "Jewtopia"*].

because, according to coauthor Bryan Fogel, he never wants to have to make another decision again (meaning, he finds the strong personalities of Jewish women attractive).[142] The men agree to help one another achieve their respective goals. The story thrives on jokes about Jewish stereotypes.

In discussing the play and the subsequent movie, Fogel explained in detail how his Jewish upbringing served as the inspiration for the play. He was raised in a Conservative Jewish home and has remarked that "Judaism was very much a part of my growing up, so much so that I think it made me run the other way as an adult. Now I consider myself a cultural Jew, but not a religious Jew. I really had my fill growing up."[143] Not surprisingly, therefore, he considers himself more like the Jewish man in the play than his Gentile friend.

Another aspect of the multifaceted millennial Jewish identity concerns the Millennials' perspective of community, specifically Jewish community. In *Living Jewishly*, a collection of essays by Millennials, the editor notes in her prologue that although Millennials often seek community and a sense of belonging as part of their Jewish journey, they tend to gravitate toward smaller, more intimate venues rather than large institutional structures.[144] This tendency has a detrimental impact on synagogue membership and federations, as they struggle to attract younger members.[145] Brown and Galperin also note the tendency among Millennials to avoid more long-term community structures in favor of the creation of "moments of community" that bring Jews together (perhaps with non-Jews) in venues such as dances, concerts, and other programs that offer opportunities for meeting, greeting, and even social networking.[146] Yet, Brown and Galperin note the following "essential paradox" with respect to these short-term opportunities to form Jewish community:

> [T]hese events are both overtly more Jewish and often more substantial in content and spiritual overtones than the purely social opportunities created by generations past. They are also more irreverent than

---

142. *See Catching Up with "Jewtopia," supra* note 141.

143. *Id.*

144. Stefanie Pervos Bregman, *Prologue,* LIVING JEWISHLY xviii–xix (Stefanie Pervos Bregman ed., 2012).

145. *Id.* at xix.

146. BROWN & GALPERIN, *supra* note 136, at 153.

the more innocent gatherings of years past, potentially undermining the very traditions with which they are playing. Jews and tattoos, Jews and plays on anti-Semitism, Jews and music that may use foul, sexually loaded language. It is this very paradox that makes older generations unsure of the lasting power and validity of such trends.[147]

One other trend typical of the millennial generation that is discussed in the literature is that they experience an "emerging adulthood" lasting from the late teens until the late twenties or longer. This phenomenon is characterized by a prolonged period of exploration of identity, instability, self-focus, and transition.[148]

It is difficult to predict how these trends will impact the future Jewish identity of Millennials, or the generations that will follow. As Millennials continue to grow and mature, and build their own families and careers, the nature of their own Jewish identity may very well change. For example, given the current economic climate, one can imagine scenarios in which ambitious Millennials will become more involved with the federation system as they begin to understand that often their clients and customers will come from the Jewish community. Moreover, as they have children, Millennials who were raised with some degree of religion and observance may gravitate toward synagogues so they can provide their offspring with some opportunity for Jewish education. In fact, given the high cost of private Jewish day school, it is likely that even some more traditionally oriented Millennials will embrace an after-school Jewish education model for their children. These possible scenarios may provide synagogues with exciting opportunities to restructure after-school Jewish education in new ways that can reintroduce more young Jews and their parents to innovative and meaningful observance.

This chapter illustrates that among Jews in the United States, Jewish identity appears to coalesce around certain types of culturally informed behaviors, political attitudes, and socially influenced responses rather than around observance of *halakhah*. Yet, a cultural analysis perspective questions whether a complete separation is possible between the realms of *halakhah* and Jewish culture. The most foundational insight of a cultural analysis of the law is the critical intersection between law and culture. According to cultural analysis, the relationship between the law and the surrounding cultural environments

---

147. *Id.*

148. Bregman, *supra* note 144, at xvii (discussing the research of Jeffrey Jensen Arnett).

is fluid and constantly in flux. This cultural-legal synergy characterizes all law, not just *halakhah*.

Based on a cultural analysis perspective, therefore, it can be argued that most markers of Jewish identity incorporate aspects of the *mesorah* (the Jewish tradition) in some form. Although the consumption of bagels and lox and the popularity of Jewish Geography may not have an origin in the *halakhah*,[149] it is difficult to come up with many other examples of Jewish behavior that lack at least some basis in the tradition.[150] Similarly, the development of the *halakhah* has been influenced significantly by cultural norms, both within and outside of Jewish communities.

The following chapter examines how this relationship between law and culture, as well as other insights of the cultural analysis model developed throughout this book, inform the issues facing Jews in the twenty-first century. Addressing these issues requires a delicate balance between maintaining the tradition's authenticity, especially for purposes of transmission, and its response to changing social realities. A culturally nuanced approach to *halakhah* provides a framework that is well suited to this challenge.

---

149. *See supra* note 3 and accompanying text.

150. Paradoxically, such can be the case even if the behavior at issue actually *violates* the *halakhah*. For example, the argument has been made that the well-known love among American Jews for non-kosher Chinese food is partially attributable to the fact that this cuisine dices the non-kosher ingredients to the point where they are unrecognizable, and therefore, regarded as "safe" by non-observant Jews. *See* DAVID C. KRAEMER, JEWISH EATING AND IDENTITY THROUGH THE AGES 143–44 (2007). Moreover, after a period of time, eating Chinese food—especially on Christmas Day—simply became something Jews did together, and eventually morphed into a staple of American Jewish identity among a segment of the Jewish population. *See* Joshua Eli Plaut, *We Eat Chinese on Christmas*, JEWISH WEEK (Nov. 20, 2012), http://www.thejewishweek.com/special-sections/literary-guides/we-eat-chinese-christmas. The famous quip by Supreme Court Justice Elena Kagan during the 2010 confirmation hearings that she was at a Chinese restaurant on Christmas Day, 2009 "like all Jews" demonstrates this cultural phenomenon. *See id.*

10 THE LESSONS OF CULTURAL ANALYSIS

The "myth of the cultural Jew" is that one can adhere to Judaism on just a cultural level. In reality, those who claim to be "cultural Jews" still are embracing a degree of Jewish law and tradition regardless of whether they are aware of this reality or acknowledge it. The hallmark of cultural analysis is the intersection between law and culture. Given this foundational principle, much of what constitutes Jewish culture and identity, among Jews in the United States and elsewhere, is driven by the norms of the *mesorah* (Jewish tradition), which includes *halakhah* (Jewish law). This influence exists even though the majority of people who claim to be "cultural" rather than religious Jews do not necessarily recognize these norms as being drawn from the Jewish tradition or *halakhah*.[1] Two examples illustrate this point. The liberal causes and social action models that attract many American Jews derive in large part from the Torah's command to leave the edges of the fields untouched to benefit the poor and others who are socially disadvantaged.[2] Further, the preoccupation among American Jews with the benefits of intellectual curiosity,[3] documented in the recent Pew Report study of the Jewish population,[4] can be attributable to Judaism's historically rich textual tradition and respect for education.[5]

---

1. *See, e.g.,* BERNARD SUSSER & CHARLES LIEBMAN, CHOOSING SURVIVAL 68 (1999) (noting that even though "Jewish cultural sensibilities lead Jews to join liberal causes, the source of their own behavior often remains obscured.").

2. *See supra* Chapter 9, notes 97–98 and accompanying text.

3. *See supra* Chapter 9, notes 42, 68, 108 and accompanying text.

4. *See* A Portrait of Jewish Americans—Pew Research Religion & Public Life Project (Oct. 1, 2013), http://www.pewforum.org/2013/10/01/jewish-american-beliefs-attitudes-culture-survey/ [hereinafter Pew Report].

5. *See supra* Chapter 9, notes 106–08 and accompanying text.

This chapter demonstrates the potential of cultural analysis to inform, and even mold, Jewish identity in the twenty-first century. Although the focus of this discussion is American Judaism, several of the cultural analysis insights applied in this chapter have relevance for Jews throughout the world, including those who live in Israel. One of the main reasons it is desirable to achieve a more accurate and nuanced understanding of Jewish identity, particularly in the United States, is that such an understanding will contribute important information concerning the survival of Judaism and the Jewish people in the Diaspora and even in Israel. Many people believe this survival is in jeopardy given the high degrees of assimilation and intermarriage. The focus of this discussion is not on developing strategies for Jewish survival per se, although some of the following analysis incorporates points relevant to the survival discourse. Instead, this discussion illustrates how a cultural analysis of Jewish law can inform the conversation about Jewish identity and Jewish survival.

Particularity and Cultural Fluidity

As discussed throughout this book, the borders of cultural systems are porous. This is as true of the culture of the Jewish tradition as it is of all other cultural systems. As a result, both Jewish law and Jewish culture reflect and have been shaped by the reality of borrowing and adapting selected cultural content from the surrounding environments. Throughout history, Jews took what they needed from these surrounding environments in order to survive and thrive, and they adapted these influences to their own needs.

In discussing this borrowing phenomenon during the medieval period, Professor Menachem Kellner observed that even the audience of Maimonides "lived in a culture suffused with elements of Greek and Muslim thought and very likely understood at least portions of their own faith in terms of categories borrowed from the host society."[6] Professors Susser and Liebman similarly noted that "Judaism…learned from and was enriched by the many cultural legacies it inherited from the dozens of countries through which Jews passed."[7] Thus, they posited that the source of "Jewish cultural creativity" may inhere in its multidimensional confrontation "with so many of the world's greatest cultures."[8]

---

6. MENACHEM KELLNER, DOGMA IN JEWISH THOUGHT 45 (1986). *See also supra* Chapter 2, note 145 and accompanying text.

7. SUSSER & LIEBMAN, *supra* note 1, at 88.

8. *Id.*

A recent article about two singers in Israel provides an interesting example of the importance of Jews living in the "real world" rather than in enclaves. The singers are two brothers and are visible *haredim*, ultra-Orthodox Jews. Yet, they are dubbed Israel's "latest national sweethearts" by virtue of their audition for Israel's renowned version of *American Idol*.[9] The brothers did not grow up religious, which probably accounts for the love they developed for modern music. One of them became a professional drummer, and the other spent time in New York playing in jazz clubs. Undoubtedly, their prior exposure to their surrounding environment facilitated their current ability to earn a living playing secular folk music.[10]

Despite the cultural fluidity that has shaped *halakhah*, Judaism is unique in its belief that God commanded the Jews to preserve their particularity and gave them a path to guide them in this endeavor. The Torah is the foundational text for this path, which was amplified by the texts produced by the rabbinic sages in the early centuries of the Common Era. As discussed in earlier chapters, the human component of *halakhah* derives from the Torah and constitutes a foundational element of the tradition.[11]

From a cultural analysis perspective, the human element of *halakhah* is of vital importance. Recall that cultural analysis of law concentrates on how law reflects and shapes humans and their world.[12] This human component of *halakhah* not only represents a searching for Divine will, but also establishes that *halakhah* is embedded figuratively in the DNA of the Jewish people, regardless of the level of religiosity of any one person.[13] Recognition of this reality may help explain why people are proud to be Jewish even if they do not explicitly recognize the role of *halakhah* with respect to this pride. In other words, *halakhah* shapes the individual and collective identities of the Jewish people, despite the fact that most Jews lack an explicit consciousness as to its role. Further, because the *halakhah* as it has been developed over the

---

9. Isaac Scharf, *Ultra-Orthodox Singers Defy Stereotypes in Israel* (Oct. 23, 2013), http://music.yahoo.com/news/ultra-orthodox-singers-defy-stereotypes-israel-152801898.html. The Israeli reality talent show is called *Rising Star*.

10. Although they are not violating *halakhah* by virtue of their musical activities, they have not shared their appearance on the television show with any of their children and few of their friends and neighbors are aware of what they are doing. *Id*.

11. *See generally supra* Chapter 1, notes 78–85; Chapter 2, notes 1–26 and accompanying text.

12. *See supra* Chapter 1, notes 16–19 and accompanying text.

13. I thank Elliot Dorff for this insight.

centuries also is a product of culture, environment, and historical circumstances, it essentially embodies the entirety of the Jewish people's existence and experience.

This cultural analysis perspective of *halakhah* highlights the importance of preservation of cultural tradition. Cultural analysis does not endorse dismantling tradition but instead seeks to conserve its essence. Further, a cultural analysis model suggests that if *halakhah* is what drives Jewish particularity, and if *halakhah* is figuratively embedded in the DNA of the Jewish people, then a failure to actively cultivate an appreciation of its role will inevitably lead to the extinction of the Jewish people. Cultural analysis highlights the idea that if Jews ignore *halakhah* and its relevance to their lives, they risk diluting their own particularity. Many, if not the majority, of Jews consider themselves "culturally Jewish," without recognizing that such a label is an impossibility according to cultural analysis. The culture embraces the *halakhah* and vice versa. One cannot exist without the other.

The cultural analysis insight that *halakhah* is a vital element in preserving the particularity of the Jewish tradition does not necessarily resonate with Jews who see their Jewishness as something completely independent of any religious affiliation or identity. Even among those Jews who associate their Jewishness with the Jewish religion, the notion that *halakhah* is vital for self-preservation may not be intuitively obvious. Moreover, once *halakhah*'s role is explicitly recognized, a difficult question surfaces: How should *halakhah* be defined, and by whom? As prior chapters demonstrate, this issue fosters disagreement among the Jewish denominations. A central difficulty in this regard is the increasing tendency, particularly common in American society, to embrace autonomy, pluralism, and customization as important societal attributes. These attributes are also highly valued in most sectors of the American Jewish community, but they potentially conflict with the traditional *halakhic* perspective that one must adhere to the commandments because they originate from God.

Despite the ongoing evolution of Judaism's particularity throughout the ages, the reality that the *mesorah* entails particularity is a constant. Still, the very existence of cultural fluidity can result in the destruction of Jewish particularity as individual members of the cultural community abandon their cultural tradition and identity. This cultural fluidity poses a particular risk for Diaspora Jews who represent a minority culture in their respective homelands.

Cultural analysis affirms the *mesorah* generally and *halakhah* specifically as fundamental starting points. They are the source of the tradition's particularity. If these elements are marginalized or discounted, not only will the continuity of the tradition be jeopardized, but also an increasing dilution of the existing culture will materialize. Thus, given the inevitable intersection between law and culture, Jewish culture is meaningless absent its grounding in *halakhah*.

On the other hand, the cultural analysis paradigm developed and applied throughout this book departs from the traditional understanding of *halakhah* solely as the embodiment of Divine command. On the contrary, it emphasizes the human element of the law's composition and acknowledges that this human component often was—and still is—the result of existing power dynamics. Further, this perspective acknowledges the role of social context in the development of both *halakhah* and the *mesorah* throughout history.

Pluralism and Authenticity

Cultural analysis actively supports a pluralistic approach to *halakhah* as well as embraces the conflict that at times may result from this pluralism. Significantly, the importance of *halakhah* does not detract from the struggle that can result in some sectors of the cultural community that are engaged in determining the ongoing application of the *halakhah*. Cultural analysis welcomes this struggle and thus reaffirms engaging with the *halakhah* on a deep and meaningful level.

Cultural analysis sees a multitude of *halakhic* interpretations and applications as beneficial. This perspective is consistent with an emphasis on a degree of human choice. The concept of choice has had a long and significant history even with respect to the decisions of membership and participation in the Jewish community and tradition. According to the text of the Torah, when Moses told the people all of God's commandments, the people answered with one voice and said "we will do" all that God commanded.[14] From the outset, therefore, the Jews elected to obey God's laws. The Book of Ruth furnishes another important example of the importance of choice. Ruth, a Moabite woman, married one of Naomi's sons, who later died. Naomi then urged Ruth to return to her own people, but Ruth refused to do so and uttered the famous pledge of loyalty including the words "For wherever you go, I will

---

14. *See* Exodus 24:3 (translation from Etz Hayim: Torah and Commentary 477 (David L. Leiber et al. eds., 2001)).

נעשה ונשמע

את

go...your people shall be my people, and your God my God."[15] The Book of Ruth concludes with Ruth marrying Boaz, a relative of Naomi's deceased husband, and bearing a son named Obed, who was the grandfather of King David. The placement of this lineage at the end of the text is especially significant because according to the tradition, the Messiah will be a descendant of King David, and of Ruth—the woman who chose to be Jewish.[16]

The concept of choice in how to observe the tradition often is seen as antithetical to the traditional precept of obedience to Divine Command. Yet, the affirmation of some degree of personal choice concerning religious practice is consistent with the inherently pluralistic nature of *halakhah*. From an ideological perspective, the idea that Judaism is a one-size-fits-all tradition never has been the norm.[17] For example, throughout Jewish history, the *mesorah* has been shaped by the bottom-up choices of the people in addition to the top-down *halakhic* rulings of the leaders. This reality also is consistent with the emphasis cultural analysis places on the bottom up working in conjunction with the top down in formulating cultural tradition.

In connection with the top-down component of the *mesorah*, the diversity reflected in the *halakhic* authorities and sources has been discussed repeatedly in this book. For example, consider Daniel Sperber's characterization of the *halakhah* concerning women's participation in public Torah reading as a stream that "does not follow a uniform course; rather, it is multidirectional,

---

15. TANAKH THE HOLY SCRIPTURES, Ruth 1:16 at 1420 (JPS 1985).

16. *See* AMY KALMANOFSKY, DANGEROUS SISTERS OF THE HEBREW BIBLE, 157–74 (2014).

17. Even with respect to matters of belief, historically the tradition always has tolerated some variability. Professor Marc Shapiro illustrates this very point in his book debunking the myth of unanimous historical acceptance by traditional authorities of the Thirteen Principles of Faith that were articulated by the renowned medieval Jewish law authority Maimonides. In his work, Shapiro notes that "Judaism is a religion of law" and "one can basically believe what one wishes." MARC B. SHAPIRO, THE LIMITS OF ORTHODOX THEOLOGY 30 (2004) (citing Modern Orthodox thinker Zvi Kurzweil as a proponent of this view). Similarly, Rabbi Norman Lamm, a contemporary Orthodox leader, has observed with respect to the presence of doubt in religious experience: "We found that there is place for doubt within the confines of cognitive faith; it must not be allowed to interfere with normative *halakhic* practice, which is the expression of functional faith." NORMAN LAMM, FAITH AND DOUBT 30 (1971).

In this regard, the Pew Report also demonstrates a wider spectrum of thought than one might expect, even among traditional Jews, concerning faith in God. The survey indicated that only 89 percent of Orthodox Jews are "absolutely certain" of their belief in "God or a universal spirit" (96 percent ultra-Orthodox and 77 percent Modern Orthodox). Pew also notes that "most Jews see no conflict between being Jewish and not believing in God." Pew Report, *supra* note 4 (follow "Chapter 4: Religious Beliefs and Practices" hyperlink). *See also* Jay P. Lefkowitz, *The Rise of Social Orthodoxy: A Personal Account*, COMMENTARY 37 (Apr. 2014), discussed *infra* at notes 23–24 and accompanying text.

moving in different directions, reflecting different aspects at different times and places."[18] Sperber's general point is one that resonates with other authorities.[19] Thus, Judaism historically has embraced the cultural analysis insight of a multiplicity of values in shaping the tradition.

On the other hand, too much choice in observance can lead to a watered-down version of Judaism that lacks meaningful content with a basis in the *mesorah*. In other words, choice has the potential to compromise consistency and authenticity of the tradition. Safeguarding authenticity is a problem for any cultural tradition, and cultural analysis is very concerned with this issue.

With respect to effectuating changes to the tradition, a key goal of cultural analysis is to retain the essence of the original blueprint so that any modifications allow the tradition to retain its authenticity. Further, a cultural analysis paradigm suggests that different segments of the cultural community need the space and the tools to make particular choices and still be considered within the umbrella of the tradition. Therefore, cultural analysis affirms that all parts of the identified Jewish community—both in Israel and throughout the Diaspora—play significant roles in perpetuating the tradition. The right end of the religious spectrum keeps the boundaries in check and sets the tone; the left end pushes the boundaries and brings new visions and energy. The middle provides a critical center that balances the energies on both sides while operating as a check against extremist tendencies. All are important components for a minority culture seeking to retain its character as a people but still function in the world outside of its own borders. Jews have many different ways of making Judaism their own, a reality that cultural analysis embraces because it responds to the entirety of human experience.

On a theoretical level, the pluralism inherent in a cultural analysis methodology stems from the recognition that law and culture cannot be separated, and therefore, neither can be the exclusive focus. No individual, and no single Jewish community, can be all about either the *halakhah* or the culture. There is the inevitable intersection between the two. This intersection requires that with respect to serious Jewish endeavors, pluralism must be not just tolerated

---

18. *See supra* Chapter 7, note 76 and accompanying text.

19. The pluralistic nature of the Talmud was emphasized in a public lecture by Shlomo Riskin, a renowned Modern Orthodox authority and the Chief Rabbi of Efrat, Israel, at Congregation Kehilath Jeshurun in New York City on November 9, 2013. *See also infra* text accompanying note 57.

but affirmatively embraced. Too often this recognition is missing from the discourse in communities both on the right and the left.

Importance of the Emerging Middle Ground

The overall fluidity of a cultural analysis perspective with respect to the *mesorah* underscores the importance of a strong middle ground in the Jewish community.[20] This perspective suggests that Judaism need not be viewed in black and white terms, from either an ideological or behavioral standpoint. With respect to ideology, Jews who advocate an historical approach to *halakhah* operate squarely within the model of cultural analysis given their acceptance of the view that Jewish law must be interpreted through a cultural lens.[21] Further, those who gravitate toward the historical approach assert that Torah law has evolved, and should evolve, to accommodate social needs. Although Orthodoxy by and large rejects this model of *halakhic* lawmaking, there is a small but visible group of self-denominated Orthodox thinkers who are beginning to embrace a historical and contextual approach to biblical and Talmudic study.[22] The very existence of this group signals an important paradigm shift that may well result in some much needed synergy on an academic level between serious non-Orthodox Jews and some who identify as Modern Orthodox.

In addition to the emergence of this potential intellectual middle ground, an interesting behavioral phenomenon appears to be surfacing in certain Modern Orthodox communities. This phenomenon has been termed "the rise of social orthodoxy" among lay Jews. One proponent has defined social Orthodoxy by the ability to "pick and choose from the menu of Jewish rituals without fear of divine retribution" and as an identity rooted "much more in Jewish culture, history, and nationality than in faith and commandments."[23] Jews who claim to be "socially Orthodox" consider themselves Orthodox, affiliate with Orthodox institutions such as synagogues and day schools,

---

20. Writing from a sociological perspective, Steven Cohen also emphasizes the importance of the "Jewish middle." *See* Steven M. Cohen, *What Is to Be Done? Policy Responses to the Shrinking Jewish Middle*, Berman Jewish Policy Archive at NYU Wagner (BJPA) (June 25, 2014), http://www.bjpa.org/Publications/details.cfm?PublicationID=21551.

21. *See supra* Chapter 4, text following note 218.

22. *See supra* Chapter 4, note 225 and accompanying text.

23. Lefkowitz, *supra* note 17, at 42.

and claim to follow an Orthodox lifestyle, although they do not necessarily accept the divinity of the Torah as a precondition for Orthodoxy. In truth, it is possible that many people who consider themselves socially Orthodox Jews are not thinking much at all about Jewish theology or *halakhic* theory on a daily basis.[24] Although their strong commitment to *halakhah* is analogous to other Modern Orthodox Jews who believe in the divinity of the Torah, their ideology may be more similar to non-Orthodox Jews. As for their overall behavior, socially Orthodox Jews may not be all that different from seriously observant non-Orthodox Jews who keep kosher homes and observe the Sabbath, although some socially Orthodox individuals may keep these practices more rigorously than their non-Orthodox counterparts. For purposes of this discussion, the identification of social Orthodoxy as a phenomenon is important because it reinforces a previously ignored commonality between serious Jews of all denominations that has long been lacking in the denominational discourse.

Writing from a sociological perspective, Steven Cohen advocates increasing "interaction between Orthodox and non-Orthodox children and young adults" as an action measure designed to enhance a much-needed middle ground.[25] Typically, such interaction takes the form of Orthodox outreach known as *kiruv*. The literal meaning of this term is "bringing close" but to the Orthodox, *kiruv* in practice means "bringing you close to me and my ways." There is indeed an important place for traditional *kiruv* given that over the years, numerous non-Orthodox Jews have found spiritual satisfaction in more observant communities. As a general matter, however, most non-Orthodox Jews are not likely to embrace either an Orthodox lifestyle or perspective. Therefore, other types of synergies that are dependent on dialogue rather than this type of outreach are necessary.

Significantly, alliances are forming between certain sectors of the Jewish community that hold differing religious views. For example, in commenting on both Dr. Ruth Calderon's introductory speech to the Knesset (Israel's legislature) following her 2013 election and the emergence in Israel of secular institutions of classical Jewish learning,[26] Rabbi Yosef Kanefsky observed that individuals such as Calderon represent "a new way of thinking and

---

24. Lefkowitz candidly acknowledges that theological matters do not occupy much of his time and attention and are not "particularly germane" to his life as an observant Jew. *Id.* at 40.

25. Cohen, *supra* note 20, at 16.

26. *See supra* Chapter 8, notes 130–36 and accompanying text.

learning and behaving as a Jew in the modern world which can actually serve as a vital partner and ally of traditional Orthodoxy."[27] Kanefsky also asserts that this type of partnership has the potential to weave "a net of Jewish life that will capture so many who might otherwise fall through the cracks."[28] Similarly, Rabbi Asher Lopatin has been particularly aggressive about trying to break down denominational barriers. In May 2013, shortly before his installation as the President of Yeshivat Chovevei Torah ("YCT"), Lopatin told a reporter of his dream for uniting the distinct Jewish institutions on the Upper West Side of Manhattan:

> My dream is to have Hebrew Union College, the Jewish Theological Seminary, Hadar, and Chovevei on one campus, to move in together. We'd each *daven* [pray] in our own ways, but it could transform the Upper West Side. I'm not talking about closing down campuses, because I want more Torah, not less…I want to hear different opinions. Disagreement is OK—I don't care if we come to a consensus, but put it all out there and continue the conversation.[29]

Although these alliances are not without their critics and have indeed spurred disagreement,[30] they have tremendous potential to implement in practical terms the theoretical insights of the cultural analysis model.

---

27. Yosef Kanefsky, *Ruth Calderon—Mother of Redemption?* MORETHODOXY (Feb. 27, 2013), http://www.jewishjournal.com/morethodoxy/item/ruth_calderon_mother_of_redemption [hereinafter *Mother of Redemption*].

28. *Id.*

29. Rich Dweck, *The New "Morethodox" Rabbi Asher Lopatin Succeeds Avi Weiss at an Influential Seminary, Offering a Pluralistic Version of Orthodoxy* (May 1, 2013), http://www.jewishpinkelephant.com/2013/05/the-new-morethodox-rabbi-asher-lopatin.html.

30. *See, e.g.*, Rabbi Avrohom Gordimer, *From Openness to Heresy* (July 18, 2013), http://www.cross-currents.com/archives/2013/07/18/from-openness-to-heresy/. Rabbi Lopatin endured further criticism from Orthodox quarters with respect to his decision to mark his October 2013 installation as President of YCT with a roundtable discussion involving Jewish leaders from the Conservative, Reform, and Reconstructionist movements. *See* Paul Berger, *Asher Lopation Gets Less-than-Warm Welcome from Orthodox World*, DAILY JEWISH FORWARD (Oct. 28, 2013), http://forward.com/articles/186116/asher-lopatin-gets-less-than-warm-welcome-from-ort/?p=all.

Aggadah and *Halakhah*

Effective Jewish education geared to non-Orthodox Jews is one of the most vital ways of fostering a stronger middle ground within the global Jewish community. From a cultural analysis perspective, effective education about cultural tradition requires understanding the essence of the past in order to arrive at new, yet authentic, interpretations of the tradition. In addressing this issue in general terms, Paul Berman proposed a cultural analysis approach grounded in "a hermeneutics of meaning, faith, and sympathetic interpretation" based on Ronald Dworkin's chain novel metaphor.[31] According to this approach, Jews must be educated with positive, authentic messages concerning the *mesorah* so they can be armed with the necessary knowledge to participate in the relevant discourse.

Aggadah, which includes not only biblical and rabbinic narrative but also wisdom, speculation, and folklore, can be especially useful in educating Jews about the beauty and particularity of the tradition.[32] From the outset of the Jewish religion, *aggadah* has played a central role in shaping Jewish identity and the Jewish worldview. In speaking of the Hebrew Bible, Professor Yosef Hayim Yerushalmi has observed that as a whole, it offers "not only a repository of law, wisdom, and faith, but a coherent narrative that claimed to embrace the whole of history from the creation of the world to the fifth century BCE, and in the prophetic books, a profound interpretation of that history as well."[33] The biblical narratives, recited on an annual basis in synagogues since the early centuries of the Common Era, not only served to educate Jews, but also reaffirmed "the inevitably cyclical quality of liturgical time."[34] Through this pattern of recitation, Jews became essentially "one" with their past as they embraced biblical events experientially on a regular basis.

Further, biblical narratives shaped Jewish thought and action over the centuries. For example, the *Akedah*, the narrative of the "binding of Isaac" on Mount Moriah that appears in Genesis,[35] furnished the ultimate paradigm for the response of medieval Jews during the Crusades. During this time, many Jews opted to kill themselves and their families rather than accept

---

31. *See supra* Chapter 1, notes 130–34 and accompanying text.

32. *See, e.g., supra* Chapter 6, notes 149–58 and accompanying text. (discussing Gordon Tucker's position).

33. Yosef Hayim Yerushalmi, Zakhor 14 (1996).

34. *Id.* at 42.

35. *See* Genesis 22:1–19.

baptism.[36] These Jews turned to "the image of Abraham ready to slaughter Isaac" as a basis for their response to catastrophe.[37]

The rabbis who wrote the Talmud augmented the more familiar biblical narratives with their own *aggadah*. Rabbi Adin Steinsaltz, who fittingly described the Talmud as "a conglomerate of law, legend, and philosophy, a blend of unique logic and shrewd pragmatism, of history and science, logic and humor," estimated that one-fourth of the Talmud may be considered *aggadah*.[38] In speaking of the medieval period, Yerushalmi noted that the "real or legendary biographies" of the Talmudic sages rendered them "familiar figures in a landscape of memory where the boundaries between history and legend were never sharply drawn."[39]

Indeed, cultures are shaped by their stories. In the case of the Jewish people, biblical and Talmudic *aggadah* have had a profound impact in shaping the Jewish psyche and in contributing to the richness and wisdom of the *mesorah*. Throughout the history of the Jews, *aggadah* has been a major component of Jewish collective memory, and in turn, Jewish identity.[40]

Aggadah can play a powerful role in Jewish education. For example, when Calderon addressed the Knesset, the section of the Talmud she chose to teach focused on the story of a rabbi who became so engrossed with his studies that he failed to come home for his annual one-day visit to his wife on the eve of Yom Kippur. At the same moment the wife shed a tear of disappointment, the floor on which the rabbi was sitting collapsed and he fell to his death.[41] Calderon explained to the Knesset that this tragedy teaches that one who adheres to the Torah at the expense of being sensitive to human beings is not righteous.[42]

---

36. *See supra* Chapter 3, notes 126–29 and accompanying text.

37. YERUSHALMI, *supra* note 33, at 38.

38. ADIN STEINSALTZ, THE ESSENTIAL TALMUD 4, 251 (Chaya Galai trans., 1976).

39. YERUSHALMI, *supra* note 33, at 45.

40. *Id.* at 94 (noting that "the collective memories of the Jewish people were a function of the shared faith, cohesiveness, and will of the group itself, transmitting and recreating its past through an entire complex of interlocking social and religious institutions that functioned organically to achieve this").

41. This narrative appears in Ketuvot 62b (Babylonian Talmud). *See supra* Chapter 8, notes 132–36 and accompanying text.

42. *See* Rabbi Yehoshua Look, *The Knesset as Beit Midrash: A Model of Hope for a Better Israel* (Feb. 25, 2013), http://www.haaretz.com/jewish-world/rabbis-round-table/the-knesset-as-beit-midrash-a-model-of-hope-for-a-better-israel-1.505685.

Consider another poignant Talmudic narrative containing a message about the importance of elevating the substance of the law over the form. In this narrative, some porters unintentionally break a barrel of wine that belonged to Rabbah, son of Hanan, who wanted to hold them accountable for this breakage by seizing their garments, because they were poor and could not pay him back. The porters went to the sage Rav, who ordered that Rabbah return their garments, even though the law would have allowed Rabbah to keep them. The workers then complained that they labored all day and were in need. Rav ordered Rabbah to pay them. When Rabbah again questioned this result because it is not according to the law, Rav replied, "Even so...And keep the path of the righteous."[43] The point of this narrative is that although the letter of the law may require one thing, the spirit of the law may require a more compassionate application in certain instances.

Although other cultural traditions might endorse the general moral of this narrative about the porters, the particular way it is presented in the Talmud represents a uniquely Jewish perspective and historical context. This is also true of the story Calderon recounted to the Knesset. Both of these examples of *aggadah* illustrate how the *mesorah* embodies the particularity of the Jewish tradition. Jews who lack education with respect to the *mesorah* are unable to access the message, content, and unique presentation of these narratives. For non-Orthodox Jews especially, education focusing on such *aggadah* not only is accessible, but also can be packaged in a way that will generate interest and a positive response. This use of *aggadah* does not entail an emphasis on the legalities of ritualistic observance that might trigger resistance by more liberal Jews who are disinterested in *halakhah*. Moreover, *aggadah* can be particularly useful for teaching children who might be especially receptive to the moral lessons these narratives contain.

The use of *aggadah* as an educational tool strengthening Jewish particularity has enormous potential in today's world. Recent neuroscience research demonstrates that emotion is "one of the more important regulators of learning and memory formation."[44] The authors of a recent paper on this topic caution that "one challenge of using emotion in a learning context is the difficulty of creating emotion-arousing events, especially ones that are positive."[45]

---

43. Bava Metzia 83a (Babylonian Talmud).

44. Lila Davachi, Tobiasi Kiefer, David Rock & Lisa Rock, *Learning That Lasts through AGES*, in NEUROLEADERSHIP JOURNAL 5 (Issue Three 2010), http://www.davidrock.net/files/AGES.pdf.

45. *Id.*

As the examples of *aggadah* furnished in this chapter illustrate, however, the *mesorah* contains a wealth of positive content upon which educators can draw to spur and deepen interest in the tradition among a wide variety of Jews.

Further, *aggadah* offers all Jews an accessible source of material for engaging in the process of "remixing" Jewish culture, a phenomenon that is receiving increasing attention in the Jewish studies literature as a result of its growing popularity.[46] Scholars of American Judaism Steven Cohen and Arnold Eisen have noted that the moderately affiliated Jews between the ages of thirty and fifty that they interviewed toward the end of the twentieth century "aim to make Jewish narratives part of their own personal stories, by picking and choosing among new and inherited practices and texts so as to find the combination they as individuals can authentically affirm."[47] As applied to the Jewish tradition, remix affords participants the ability to create a personally authentic version of the tradition fashioned "from the large repertoire of possibilities available."[48] Remix entails "creative originality that breathes life into the script and makes each performance unique, thereby keeping the ritual alive as one that people seek to perform."[49] Those who are engaged in this process are "defined as much by what they have embraced Jewishly as by what they have rejected of the tradition" and even more by "*how* they have embraced" the tradition.[50]

Although the term *remix* may be of recent origin, the phenomenon is not new with respect to the Jewish tradition. Yerushalmi discusses the work of Azariah de'Rossi, an observant Italian Jewish scholar-physician, who

---

46. *See, e.g.,* Erica Brown & Misha Galperin, The Case for Jewish Peoplehood 161–64 (2009).

47. Steven M. Cohen & Arnold M. Eisen, The Jew Within 8–9 (2000). *See also supra* Chapter 9, notes 121–22 and accompanying text.

48. Cohen & Eisen, *supra* note 47, at 14. *See also* Chapter 9, notes 124–25 and accompanying text.

49. Cohen & Eisen, *supra* note 47, at 96. Cohen and Eisen do not use the term *remix* but the process they describe is consistent with its application. They also caution that this process can "go too far," thereby "precluding the experience of tradition and community" that is important to their subjects as "a primary motivation, meaning, and satisfaction." *Id.* at 96.

50. *Id.* at 42. The concept of "remix" initially became popular in academic intellectual property circles through the efforts of professors such as Lawrence Lessig. In this context, "remix culture" allows users of copyrighted works to be able to use and remix these works liberally as a basis for creating new, derivative works that play an important role in creating cultural wealth. *See* Lawrence Lessig, Remix: Making Art and Commerce Thrive in the Hybrid Economy (2008). Brown and Galperin explicitly acknowledged that Lessig's "definition of remix may be applicable to the current state of American Jewry." *See* Brown & Galperin, *supra* note 46, at 162.

evaluated rabbinic *aggadah* from the standpoint of "profane history" and non-Jewish historical sources "drawn from Greek, Roman, and Christian writers."[51] This approach can be characterized as sixteenth century remix, although Yerushalmi also notes that "Azariah's experiment…remained his alone" and that there were "no heirs to his method."[52]

Today, however, Doctors Erica Brown and Misha Galperin explicitly call for an application of remix on the part of American Jewry. They argue that we need to use the current trend toward customization in an advantageous manner by embracing "the beauty of remix identities," particularly "for younger generations of Jews who respect the 'original' enough to take hold of it and make it their own."[53] *Aggadah* provides a particularly useful foundation for remix given that stories are especially accessible and appealing to Jews who lack rigorous Talmudic training. *Aggadah* has the potential to effectively transmit the particularistic aspects of the *mesorah* that can serve as the basis for remix and appropriation by future generations.[54]

Significantly, however, *aggadah* cannot be the only ingredient of Jewish remix in furnishing the necessary building blocks for crafting positive and authentic messages that are steeped in the entirety of the *mesorah*. *Halakhah* works with *aggadah* in this process, and together, they illustrate the *mesorah*'s incorporation of a cultural analysis paradigm in which law and culture are deeply intertwined.[55] The poet Hayim Nahman Bialik's famous essay on *halakhah* and *aggadah* exemplifies this very point, although he does not specifically rely on a cultural analysis methodology. Instead, he analogizes both Jewish law and narrative to art forms and emphasizes their interdependence upon one another. Writing in the early years of the twentieth century, Bialik claims with respect to *halakhah* that "our artists are at present quite content to labor with borrowed vessels and engage in the bad imitations of forms which they find ready at hand."[56] In reading this passage, one cannot help but

---

51. YERUSHALMI, *supra* note 33, at 72. Yerushalmi singles out Azariah for his "reluctance to set up predetermined boundaries between his general and his Jewish knowledge, in his readiness to allow a genuine confrontation between the two spheres, and in his acceptance of whatever conclusions seemed to flow out of it." *Id*. at 70.

52. *Id*. at 73.

53. BROWN & GALPERIN, *supra* note 46, at 162.

54. For a powerful example of how *aggadah* can be used in this way, see RUTH CALDERON, A BRIDE FOR ONE NIGHT (Deborah Harris Agency trans., 2014).

55. *See supra* Chapter 1, notes 125–28 and accompanying text.

56. H.N. BYALIK, LAW AND LEGEND OR *HALAKAH* AND *AGGADA* 26 (1923).

think of Asher Lopatin's critique of Steven Greenberg, discussed in Chapter 6, for failing to play sufficiently with the *halakhah* in a creative way in order to arrive at solutions to problems facing homosexuals within the Orthodox community.[57] Remix can be accomplished by a willingness, in Lopatin's words, to plunge "into the great pool of our tradition, certain that [one] will be received by water rather than a dry cement bottom."[58]

Cultural analysis suggests the need for a greater appreciation for *halakhah* among some Jewish communities and a greater appreciation of the cultural attachment to Judaism among other communities. In addition, cultural analysis emphasizes the need for a mutual appreciation of a multitude of roles in the enterprise of transmission. This approach contrasts with the belief by some Jews that *halakhah* in its entirety is the only legitimate content for transmission of the tradition. The analysis developed in this book recognizes the validity of this approach but sees it as under-inclusive in light of the cultural analysis paradigm. If Judaism is defined solely in terms of *halakhic* observance as those practices have been developed historically, the majority of Jews are effectively eliminated from the Jewish community and from the discourse. This approach also fails to appreciate the multivalent possibilities with respect to cultural attachment and its transmission.

On the other hand, sometimes the progressive end of the Jewish community's spectrum can be faulted for its assumption that Jewish identity can be defined solely in cultural terms.[59] This perspective neglects the importance that cultural analysis ascribes to the particularity of the tradition derived from *halakhah*. *Halakhah* and the language of the traditional Jewish sources furnish the specialized vocabulary necessary to engage in the discourse. This language is important for connecting the past with the present.[60] It also provides not only

---

57. *See supra* Chapter 6, note 57 and accompanying text.

58. Asher Lopatin, *What Makes a Book Orthodox?* Wrestling with God and Men *by Steven Greenberg*, 4(2) EDAH J. 1, 9 (2004), http://www.edah.org/backend/JournalArticle/4_2_Lopatin.pdf.

59. A recent proposal by sociologist Steven Cohen and Rabbi Kerry Olitzky relates to this point. They call for a new means of joining the Jewish people that would not require a formal conversion according to *halakhah* but instead would allow non-Jews to acquire a Jewish social/cultural identity without a Jewish religious identity. Steven M. Cohen & Kerry Olitzky, *Another Way to Join the Jewish People?* (Dec. 9, 2013), http://forward.com/articles/188947/another-way-to-join-the-jewish-people/. They tentatively call their method a Jewish Cultural Affirmation. It seems as though they are contemplating the addition of people Pew identified as "Jews of no religion" to the overall number of American Jews. Their proposal seems to overlook the vital synergy between Jewish law and Jewish culture.

60. *See* RACHEL BIALE, WOMEN AND JEWISH LAW 9 (1984) ("If we master the language of these sources and use them as an anchor, we can talk about contemporary problems in a way that connects them to what is already known and crystallized."). Biale, a secular Jew,

the basis for transmission of Jewish particularity to future generations, but also essential ingredients for authentic remix of the tradition.

* * *

A cultural analysis model understands the *mesorah* as a cultural product composed of law, wisdom, and narrative, all of which have been shaped by social forces over the centuries. Bialik's essay illustrates that the *mesorah* also can be understood as a work of authorship. More precisely, it is a "joint work" given its many human authors as well as its Divine origin. The issue of how much change and evolution it can tolerate and yet retain its authenticity is one that has occupied much of *halakhic* discourse in certain circles of Jewish thought since the inception of the Enlightenment. This discourse also has focused on the issue of who can legitimately claim the ability to make these interpretative decisions.

Cultural analysis is a valuable methodology for addressing these issues. It reminds us that there is something inherently special about cultural particularity that deserves preservation even if the mechanics and details of this process constitute a messy enterprise. Whether one agrees with a cultural analysis approach to the development of *halakhah* and the *mesorah* probably depends upon one's comfort level with living in the gray rather than black and white. For some Jewish people and for some Jewish communities, gray is preferable. For others, black and white works better. Moreover, sometimes the same individuals and communities will opt for gray and at other times black and white. The important point, however, is that the color gray is a combination of black and white. In the end, they are all part of the same family.

---

also focuses on the need for acquiring a "shared 'Jewish language'" in order "to engage in meaningful Jewish discourse today, and to formulate personal and communal ways of 'being Jewish'." *Id.*

INDEX